Dropping Anchor,
Setting Sail

Dropping Anchor, Setting Sail

GEOGRAPHIES OF RACE IN

BLACK LIVERPOOL

JACQUELINE NASSY BROWN

PRINCETON UNIVERSITY PRESS

PRINCETON AND OXFORD

Library of Congress Cataloging-in-Publication Data
Brown, Jacqueline Nassy, 1961–
Dropping anchor, setting sail: geographies of race in Black Liverpool / Jacqueline Nassy Brown.
p. cm.
Includes bibliographical references (p.) and index.
ISBN 0-691-11562-1 (cl : alk. paper) – ISBN0-691-11563-X (pbk. : alk. paper)
1. Blacks—England—Liverpool. 2. Liverpool (England)—Race relations.
3. Liverpool (England)—Social conditions. I. Title.
DA690.L8B76 2004
305.8961′0427′53—dc22
2004044426

British Library Cataloging-in-Publication Data is available
This book has been composed in Times
Printed on acid-free paper. ∞
pup.princeton.edu
Printed in the United States of America
1 3 5 7 9 10 8 6 4 2

FOR MY MOTHER, MINGA,
WITH ALL MY LOVE

C O N T E N T S

"WHY LIVERPOOL?" Since American friends and colleagues often ask me how I chose to study Black folks in this place, it makes sense to begin with a meditation on that question. The query is actually apropos for a book that is about spatial knowledges. What is it that Americans know or don't know about England that would consistently prompt that query?

In 1987, a few weeks before leaving my hometown of New York City to attend graduate school in anthropology at Stanford University, I met a Black Londoner, Ingrid Pollard. Ingrid is a photographic artist of renown in Britain, and my initial curiosity about Blacks in that country was born in the context of our friendship. I confess that she was totally exotic to me. I had never heard an English accent issuing from a Black person's mouth. I'm embarrassed to admit that Ingrid only made sense to me when she finally told me that her parents were from Guyana, where Ingrid was also born. I remember vividly how that knowledge filled me with relief. How provincial I was! Now that I could place her in a "Black" country, my racial map of the world was put nicely back in order.

I moved to California, and Ingrid returned to London. From there, she sent me a set of books about race and nationalism in Britain that determined the course of my life. If it were not for those books, this one would be about Brazil. As a Black American, I had never been forced to think about race through nation precisely because in the United States there is no discourse about Black Americans' Americanness. Blacks get swept into (and away by) American nationalism rather than cast on the other side of it, as has been the case in Britain. Is there anyone in the United States who seriously believes that we are out of place? That we all really belong elsewhere? Or that we are not central to the national community even, ironically, in our marginality? I do not deny that there have been moments, particularly in every war since the American Revolution, when these questions would have been answered very differently. Nevertheless, the Black American case cannot compare to the Black British one. The latter term, to some, is an oxymoron. "Black English" is a near impossibility. Being "just" English—without the Black qualifier—is unheard of. I needed to know more about how Black people understood their relationship to Britishness and especially Englishness, since that is far and away the more racially weighted category.

Why Liverpool? In the summer of 1989, I stayed at Ingrid's house while doing exploratory research in London. I hung out for hours on end in pubs that Black people frequented, striking up conversations over friendly games of pool. After a few months I realized that most of my reading as well as my friendship with a Londoner combined to make the capital seem like the natural choice for my field site. Indeed, I suspect that since Americans generally equate England with London, I probably would not have been asked, "Why London?" if I had chosen to do fieldwork there.

I knew that Bristol and Liverpool had older Black communities than other English cities, so I decided to venture out of London to see if I could learn anything different. Ingrid found friends of friends for me to stay with in each city. I went to Bristol first. I had an amiable host, but I explored the city on my own. It was difficult to find Black people and to meet them once I did. I went directly from Bristol to Liverpool, where I operated with a fantastic advantage. Ingrid had found me the gem whom I call "Cecelia" in this book. Cecelia could not have been a more generous host nor, over the years, a better friend. I stayed with her for five days in 1989, and then for nine months in 1991. For three months of the following year, I stayed with a friend of hers, Yvette.

Cecelia is a beloved person around town. She had a propensity to barge into community centers and organizations, where she was known by one and all, and immediately command everyone's attention. One man I knew affectionately called Cecelia "the little general." Her friend Yvette never called her by her name, addressing her instead as "Leader." Cecelia is a tad bossy but in a very endearing way. The day after I arrived, Cecelia gave me a tour of the city center on foot, while also taking me to various race relations organizations in and around Liverpool 8, the neighborhood where Blacks are thought to live in largest numbers. ("Liverpool 8" is also synonymous with the district called "Toxteth.") She took me to Liverpool University, a few blocks away from Liverpool 8, where she introduced me to a longtime activist who worked with policy advisors on the faculty. And she took me to the Merseyside Community Relations Council, also known as the CRC. (Merseyside, named for the River Mersey, is a county that includes the city of Liverpool and neighboring towns.) On arrival, Cecelia quickly corralled a couple of politicos, a group that included Cecelia's sister and a few other women. She made quick work of the introductions and then issued her first command: "Tell them what you're doing, Jackie." Her order made me even more shy than usual, but I managed to tell them that I was in Liverpool to conduct research about Black people's relationship to Britishness, considering the dominant view of Blacks as non-belongers to the nation. Cecelia's sister led a chorus of spirited responses that went on for about five minutes. I understood not a single word. All I was able to make out was that they thought this was a good idea. Until that moment, I had no clue of the existence of what has been folklorized in Liverpool as "an accent exceedingly rare." I caught myself thinking, "This is English?!"

In her early forties, Cecelia had graduated from Oxford University some time ago. Though she can and does speak with a Liverpool accent, she did not use it with me. And so the surprise awaited me at the CRC.

Cecelia took me to the Merseyside Caribbean Centre, a community institution in Liverpool 8. After introducing me around, she asked the officials there to arrange a group interview with some kids the next day. They warmly obliged, and the next day I spoke with about ten kids, about thirteen years old on average. I asked them a set of basic questions like, "Black people have been in this city for hundreds of years, so do you see yourselves as English?" The gist of the answer was "no." That term refers to White people, they said, with far more flair than I can re-create here. I asked another question having something to do with

Black identity. Waxing historical, one young girl quoted Malcolm X in her response. They answered all my questions with ease and great interest—except for one. Everyone—adults and children—froze when I asked these kids whether they were of Caribbean background, and whether they consider themselves Afro-Caribbean. We were in a place called the Caribbean Centre, so I thought that an ethnicity question was called for. As the kids drew their first and only blank, I spied a woman in a corner of the center making frantic gestures in an effort to get me to cut off this line of questioning—which I did. I penetrated an open wound, as I learned later. After the interview, a couple of kids approached me with a question of their own. Could I teach them some new dance steps from America?

For all the sound scientific reasons there were for choosing this city as a field site, it was these kids who made Liverpool irresistible. In view of the heavy political content of their answers, I surmised that their parents must be *really* interesting. As well, these kids were warm, forthright, and terribly expressive. And, for whatever it's worth, the people of Liverpool reminded me of home. The edgy and raw but always friendly affect of everyone I met, White and Black alike, took me back to my roots in working-class Brooklyn-Queens. They reminded me of "New Yawkahs."

When I got back to London, one of Ingrid's housemates, who was about twenty years old, asked me how I liked Liverpool. I said I *loved* it. With a gut enthusiasm, she responded "Yeah, I thought you'd really fancy it! It's brilliant!" Her comment sticks out in my mind because it is the only genuinely, unabashedly enthusiastic comment about Liverpool that I've ever heard from a Briton who is not from that city. For example, I once mentioned to one of Ingrid's artsy-intellectual friends, another Black Londoner, that I was on my way to Liverpool. He groaned, "How depressing." For another example, I made fleeting acquaintance with an English student in California. I asked him where he was from in England, and he was evasive in his response. Perhaps it was none of my business. I told him I had spent a year in Liverpool. "There are *much* nicer places in England than Liverpool," he informed me. Over the years, I have amassed an impressive collection of little anecdotes like that.

Why *Liverpool*? Why does it provoke such responses? But then again, "London" does not inspire very nice comments in Liverpool either.

A few days after I returned to Liverpool in 1991, Cecelia packed me up in her little car and took me to meet one of her former professors, now retired from Oxford. She lived in a rural area just outside of the small town of Chester. Over tea and biscuits, Cecelia issued her usual command. "Tell her what you're doing, Jackie." This time, I did not refer to Black people or Britishness. I just said I was researching Englishness in Liverpool. The professor gasped, "In *Liverpool*?!" Then she muttered, half to me and half to herself, "What a bizarre place to study Englishness." Although I get it now, I was too stunned then to pursue her cryptic point. Instead, I started second guessing myself. *Why* Liverpool? Maybe I should consult a map. Maybe Liverpool is not in England after all.

This book could be described as one long meditation on the question, "Why Liverpool?" I pursue that question not out of my abundant affection for Liverpool but because the answers can contribute to our knowledge about how race works in Britain and maybe elsewhere. I went to Britain to study race through nation. In search of something different I went to Liverpool, where I found place *as* difference.

Much of the analysis is written with a British audience very much in mind. Yet Britain is not seriously studied in the United States—the popularity of the writings of Stuart Hall and Paul Gilroy in graduate seminars notwithstanding. The question of audience has thus created an unavoidable awkwardness in this book. I do, at points, take some care in elaborating salient aspects of British politics and history—a move that Britons may find tiresome. I have chosen not to compromise on this score, believing that Britain should be subjected to the same methods of ethnographic exposition, including occasional doses of history, as any other society.

On the long and winding road that culminates in this text, I have benefited from the love and support of about a thousand people. I am really humbled to remember what wonderful hosts and friends the people of Liverpool were to me. I hope that my great respect for them shines through in this book. Indeed, I offer this ethnography in the spirit of the precious, intimately diasporic relationship between Black Britain and Black America—an albeit one-sided relationship that people actually invoked in agreeing to participate in this research. While this book cannot fully be what my friends and informants wanted it to be, I do hope that it participates constructively in the tough and ongoing work of community formation in that city.

For their support and for their enduring pride in me, I thank my family, including Ernece Kelly, the Nassys, and the Browns. Much love also to my father, who died before I could give a satisfactory answer to his question, "Why anthropology?" This book is my answer. No one would have been prouder of me than him—except my mother. For the boundless love that she has always given me and for being such a thoroughly fabulous human being, never mind a superlative mother, this book is for her. If I did not have a perfect mother, I would have dedicated this book to Lisa Rofel. She did more than respond enthusiastically, critically, and constructively to every two words I ever put together. Lisa also worked tirelessly to convince me that I had something well worth saying. Some of the core insights of this book came out of conversations with her.

Many friends and colleagues have sustained me since the inception of this project. The special gifts that they have given me lie less in their generous comments on parts of this book—although these were often considerable—than in the inspiration they have provided. For ruthless but loving criticism when I most desperately needed it, I thank Hugh Raffles, Tina Campt, and France Winddance Twine (who, in her inimitable way, bluntly advised therapy). Other cherished interlocutors have been Rudolph Byrd, Susan Reinhold, Anna Tsing, Susan Harding, Daniel Linger, Bruce Knauft, Donald Donham, Donald Brenneis, Donald Moore, Brian Larkin, Deborah Amory, and the ever-fabulous Kathryn Chetkovich, whose special gift is to make the impossible seem utterly doable. For setting me on the right path, I thank my wonderful faculty advisors at Stanford University including Sylvia Yanagisako, Akhil Gupta, Renato Rosaldo, and Paulla Ebron. My colleagues at Hunter College, especially Gerald Creed, Susan Lees, Marc Edelman, Greg Johnson, and Yvonne Lasalle, have been wonderfully supportive during this book's final stages. In sisterhood and with so much love, I thank Ingrid Pollard first and foremost, for the inspiration of her friendship and of her art, but also for all the fig rolls and the occasional newspaper clippings that she sent me from England. Ingrid took a special trip to Liverpool in order to take the photograph that appears on the cover—a "setting sail" image that exquisitely captures the spirit of this book. I also thank Karen L. Stroud (I owe you everything!), Crystal Terry, Clara McLaughlin, Paulette McKenzie, Claire Prymus, Lisbet Tellefsen, Susan Callender, Jennifer Gonzalez, Kim Robinson, Jacqueline Francis, Jeryl Sobers, Marien Elizabeth, and Lisa Baltazar, who saw this book out with love, grace, and the patience of Job. As for the men in my life, I thank Leonardo Stroud, Gregory Campbell, Gary Collymore, Gordon Barr, Henry Goldschmidt, Herman Gray, Jeffrey Swinkin, and Louis Chude-Sokei for their love, care, and support over the years. For excellent research assistance, I am indebted to Bregje Eekelen, Conal Ho, Michelle Rosenthal, and James Pile. I thank the community of scholars (including the many undergraduate and graduate students who have commented on my work) at Emory University, the University of California at Santa Cruz, and Hunter College of the City University of New York. All of these people know more about Liverpool than I do at this point. Yet any critical concerns with the arguments advanced here must unfortunately be addressed to me. I gratefully acknowledge the support of the National Science Foundation (BNS#9024515), the Wenner-Gren Foundation for Anthropological Research, and the Center for European Studies at Stanford University. For her incredible patience and cooperative spirit, I thank Jenn Backer, who did the copyediting on this book. Finally, I thank Mary Murrell, to whom I gave many headaches as she left Princeton University Press. Considering the delays I have caused in the completion of this book—in the foolish quest, that is, for perfection—it is only appropriate that I offer it in humble tribute to Mary for the many, truly amazing ethnographies that she helped to bring into the world.

TABLE OF CONTENTS

Setting Sail

"To UNDERSTAND Black people, you've got to understand Liverpool." So argued my friend Scott, a sixty-year-old Black man born and raised in that city. I first met Scott in 1991, a few weeks after beginning fieldwork there, back when I still thought my research was just set in Liverpool rather than being about "Liverpool."

On the occasion of my first interview with Scott, he came over to where I lived bearing a folder labeled "Anti National Front," a reference to a political party on Britain's far right. The folder's voluminous contents forced its seams to burst. The newspaper clippings and other documents he pulled out over the course of the evening also overflowed the folder's topical boundary. One of his clippings, for example, concerned Colin Powell, then Chairman of the Joint Chiefs of Staff. Powell's position implied to Scott that in America, Blacks have been given their due recognition, social status, and position, even in the military. He pulled out a copy of the original charter for Stanley House, a cherished but defunct community center established in 1946 for Blacks of south Liverpool. In the midst of describing the center's aims he stopped short, interrupting himself to say, "To understand Black people, you've got to understand Liverpool." He explained that Stanley House was established by charitable White people. But their charter referred to the children of African seamen and the White women to whom they were often married as "half-castes," a much despised term now. He went deeper into his folder, pulling out a series of newspaper articles about the various affronts to Black people—and their responses to these—that had occurred in the last ten to fifteen years. After discussing these materials, he suggested what we might do on the occasion of our second meeting: he wanted to give me a tour of Liverpool.

Scott's tour brought Liverpool's past as an international seaport to life. He took me to Pitt Street, where most Black families lived when he was a boy. Pitt Street was bombed in World War II, and what survived was later destroyed by slum clearance. The Pitt Street of old no longer exists—physically. But it does psychically. Cars whizzed by as Scott and I stood on a corner that approximated where Pitt Street would have been. He asked me to visualize Chinese, African, and Arab people, all wearing traditional garb. I was to imagine them walking around. The picture he painted was not in Black and White. Rather, he emphasized the racial, ethnic, and national heterogeneity of this dockside neighborhood. Liverpool's shipping industry died years ago, and Blacks like Scott mourn the internationalism that seemed to die with it. In its invisibility, Pitt Street symbolizes the disappearance of all things related to the shipping life, including, some say, young Black people's sense of imagination and adventure, their desire to experience the world beyond Liverpool. Scott told me that if I were a young Black person in Liverpool 8—which is, strictly speaking, a postal code that also serves as a place name and as a synonym for "Black people"—I would have never ventured so far from home. I would have scarcely left my neighborhood, much less traveled abroad. Scott then told me what motivated him to participate in my research. He feared that if I let Blacks around Granby Street, the symbolic heart of Liverpool 8, tell the community's history, I would come to believe that it was born there, in Liverpool 8, and that it originated in the 1950s with Caribbean immigration. He said he wanted to show me the Black community's real history. Blacks descended from *this* place, Pitt Street, invisible though it may be. Just a few blocks from the once busy docks, Pitt Street was the site of settlement for nationals—mainly men—from around the globe. Their origins lay less in other places, by Scott's account, than in the shipping industry that brought them to Britain first as seamen and eventually as settlers.

The most striking aspect of Scott's tour was that it consisted largely of places that no longer exist. To make his points, he often had to narrate around the physical environment. This or that building didn't used to be there. Instead, there were houses where such and so people used to live, or places where they used to shop, or where some other events, integral to the daily life of a seaport, used to happen. When Scott took me to important places that did physically exist—a rice mill and an old police station, neither operative in the present day—he insisted that I take pictures of them, perhaps for fear that they, too, might sail away without notice. He would not move on until I took a shot.

The places that hold the dearest meaning for most Black people I knew are those that are no longer visible to the eye. For Scott and others of his generation, this would be Pitt Street. For Blacks a generation or two younger, it would be Granby Street. The latter place does exist, physically, but it bears no resemblance to the way Granby was "back when all the ships were coming in," as one Black woman in her thirties memorialized it. The constant arrival of ships is what made Granby glorious. Commodities from around the world could be found in the international shops that lined that street. Back then, Black people were confined to Liverpool 8 on threat of the violence or verbal abuse of Whites. But never mind—Black life was gloriously cosmopolitan in Granby's environs. Blacks' corner of Liverpool, by absolutely all accounts, was once vital and teeming. Filled to overflowing. Now, unimaginably, Granby Street is a ghetto. It is commonly described as "dead." So much did I hear about how exciting Granby used to be, and how great Pitt Street was, that I started asking people if they had pictures of them in their glory. No one did.

As we walked from one neighborhood in south Liverpool to the next, Scott told me about race in the city and in Britain more broadly. He showed me exactly where it was that a White person made some unsavory comment to him when he was a boy. A superlative informant, Scott was careful to elaborate the racial implications that made it a slight. He showed me the former location of his school—now gone—where he first learned that he was different. And so it went. We would stand in a little spot, Scott would tell me a vivid story that defied the actual surroundings, and then it was on to the next place that wasn't there.

As we passed the offices of a state-funded race relations organization, the Merseyside Community Relations Council, his geography of race opened up. He observed that race relations had become an industry in Britain, and he asked me whether this was the case in the States. He took this opportunity to describe Granby Street again, not in terms of its physicality but its "mentality." I would get a hopelessly distorted picture of Black life in Liverpool, he reiterated, if I were to talk to Blacks around Granby Street. They would tell me that they cannot get jobs. Scott, himself a longtime and passionate antiracist activist, opined that this is not the case at all. If only they would just travel out of the Granby area and into town, then they *could* get jobs. They're "putting shackles on themselves," he explained. Granby Street was not part of his tour at all, despite how much it figured as a foil in his narrative.

Scott was born in 1932 to a Black woman, originally from another English city, and a seaman from Barbados who settled in Liverpool. After his parents divorced, he and his siblings had no further contact with their father. As Scott grew up, his mother expected him to help provide for the family. She wanted him to find a living in the city, and thus Scott never went away to sea—which he deeply regrets. Yet, as he went on to explain, men of his generation came of age as the shipping industry was in decline. Seafaring became less of an option. For much of his adult life, Scott was employed as a laborer doing repairs in houses owned by the Liverpool City Council. By the time I met him, he had risen within the council's ranks. In his spare time, he organized within and outside of his labor union on issues of workers' rights and race. And he nursed a healthy obsession with the history of Liverpool.

If Granby embodies stasis, other places are the picture of mobility. As we approached Park Lane, Scott said that any sailor in the world of his own age could tell me about that street. Two blocks away from the city's busiest piers, Park Lane was the first stop for many foreign sailors docked in Liverpool. It was lined with big pubs that occupied several floors and included accommodations. Women were also frequent visitors to Park Lane, Scott said. Shipping companies encouraged foreign—often colonial—men in their employ to mix with women in Liverpool, he continued, because the greater the ties between them, the less likely sailors would be to jump ship and settle elsewhere, reneging on their contracts.[1] Despite the vibrant picture Scott painted of its past, the street was absolutely desolate. Not a soul passed us as we toured the former life of Park Lane. The sight of a sign for Jamaica Street prompted an abrupt turn in Scott's narrative. In a previous life, Liverpool was also a slave port. All local shippers were involved in the trade in Africans, the profits of which built the city, he told me. Even small-time merchants of the eighteenth century would get in on the action, investing little bits of money in the voyages. I failed to ask Scott whether he had mapped out this route for dramatic effect—in order, that is, to exploit the strange and disturbing contradictions that could only be summoned up at the point where Jamaica Street greets Park Lane.

Scott's narrative testifies to the manifold politics of race, sexuality, nation, and gender forged at the intersection of the sea and this port. His tour of invisible places, and of others that were only nominally there, conveyed not only Blacks' "real" history but the poignancy of their fate. The gulf he placed between Pitt

Street and Granby reflects the city's own painful transformation from an international seaport of global importance and world renown to an out-of-the-way place. To understand Black people, you've got to understand Liverpool. In view of that thesis, the racial knowledge that Scott imparted could only be situated in and through place.

GEOGRAPHIES OF RACE

This ethnography argues that British cultural notions of place and localness have shaped all aspects of racial politics in Liverpool. In so arguing, this book affirms Scott's straightforward but arresting thesis, although not in ways that he might have predicted. At first blush, Scott's words seem to rely on the reasonable premise that any phenomenon should be understood in its larger social context. But here I inquire into the very question of "context" by showing the effects of its conflation with the constructs of place and localness. In their seeming transparency, these constructs mediate racial phenomena of all kinds: racial classification, racial subjectivity, racial community and identity formation, as well as understandings of racism and resistance to it. The naturalization of place through ideas about its efficacy is beautifully captured in Scott's own thesis, which hands ultimate explanatory power directly over to Liverpool—or *place*—which you've *got* to understand. I would argue, though, that what one must really understand is not Liverpool, per se, but "Liverpool," the signifier.

For its rich and tortured history, Liverpool is an endlessly fascinating site for the study of race and place. Located in England's northwest, Liverpool was once a seaport of incalculable national and global significance. Its merchants, shippers, and financial elites were among Britain's most active and prosperous colonial traders. As well, Liverpool held a monopoly on shipping in the North, where most of England's manufacturing towns and cities—most famously, Manchester—were located. Manchester's workers may have been spinning tons of cotton into cloth during the Industrial Revolution, but without Liverpool's ships and its perfectly located and highly developed port, that tonnage would have had a formidable route out of England and into international markets. Speaking of cotton, and as Scott suggested, Liverpool also played a prominent role in the British slave trade. Liverpool shippers raked in untold millions in the traffic in Africans.

By the time of my fieldwork in 1991 and 1992, though, shipping—for three hundred years Liverpool's one cash crop—had long since died. Once Britain's "second metropolis," Liverpool currently occupies very marginal status nationally. The city has become one of the poorest not only in Britain but in Europe. In 1993 it received "Objective One" status from the European Union—a status that likens the city, precisely through its abject class positioning, to a third world country in need of development. As chapters 6 and 7 elaborate, Liverpool's precipitous fall from grace perhaps encourages the narratives that circulate in Britain about this place *as* disgrace. Its designation as "the capital of the slave trade" is one of many powerful examples of the way race and place intersect in the production of "Liverpool."

Liverpool's Black community dates its history back at least as far as the mid-nineteenth century when British shippers hired African seamen who eventually settled in the city, marrying (mostly) White English and Irish women. This ethnography examines Blacks' uses of that origin story in the context of racism, nationalism, and localism in Britain and in relation to the myriad transnational dimensions of Liverpool's political economy, identity, and social life. As they narrate distinct moments in their emergence as a political collective and as a social group, self-described Liverpool-born Blacks construct geographies of race that render some histories, experiences, and subject positions visible, and others less so. Hence, the various and protracted episodes of local-cum-global racial history outlined above and further elaborated below do not serve as background material for this ethnography. Rather, I show their contemporary bearing on the production of hegemonic and oppositional racial identities in the city, as well as those projected *onto* the city.

This goal requires careful ethnographic attention to the meanings of "the local." The drama that attended the reversal of the city's fortunes mirrored the larger crisis of the fall of the British Empire—although in Liverpool that fall is narrated, like almost everything else, in terms that distinguish the local from the national. If Britain's decline resulted in racialized contestations over nationhood and citizenship, Liverpool's own spectacular fall created a greater investment in all things local (Belchem 2000). Blacks share in this investment, and they do so in distinctly (though not exclusively) racial registers. They boast of being the oldest Black community in Britain; Blacks elsewhere, but especially London, are mere immigrants in Liverpool-born Blacks' view. Bristol and Cardiff, as British seaports with similarly old Black communities, are oft-noted exceptions. Nevertheless, the meanings they invest in "Liverpool" and its singularity serve as frames, at nearly every possible turn, for their understandings of what Blackness means and who gets to claim it. The subjectivities and concrete practices that enabled Scott's thesis thus forced the primacy I give to localness in this book. Scarcely could Blacks discuss a racial issue without appealing to Liverpool and its apparent distinctiveness. As assertively *Liverpool-born* Blacks, they have deployed the local to tremendous effect in their historic struggles against various forms of racism. The cultural and political dilemmas that arise from the mutual constitution of spatial and racial subjectivities form the substance of this ethnography.

In a historical milieu consumed with the theory and politics of globalization, Blacks in late twentieth-century Liverpool compelled attention to localization. Their unwitting intervention is fortuitous, for it allows us to ask how we might theorize the local in view of increased scholarly attention to transnational processes of racial formation. The still-reverberating effects of Liverpool's past as an imperial seaport, one that drew colonial seamen from all parts of the world as both transient visitors and eventual settlers, makes the city a novel vantage point from which to pursue such an inquiry. In terms equally broad, the Liverpool case prompts the question: How might the local be theorized in a way that does not feminize it either by reducing it to an outpost of global penetrations of whatever form, or by fetishizing it as the site of resistance to globalizing agendas? In what ways, indeed, might "the local" and "the global" be understood as cultural categories implicated in the production of race and gender rather than simply analytical indices of scales, scopes, and scapes? What racial formations would result from the encounter between "global men," many of whom were African, and the "local women," most of whom were White, over there on Park Lane, the desolate street where Scott took us on his tour?[2] In the sexual tensions of empire unfolding in this once jointly local and global space, when and where does the nation enter? Scott specified that *Liverpool* explains Black people. Liverpool may very well be in Britain but the city's national citizenship, as it were, cannot be assumed.

Scott's tour presents in miniature the monumental racial histories that alternately combine and fragment in the construction of Black experience and identity. The importance of slavery and colonialism to understanding Liverpool and hence Black people raises the question of diaspora. As a complex formation of community, identity, and subjectivity, diaspora is generally studied in relation to international migration, nations and nationalism, ancestries and homelands, roots and routes, postcoloniality and globalization. Here I pursue diaspora through place and localness, which receive little attention in ethnographies about Black folk here and there.[3] The cultural studies literature on diaspora—caught up in the claustrophobic vortex of globalization—analyzes place and localness even less. My intention is not to celebrate place or to exalt the local, much less to reduce diaspora to "another Black community heard from." Rather, this book elaborates diaspora by analyzing the geopolitics of diverse Black histories, experiences and constructions of race and identity, as they have alternately and contentiously come to bear in the formation of Black Liverpool. Here diaspora attends to the production of affinities and the negotiation of antagonisms among differently racialized Black subjects—Liverpool-born Blacks, West Africans, Afro-Caribbeans, and Black Americans—not simply in Liverpool but in view of "Liverpool." The analysis also shows how the very histories that produced a "global" Black world— histories that implicate Liverpool directly—find themselves reverberating in a space ideologically defined as "local."

Arguably, no scholar traffics in the local like the anthropologist, who often conflates it with the ethnographic, the specific, and, ultimately, the cultural.[4] The terms *local specificity* and *ethnographic specificity* are interchangeable in anthropology. Because this book is so heavily invested in showing the racial effects of similar conflations in the context of everyday British life, it behooves me to situate this project in relation to two very important ethnographies that analyze race through place and localness in national contexts: John Hartigan's *Racial Situations: Class Predicaments of Whiteness in Detroit* (1999) and Steven Gregory's *Black Corona: Race and the Politics of Place in an Urban Community* (1998). A comparison of their spatial frameworks shows the implications of constituting the local as either a site of ethnographic and therefore cultural specificity within the nation, or as a location from which national processes of race can be seen in all *their* cultural specificity.

From the vantage point provided by his field site, Hartigan argues, essentially, that to understand White people one must understand Detroit. That argument is premised on Detroit's uniqueness, for not only is the city predominantly Black—perhaps "the blackest city in America" (1999: 4)—but it is also home to a larger percentage of poor Whites than any of the ten largest cities in the United States (9). A second-order differentiation follows: the racial situations he studies unfold in three predominantly White neighborhoods, each with a distinct class composition. Class is the basis of Americans' sense of place, Hartigan suggests, and hence each neighborhood can be considered a unique "zone." These distinctions provide the theoretical anchor for his project, which is elaborated in a section called "The Localness of Race." There he argues that "race functions as a local matter" (13) and announces his intention to show "the distinctive role of *places* in informing and molding the meaning of race" (14, original emphasis). As he explains, "This approach derives from a developing tendency among anthropologists to regard race as they do culture—as a relentlessly local matter" (14). For its bigness and heterogeneity, the United States can be neither the site of "local" (read: "specific" and "distinctive") processes nor a site of culture. For a matter to be cultural, it must be spatially contained in a small place and, presumably, have a fairly homogeneous expression. The more homogeneous, the more distinctive is the place being cordoned off. The racial makeup of Detroit, and the class composition of the three neighborhoods studied, render place stable. Race is the only moving target—albeit a crucial one, of course. Hartigan's work in Detroit leads him to conclude that "racial identities are produced and experienced distinctly in different locations" (14). These racial identities may very well be *experienced* as if they were distinct, but that does not mean that they are. As well, the social forces that *produce* experience do not necessarily originate in those neighborhoods. Rather, those forces may derive from a site that *Racial Situations* renders invisible: the cultureless nonplace lying seemingly beyond Detroit called the United States. These concerns notwithstanding, *Racial Situations* achieves its goal of complicating generalizations about when and how race matters in that country.[5] Yet that aim could have been accomplished just as well without reifying place and localness in the process.

Steven Gregory's objective in *Black Corona* is to challenge the racial construction of "the Black ghetto" as a social isolate, one explicitly marked "distinctive" and therein cordoned off from so-called mainstream American society. Social scientists (especially sociologists) and social policy makers are implicated here. Of his own project, Gregory writes: "This is not a book about a 'black ghetto' or an 'inner city' community. . . . These concepts have become (and perhaps always were) powerful tropes conflating race, class and place in a society that remains organized around inequalities in economic resources and political power that stretch beyond the imagined frontiers of the inner city" (1998: 10). Gregory does not refer to the neighborhood of Corona, in Queens, New York, as a unique place but rather as a vantage point from which to examine the formation of "place" as an object and symbol of Blacks' class-based desires and politics, as shaped by national histories of racial inequality. An ethnography and social history of impressive detail, *Black*

Corona never makes the local serve as a signifier of specificity. In what follows, for example, Gregory makes an implicit call for "specificity" without locating it "locally": "[T]idy sound bites for discussions and debates about the 'state of black America' in the mass media and the academy . . . fail to reveal not only the complexity of black identity but also the social processes through which that heterogeneity has been produced, negotiated, and contested in the everyday lives of African-Americans" (156). Indeed, Gregory does not localize the Black people of Corona. Rather, he specifies the ways that bureaucratic government structures and experiments localized *them*, "producing knowledge about neighborhood needs and problems that obscured the origins of urban deterioration and black poverty in practices of racial subordination" (86). This knowledge, Gregory suggests, shaped the ways that Black political activists in Corona framed their actions and interests. From there, he details actors' initial difficulty in seeing beyond naturalized spatial boundaries and shows their ultimate success in recognizing their artificiality. In sum, Gregory's critical intervention is to lend ethnographic "specificity" to the *normalization* of the local.

Corona, despite its "smallness," serves as a vehicle to expose the specificity of *American* racial politics. One could, of course, say that Corona is not Detroit. For that matter, it might not be like other neighborhoods in New York City. But what would be the point of arguing that any of these other places are, therefore, departures from the United States rather than—in equal measure—productions of the United States? Even if Corona is not like every other spot on the American map, its possible difference from other places need not imply an exceptional status. Similarly, to the degree that Corona does seem to function well as a mirror onto the United States, it need not be confused as an exemplar of it. Rather, what begs analysis is why and to what effect a particular group of historical actors might be moved to make place serve such functions. These are not Gregory's concerns, nor should they necessarily be. These are my obsessions, and they grow out of the conundrum presented by the racial politics of place and localness in Liverpool—or is it Britain?

With a bit of rearranging, then, Scott's thesis can stand as my argument. To understand race in Liverpool, you've got to understand place in Britain. The ambiguous and sometimes tense relationship between Liverpool and Britain is perhaps the most important instantiation of a national politic of place that shapes race in that city. I often use the phrase *Liverpool/Britain* in order to highlight the instabilities at work and to keep Britain in view at precisely those moments when one might be tempted to view Liverpool as "specific," "particular," and hence a place apart. Along similar lines, I use the term *localness* rather than *locality* because the latter is synonymous with *place*. One of this book's goals is to analyze the ways that place takes on meaning in relation to ideologies of localness, while also showing that neither place nor the local is limited to the terms set by the other.

Place is an axis of power in its own right. As a basis for the construction of difference, hierarchy, and identity, and as the basis of ideologies that rationalize economic inequalities and structure people's material well-being and life chances, place is a vehicle of power. While I follow a host of other scholars in treating it as such, my contribution is to show the mediating effects of place on race, emphasizing in the process that race is not autonomous.[6] Race takes its changing and contradictory shape in dynamic interaction with other forms of power—an argument most commonly made in relation to class and gender. Place, I further argue, must be understood first and foremost as an abstraction, not a set of physical properties just there for the eye to see.[7] Like race and gender, place operates powerfully, though not exclusively, through the invocation and naturalization of matter. Yet one cannot see, touch, or in any other perceptual way "sense" or physically occupy, all that gave rise to Scott's tour, which advanced the thesis that (a largely invisible) Liverpool explains. The very urge to make meaning out of the materiality of places—what they look like, feel like, and where they are, for example, and who occupies them, what social relations define them, and what processes unfold within them—is produced through an axis of power and subjectivity that we might call *place*. Understood thus, *place* is not photographable (hence the absence of pictures in this book), although places are. Moreover, the materiality of a place lies not merely in its physical, visible form (and visibility itself is a moving target) but in its identity as, for example, a seaport, or as the original site of Black settlement, or as a site hospitable or hostile to capital investment, or as one of Britain's problem cities. In similarly discursive terms, place's materiality is produced through enactments of the very premise—implicit though it might be—that place matters. "You've got to understand Liverpool." Power further manifests in the naturalization of place *as* matter—that is, in the ways that a place's physicality is "read" and rendered significant. For example, in 1981, in the aftermath of three days of very violent, very racialized riots in Liverpool 8, where most Blacks lived, state officials deemed that the roots of Black people's "problem" lay in their uncheery environment. So the government arranged for trees to be planted on Princes Avenue, Liverpool 8's main thoroughfare. I shall have more to say about those trees, but for now they introduce this book's critical concern for the attribution of agency to place's *apparent* materiality or, put otherwise, the use of place-as-matter to explain the social.

Toward those ends, I find phenomenology quite useful—not as a theoretical tool but as an interpretive frame. Philosophers, urban planners, and anthropologists draw from that school in suggesting that place is significant, primarily, as physical matter—particularly as an object of people's everyday perceptual activities. But not only that. Place is defined by its physical *particularity*, which exerts an intense effect on human experience. The cultural logics of place through which England and Englishness are constructed, I would suggest, can be productively considered a folk version of phenomenology.

So what is phenomenology? In short, it is the study of experience and perception. Philosopher Robert Sokolowski defines it as "the science that studies truth" and the method through which that truth can be accessed (2000: 185).[8] Through phenomenology, one hopes to achieve a "transcendental attitude," which enables the apprehension of things—objects—as they are rather than how they are preconceived to be ("the natural attitude"). In reflecting on the object in question, one comes to understand how human consciousness and being are constituted through

the experience of that object; as part of that same process of reflection, the nature of that object's being also comes to be fully (transcendentally) apprehended.

> When we shift from the natural attitude to the phenomenological, we raise the question of being, because we begin to look at things precisely as they are given to us, precisely as they are manifested. . . . We begin to look at things in their truth and evidencing. This is to look at them in their being. We also begin to look at the self as the dative to whom beings are disclosed: we look at the self as the dative of manifestation. This is to look at it in *its* being, because the core of its being is to inquire into the being of things. (Sokolowski 2000: 64–65)[9]

The poststructuralist might worry about the appeal to truth and the search for meaning in things as they are, not as they are preconceived to be. All of this implies that things have a prediscursive, pure, unmediated form, an essence unaffected by human activity and social process.

The phenomenologist strives for an identity with the world of objects, a world that is always already acting on him or her anyway. The self, in this view, is at once paramount—for it is the self that we ultimately desire to understand—and sublimated to something else, whose own being must be apprehended transcendentally. The key question thus becomes, as Martin Heidegger puts it, "In *which* entities is the meaning of Being to be discerned? From which entities is the disclosure of Being to take its departure? Is the starting-point optional, or does some particular entity have priority when we come to work out the question of Being? Which entity shall we take for our example, and in what sense does it have priority?" (1996b: 28).[10] That entity, for some phenomenologists (including Heidegger), is place, which is determining on at least two levels. First, as the locus of the self, the perceiving human body is itself a place. And second, the body inhabits place (Casey 1996: 34). A hallmark of the phenomenological view of place is that *its* being dynamically affects *human* being and experience. As Edward Casey explains,

> place . . . functions like a general feature, even a condition of possibility, of all human . . . experience—however expansive the term "experience" is taken to be. On the other hand, place is also a quite distinctive feature of such experience. Place is not a purely formal operator empty of content but is always contentful, always specifiable as this particular place or that one. . . . The deconstruction of this distinction will already be effected by the character of place itself, *by its inherent generative force.* (1996: 29, emphasis added)

Place is matter that acts—and acts *first*. Through its particularity, place generates effects on human consciousness and experience, even if the affected humans remain oblivious. In their introduction to *Senses of Place*, Steven Feld and Keith Basso suggest that "no one lives in the world in general. . . . What could be truer of placed experience . . . than the taken-for-granted quality of its intense particularity?" (1996: 11). Motivated by the desire to identify what human beings most fundamentally require for the spiritual nourishment of their souls, Heidegger famously examined place in terms of dwelling (1977).[11] As Casey suggests, "Heidegger . . . insist[s] that it is in dwellings that we are most acutely sensitive to the effects of places upon our lives" (1996: 39).

Again, my point is not to endorse such perspectives but to lay the groundwork for one of the arguments that follows, which is that a folk phenomenology undergirds constructions of England, English places (and un-English ones), and Englishness. I study how people make sense of place-as-matter, a practice that includes reading landscapes and acting on the view that place acts, that it shapes human consciousness. To return to the example above, the British government of the early 1980s seemed to believe that the physical environment of Liverpool 8 affected its residents in some terribly adverse ways, making it impossible for them to dwell in ways that nourish the soul, to use Heidegger's terms. That is, for the government, "trees" made sense as an answer to the questions posed by the most destructive riots of twentieth-century Britain (chapter 3). Undeniably, the state could have devised the tree solution as part of a political maneuver in which it feigns interest in the residents with this *visible* display of largess while discounting their explanations of the riots and ignoring their grievances. Perhaps there were additional impulses at work. For centuries, English folklore and literature have invested trees with spiritual powers over humans. According to Peter Ackroyd's gushing study of the English imagination, trees appear again and again as the guardian spirits of English people and places (2002: 3–7). Moreover, greenery of all kinds, especially gardens, have been central to both English senses of place and English senses of self—again, for centuries (Ackroyd 2002: 411–18).[12] For the elevation of spirit that it alone makes possible, the "green and pleasant land" of the Lake District has been, arguably, an unrivaled symbol of Englishness. Being bleak, Liverpool 8 was completely out-of-place, fundamentally inconsistent with the (imagined) English pastoral and hopelessly incapable of nourishing the soul. Could the trees have been planted as an effort to spawn a more "pleasant" disposition among the people of Liverpool 8?

In addition to addressing the effects of places on selves, phenomenology also treats place-as-self. In his ethnography of the Western Apache, Keith Basso makes the connection by observing that both places and selves are reckoned to be individuals; both go by names (1988, 1996). This ethnography takes that formulation in a critical direction, analyzing the ways that historical subjects are encouraged to perceive—in the sense of "to conceptualize"—a place as "individual." More to the point, I draw attention to how a place is "individuated," to invoke Foucault's term for the production of "specific" kinds of bodies and selves (1977). I show how racial subjects come into being—in all their "specificity"—through the *idea* that places are essentially selves.

The Place of Britishness and Englishness

Not much distance lay between Scott's thesis, "To understand Black people, you've got to understand Liverpool," and Doreen Massey's argument that "Places are spaces of social relations" (2000: 458). A tour-like, autobiographical passage follows that statement:

> Take this corner of a council estate; on the southern outskirts of Manchester. . . . My parents lived here for nearly fifty years and have known this spot for even longer.

Their lives have taken it in, and made it, for over half a century. Both they and it, and their relationship to one another ("place" and "people") have changed, adjusted, readjusted, over time. (458)

Currently a growth area in American anthropology, place has long been the object of rich and prolific theorizing in Britain. In the United States, the most well-known and commonly cited geographers, including Doreen Massey, David Harvey, Neil Smith, and Michael Watts, all hail from Britain. Geography is institutionalized in Britain to a far greater degree than in the United States, a difference attributable, at the very least, to the field's importance to imperialism.[13] It might also owe to the fact that British conceptions of the social—and the hierarchies supported by them—have long been routed through place. Let's begin with place's changing relationship to race, as manifested in the historical constitution of the categories *English* and *British*.

In his brilliant book, *Out of Place: Englishness, Empire, and the Locations of Identity*, Ian Baucom makes an argument to which I shall refer on numerous occasions. He argues that "Englishness has consistently been defined through appeals to the *identity-endowing* properties of place" (1999: 4, emphasis added). Baucom traces this reification to the early nineteenth century, when English historians sought to pinpoint the definitive basis of English identity. Their concerns about their bloodlines made that project both difficult and necessary. In 1700, for example, Daniel Defoe made a mockery of Anglo-Saxons' pretensions to racial purity in his satirical poem, *The True-born Englishman*. Their blood had been contaminated by all manner of foreign invaders. The writing of nineteenth-century English historians reflects their anxious efforts to explain authentic Englishness without relying on race. In the end, Baucom argues, they proposed that distinctly English places produced Englishness. Deploying what I am calling a folk phenomenology, these historians suggested that traditions emerged from uniquely English places such as cricket fields. An essential English spirit arises mystically from the very soil of England and accounts for historical processes. Just *beholding* an English place could put one under its irreversible spell. Even Indians, it was suggested, could become English thus. Their "blood" did not render them immune from the power of English places. As for Anglo-Saxons, their bloodlines may have been murky, but, these writers suggested, place was stable and continuous.[14] The unitary, racially uncompromised Englishness these historians sought was eventually found in the intrinsic place/self isomorphism.[15] Place supplanted race. While the phenomenological underpinnings of English cultural logics of place recur—as the tree solution suggests—the racialness of Englishness has been reinscribed, most notably through a discourse on Whiteness.[16]

Historically, place has also been fundamental to Britishness, forming the customary basis for reckoning subjecthood in the kingdom encompassing Wales, Scotland, England, and, until 1922, Ireland. (Presently, of course, Northern Ireland remains part of the United Kingdom.) An important digression is necessary here. It bears emphasis for some American readers that *British* and *English* are not synonymous terms.[17] More often than not, the difference matters profoundly.

It is through Britishness that Wales, England, Scotland, and Northern Ireland (the United Kingdom) are linked into collective (though often contested) state-legitimated nationality. The fact that *British* and *English* are often taken for synonyms is both symptom and effect of English hegemony.

From medieval times through 1981, and through prescriptive custom, British subjecthood was reckoned through the principle of *ius soli,* or "law of the soil" (Baucom 1999). If one was born on British soil, one was a British subject—beholden to the Crown. By the late nineteenth century, British soil consisted of one-quarter of the world's land mass. Law of the soil presented a special complication when, at various points, colonial and postcolonial subjects laid claim to British nationality within mainland Britain itself. As will be discussed fully later, British nationalists of the 1960s and through to the present day have been arguing that Blacks could never properly belong to the nation and, even more pointedly, that they could never share culture with Irish, Welsh, Scottish, and English people. In 1981, the government of Prime Minister Margaret Thatcher codified these racist exclusions with the passage of the British Nationality Act. To be a British citizen, one now had to have a parent born in Britain. The government obviously intended to exclude Blacks from British nationality, as most of them would not have had a parent who qualified. Baucom sums up the radical transformation thus: "Discarding nine hundred years of legal precedent that recognized a *territorial* principle as the sole absolute determinant of British identity, the [British Nationality Act] determined that Britain was, henceforth, a *genealogical* community" (1999: 8, emphasis added).[18] Race supplanted place.

The 1981 Nationality Act may have made state-legitimated forms of Britishness dependent on genealogy for the first time ever, but this racially motivated move did nothing more than capitalize on the already existing link between place and ancestry in the British Isles.[19] In rural and urban British communities alike, genealogy often establishes place-based belonging. A few ethnographic examples may illustrate the point. In her study of a rural community in Essex, Marilyn Strathern deconstructs the notion of the "real" Elmdon, which villagers define through "old families" among other kinship idioms (1982). Anthony Cohen argues that in the fishing community of Whalsay, in the Shetland Islands, "'Belonging' implies very much more than merely having been born in a place" (1982b: 21). Rather, it is conferred through a rhetoric of continuity dependent on genealogies, which are further mapped onto neighborhood and occupation (membership in a fishing crew). Kinship, neighborhood, and occupation combine to situate all individuals vis-à-vis the community. This use of a jointly genealogical and occupational idiom has broader significance. Like Whalsay, many towns and cities developed through one or two industries (Waller 1983). People often use these industries, even in their obsolescence, to define a place and to produce ideologies of belonging. The nickname for people from the Newcastle area, "Geordie," was traditionally synonymous with the term *pit worker*, a reference to the prominence of the coal-mining industry there (Colls and Lancaster 1992). With the decline of that industry, young, White, unemployed, men now constitute themselves as "real Geordies" by invoking the "labouring heritage" they trace through their fathers and grandfathers (Nayak 2003: 14). My friend Scott traced Black Liverpool's authentic history through seafaring. As we see in the next chapter, Blacks trace their genealogies as locals through their male ancestors' participation in that place-based tradition. Chapter 4 shows Blacks tracing still other kinds of genealogies in reference to place.

Genealogy establishes local belonging and authenticity in Elmdon, Whalsay, Newcastle, and Liverpool. Interestingly, Doreen Massey advanced her argument that "Places are spaces of social relations" very nearly by tracing her genealogy in reference to Wythenshawe, on the outskirts of Manchester. Although she certainly does not appeal to ideologies of local authenticity and belonging, much less to nationalism, her use of that method is further evidence of the Britishness of that cultural practice.[20] Strathern draws out the larger, again *cultural* significance of the "real Elmdon" by linking it to forms of hierarchy and differentiation that define the society at large: "[T]he idiom of village identity is precisely attuned to an outside world which is highly 'class' conscious, and provides a model for the same articulation of open and closed factors in status structures which preoccupy most English" (1982: 274). Elmdoners may use kinship to define the real villager but, Strathern stresses, these practices are relevant to the world outside of the village because that is where their impetus lay. Though these case studies straddle the historical event in question, the passage of the 1981 British Nationality Act, they collectively suggest that the Act's elevation of genealogy as a determinant of national citizenship was not out of step with British (not just English) ways of reckoning belonging.[21] This point is not offered as a "cultural defense" of racist exclusions but as evidence of place's centrality to the politics of difference in Britain.[22]

Just as traditional occupations imbue place and people with identity, so too does social class give places their meaning. The *Geordie* of Newcastle has counterparts in the *Cockney* of East London and the *Scouser* of Liverpool. These nicknames, for want of a better word, express inextricably place-based and working-class identities. Moreover, on an individual level, one's class background, among other attributes, is reckoned through one's birthplace; the politics of accent shows this clearly. As is commonly known, accents are indelible markers of social class in Britain. Generally, to speak the English standard, known as "Received Pronunciation" (RP), is to speak "posh," a word with obviously elite class associations. Yet the key criterion of the standard is that it defies geographical placement—notwithstanding, of course, its historical origins in London and its continuing association with middle- and upper-class Londoners.[23] At its inception in the late nineteenth century, RP encouraged the view of speakers of "provincial" (a term used for localities distant from the metropole) variants of English as cultural inferiors (Rawnsley 2000). That inscription has relevance to anthropologist Charles Frake's observation that in present-day England it is considered rude to inquire into another person's provenance.

[T]he impression that one does not casually ask the provenance of someone one does not know well is certainly widespread. It is mentioned in humourous treatises on

English-American differences: "Curiously, for people who identify so closely with region of origin, Brits refuse to tell outsiders where they're from. . . . [If you ask one] he freezes, tongue-tied. You have intruded somehow on private matters, and embarrassed him." (1996: 233)

One has to wonder about the middle-class and other privileged positionings from which these generalized cultural rules are articulated. Certainly, they are not as hard and fast as they are represented to be. Not all English people want to be seen as posh and to escape an association with place. Indeed, local identities are often oppositional and proudly anti-English, as the case of Liverpool's "Scousers" will certainly show.

With these caveats in mind, I offer an anecdote illustrating place-of-origin as a private matter. In 1999 I visited the exceedingly posh town of Bath, whereupon I made brief acquaintance with a White woman, perhaps in her mid-twenties. She was a sales clerk in a charming little crafts shop. A few minutes into our warm and amiable exchange, I noticed the faintest trace of a Liverpudlian accent. And so I popped the question: "Are you from Liverpool?" With that, our friendly encounter came to an abrupt close. Positively glaring at me, she replied, "Yes." She uttered not a single word to me thereafter. She handled my eventual purchase in icy silence. If a lowly American can hear Liverpool in her voice—after all, we are not known for our ability to discern different British accents—maybe the people of the incurably precious town of Bath hear it too? And maybe they, unlike crass Americans, are too "polite" to inquire into or otherwise invoke her provenance? To the degree that Britons see origins as a private matter, there must be something about place that defines one's personhood on some terribly deep level. This woman's origins, if discovered, would immediately associate her with everything that marks Liverpool's difference; an abject class positioning would only be the beginning (chapter 6). Indeed, the trenchant emphasis on *origins,* which connotes fixity and nature, implies that one can no more reverse the effects of *birth*place by, for example, migrating, than one can change one's "race."[24] But one can try to "pass."[25]

Interestingly enough, the rules prohibiting inquiries into provenance are suspended when it comes to Black people. To the degree that some White Britons refuse to reveal their own birthplace to outsiders, this does not stop, again, *some* of them from popping the question to their would-be Black counterparts: "Where are you from?" Blacks' phenotype cancels out the identity that their particular British accents would otherwise secure. A Black Londoner tells me that her response of "north London" never satisfies. So the question gets revised: "No, I mean, where are you *really* from?" Blacks interpret Whites' insistent questions on provenance as an effort to establish their "real" identities and hence the place where they really belong, which cannot be, for example, north London (much less England).

The centrality of place to constructions of personhood, especially class-based ones, manifests on another, even broader scale. While individual places are identified with one or two industries, the North of England has, historically, symbolized industry itself. Northern otherness is important to the present work not only because Liverpool is—at least technically—in the North, but because it indicates the confluence of representations and economic factors in the production of place-based inequalities.[26] While northern difference and consciousness are as old as England itself (Jewell 1994), their basis in industrialization and then deindustrialization is most salient in the present day. The North's inescapable association with the environmental and social ills of industrialization was etched in Charles Dickens's depiction of Coketown (based on Preston, Lancashire) in *Hard Times*:

> It was a town of red brick, or of brick that would have been red if the smoke and ashes had allowed it; but as matters stood it was a town of unnatural red and black like the painted face of a savage. It was a town of machinery and tall chimneys, out of which interminable serpents of smoke trailed themselves for ever and ever, and never got uncoiled. It had a black canal in it, and a river that ran purple with ill-smelling dye, and vast piles of buildings full of windows where there was a rattling and a trembling all day long, and where the piston of the steam-engine worked monotonously up and down like the head of an elephant in a state of melancholy madness. It contained several large streets all very like one another, and many small streets still more like one another, inhabited by people like one another. (1980 [1854]: 30–31)

This passage is notable as *the* classic description of an English industrial town—the basis of many stereotypes of the North that would follow (Shields 1991). The place's harsh physicality bears down on its inhabitants.[27] Generally, the cultural attributes of "gritty England" are working class in nature; they include plain-talking and good humor, tough masculinity and raw manners.

The obsolescence of some northern industries and the migration of others southward forced attention, in the 1980s, to the national geography of economic inequality. Recognizing great disparities from one end of the country to the other in terms of wages, unemployment rates, housing prices, and the cost of living, the press launched a nationwide debate about what it termed the "North/South divide" (Shields 1991). The North and the South were increasingly recognized as two nations, separate and unequal (Massey 1984). Yet comments on postindustrial decline sometimes reinscribed a centuries-old discourse on northern otherness, projecting a disabling social malaise onto entire regions. One method drew on a folk phenomenology in which the physicality of place was assumed to betray an important truth about its inhabitants' selfhood, explaining their actions in turn. In the late 1970s, a serial killer stalked women in the northern cities of Leeds and Bradford. For an academic who studied the murders, the "particular" physical signs of postindustrial decline were informative: "You couldn't help wondering what connections there were between the socio-economic dereliction which much of the geography expressed and the type of violence which was at work in the nooks and crannies of those landscapes" (Noele Ward Jouve, quoted in Walkowitz 1992: 240). The givenness of a place's sorry state explains the pathological actions of the persons who inhabit them.

The same logic suffuses an article that appeared in *The New Yorker* as a "Letter from Liverpool," written in 1994, on the tragic occasion of a little boy's murder at the hands of two older boys.[28] Addressing an American audience assumed to be unfamiliar with the North of England and Liverpool in particular, the author draws the following picture:

> In a northern working-class environment, where to be thought "dead 'ard" is a tribute, boys were left to be boys. . . . The roads near that part of the route [where the boys walked their victim] have the names of Oxbridge colleges. . . . But nothing could be less like Brideshead than this part of Liverpool. To imagine it, you have to set aside images of college quads—and of chamomile lawns, bluebell woods, country lanes, mazy rivers, dappled meadows, rolling downs, and all the other pastoral myths of southern England—and think instead of a vast tract of brick and concrete. Between Breeze Hill and the railway track where James Bulger died, the only grass to be seen grows between the graves in Walton churchyard. . . . [T]he view from the reservoir on top of Breeze Hill is as mean and dispiriting a panorama as you will ever see. The roofs of houses stretch to the horizon: pebble-dash semis, low prefabs, dirt-encrusted red brick row houses, mock-Tudors, a handful of high-rises, boarded-up shops. A large, squat pub called the Mons—"short for the Monstrosity," say the locals—stands, in its bleak anonymity, as the inverse of whatever cozy virtue English pubs once had. This is a landscape emptied of energy and innovation—a city that no longer knows what to do with itself.

This passage evokes the North's abject working classness to perfection. It stereotypes the North with its shorthand reference to unreconstructed masculinity and its relentless description of the landscape's utilitarianism. The harshness of the North is thrown into relief by what the author admits is the mythical "sweetness and light" of the pastoral South.

But there is something more insidious at work in this rendering. In a passage intended to provide some basic context for understanding James Bulger's murder, Liverpool itself is depicted as death. There is a bit of grass, but it grows in a graveyard. The panorama is dispiriting. Emptied of life forces, the landscape sucks the same from its inhabitants. Place's mean and unforgiving physicality explains a despicable, deadly act. With condescension, the author asserts that the city no longer knows what to do with itself—an allusion to the death of shipping, perhaps. Once so vital, Liverpool has become lifelessness incarnate.

THE BIRTH OF LIVERPOOL

> "The discoverer of America was the maker of Liverpool." In the Middle Ages Liverpool lay near the fringes of the known world; she could not compete with ports like Venice which lay near its centre. After the rediscovery of America, Liverpool lay mid-way between the Old and New Worlds. No longer was she almost the last station on the line, but an intermediary station with later stops at New York, Chicago and ultimately, San Francisco.

> The geographical advantage of being situated on the western coastline
> of Europe was shared by other ports, such as Bristol, Bordeaux, Bilbao,
> Lisbon, and Cadiz, which have long been eclipsed by Liverpool, for they
> had not our industrial North and the Midlands behind them.
> —Chandler 1973: 9

This quotation is drawn from one of many popular histories of Liverpool. This sweeping panorama all but sets Liverpool apart from Britain. Another British port, Bristol, appears on a list with a set of foreign ones. Other British places are important as aids in Liverpool's rise to greatness. Indeed the city is conjured here as a quasi-imperial power unto itself: the industrial North and the Midlands seem to be Liverpool's own little colonies.

Chandler's opening statement, "The discoverer of America was the maker of Liverpool," quotes the inscription on the city's infamous statue of Columbus. Liverpool's debt to the explorer is commonly acknowledged but extremely contentious—so much so that the statue is kept from public view out of fear that it might be vandalized. Such was the fate of a statue of William Huskisson, a political figure of the late eighteenth century who, two hundred years later, was thought to be a slave trader. Prior to the 1981 riots, Huskisson's statue stood at the entrance to Liverpool 8, right at the top of Princes Avenue, where some trees have since been planted.

In contrast to Chandler's triumphant account of the seaport's beginnings, Peter Fryer indicates that "without the slave trade, Liverpool would have remained much as it had been towards the end of the seventeenth century: 'an insignificant seaport,' 'a small port of little consequence . . . a few streets some little distance from the creek—or pool—which served as a harbour'" (1984: 33). A couple of young Black men I knew could quote this passage from Fryer's *Staying Power: The History of Black People in Britain* almost verbatim. Meanwhile, some of their fellow citizens, members of the mysterious Luso-American Society, have the huge Columbus statue hauled out once a year on his birthday. After a quick, clandestine, nighttime ceremony at the Pier Head (the focal point of the docks), Columbus is returned to his resting place, the Palm House in Sefton Park. With a weird mix of pride and embarrassment, the daily tabloid, the *Liverpool Echo,* reports on the ceremony— but safely after the fact and in a little blip of a story buried deep inside the paper. Liverpudlians make sense of race through the contested histories of place.

Notwithstanding its enormous debt to the Atlantic slave trade, the port of Liverpool, it should be noted, was first developed in the seventeenth century as part of a strategic, military maneuver to control Ireland. This and other aspects of the port's imperial function bespeak what is arguably the defining paradox of Liverpool. Until the death of shipping, Liverpool had always advanced British political interests. But in doing so, Liverpool fashioned an identity for itself that disavowed Britain. Facing the Atlantic Ocean and the world beyond, Liverpool's orientation was always international. Chandler's vainglorious account is one of many locally published histories that imbue the city with a mammoth and quite individual agency of world-historical significance. In another version, Liverpool is a "gateway of Empire" (Lane 1987). "Liverpool's story is the world's glory." Less popular histories show the interdependence between the city and the nation-state, while also staging the encounter between Liverpool and the world in decidedly racial terms rather than in happily cosmopolitan ones.

Over the course of Liverpool's life as an international seaport, many kinds of ships depended on African workers. Slavers were the first (Frost 1999). Owners of those ships employed the Kru of Liberia as wage laborers, inaugurating a racial organization of labor that would become the basic mechanism of imperial exploitation henceforth. In African ports of call, labor was recruited first to extract local resources and then to assist in their global transportation. With the abolition of the slave trade in 1807, British shippers swiftly developed other kinds of ventures with West Africa, intensifying its economic and political ties as well with India and China. Accordingly, the employment of foreign labor picked up much more steam and drew from more sources.

In the mid-nineteenth century, Britain's merchant fleet was the most dominant force in the circulation of the world's goods. Beginning in the 1870s, and for roughly a hundred years thereafter, Liverpool shipping firms hired thousands of West Africans (particularly from the Gold Coast, Sierra Leone, the Gambia, and Nigeria). A watershed moment occurred in 1879 with the formation of Liverpool's Elder Dempster and Company, which brought together firms already trading with West Africa, as well as some of shipping's most powerful moguls. By the early twentieth century, and through the exploits of Elder Dempster, Liverpool came to monopolize the British trade with that region (Frost 1995b: 24–25). Shippers based in Liverpool and other ports also hired Afro-Caribbeans, Lascars,[29] Chinese, Liberian, Arab, and Somali seamen in large numbers. It is impossible to specify the size of any of these groups, either in the shipping workforce or in their presence or eventual settlement in various British ports.[30] Historian Laura Tabili offers a general picture, however. Between 1901 and the 1950s, one-third of the labor force working British ships, or 66,000 men, were from East and West Africa, the Caribbean, and the Arabian peninsula (1994: 42). Within that period, however, the numbers of "colored" seamen working British ships waxed and waned, according to both the availability of White British seamen and the degree of patriotic loyalty shown by shipping companies. For example, during World War I, White British seamen were less available due to their wartime service, and thus the use of colonial labor picked up. At the war's close, the latter fell into disfavor (Rich 1986: 121). The pattern repeated in World War II (Tabili 1994: 12).

In addition to the useful purposes they served in their home ports, colored seamen offered other advantages. Shippers could easily justify paying them less than White British seamen, despite sometimes considering Africans in particular to be better-skilled than Europeans (Frost 1995b: 25; Sherwood 1995). On a less positive note, Africans were thought to be well-suited for the more backbreaking work onboard ship and were, along with Lascars, considered naturally amenable to the punishing tropical climes to which British ships sailed. And with the advent of steamships in the mid-nineteenth century, Africans were, for the same

reason, put to work in the exceedingly hot spaces below deck, in the engine room and stokehold. For their part, the Kru and some Arab men considered employment on British ships to be a relief from the poverty of agricultural work (Frost 1995a: 3). Moreover, colonial seamen, especially West Africans, were attracted to the shipping life because it offered the possibility of jumping ship in a British port, where they sought relief from what they saw as their total subordination under British rule in Africa (Tabili 1994; Rich 1986: 122).

However, colonialism also structured the economic and political terrain of early twentieth-century Liverpool and other British ports, even if in contradictory ways. As we will see below, the ideologies of racial inferiority that justified colonialism were in full force in Britain, both shaping colored people's subordination and providing them a set of idioms with which to condemn racism. In turn, Britain's determination to maintain its empire at all costs sometimes put local and state officials at odds with each other on matters of race, nationality, rights of abode, and repatriation. The imperial imperative served, albeit to a small degree, as a check against racism.

Prior to 1925, colonial seamen had free entry into British ports because they were British subjects. Oftentimes the shipping companies hired these men in West African ports for voyages ending in British ones, where they would have to find accommodations until they got another ship—which could take months. Seamen's unions strongly opposed the use of colonial labor because their constituents were White British sailors whose labor was being undersold. With the exception of the two postwar periods, shipping firms showed no strong preference toward hiring White seamen. Rather, they capitalized on the poverty of the African sailors languishing, often starving, in British ports. African seamen could rarely find other work while waiting around, so to speak, for their ship to come in. Shipping agents would visit various hostels and missions to recruit the labor of these men, who had little choice but to accept the exploitative wages offered. But these men did not passively accept this situation. They drew on the resources of British imperial rhetoric and invoked their own wartime service to assert their status as loyal British subjects and, with that, their rights to fair terms of employment. Mr. D. T. Aleifasakure Toummanah made the case thus in June 1919 at the Ethiopian Hall in Liverpool:

> The coloured men have mostly served in the Forces, Navy and transport. They are largely British subjects, and are proud to have been able to have done what they have done for the Empire . . . the majority of negroes at present are discharged soldiers and sailors without employment; in fact, some of them are practically starving, work having been refused them on account of their colour . . . some of us have been wounded and lost limbs and eyes fighting for the Empire to which we have the honour to belong. . . . We ask for British justice, to be treated as true and loyal sons of Great Britain. (Quoted in Tabili, 1994: 15)

The presence of Africans and other colored seamen in the ports of Cardiff, South Shields, London, Bristol, and Liverpool was, generally speaking, anathema to unemployed White seamen. Although there is evidence that White and colored seamen, at times, joined forces in seamen's organizations and unions and that Africans were savvy to the role of the press in creating tensions between themselves and White seamen (Tabili 1994), the relationship between foreign and British seafarers was generally antagonistic. No more dramatic example exists than the 1919 riots that occurred across Britain, in most of its major ports (except Bristol). In late May and again in June of that year, Blacks in Liverpool were mobbed and randomly attacked by roving gangs of White men. In the June riots, these men numbered in the thousands. Historian Paul Rich described the June riots thus: "With covert support from the local police, who perceived the blacks, in the words of one police officer, as 'only big children who when they get money like to make a show', the crowds had all the trappings of lynch mobs and were often goaded on by demobbed servicemen" (1986: 121). One seaman, Charles Wootton (also known as Wooten), originally from Barbados and a resident of Upper Pitt Street, died in these attacks. Fleeing the mob, he perished after jumping into the River Mersey to the chants of "Let him drown!" Charles Wootton is a name known by every member of Liverpool's contemporary Black community.[31]

The official response to these riots was to render the colored peoples in Britain the source of the problem. Liverpool's Lord Mayor, for example, referred to these men as an irritation that should be removed (Tabili 1994: 137). Such removal required an explicit racial policy on the part of the state, a responsibility that fell ultimately, if reluctantly, to the Aliens Department of the Home Office (Tabili 1994: 116). The Home Office agreed in principle that non-British subjects should be deported. But, of course, the colored seamen whose expulsion was sought *were* British subjects. In the years immediately following the 1919 riots, the Home Office hemmed and hawed and otherwise resisted the pleas for deportation being made by officials in various British ports. The double bind of the irritants' color and their British subject status posed a major constraint on British state officials, who were acutely aware of the possible repercussions in the colonies if knowledge were to spread of colored men's ill-treatment in Britain, much less if they were to deport these men.

Their fears were well-founded. A riot that erupted in Freetown, Sierra Leone—also in 1919—was initially sparked by the local politics of colonial rule, but developed into a condemnation of the racism suffered by Africans in England.[32] In a petition to the government, the Creoles reported, "There was considerable indignation in some parts of the city at the report of racial disturbances in Liverpool, Cardiff and a few other places in England and Wales which gave rise to considerable apprehension that the 'sea-boys' repatriated from those places with a deep sense of injury would instigate reprisals in Sierra Leone against the white residents" (quoted in May and Cohen 1974: 121). Conscious of the potential effects of unrest in England on political mobilization in the colonies, the Liverpool press called for calm. As one editorial put it: "Careful and commonsense handling of the colour disturbances is necessary if what at present is little more than local hooliganism is not to develop into an Imperial problem. There would be unfortunate possibilities of mischief if any idea gained ground in India and Africa that the attitude of the [rioters] reflected British attitudes" (quoted in May and Cohen

1974: 121). The 1919 riots in England did spark a desire for repatriation among some African men. In Sierra Leone, a collection was taken up to facilitate it (May and Cohen 1974: 123).

African men in Britain were an "irritation" not only because their presence incited riots but also because they were in the business of making political statements about their rights as British subjects. They were also organizing, both within and outside their seamen's unions and organizations, and sometimes with Whites (Tabili 1994; Sherwood 1995). May and Cohen (1974) unearthed intelligence reports suggesting that British state officials in the early twentieth century were extremely concerned about the increasingly transnational political mobilization among colored peoples.[33] Only a decade later, the Pan-Africanist and the Garveyite movements would be a source of even greater concern (Rich 1986: 122). In what follows, a West Indian seaman echoes the sentiments of above-quoted Mr. Toummanah in precise detail, here with the desire to influence Colonial Office policy:

> We have never regarded our selves as aliens to Britain in peace or in war. . . . So long as the Union Jack flies . . . so long will we regard the word alien as a totally unsuitable word. . . . [A]ll these years all the British Black people have such love for the Mother Country England but since the great war things is turn look what happens to us in England in 1919 dont it ashame on Britain part. (West Indian seaman in Barry Dock, Wales, to the Colonial Office, May 5, 1925, quoted in Tabili 1994: 30)

The quoted seaman was part of a group of twenty-six West Indians and Africans who mobilized to contest the mutual and effective diminution of their British subject status in the form of the Coloured Alien Seaman Order of 1925 (Tabili 1994: 125). Its racist intent would presage many other twentieth-century efforts to codify the relationship between race and nationality, especially the 1981 British Nationality Act.

Colonial subjects, it bears repeating, had rights of abode anywhere in the empire, including Britain. The Order respected those rights, if minimally; its ostensible target was colored seamen without British subject status. Yet, the burden of proof of British nationality fell upon colored seamen, who generally lacked the paperwork proving such. The Order hence rendered all colored seamen de facto aliens and, indeed, criminals. They were required to carry a "document of identity," which was to be produced at their British ports of call and registered with the local police. The documents specified a seaman's origins, providing as well a minute description of his physical features (including distinguishing marks like tattoos) and a perfectly clear photograph—the latter deemed necessary by officials who complained of the difficulty of telling these men apart. The document bore a conspicuous red stamp that read "seaman." Moreover, the Order required that their voyages be round trip and that they not be paid while in Britain, hence ensuring that they did not stay (Rich 1986: 122–26).

In practice, the Order did not produce the desired effect. Colored seamen, whether "alien" or not, managed to work around it. Further, the law was differently understood and applied in the various British ports. It also depended on the still murky distinction between race and nationality. Racial categories were themselves uncertain (were the Maltese "colored"?) and were left for local bureaucrats to figure out (Lane 1995). Rich argues that the passage of this order was a direct, long-term effect of the 1919 riots and that it "exemplified that the ideas on race and empire generated at the heart of British imperial culture could penetrate down into the administrative petty bourgeoisie within the metropolis" (1986: 121). Ultimately, the Order sparked protest and collective action among the seamen targeted, as exemplified in the action above.

In the longer term, such incidents in the history of race and empire have penetrated into, and helped form, the present-day political subjectivities of Liverpool-born Blacks. One of the artifacts that Scott pulled out of his "Anti National Front" folder was a photocopy of a letter addressed to the late father of one of Scott's friends. The letter thanked him for his courageous service during World War I and issued him a check for seven pounds sterling. Scott described the significance of the letter thus:

> In the first world war he was a seaman. He was away at sea and his ship was attacked by a U-boat. They fight the U-boat off and they take the ship back safely to port and they're given the sum of seven pounds, which is a lot of money in those days. But he worked for the Elder Dempster shipping company. When the ship docked, he was hauled off as an alien! [Scott laughs heartily.] Would you believe it? And this proves my point about the way Black people fought in two world wars—and he's just a merchant seaman! Some actually went out on bombing missions in the Air Force. Never mentioned! Very rarely is it shown on television. They don't tell you the history that Black people played in this country in two world wars.

Far from being relegated to the past, the histories of slavery and colonialism resound in contemporary Liverpool: Blacks destroying a statue of a reputed slave trader in their neighborhood; the Luso-American society hauling out its Columbus statue in homage but under cover of night; popular historians thanking the explorer for making Liverpool, while claiming other parts of England as the city's own colonial possessions; Blacks keeping the memory of Charles Wootton alive, rehearsing verses from Peter Fryer's *Staying Power*, and pulling out tattered documents to prove the indignities suffered by Britain's Black war heroes. Along similar lines, the living history traced above reveals the intense politic of empire that unfolded in the interactions among Liverpool shippers, seamen's unions, their rank-and-file members, colonial workers-cum-activists resident in the city and across the country, the Liverpool press, the British state, and the colonizers and colonized in various British possessions. Where would one place the local in any of these pointed encounters? Where would Liverpool and/or Britain leave off and the global begin?[34] The local/global dichotomy on which that question is premised must be left behind. In much theorizing on the local and the global, the latter stands in for the universal, and the former is reduced to a site of ethnographic specificity. Liverpool presents the case of a decidedly local site— which is to say, a place that is relentlessly constructed through a discourse on the local—that is global by definition. This section has already shown that the local

is defined—critically by Blacks and ceremoniously by White Liverpudlian
elites—through its complete exploitation of a host of worlds beyond Britain. And
not only that: the local's exploits dominated the region in which it was situated,
and often outpaced the rest of Britain in pursuing national-imperial goals
(chapter 6). The Liverpool case inverts the premises of dominant models, in
which the global acts (and acts *first*), leaving the local only to *re*act.

It remains to outline the sexual tensions of empire that gave birth to "Liverpool."
Like London and other important British ports, Liverpool was the ground where
the metropole first met the colonies, both in their colorful variety and their albeit
contested masculinity. The front-page news of the 1919 riots afforded White
Britons their first realization that there were so many colored people resident
among them (Rich 1986: 120–22). Certainly, those who lived near the docks of
these port cities would have known, but even in London the dock areas represented an underclass netherworld. In Liverpool, the presence of colored men was
harder to avoid, for the docks were very much a part of the general downtown
bustle. "Unlike London," Belchem writes,

> Liverpool docks were not distant and separate from the city: goods moved freely (if
> not always securely) between the unenclosed waterfront and warehouses dispersed
> throughout the city centre. The open-access economy of perks, ploys and pilfering
> was put at risk in 1846 by the opening of the Albert Dock, "constructed upon the
> model of those in London—surrounded by its own warehouses, worked by its own
> porters, and denying access within its gate to ragged children, beggars, thieves, and
> all who can give no account of their business." (1998: 2)

Even if the 1919 riots occasioned the first widespread dissemination of the
racial composition of port cities like Liverpool, an earlier reading public, lapping
up the series of travel accounts written by Charles Dickens, would have certainly
been aware. Writing anonymously, Dickens produced a set of essays about his
travels across the British Isles and abroad. Originally published in a journal
called *All the Year Round* in 1860 and again in 1865, his essays were eventually
collected in a monograph titled *The Uncommercial Traveller*. As we join him
below, he is being treated to a tour of Liverpool. He has stopped at a public
house, perhaps on Park Lane. Using the term *jack* (a nickname for a sailor) as a
trope, Dickens defines each seaman by his nationality: British Jack, Scandinavian
Jack, and so on. Until he gets to "Dark Jack" who has only race:

> [I]n the little first floor of a little public-house . . . in a stiflingly close atmosphere,
> were Dark Jack, and Dark Jack's delight, his *white* unlovely Nan, sitting against the
> wall all round the room. More than that: Dark Jack's delight was the least unlovely
> Nan, both morally and physically, that I saw that night.
>
>   As a fiddle and tambourine band were sitting among the company, Quickear sug-
> gested why not strike up? "Ah, la'ads!" said a negro sitting by the door. "Gib the jeb-
> blem a darnse. Tak'yah parlers, jebblem, for 'um quad-rill. . . .
>
>   The male dancers were all blacks, and one was an unusually powerful man of six
> feet three or four. The sound of their flat feet on the floor was as unlike the sound of

white feet as their faces were unlike white faces. They toed and heeled, shuffled, double-shuffled, double-double shuffled, covered the buckle, and beat the time out, rarely, dancing with a great show of teeth, and with a childish good-humoured enjoyment that was very prepossessing. They generally kept together, these poor fellows, said Mr. Superintendent, because they were at a disadvantage singly, and liable to slights in the neighbouring streets. But if I were Light Jack, I should be very slow to interfere oppressively with Dark Jack, for whenever I have had to do with him I have found him a simple and a gentle fellow. (1958: 45–46, original emphasis)

It might be best to leave aside the references to all that shuffling and grinning and proceed to more important matters. Let it be known from the outset that Dickens's account is not uncommonly quoted in popular texts on the Black presence in Liverpool, owing less to its racial overtones than to the time depth it establishes for that presence (for example, Law and Henfrey 1981). It was written in 1860. To wit, Dickens does not imply that there is just one isolated Dark Jack; there seem to be lots of them on the scene. And Dark Jack, Dickens emphasizes, has a *white* unlovely Nan. In contemporary British usage, a nan is a grandmother. But this meaning might have been different in Dickens's time. And she is the "least unlovely Nan, both morally and physically" that he met that night. The qualified loveliness he ascribes to her derives from his assessment of Nans he encountered elsewhere, in the back alleys and cellars of the slums—specifically, in "a nauseous room with an earth floor, into which the refuse scum of an alley trickled" and where "the stench was . . . abominable." And the place constructs the people: Dickens describes the Nans there as "three old women of transcendent ghastliness" (1958: 50) and proceeds to name them Witches One, Two, and Three. In this light, the White women keeping company with Dark Jack, in the gay environment of the public house, become lovelier, morally and physically—but still unlovely, after all. Although my emphasis here is on the social intercourse between White women and Black men—intercourse that can clearly become sexual at any moment—Dickens actually describes Liverpool's milieu through the presence of all sorts of global men: Spanish, Finnish, Maltese, and Swedish, for example.

The contemporary racial identity of Liverpool, the place, depends greatly on the fact that it played host to men from around the globe. The local was global by definition. Of course, London was also an international seaport. It, too, was a revolving door for the world's men. But London was also other things. It defied singular inscription. Besides, its docks were in the East End, off the city's beaten track. Liverpool, by contrast, was full of portness. It was portness personified. It was nothing if not seven miles of very busy dock, as many English (and American) travel writers from the eighteenth century onward confirmed (Defoe 1971 [1714]; Priestly (1984 [1934]). Hence has Liverpool long been singularly available for one wishing to make a swift point that depends on racialized forms of international movement. We see this most clearly in Emily Brontë's 1850 novel *Wuthering Heights*.

The story takes place on the Yorkshire moors and centers on the relationship between Catherine Earnshaw and Heathcliff. The circumstances of Heathcliff's arrival in the Earnshaw household are most relevant here. Emily Brontë sends Catherine's father, Mr. Earnshaw, off to Liverpool. Amazingly, she gives absolutely not a single reason for him to need or want to go there, although she does make a point of sending him there on foot. And it is a sixty-mile walk each way! Although it seems to lack reason, his journey is actually critical to the novel's nature-versus-nurture concerns. In Liverpool, Mr. Earnshaw finds Heathcliff and brings him home. Here is how Heathcliff enters the Earnshaw household. Mr. Earnshaw, bringing out a bundle from beneath his coat, says "See here wife! . . . [Y]ou must take it as a gift of God; though it's as dark almost as if it came from the devil." The story's narrator, a housekeeper, then says this:

> We crowded round, and over Miss Cathy's head I had a peep at a dirty, ragged, black-haired child; big enough both to walk and talk; yet when it was set on its feet, it only stared round, and repeated over and over again some gibberish that nobody could understand. I was frightened, and Mrs. Earnshaw was ready to fling it out of doors: she did fly up, asking how he could fashion to bring that gipsy brat into the house . . . . The master tried to explain the matter . . . and all I could make out . . . was a tale of his seeing it starving and houseless, and as good as dumb in the streets of Liverpool; where he picked it up and inquired for its owner. (31)

The narrator continues in the same vein, consistently referring to the young Heathcliff as "it." It was clearly human but, strangely, it had black hair and spoke in gibberish. (Dickens's use of gibberish for Dark Jack's speech might be remembered here.) Earnshaw said it was dark, as if it had come from the devil. In a thoroughly unscientific investigation, I surveyed my British friends: did they remember anything about the circumstances in which Heathcliff arrived in the Earnshaw household? Not a single person failed to remember that he was brought from Liverpool, even though the city is only named twice, early on in the novel. The significance of "Liverpool," of course, went over the heads of the American readers I asked, but they did remember something vaguely carnivalesque about the environs from which Heathcliff was rescued.

Why would Brontë send Mr. Earnshaw to Liverpool, then, to get such a thing? To establish with extreme economy that the child was racially ambiguous. Where else but the busy international port of Liverpool could one find a child of unknown racial background wandering around homeless, dirty, and begging? Sexuality and race are co-implicated by the kind of space that Liverpool was and by the age of the child; clearly, since he was born in the city, he must be the product of a local woman and a global man. As the story proceeds, the characters variously imagine Heathcliff as a gypsy, or perhaps American or Spanish. One character hypothesizes that Heathcliff's grandfather may have been a Chinese emperor. Cultural critic Terry Eagleton suggests that Heathcliff can productively be considered Irish (1995). But to try to pinpoint Heathcliff's exact racial positioning is to miss the point, for Brontë is intent on denying him such exactitude. In 1850, racial *in*determinacy would have induced far more interesting anxieties than certain knowledge, as I pursue below. This method also allows the characters to constitute Heathcliff as whatever they like. He could be wild, savage, tough, and satanic (all of these descriptors appear), or he could be of noble birth, a descendant of a Chinese emperor. Heathcliff, in short, is a "half-caste." As such he is perfectly set up for his role as the object of an experiment: given the unruly nature that his phenotype suggests and that his behavior confirms, can he be re-formed in the civilized environs of the Earnshaw household?

Variations of that question were being posed in seaports all over Britain and in the overlapping arenas of social work, philanthropy, and academia, which would, in the mid to late nineteenth century, include physical anthropology and ethnology.[35] In contrast to eighteenth-century British ideas about human varia-tion, which considered religion and clothing as key indices of civilization and posited climate as an explanation of different human potentials, the 1840s saw the emergence of a more biological argument (Wheeler 2000; Hamer 1996). Physical types, which were correlated with areas of geographic origin, became the basis of racial distinctions and served to explain differential human capaci-ties. Classificatory schema abounded. In this respect, Brontë's mysterious, some-what monstrous representation of the racially ambiguous Heathcliff is intriguing; it accords with the fearful image of the half-caste conjured up in Gothic literature and other discursive contexts. As H. L. Malchow provocatively explains, "[O]ne may define [the Gothic] genre by characteristics that resonate strongly with racial prejudice, imperial exploration and sensational anthropology—themes and images that are meant to shock and terrify, that emphasize chaos and excess, sexual taboo and barbarism, and a style grounded in techniques of suspense and threat" (1996: 102). Just as the unpredictable and brooding Heathcliff posed an ever-present danger, so too were the "hundreds of half-caste children" in 1920s Cardiff said to have "vicious tendencies." These children also confused the cate-gories of science, exhibiting, according to the press, a "disharmony of physical traits and mental characteristics" (Rich 1986: 131). In an era when science had attained unprecedented legitimacy (Lorimer 1996), the racially ambiguous or mixed person was a threat to the social order. Again, Malchow writes, "The terms 'half-breed' and 'half-caste' are double, hyphenated constructions resonat-ing with other linguistic inadequacies and incompletes—with 'half-wit' or 'half-dead', with 'half-naked' or 'half-truth', and of course with 'half-civilized'" (1996: 104). The person of mixed race was a pathology to be studied from both literary and "scientific" points of view. Their sexuality was of particular concern. It was one thing to be born of immoral unions in immoral circumstances; but as freaks of nature themselves, what moral predilections would *they* reproduce? *Could* they reproduce? (Malchow 1996; Young 1995).

Sexuality was the lightning rod of power relations of all kinds. As is commonly known, in nineteenth-century Britain social traits were commonly thought to be inherited, "race" was conflated with culture, and social classes were veritable racial groups (Young 1995). "Diseases" that bred unchecked among the working classes—laziness, slowness of wit, physical predisposition for backbreaking labor—posed a threat to the middle classes and elites of higher class status. For a society struggling to maintain social hierarchies based on innate differences, sexu-ality would have to be of absolutely primary concern. In the burgeoning but poor and overcrowded Victorian cities of London and Liverpool, working-class women, the most likely candidates to take up prostitution, became the targets of moralizing discourses. Fears of degeneration caused their sexuality to be policed most aggressively, even though it was middle-class boys and men who were so often their clients (McClintock 1995; Walkowitz 1992, 1980).

Into a milieu defined, at the very least, by the above-described dynamics of colonialism, race, nationality, place, sexuality, class, and gender entered one Muriel Fletcher, infamous in present-day Liverpool for a study she conducted in 1928 under the auspices of the Liverpool Association for the Welfare of Half-Caste Children. Fletcher was trained in social research at the Liverpool University School of Social Science, where her circle included eugenicist anthropologists (Rich 1986). The subjects of Fletcher's research were White women who were formerly involved with African men and their "half-caste" children. She published her conclusions in *Report on an Investigation into the Colour Problem in Liverpool and Other Ports*. Ultimately, the *Fletcher Report*, as it is commonly called, concludes that "the colour problem" in that city owed not to the racist structuring of British society, the ideologies promulgated by the British state and its institutions, nor those circulating within Liverpool's social welfare establishment, nor to the everyday racism of White Liverpudlians who routinely subjected colored seamen to violence. Rather, Fletcher attributed the colour problem in Liverpool to African seamen. It would be hard to state emphatically enough how thoroughly racial politics in Liverpool/Britain reflect the legacy of the *Fletcher Report*.

Fletcher argues that the Coloured Alien Seamen's Order (which really should have been named more appropriately the Coloured Alien Semen Order) was of little use in curbing West African men's presence in Liverpool. They formed a large part of the "color problem," as Fletcher suggests in her reference to these men's unknown numbers in Liverpool: "There was . . . no information to hand as to the exact size of the problem" (1930: 9). Fletcher goes on to explain these men's desires for life in England thus: "In their own country they are not allowed to mix freely with white people nor to have relations with white women. Once having formed unions with white women in this country, they are perhaps loath to leave England and later, should they not obtain employment, it is comparatively easy for them to obtain out-relief or unemployment pay" (14). The *Fletcher Report* is, quite simply, colonialist to the core: "In his own country the West African's relations with women are definitely restricted by a stern and rigid tribal discipline. In this country he is cut adrift from these restrictions before he has developed the restraint and control of Western civilization. In Liverpool there is evidence to show that the negro tends to be promiscuous in his relations with white women" (19).

The supposed moral vacuity of the African seaman contributes to that of the White woman (who is never specified as either English or Irish): "In the other ports 90 percent. of the white women who consort with coloured men are said to be prostitutes; in Liverpool, however, although a number of the women live on immoral earnings, they appear to do so because of the fact that they are living with a coloured man rather than because they were originally prostitutes" (21). Fletcher dismisses White women's own explanations for their choice to partner colored men: "To the ordinary casual visitor these women will say that they married a coloured man because he makes a better husband than a white. Such a statement, however, appears to be merely an excuse on the part of the women for conduct which she feels has set her apart from other women. They almost invariably regret their alliance with a coloured man, and realising that they have chosen a life which is repugnant, become extraordinarily sensitive about their position" (21). From there we learn that these men's "sexual demands impose a continual strain on white women" (21). Below Fletcher delineates, with authority, the roots of these women's pathology:

> The white women in Liverpool who consort with coloured men appear to fall into four classes—
>
> (1) Those who took the step because they had an illegitimate child by a white man who refused to marry them, or because they had an illegitimate colored child.
>
> (2) Those who are mentally weak.
>
> (3) Prostitutes.
>
> (4) Younger women who make contacts in a spirit of adventure and find themselves unable to break away.
>
> Those in the second and third classes are often interchangeable, while (3) can be subdivided into:
>
> (a) Those women of a somewhat lazy nature, who choose such a life more or less deliberately and who take care to have no children; (b) Those who have children dependent on them and are willing to earn money in this way for their support (22).

The African man creates the White woman's problems, while they both create the myriad crises said to befall their "half-caste" children. Fletcher uses the term *half-caste* in various ways. At times she distinguishes between "Anglo-Negroid" and "Anglo-Chinese" children; yet both of these groups belong to the *half-caste* category. Fletcher remarks at the outset, however, that "Anglo-Chinese" children are quite well-adjusted. Since they pose no problem, we need not hear anything more about them. As well, in the early pages, Fletcher uses the term *Anglo-Negroid* for children of African men and White women. In detailing the minute phenotypical features of "half-caste" children, the *Fletcher Report* marks some of them "English," as in "30 per cent. had English eyes. . . . A little over 50 per cent. had hair negroid in type and colour. 25 per cent. had English, while the remaining 25 per cent. exhibited some curious mixtures. . . .About 12 per cent. had lips like the average English child" (27).[36] She refers to these children's social characteristics in similar terms. While she does not suggest that biological inheritance is at work, the children nevertheless manifest a troubling duality, exhibiting the worst trait of each parent. Here speaking about "half-caste" girls, Fletcher argues, "From her mother the half-caste girl is liable to inherit a certain slackness, and from her father a happy-go-lucky attitude towards life" (34). The problems of the program chairpersons to give the students some opportunity to know what life looks like ahead. The students would be much better off to be attracted into a real position rather than pushed out of the program. As a matter of fact, most of the students know what a degree means to them and want to finish it as soon as they can, unless there is a special reason for holding their student status (e.g., foreign students waiting for job offers before they can leave school and change immigration status). Therefore, time is actually a greater pressure to the student than is usually thought. If a doctoral student has spent two or three or even four years pursuing his coursework and satisfying other pre-dissertation requirements, he certainly cannot be that prodigal in consuming time writing the dissertation.

The students are also limited by other kinds of resources, particularly by the money they can spend on their thesis/dissertation research. For the doctoral students, there might be some chances for them to get their dissertation projects funded. Since the award of a grant is considered an achievement in itself, the students would be strongly encouraged by some faculty members to search and apply for such funding. Yet this kind of opportunity is not always available in your particular field; hunting for the grants and competing for them also means an extra cost of your time. Therefore, you might be discouraged from using time seeking out small awards by your advisor, who would instead urge you to focus on carrying out your project and finishing your degree as soon as possible.

Finally, the students may have very limited experience. If a student has never done any independent research before, the time she needs to prepare for the very formal project could be prolonged. It is unreasonable to expect a student to conduct such a project as smoothly as an experienced faculty member can.

It is important, therefore, to be realistic when thinking about your thesis or dissertation project. You may have some great ideas in your mind, but if they are not feasible at this stage you can put them in your long-term plan and continue your pursuit later. At this moment, you should lay a solid groundwork for your future by launching a manageable project. You may create new opportunities for yourself by finishing the degree. This does not mean that you cannot engage in a grand topic; rather, it is the value of a practical or pragmatic attitude that matters, which will help you survive the challenges and successfully transfer to a new stage.

In reality, there are probably as many students who are more concerned about minimum requirements as those who are more interested in their ambitious dreams. When "thesis/dissertation anxiety" occurs, the students would become more sensitive to the standards of an "acceptable" work. This is understandable

half-caste children are not of their own making, then. They are victims. They attend earnestly to their schoolwork and seem amiable enough. But the immorality that characterizes their home life, given the low character of both parents, cannot help but be reproduced in these hapless children.

The only aspect of the *Fletcher Report* that even slightly redeems it is the genuine care that she expresses for these children. She seems quite moved, for example, by the certainty of the girls' future unemployment. The boys will surely become seamen—a precarious occupation, Fletcher admits, given that they will compete with Whites. But the girls will face complete discrimination in the workforce. A survey Fletcher conducted among businesses in Liverpool confirmed that none would be disposed to hiring a "half-caste" girl. Fletcher and her colleagues also found that these girls do not frequent the neighborhood clubs for juveniles. So, they set one up in the African and West Indian Mission for their exclusive use. The club was a success except that the girls would occasionally become distracted: "Much as they appreciated the club it is a significant fact that whenever there was a ship in port with coloured men on it practically none of the girls would come to the club but they returned the following week displaying scarves, necklaces, wrist watches, etc., while two invariably brought money to be saved up for them." Here is how Fletcher explains this behavior: "All the circumstances of their lives tend to give undue prominence to sex; owing to the nature of the houses in which they live their moral standards are extraordinarily low, and owing to the persistence of the men it is practically impossible for the coloured girls to remain pure." She concludes this section soberly: "[T]hose mothers of a better type regretted the fact that they had brought these children into the world handicapped by their colour" (32–33).

In all, Fletcher only once implies that racism might just be part of "the colour problem" in Liverpool and other ports. She says the "half-caste" girls will face sure discrimination, but she stops short of criticizing the racist hiring practices of local businesses. Instead, she suggests that the color problem can only be eliminated through the repatriation of African seamen. While she admits that mass deportation could result in "political reactions"—probably a reference to the response in African colonies—Fletcher is certain that it remains "the only real solution" (39).

Through the *Fletcher Report* all the moral panics that defined the Victorian era were recirculated. The studied attention the report gives to White women's virtues, or supposed lack thereof, reflects the tremendous threat that these women's sexual practice posed to the British imperial order (Tabili 1996). In the 1930s, the only colonial men immune from the threat of deportation, lacking as they often did the paperwork to prove their British subject status, were those who had fathered children there (Tabili 1994: 155). Colored men lacking "family ties" or passports were to be deported immediately (and British subjects in West Africa were actually denied passports). White women's sexuality was also at issue because their colored male children would be entitled to the same wages that White British seamen earned. Fletcher's concerns were further shaped by her sympathies with eugenicism (Rich 1986). The fate of the race was in the hands of some incorrigible women with little if any commitment to the boundaries of colonial rule. Although Fletcher does not say so, these women were more likely to be working-class Irish Catholics than middle-class English Protestants. The report itself was distributed to government departments, social work and philanthropic organizations, ministers of parliament, the media, and, crucially, the police. For the National Union of Seamen, the report justified the use of White sailors over colored ones. The union and the local police used the report's findings to bolster their objections to African men's rights of abode in Britain. For their part, Fletcher's informants, and the nascent Black community at large, were hurt and angered by the report. People trusted her enough to answer some very sensitive questions in what was a highly charged political milieu. In the end, she was driven out of Liverpool.

The *Fletcher Report* is not a text that I just managed to unearth in a library or archive. Black people in Liverpool referred to it, denounced it, made me photocopies of it. Black people I knew were alive to the politics of ethnographic and similar forms of representation, whether these emanated from the academy, the media, the government, or from within the institutions of their own community.

SITUATING BLACK LIVERPOOL

Scott's insistence that his version of the Black community's history is the real one instantiates the power/knowledge relationship with which this book is critically concerned. James Clifford (1988) has rightly warned of the dangers of regarding ethnography as the scholarly discourse that tells a people's complete, unmediated, and ultimate truth. While I respect Black Liverpudlians' ability to tell their version of their story, I in no way deny my role as interlocutor here. Similarly, I realize that the memories that have produced their narratives are highly selective. I try indeed to highlight the ways these memories speak to informants' own positions within community debates.

While this ethnography supports Scott's thesis that "to understand Black people, you've got to understand Liverpool," it really presents the genealogies of that truth claim, as well as an often interventionist analysis of its political effects. In the foregoing sections, for example, I presented two main vehicles through which Britons make place matter: first, through phenomenological premises that explain the social through ostensibly unmediated visual perceptions of place; and second, through the use of "specific" or "particular" social characteristics and relations to define a place, which we saw, for example, in the discussion of Britons' uses of traditional industries to imbue place with meaning. Filling a place with people and, likewise, defining a place through characteristic social relations are no less innocent as cultural practices than the phenomenological operations whose productive, powerful effects I discussed above. Insofar as social actors like Scott define place through, for example, seafaring, they are participating in the individuating process that, in no small measure, also constructs them as particular kinds of racial subjects. Thus, to understand Black people in Liverpool one must understand the ideological labors that place is made to perform.

I argue here that cultural logics of localness and place have profoundly shaped racial identity and community formation—so much so that the local could be profitably understood as a racial category. I show localization as racialization. With this argument as my singular concern, let me offer an important disclaimer before suggesting how this ethnography is structured and how it might be read. Liverpool's diversity is not truly captured in this ethnography, although it is that very diversity that is so much at issue here. One Liverpool-born Black informant stated the case perfectly, saying that "this is a multiracial, multicultural, whatever community." This book centers on the multiply fraught politics of place, localness, and Blackness. It will not help one understand much about, for example, the Chinese, Yemenis, Pakistanis, Rastas, and Somalis of Liverpool. There are many potent references to Africans and Afro-Caribbeans here, but very few members of those groups do any speaking. There is formidable diversity within these two latter groups, too. Africans themselves belong to ethnic collectives such as Igbo and Yoruba, categories that carried great salience in Nigeria and that have been reconstituted in Liverpool. Africans are also Nigerians, Ghanaians, Gambians, Sierra Leoneans, and Somalis. Some immigrated to England before the postwar era and some afterward—which makes a big difference to Liverpool-born Blacks (chapter 5). Afro-Caribbeans (often called West Indians) also straddle the post–World War II era. White Liverpudlians are also critical to this story—as Black people's neighbors, friends, mothers, and partners, and, crucially, as local subjects, also known as "Scousers" (again, a common nonderogatory nickname for Liverpudlians). They, too, are deeply involved in the discursive production of "Liverpool." Members of the above-listed groups come into view to different degrees, and only as they enlarge on the politics of place, localness, and race. The ways that these groups come to feature, then, are shaped by the dictates of an ethnography that is fundamentally about Liverpool-born Blacks. For example, the chapter that follows is about the Black America that lives in Black Liverpool's positioned experience and imagination. Despite how present Black America is in that chapter, it is not about Black America. It is about Black Liverpool.

The exact size of Liverpool's Black population confounds scholars and policy makers alike. Census data have always been particularly unreliable. Figures on Blacks resident in Liverpool in the eighteenth and nineteenth centuries are compromised by the very transient nature of seamen's lives.[37] Add to this the great variability and flux in the construction of racial categories over time, and Black people's unwillingness to answer census questions on race for fear that the data might be used in all manner of unsavory ways, and the problems mount. In 1989, a government inquiry into racial discrimination complained about the lack of definitive figures on the size of the Black community, noting that the most commonly quoted figures are "based on informed speculation rather than science" (Lord Gifford, Brown, and Bundey 1989: 37). Following the hegemonic usage of the term *Black* in Liverpool—which should only be provisionally indicated here, since that point will be pursued at length in what follows—the estimated size of the combined population of Africans, Afro-Caribbeans, and Black Britons was between 12,000 and 18,000 (37). In 1992, the Office of Population Censuses and Surveys announced that "science" had determined there to be 6,786 Blacks in the city, which would amount to 1.5 percent of the total population of 452,000 (OPCS 1992).

In lieu of a chapter-by-chapter outline of the entire book, let me offer the following guide. Thematically, this ethnography follows an arc. It proceeds, in the next chapter, with the liberating yet contentious emergence of Black identity in Liverpool and goes on, in subsequent chapters, to show the rise of the local as a frame for particularizing the racial positioning named *Black*. Generally, Liverpool-born Blacks narrate these times in triumphant tones. Black identity and then Liverpool-born Blackness came into being against some formidable odds, and people detail these processes—for the most part—with no small bit of satisfaction. These were the glory days of Black Liverpool in formation. The ethnography goes on to study the ambivalences and instabilities that surround both Blackness and localness.

This book does not pretend to represent "the history of Black Liverpool." Rather, it is an ethnography about people's deployment of a historically attuned and alternately expanding and contracting geography of race. While I do struggle to convey a sense of a process unfolding, my analytical objectives ultimately determined the placement of particular events. For example, I detail the decline of Liverpool's shipping industry fairly late in the book, when it can be most usefully—that is, ethnographically—exploited. As well, events belonging to the formative period of the late 1970s/early 1980s are spread out over a few chapters, and are presented somewhat out of order, so that particular dimensions of the intersection of place and race—rather than strict chronologies—can be brought out. And even though the category *Liverpool-born Black* was hegemonic by 1991 and 1992, I nevertheless reserve use of that term until we arrive at the point in the ethnographic arc when it comes into existence. Early chapters, hence, refer to Blacks from Liverpool as *Black Liverpudlians*—a term that, indeed, no one uses. On this point I should note that throughout the book, I reserve the latter term for moments when it bears remembering that not all Blacks born in Liverpool are considered or consider themselves Liverpool-born Black. Or, I use it to signal that the specific positioning named *Liverpool-born Black* is not necessarily being engaged in the matters under discussion.

Of course, all the narratives about times past were spoken through subjectivities of race and place that belong to the ethnographic present. The closer we come to the nether end of the arc, the more the ethnography reveals the dilemmas and disappointments that motivate the glorious evocations of past times and places, as exemplified by Scott's tour of an invisible Liverpool. To get to the beloved Pitt Street of the 1930s, the subject of the final chapter, we have to travel the ethnographic route traced by the arc.

Black Liverpool, Black America, and the Gendering of Diasporic Space

Afraid is a country with no exit visas.
—Audre Lorde, "Diaspora"

If the paper seems preoccupied with the diaspora experience
and its narratives of displacement, it is worth remembering
that all discourse is "placed", and the heart has its reasons.
—Stuart Hall

THE TERMS *Black Liverpool* and *Black America* refer to racialized geographies of the imagination. The mapping of racial signifiers onto geographical ones lends such terms the illusion of referring to physical rather than social locations. The fact that there is no actual place that one could call Black Liverpool points attention to the ways that social spaces are created in tandem with processes of racial formation. Black Liverpool was born in the context of its joyous but contentious engagement with Black America, as imagined from a distance and as experienced up close.[1] The radical Blackness engendered in that diasporic encounter is the subject of this chapter.

Black Liverpudlians commonly narrate their history through three related processes. The first highlights the generation-spanning participation of Africans in the city's shipping industry; the second concerns the role of interracial unions in producing the contemporary Black population; and the third traces the transformation of that population's racial identity from *half-caste* to *Black*. As outlined in the previous chapter, African men were hired as seamen by Liverpool shippers during the slave-trading era, and increasingly so in the late nineteenth century. There are, of course, other migration histories that account for the Black presence in that city, notably post–World War II Caribbean immigration and postcolonial West African immigration in the mid-1960s. Nevertheless, the dominant narrative in Liverpool positions "the old Africans," or the original seamen, as the community's founding fathers. To no small degree, Black men and women stake their claims on local belonging through reference to these men's participation in the tradition that defines Liverpool itself: seafaring.

Sean, a forty-year-old Black man born in the city, was the youngest seafarer I knew. His late father, also a seaman, was from Barbados. But Sean traces his lineage as a seafarer through African reference points. Here he explains why he became a seaman, naturalizing the occupation through his genealogy: "Me mum's father originated in Africa—he went away to sea. All her brothers went away to sea. So all the males in the family that I know of all went away to sea at one point. So for me that was just a natural thing to do." In addition to the seafaring background of his family, his entire environment served as an enticement. He recalled:

The house where we used to live in Upper Warwick Street was next door to an African social club. So even people going in there I knew were going away to sea as well, on the African ships. We used to call them "the palm boats." It's a nickname for any ships going to Africa and bringing oils and all the rest of it back. So even then, I knew I'd be going away to sea, and everything revolved around that, really.

Women also trace family lineages through seafaring. Clara Ewing, in her sixties, was born in the city, as were her parents (who were both Black). In one interview, I asked her son why he went away to sea. He responded simply, "I wanted to travel." His mother immediately chimed in to revise his answer: "Because my father—his granddad—did it. His father did it. His grandfather on the other side did it. His great-grandfather did it. It's a seafaring family, you see? As I say, Liverpool, [they] were all seafarers, weren't they?" In addition to the employment it provided, seafaring is important to Black men and women alike as the very basis of their local identity.

People spoke glowingly of the seafaring activities of the men in their families and what these activities afforded them. Seafarers never returned to Liverpool empty-handed. They brought back clothing for their children; they brought food, novelties (Clara always requested copies of *Reader's Digest*), and downright luxuries. These men's contributions were especially important during the wartime and postwar periods. My friend Scott had childhood memories of these times. He noted that despite the fact that "we won the war," rationing of meat and bread went on for years after hostilities ended. If it were not for ships coming in from Africa and the Caribbean, he said, they would not have had fruit for years. Yet despite the poverty, by many people's accounts, Black people had an active social life, some of which centered on the rituals that celebrated seamen's comings and goings.

During the war, [as regards] the type of parties and music we used to have, almost every Black family regardless of how poor they were, there would always be someone in that family who could play some kind of musical instrument—mainly guitars. When it came to people mixing, the club life didn't exist. Community centers didn't exist. When someone's uncle or father would come home from sea, you couldn't go to the pubs, so they'd arrange a party that would be mainly of an African style. There'd be yams, and there'd be fruit. . . .

Scott's nostalgic feeling was also evoked by others even older than he was. Mrs. Smith, who was born in 1907, relayed her own joyful memories about Liverpool in the age of sail. She grew up in her grandmother's home, which was a boardinghouse for African seamen. It was on Beauford Street, she remembered. "All seamen. We didn't live far from the docks. Just down Hope Street, there's the docks. Just down the bottom, and there was the docks." In Mrs. Smith's youth and through to the 1980s, Blacks were confined to small corners of Liverpool; first around the docks in the city's south end (the Pitt Street area) and later to Liverpool 8, several blocks inland. Even as Black people criticize the racism that restricted them to these areas, they lovingly recall the vibrant life within them. Mrs. Smith continued,

> It was hard for a person to get a job. Very hard. Couldn't go anywhere. You know when you're going out at night, like going out to a dance? You couldn't! You had a big house and the seamen would come there, and you have a dance in your house and people pay to go in there. It was somewhere to go! 'Cause you couldn't go anywhere. They all pay so much to go in. All colored. Dance all night. All African dancing and all that. It was like that, and playing guitar and dancing all night. It was somewhere for people to go; you go to a dance at such and such a house. People had big cellars and you'd go in there and dance. That's the only place we could go. We couldn't go anywhere else because it'd be "nigger, nigger, nigger." We used to go to cellar dances. Some White people would go and make friends, but not all. They'd say "nigger, nigger." They go and teach the kids that, "nigger, nigger."

In addition to their central role in producing the glorious nightlife of early twentieth-century Liverpool, African seamen are also noted for setting into motion the institution of interracial marriage. Its prevalence is a crucial theme in narratives on local history. During their careers at sea, African men commonly docked in Liverpool's port, formed romantic relationships with the women there, who were mostly White, and later married them, had children, retired from seafaring, and settled in the city. So the origin story goes. Since Africans' presence dates back furthest, the history of interracial marriage gets traced through them. Male versions of the origin story highlight the shortage of marriageable Black women in Liverpool in the early years of the African presence. And when the numbers of Black women did begin to rise, their male counterparts did not consider them potential spouses. Black men I knew reported that they had grown up with these same women, concentrated as they all were into one small neighborhood. Black men felt a degree of familial intimacy with Black women that precluded the formation of any sexual desire for them. Another common narrative on interracial marriage, this one also articulated by Black men, argues that it is an expression of "freedom of choice." Although some Blacks I knew observed that this generations-old practice is now on the decline, interracial marriage, which consists most visibly of Black men and White women, is still prevalent in Liverpool. Although no reliable statistics are available, it is fair to say that at least half of Liverpool's locally born Black population is of mixed racial parentage. Most Black Liverpudlians whom I knew had White mothers and Black fathers, who were either African, Afro-Caribbean, or Black Liverpudlian.[2]

A major chapter in Blacks' origin story focuses on the publication of the *Fletcher Report* (1930), discussed previously. Scholarship on Blacks in Liverpool always condemns the *Fletcher Report* for arguing that racially mixed families were not viable, that African men were hypersexual, that the White women

partnered to them were of ill-repute, and that the children of these unions, referred to as "half-castes," had no hope of becoming moral, respectable members
of society.[3] Although the *half-caste* category did not originate with her *Report*,
Fletcher's name lives in infamy for contributing to its legitimacy. The struggle of
people of mixed racial parentage to recognize and overcome the stigma of the
half-caste inscription features centrally in their accounts of how they became
Black. People of mixed parentage whom I knew cited Black American influences
on the rise of a specifically *Black* identity there, while people with two Black
parents tended to boast that "we were *always* Black in our family"—speaking
disparagingly of those who have claimed that identity more recently. Yet people
of mixed racial parentage, as we will see shortly, testify to the difficulty of that
process. They indicated rather painfully that their African fathers, whom they
said they looked to for racial as well as cultural identity (as Nigerian or Igbo, for
example), also regarded them as half-castes.

As they spoke of these matters, my informants frequently made discursive
forays into Black America. Nested at key moments in their accounts were references to the formative influence that Black America, in many forms, has had on
racial and cultural identity in their city. The experiences they narrated were varied, and the narratives themselves were rich, poignant, and deeply gendered.
Black Liverpudlians told of their relations with the Black American servicemen
(or "GIs") who were stationed outside their city for some twenty-five years, beginning in World War II. Men and women also spoke about the travels of the
city's Black seafarers who, in their global wanderings, often brought back cultural riches from Black Atlantic ports of call, many in the United States. Narratives of Black Liverpudlians' diasporic encounters also referred to the immigration of Liverpool's Black women to the mythical place called *Black America*.
Finally, and crucially, men and women told of how and why they accessed the
many Black American cultural productions circulating around Liverpool.

Black Liverpudlians' narratives on these diasporic encounters are the subject of
this chapter. I focus on the politically, culturally, and sexually intimate relationship that unfolded between Black Liverpool and Black America over two historical moments: the postwar period, and the era of the U.S. civil rights and Black
Power movements. In addition to analyzing the effects of a nascent American
hegemony on the emergence of Blackness in Liverpool, I focus on the gender
politics of Black America's role in that process. The next three chapters examine
the rise of a specifically local politic of community, even though the debates about
Black America described here reflect its imprint. The local comprises a racial and
spatial formation of community of premier importance for Black Liverpudlians,
one that mediated and sanctioned appropriations of Black America. I argue that
gendered ideologies about localness have effectively produced Black America
and Black Liverpool as diasporic spaces to be differently occupied, experienced,
bridged, and traversed.

The case of Black Liverpool, then, presents a rich opportunity to invert the
dominant premises in the study of diaspora. A brief critical analysis of those is
followed by a discussion of people's narratives on the ways social relations in

what has become Black Liverpool have produced contradictory gender positionings vis-à-vis Black America.

GEOGRAPHIES OF DIASPORA THEORY

The foundational tendency in the study of diaspora is to define it quite simply as
any population that lives outside of the place thought to be its original homeland.
For example, James Clifford begins a review article on diaspora by asking, "How
do diaspora discourses represent experiences of displacement, of constructing
homes away from homes?" (1994: 302). In a similar vein, Basch, Schiller, and
Blanc say quite definitively, "To see oneself in a diaspora is to imagine oneself as
being *outside* a territory, part of a population exiled from a homeland" (1994: 269,
emphasis added). Or diaspora refers to "the doubled relationship or dual loyalty
that migrants, exiles and refugees have to places—their connections to the space
they currently occupy and their continuing involvement 'back home'" (Lavie and
Swedenburg 1996: 14). Avtar Brah uses the same social categories to suggest that
diaspora refers to "contemporary forms of migrancy" (1996: 186).

Displaced from the homeland by a combination of political and economic
forces, exiles, refugees, and migrants cross nation-state borders and, according to
conventional theory, enter "diaspora"—which often seems to be both a place and
an existential state. They are "in" diaspora, which some scholars refer to as a
"condition." Its symptoms are feelings of loss, alienation, and displacement.
Above, Clifford explicitly equates diaspora with displacement, as do Lavie and
Swedenberg in the very title of their edited volume *Displacement, Diaspora and
Geographies of Identity*. Displacement from an original homeland is rendered
axiomatic of the phenomenon. Diasporics are completely defined by their longings for home. They are pining for a past rooted in some other place.[4] "Diasporas
are populations that, while dispersed across boundaries and borders, salvage
from their common *loss* and *distance* from home their identity and unity as 'a
people'" (Basch, Schiller, and Blanc 1994: 269, emphasis added).

Diaspora is better understood as a relation rather than a condition. Theorizing
it as such, I do not want to propose that migrants do not suffer displacement, nor
that migration and dislocation are not matters properly studied under the rubric
of diaspora. I am concerned, however, that these phenomena tend to monopolize
the category, rendering it surprisingly static and staid. Despite over a decade of
prolific theorizing—much of it addressed to the effects of contemporary globalization—diaspora is still largely approached in ways not too far afield of the
term's classical Greek and biblical heritage.[5] The foundational premise still
stands: an initial, traumatic moment of dispersal becomes the starting point of
analysis, at the expense of examining how historically positioned subjects identify both the relevant events in transnational community formation and the places
implicated—or perhaps even produced—in that process. Black British cultural
critic Paul Gilroy theorizes transatlantic Black cultures and identities in a diasporic framework that does not privilege contemporary forms of migrancy, nor

migration itself, nor origins and homelands. Two of his major books, *There Ain't No Black in the Union Jack: The Cultural Politics of Race and Nation* (1987) and *The Black Atlantic: Modernity and Double Consciousness* (1993a), deserve close examination for their innovations and limitations.[6]

Gilroy's enthusiasm for diaspora grows out of his impatience with what he characterizes as the "ethnic absolutism" of nationalist discourses on culture and community in Britain.[7] The first of his many weighty pronouncements on the limits of nation occurs in the introduction to *There Ain't No Black* where he confesses to being weary of "having to deal with the effects of striving to analyse culture within neat, homogeneous national units reflecting the 'lived relations' involved" (1987: 12). With considerable force and subtlety, he goes on to argue that the language of nation is racialized to its core, operating through a wholly biologized notion of culture. That language, then, is inappropriate for Britain's Black movements (68). He further states that the emphasis on nationhood obscures the salience of local and regional identities, which often contest and fracture English and/or British identity and sometimes welcome Black membership (54). In a more crucial vein, he presents the plurality of diaspora cultures as the antidote to the putatively homogeneous nation. In order to advance that argument, Gilroy must show how diasporic identity transcends the biologistic and ahistorical terms in which racial and national identities get constructed. Toward these ends he offers this insightful example: Black Britons' connection to Black South Africans under apartheid was based neither on a primary affiliation to Africa, romantic visions of a homogeneous African culture, nor shared Africanness.[8] On the contrary, it derived from "a common experience of powerlessness" understood in racial categories and giving voice to an "identity of passions" (158–59). Although Gilroy does not pursue this illustration further in *There Ain't No Black*, the point may profitably be considered one of the cornerstones of his approach to diaspora—an approach that is more fully elaborated in *The Black Atlantic*. The passages that follow, also from his first book, introduce two other foundational premises:

> Black Britain defines itself crucially as part of a diaspora. Its unique cultures draw inspiration from those developed by black populations elsewhere. In particular, the culture and politics of black America and the Caribbean have become the raw materials for creative processes which redefine what it means to be black, adapting it to distinctively British experiences and meanings. (1987: 154)

> The social movements which have sprung up in different parts of the world as evidence of African dispersal, imperialism and colonialism have done more than appeal to blacks everywhere in a language which could invite their universal identification. . . . They have communicated directly to blacks and their supporters all over the world asking for concrete help and solidarity in the creation of organizational forms adequate to the pursuit of emancipation, justice and citizenship, internationally as well as within national frameworks. (1987: 156)

Gilroy's difference from other diaspora scholars is marked, in the first instance, by the simple choice of referent for the word *elsewhere*, for it does not

signify Africa, but the plethora of places where African descendants live. Black communities are linked transnationally by the mutual perception of a shared, wholly racialized condition and through the cultural and political resources they make available for overcoming the racial oppression that grips them all, albeit in different ways.[9] With this he productively pushed diaspora beyond the migration fixation. The foregoing passages reveal two other important premises: that the quest for "emancipation, justice and citizenship" characterizes Black diasporic political culture, and that the national and transnational dimensions of Black British life and politics are linked, though it remains important to distinguish their domains and effects. I would argue that the contentious aspects of Gilroy's approach lie not in these premises, per se, but in the ways he chooses to apply them. The effect of these choices is that *There Ain't No Black* avoids discussion of power asymmetries within national Black communities, while *The Black Atlantic* does not attend to relations of power extant across them.

Gilroy forcefully resists the hegemony of the nation, yet he is very careful to preserve some of its usefulness. As he remarks wryly in another context, "I am not against the nation . . . we have to put it somewhere" (1993b: 72). But in his considerable revamping of diaspora, the national functions, rather selectively, as a sign for specificity, while the transnational operates under the sign of universality and political affinity across national difference. In this way, the national reverts to its traditional role, permitting an understanding of specifically Black *British* experiences and meanings. Likewise, in his suggestion that "unique" Black British cultures are being created based on particularly British "experiences and meanings," two phenomena he works so hard to pull apart—nation and culture—again get collapsed. Meanwhile, he lauds the eminently useful and translatable in Black *American* culture. Together, these moves effectively grant one Black population the luxury of particularity, while endowing the other with the burden of universality. Black American cultural products that make the journey across the Atlantic must invite universal participation despite the fact that they may actually spring from specifically American "experiences and meanings" that do not translate well. As I elaborate below, this tension makes exceedingly difficult the realization of the project he identifies in *The Black Atlantic*: to locate common ground within the transnational.

In *The Black Atlantic,* Gilroy calls for a more geographically expansive understanding of Black political culture. The aforementioned premise concerning "emancipation, justice, and citizenship," first announced in *There Ain't No Black*, seems to have busted through the seams of that text, as evidenced by the richness and length of the diaspora chapter. So it returns, slightly amended, as the driving force of *The Black Atlantic*, a space formed in the first instance by the hemispheric—not national—racial order inaugurated by slavery, and thereafter by Blacks' constant movements through and engagements with multiple places in their search for freedom, citizenship, and autonomy. This ongoing search, he argues, constitutes the link among Black cultures across different times and spaces. If his first book emphasizes the influence of Black America on Black Britain, the second is premised on a strategic reversal. *The Black Atlantic* unearths data on the profound influence that European thought had on Frederick Douglass, Richard Wright, and W.E.B. Du Bois, and presents similarly convincing evidence on the Black American tendency to discount these sources, and the works inspired by them (such as Du Bois's *Dark Princess*), as racially impure. Gilroy argues convincingly that the international travels of these and other Black American intellectuals fundamentally shaped their lives and works—which nevertheless get studied, he justifiably protests, in the inexcusably provincial, national frame of Black American particularism.[10] He indicts Black American cultural historians and critics for promoting cultural or ethnic exclusivity in a way that allows Black Americans to claim ownership of resources that are only partially, as Gilroy says, their "ethnic property." This ethnic particularism prevents the Black public sphere from functioning as a conduit of intercultural exchange of raw materials that are themselves hybrid in origin and that could invite universal belonging and participation—particularly from Europe. To state it more pointedly, Black American exceptionalism marginalizes Black Britons and other Black Europeans from what their American counterparts myopically constitute as "real" Blackness. Invoking Du Bois to great effect, Gilroy poignantly conveys the gravity of these identity politics in the very first sentence of *The Black Atlantic*: "Striving to be both European and Black requires some specific forms of double consciousness" (1993a: 1).

Despite the obvious appeal of a hybrid transnational culture that could invite belonging among Blacks everywhere, merely celebrating the ideal without attending to the power relations that thwart its realization invites the discrepant policing of cultural borderlands and boundaries noted above. A hybrid transnational culture is only ideally a source of affinity; in practice, that hybridity could just as well produce antagonism. In searching out antagonism's roots and routes, we might begin by inquiring into the way particular Black communities outside the United States are affected by the global dominance of American culture. Britain is surely more inundated with things American than the reverse. As the case of Black Liverpool will show, American hegemony shapes the antagonistic relations between Blacks on either side of "the pond," even as that same force may be credited with providing the very means for Black identity to become such a formidable political force in this particular British context. Diasporic power asymmetries may also be identified in the ways Black American cultural products are differently absorbed, translated, and utilized within the individual Black European communities into which they travel. It is worth asking what kinds of ideologies on culture and community—ethnically absolutist, exceptionalist, or otherwise—work within localized racial communities to determine how they process the raw materials they access. How do Blacks within particular communities draw on those ever so contested concepts of nation, ethnicity, place, and culture to distinguish and mark particular materials originating "locally" and elsewhere, assigning them meaning and significance accordingly?

The gender politics of this particular process of classification, as well as the broader one of fashioning Black American raw materials into localized Black cultures, communities, and identities, represent other questions central to this kind of interrogation. Appeals to "heritage" and "tradition"—the touchstones of conventional studies of diaspora—here refer us to the gendered politics of the local; these politics split the category *Black*, providing people with quite different motivations for seeking affirmation from Blacks elsewhere. A serious elision in Gilroy's work, then, concerns the possibility that actors may assign mutually contradictory meanings to the Black cultural productions they appropriate. Diaspora may very well constitute an identity of passions, but these passions may not be identical within particular Black communities. These points force the sober realization that despite invitations to universal identification, not everyone partakes in the privileges of membership to the diasporic community with impunity.

There Ain't No Black and *The Black Atlantic* are integrally linked. Yet, it is in the gap between them that the greatest analytical potential lies. Broadly speaking, these books are distinguished by the fact that one studies the formation of Black culture within a national context, and the other studies it across national contexts. Gilroy acknowledges the importance of analyzing Black culture both in national and transnational frames, noting that "[b]oth dimensions have to be examined and the contradictions and continuities which exist between them must be brought out" (1987: 156). Yet the questions his work prompts are even more complicated than this. He leaves us to explore how power differentials extant *across* Black communities might mediate power relations *within* them. The inverse also merits interrogation: how do power relations within the diasporic space of particular Black communities shape participation in the transnational space of diaspora?

For the purposes of exploring the power-laden symbiosis between the "within" and "across" of diaspora, I will analyze those practices in which Black people in Liverpool make use of any of the vast resources of what they construct as the Black world, yet within the political economy of what has been available to them. Diasporic resources may include not just cultural productions such as music, films, and literature, but also people and places, as well as iconography, ideas, and ideologies associated with them. "Place" is an especially important resource, for the practice and politics of travel serve to map diasporic space, helping to define its margins and centers, while also crucially determining who is empowered to go where, when, under what conditions, and for what purposes. I use the term *diaspora's resources*, then, to capture the sense that Black Liverpudlians actively appropriate particular aspects of Black America for particular reasons, to meet particular needs—but do so within limits, within and against power asymmetries, and with political consequences.

To give life to the debates on local and diasporic community formation, I shall, in the remainder of this chapter, draw heavily on the words of Black Liverpudlians whom I knew, essentially putting their narratives into conversation with each other, therein allowing the bases of commonality and contestation to emerge. With this strategy I hope to reveal people's highly mediated representations of the past, focusing attention on the ways their own positioning vis-à-vis the racialized politics of gender, sexuality, and localness have shaped their desires vis-à-vis Black America. The ethnographic material is also structured to show these desires unfolding across two critical moments in the formation of Black identity. The older voices belong to Blacks in their fifties and sixties who

THE GENDERING OF DIASPORIC SPACE

were born and bred in Liverpool and who were young adults during the wartime and postwar periods. The younger voices belong to the next generation, people in their thirties and forties who were just coming of age when the U.S. civil rights and Black Power movements began "reverberating" around Liverpool, as one informant put it. One crucial subjective element links all of these informants, across generation and gender. All of their narratives portray, essentially, an invisible Liverpool. Despite the many contestations that bubble up in discussions of Black America, its presence as well as the exciting contributions made by the comings and goings of African seamen are relayed with unrestrained joy—as if that bygone era is being relived, and all those people brought back, in the very act of storytelling.

BLACK AMERICANS DROP ANCHOR

World War II was a formative moment in Liverpool. The city was heavily bombed and many of its men, Black and White, were killed on the high seas. Moreover, the war created dire economic circumstances with which Liverpudlians had to cope. Also, very importantly, the end of the war saw the rapid acceleration of U.S. global hegemony (West 1993). This hegemony would carry through not only the postwar era but into the next when the U.S. civil rights movement would begin reverberating around Liverpool.

In a previous section, Scott noted that the global travels of Black seamen during the war gave the local community access to foodstuffs unavailable in the rest of Britain. Yet it was not only food that the seamen brought into Liverpool, but music. As Scott spun these tales for me in his home on a summer afternoon, he was also spinning all the appropriate tunes. With pride and pleasure, he treated me to a soundtrack of those times. In the 1940s, he said, people were able to enjoy Billie Holiday and Lena Horne recordings because "in some instances, fathers and uncles had been over to America as seamen, and had brought records back. So within the Black community of Liverpool, we've always grown up with a type of traditional Black music. If it wasn't African, it would be American—it wouldn't be so much West Indian, Caribbean music around at that time." Although there are distinctions to be made among styles classified as African, American, and Caribbean, they all intermingle and distinguish themselves from styles classified as White and account for Liverpool's rise as a musical center. "White people," Scott continued, "found the Black community of Liverpool, musically, so interesting because it wasn't the White Victor Sylvester, it wasn't the White Harry James music. When they came into the Black community they were able to hear a mixture of music." As will be elaborated below, African seamen's contribution would soon be augmented by the offerings made by another group of Black men: American GIs.

Into the impoverished yet lively wartime environs entered American servicemen, Black and White, who were stationed at bases across Britain; Liverpool was sandwiched between two of them. One base, called Sealand, was thirty miles south of the city, and the other, Burton Wood, was even closer to Liverpool, short of Manchester. Scott described the social scene in the mid-1950s that was created, in part, by the presence of these men, who are commonly referred to as either "the Yanks" or "the GIs."

> By that time we had our own community centers as well as nightclubs. But the actual nightclub scene was fantastic. The Black American GIs—'cause *that's* what they were called—would come in with their big cars. Some of them were regular servicemen . . . [but] some, in comparison to British servicemen or to the Black population, were quite rich. So they could afford to have their cars shipped over from the States. And they would drive into Liverpool with these American Cadillacs. Some of them would be in their uniforms, and some of them would be in their American-style civilian clothes. And they'd come into the nightclubs. . . . You'd have a bit of a dance floor, and everybody would come in and enjoy themselves. . . . It was the first time that you'd hear the likes of the Platters, and a lot of the old Black groups that are dying out now.

An important site in the cultural geography of race in the city, across generations, was a place called the Rialto. It consisted of a ballroom that excluded Blacks and a cinema that did admit them. A popular nightspot in Scott's youth, it was burned to the ground in the 1981 riots (see chapter 3). Yet the Rialto featured prominently in happier Black Liverpudlian memory. Through the legendary Rialto, another informant, a Black man in his thirties, made connections like Scott's that drew distinctions between White and Black cultural production. Here he speaks of his mother, a White woman who sang Black American jazz at the Rialto Ballroom prior to the arrival of the GIs: "Before I was born, my mother and her friends used to sing Billie Holiday and that. They were heavily into that music. So when the GIs came, it was like the real thing. Like these were the people whose culture it really was."

Although they were stationed in England, the GIs had complete access to music from home, which they shared with their "host community" and which added to the city's already growing status as the cutting edge of popular music. White musicians were displaced and the Black section of Liverpool began to draw the attention of neighboring areas for its booming musical life. Indeed, some of my older informants alleged that the Beatles "pinched" their musical ideas—and some say actual songs—from the music they heard in the Black clubs of Liverpool in the late 1950s.

The nostalgia of some of the city's Black men, across generations, revealed an unwavering reverence of Black America for its musical contributions to Black Liverpool. However, another common theme in Black men's response to the presence of Black America in the city concerned its embodied form—that is actual Black American men as opposed to just music. Black Liverpudlian men were critical of the GIs for their apparent wealth. Scott described the monied image they struck: "The high-ranking ones drove big Pontiacs; it was the first time I had seen these cars apart from seeing them in American films. And you'd see one of the GIs walking down Upper Parliament Street with conked hair, and he'd be flashing his wallet and sweet-talking the women." Some Black men of the city joined White British men in commenting on this politic of location, saying that "there's nothing wrong with the GIs except that they're overpaid, oversexed, and over here."[11] Black women of this era had a different opinion. Invariably, Black women who spoke of "the Yanks" and their appeal referred to the good times the GIs gave them. What follows is the description that Claire, in her fifties, provided of the postwar dating scene.

> We always looked forward to the weekend because Friday to Sunday, around the Rialto area, it was packed with either men with blue uniforms or brown uniforms. At Burton Wood Club they all had the brown uniforms on. And at the Sealand Club, they were Air Force, so they all had the blue uniforms on. So there was this color of brown uniforms and blue uniforms, and we would be looking for stripes. If they had no stripes they wouldn't get a look in. One stripe, you didn't get a look in. You had to have *two* stripes and over before we would entertain them.

I asked Claire what the Black men of Liverpool had to say about all this, and here is her response:

> Well, there was a fight! The Black men said that the Americans—"the Yanks" is what they said—the Yanks were taking away our women. So there was a fight. They beat each other up! They beat each other up terrible. But the women stayed firm and said "We don't want homegrown!" When the Rialto was a cinema they'd come and pick us up and sometimes they'd have a car. Well! And it'd be an American car. And if you got one—an American man who had a car—oh, you were a star! And they'd take you to the Rialto. Or, if they didn't have a car, just to be seen walking up the road and going into the Rialto with this man, in this uniform, was something you knew that people were looking and nudging one another, and we just thought it was wonderful! When you go up the stairs to the Rialto, they would put their hand on your elbow and help you up, and we just thought that was marvelous! Now we did *not* get that attention from the Blacks in Liverpool. So after we had experienced these wonderful manners, this is what we wanted. We wanted to be treated like we were queens. And we were getting that treatment from the Yanks. And that's why we didn't want anything to do with the men of the area.

Claire gives evidence to a view Black Liverpudlian men commonly articulated, so it may be important to keep in mind her references to the glamour of the Black Americans, with all their stripes and their cars. That is, she intimates that Black women were attracted to the American men for what they could offer. Yet Claire also notes, importantly, that women were not getting that kind of attention from "homegrown" Black men.[12]

Two sisters of the World War II generation, Caroline and Jean, were in their absolute glory reminiscing about these days. Caroline showed me her photo album, crammed with pictures of herself, Jean, and their various American beaus. With a devilish little gleam in her eye, Caroline nudged her sister, "We had some good times, didn't we, [Jean]?" Her sister responded so viscerally, she seemed to be in pain: "Oh, honest to *God*!" Their private exchange suggested that they were calling up some rather racy memories indeed. In the memories they did verbalize, they represented the GIs' presence as key to the making of

Liverpool, even if these men were a tad unsophisticated. As Caroline commented, "Liverpool used to be a *smashing* place! All the smart ones got out. The GIs used to come in from Sealand and Burton Wood. Most of them were into partying here and partying there. But they were nice, you know?! They spoke nice. You know—they had the accent! They were good company—that is, every now and again you'd get one that you *could* converse with!"

Caroline and Jean are the daughters of a White Irish mother and a Nigerian father—"a Yoruba man," as Caroline would proudly refer to him. Her photo album was crammed with pictures of him, too. Caroline particularly enjoyed pointing out his dignified poses and how he was dressed: in stunning English attire. Part of what she loved about him—and indeed the generation of African seamen to which he belonged—was the way he traversed two cultural worlds with seeming ease. He would dress fashionably English, expressing no sense of contradiction, yet also took pride in teaching his English-born children to cook Nigerian food. The sisters' representations of their father and his compatriots contrasted dramatically with those of younger Black Liverpudlians whose relations with their own African fathers were fraught with tension (as will be discussed shortly).

In speaking about their father's identity, these women added another very important dimension to the unfolding drama of 1950s Liverpool. They condemned the Black Americans for speaking so disparagingly of Africans. Caroline recalled, "One of them asked me—now I'm going back a long way—he asked me where my father was from and I said, 'My dad's African.' And you know what that man said? 'Oh, one of them jungle men.' I said [to him], 'You don't know what you are! You're only government issue!'" She and Jean added that when they would go to the cinema with the Americans, these men would make racist comments about the Africans occasionally depicted on the screen. The sisters explained the Americans' unsavory behavior in sociological terms, through reference to their class backgrounds. Caroline supposed that in comparison to her own father who was a chief chef onboard a ship, most of the GIs came from poor backgrounds. She speculated that it was only through their employment in the services that they came to have "a few dollars in their pockets," as she put it.

Just as Black American men would descend upon the Rialto area on the weekends, so too would Black women travel to the American bases to attend dances and meet men. Kathleen, in her fifties, explained:

> The two American bases were within commuting distance; it would take an hour and a half to get there on the bus. And the buses would be at Lime Street Station and they'd pick up the girls and go to these dances, which is how a lot of the romances got started, including my own. Black men in Britain—and these were the home-grown ones—were not into us "half-castes" as we were called in those days. They were only interested in the White girls. The Americans came in and they were interested in anyone in skirts, basically.[13]

As indicated earlier, interracial relationships in Liverpool are composed most visibly of Black men with White women. Many Black women I knew expressed intense emotion when talking about the practice of interracial dating. Although they often struggled to find some charitable explanation for Black men's behavior toward them, inevitably they would talk about the pain of their perceived rejection. One woman's search for an explanation follows. Crystal was in the midst of comparing Britain to the United States on the matter of affirmative action policies and was concluding that the latter is far ahead of her own country on this and other race matters. She proceeded to make the following comment in a tone revealing both confusion and pain:

> The Black British culture is different than the American Black culture. There's a problem here because—[saying] this is going to cause so much of a problem but it's true—if you talk to Black ladies in Liverpool, they'll say to you, "The Black men in Liverpool never seem to want to date us." I know a lot of Black men in this community and they do not date Black women. And that's why when the men from America— the Black men—came from the base it was like, "Hey, thank you!" And we are so proud to be asked out by a Black man. When I go to America, I'm asked out by a Black man, never White guys. Here I am always asked out by White men. It's a crying shame. It really is. Maybe it's because you go to school together, you grow up together and you don't want to date each other. If I'm looking for a partner, I know it won't happen in Liverpool! I asked my brothers why and they couldn't answer me. They have never dated a Black woman. They say it's a personal choice. I think that's why Black women marry Americans and go and live in America.

Here we begin to see that it is exclusionary practices occurring within the racial community, along distinctly gendered lines, that send some Black Liverpudlians down the diasporic path. Black women's responses to their perpetual exclusion from local Black male desire sparked the joyful reminiscences of Claire, Caroline, and Jean. Indeed, many Black Liverpudlian women, including Crystal, married Americans and moved to the United States.

Together, the perceived class differences between Black Americans and Black Liverpudlians, and the controversial dating practices among Liverpool's Black men and women, gave rise to a now institutionalized debate of the classic chicken-and-egg variety. Black women said they were perpetually overlooked by Black men, while the latter commonly recited the refrain that "the Yanks stole our women." The older generation of men—that is, those who were young adults in the 1950s—say that they did not have fancy cars, that they were poor and skinny from having lived off of rations for years, and that they could not offer Black women what the Yanks were offering. There grew, then, some animosity between Black American men and Liverpool's Black men that would extend into the next generation. Yet it is important not to overstate the case, as it concerns the men of the World War II generation. Scott told me, for example, that one of his best friends was a Black American, adding that his own attitude, and those of his peers, was that since they couldn't beat the Yanks, they'd join them.

As the postwar years gave way to the period marked by the civil rights movement, new images of Black America were ushered into Liverpool. These contrasted sharply with the image that the Black American servicemen, themselves products of an earlier era in the formation of racial identity, had hitherto embodied. Caroline and Jean indicated the transformation that took place across generations. Caroline said that "when all this American civil rights happened in the sixties, the GIs changed their tune. They all wanted to be Black African and that kind of thing. It's like today some of these people are wearing African things and it's all like a fashion to them, you see." About the Americans, Jean added, "They haven't got a clue about Africans and the different tribes, and that. After the civil rights started . . . they all wanted to be dressed in the caftan or whatever, with the big afros." Like Jean and Caroline, Black people commonly, and proudly, represented Liverpool as a distinctly "African" city, a place where most people know their ancestors' exact origins on the continent, even if they have been in Liverpool "for generations and generations," as they often say. They also construct Liverpool's African identity by referring to the fact that many of the nightclubs in Liverpool 8 have borne African names—such as the Sierra Leone Club, the Nigerian, the Yoruba, and the Igbo. In leaving this generation and proceeding into the next, it should be noted that Caroline and Jean were the only two people who commented on the perceived lack of African identity as it concerned the Black Americans of the 1950s and early 1960s. The next generation of Black Liverpudlians had much more to say about the positioning of the Black Americans vis-à-vis "Africa."

But before examining this new phase of diasporic identity politics, and the class, gender, and sexual tensions at their core, it bears note that in the early 1970s Liverpool's shipping industry was dying a slow death. Within ten years, it would grind almost to a halt. It became increasingly difficult for Black men to get work sailing around the world. Yet a new trend in Black Liverpudlian travel had begun to attract attention: Black women were boarding airplanes in droves, leaving Liverpool with their American husbands.

CIVIL RIGHTS AND BLACK POWER IN THIS "VERY AFRICAN" CITY

In the late 1960s and early 1970s, the imaginations of young Blacks were captured not only by Black American music but also, increasingly, by the resistance practices they associated with Black America. They seized and appropriated the wealth of diasporic resources available to them, imbuing all manner of iconography and cultural productions emanating from "Black America" with a racial meaning and significance that could be productively utilized in Liverpool. Black youth fashioned these materials, in all their variety, into a distinctly—and distinctly gendered—Black politic. For example, this generation of Black men adopted the strategies of the Black Panthers in defying neo-fascist youths who, at once, sought to restrict Blacks from traveling into exclusively White areas of the city and who also went into Liverpool 8, terrorizing them there. One Black man spoke of such incidents in an interview that took place just outside of Liverpool 8:

> You wouldn't want to be in this area in them days because you'd be at risk. At my age—then I was in my teens—you were at risk of being beaten up by the police or the skinheads. And where I was was the heart of it, where these guys lived and hung

out. This was *their* homeland not mine. It's funny—up by Lodge Lane there's a pub called the Boundary. And it actually *was* the boundary for Black people as far as I was concerned. You actually couldn't go down there and down by Wavertree Road—it was like South Africa. Cops would actually say, "What are you doing going out of your area?" We didn't like it, but. . . . The Black community was Liverpool 8, Granby Street, Carter Street. To go into town meant hand-to-hand combat. And also around then—you're talking about the late sixties and early seventies—you were not only being around Black people and a Black family, but also the Black Panthers. . . . We were reflecting what was going on in the States. . . . [W]e couldn't see why we couldn't go here, there, and the other place. So we organized.

Others spoke of similar contributions Black America made to their racial sensibilities. Joseph, in his thirties, described the diasporic resources that helped him to cope with growing up in an all-White part of Liverpool. He recalled that Black American music during the civil rights era was always "reverberating around the house." Joseph said that he gained a perspective on racism by studying the lyrics of the Temptations—lyrics he described as "pure philosophy"—and by reading the backs of their album covers. He added that as a child, he idolized Muhammad Ali for the pride he showed in Black people and for his rejection of "mainstream, White-dominated, American values." With that, Joseph said that if Whites in his neighborhood were calling him a "nigger," he was proud to be that because, as he put it, "There are some powerful niggers in the world. Look at Muhummad Ali." In the quotation below, Greg, another Black man in his thirties, gives further evidence of the variety of diasporic resources that people of his generation appropriated from Black America. In so doing, he articulates a process of diasporic identity formation that mirrors that of other informants of his generation. He recalled his struggle to understand the racism of his schoolmates, as well as his parents' inability to respond to his troubles. His comments below followed from his discussion of a song that was sung in school when he was a young boy. The refrain contained the word *coon*, which Greg said his White classmates particularly enjoyed singing.

I definitely became aware of being non-British, non-White. I can't say I became aware of being "Black" because I was too small to have a political context in my head. I became aware of new things, new words that were designed to either intimidate me or put me under pressure from peers, from students, other people, and from teachers to a certain extent.

. . . Because I'm from a mixed background—my father's Nigerian, my mother's White—you had separate answers to questions anyway. My dad deals with colonialism in Nigeria and his thinking was that "they're all crazy, they're all mad, they're White—they're all crazy." I'm supposed to just dismiss these things on that basis and rise above it because my dad had the whole traditional cultural background firmed up and established, so his answer was just to ignore it. It still left the question. Going toward me mum, me mum's usually quite angry about it, and dealt with it on an immediate level. She'd say, "Well, you say this and you say that." But it still left the questions. It was all

coming out of me not being the same as the majority in the school. I'm aware that the majority of the school is British and Liverpudlian on a White basis, and aware that I definitely wasn't in that area. I wasn't quite sure of the area I was in. I wasn't fully positioned in any position.

By the time I went to secondary school I was definitely seeing myself as Black; there was a political context to how I was looking at myself. That was informed by international things: afros, and style and fashion, my sisters' contact with the American air base and things like that. It brought politics on a wider scale than just immediately in Liverpool 8. Yeah, it informed things! It was in an international context that I was starting to get feedback on things. Youth in the area were taking on things. Growing afros, wearing arm bands, wearing one black glove to a certain extent. I was brought out of this sort of West African upbringing where they put you in a bubble. I could set my own agenda. It opened up things and my identity was, like, being informed by wider things rather than just being informed by the family.

Importantly, Greg notes the futility of looking to his parents for answers. People of his age, also of mixed parentage, said that racial issues were not generally discussed in their households. And unlike Blacks of Caroline's generation, younger ones often perceived their African fathers as gatekeepers, describing their steadfast refusal to share with their children any aspects of African culture. As embodied in their relationships with their fathers, these youths' experiences of "Africa" were tinged with the pain of exclusion. Greg said his father "wanted to keep bits of his self and not necessarily share them with English people—which we were really perceived as. I mean English-mixed-race-Nigerian-British people." Veronica, a woman of Greg's age and also of mixed parentage, said she wanted to learn Yoruba, but her father "seemed to want to put her off it" because, as she put it, he was prejudiced against her because of her color. She poignantly offered her understanding of her father's position:

> To be honest, I don't know if he was a bit prejudiced against his own daughters because of our color. I think he was a bit disappointed because, like, three of us were very light (not me, I was one of the darker ones), and they seemed to get a lot of pressure. . . . He was a funny man, mentally. His mentality was different, like. Sometimes he'd go on, "Oh, you don't know what them White people done to my father," and all like this. And he'd take it out on us. These African men—these old ones what come from back home—they have some heavy mentality that is very difficult to understand. You don't know if they love you or hate you. Your own flesh and blood.

The sensibilities Greg and Veronica express above do not index desires and longings for Africa as a generalized and idealized ancestral homeland but rather betray a profound sense of displacement from their African fathers' affections. Such pained relationships to "Africa" live side by side with Blacks' pride in how "African" their city is. Put another way, "Liverpool" was more African than they were. It was in this context that "Black America" became the object of diasporic longing, for it answered these and other problematics—however partially and contentiously.

Black American iconography and ideologies traveling into Liverpool helped some people of this generation grapple with issues of both racial identity in the face of the pathologized half-caste inscription and White British nationalism (see chapter 3) and cultural identity in the face of what they perceived as their African fathers' distancing posture. In what follows, Greg suggests that through the gripping, mutually class-based and masculine image these men embodied, Black Americans inspired African identity among the people of his generation. He does so by describing the way the GIs, with their trappings of glamour and wealth, ever so visibly occupied Granby Street, the symbolic heart of Black Liverpool.

> [T]he American bases would accommodate a particular type of American Black culture. They would accommodate it in style and fashion and big cars. The thing about poverty in Liverpool—you didn't see big cars. You see them now, but [then] you didn't see big cars and flash clothes. And although you didn't fully understand what was going on, you actually did get a vibe from it: a serious uplifting feeling from seeing someone in a huge car with black skin driving down Granby Street! And that opened up other areas like the crème de la crème of the whole dancing culture within Black people. So you picked up on that level as well. There wasn't a lot of connection to Africa other than via America. There wasn't that direct connection. There *is* that massive connection within the large West African settlement in Liverpool, [but] at that time it really wasn't an "African" agenda. It was an American agenda and you got your information of Africa via America.

It would be tempting to read young Black Liverpudlians' interest in Africa, even though influenced by Black America, as expressive of a romantic reverence for an ancestral culture. A better way of accounting for it may lie in the authority the GIs, and Black America more generally, had already gained there, for the resources they provided proved eminently useful and translatable in the struggles around "race" unfolding, quite materially, on the streets of Liverpool. The GIs' influence might also be a function of transformations in Black Liverpudlians' class status.

Significant changes were afoot in the ways Blacks were positioned by their city's political-economic structure, as the death of the shipping industry left the younger generation with few job prospects.[14] For this reason, it is worth comparing the different class positionings of Black Americans and Liverpudlians over the two historical moments under investigation, for these seem to bear directly on the discrepant ways the two generations of Liverpudlians interpret the Americans' authority on Africa. It will be remembered that Caroline, speaking from the World War II generation, made an explanatory link between the GIs' *lower* class status and what she perceived as their lack of African identity; she observed that these men denigrated Africans because they were too poor to know any better. A similar, though inverted, class analysis may now be operating in Greg's generation which, as I have already noted, is marked by the Black Power era. It may be conjectured that the rising rate of Black unemployment that accompanied the steady decline of Liverpool's shipping industry lent the GIs, and their *apparent* wealth, even more prestige in Greg's generation than in Caroline's. In her generation, as

Scott relayed in his narrative about the 1950s, cars signified America's affluence relative to Britain; in Greg's 1970s version, these same flashy accoutrements were reconstituted as signifiers of Black possibility. The Black American men who drove these spectacles down the now impoverished streets of Liverpool became entrusted with unprecedented authority on Africa. And in contrast to Caroline and Jean, who remarked on the hollowness of the GIs' African identification in the civil rights/Black Power era ("They haven't a clue about Africans and the different tribes. . . . It's all like a fashion to them"), Greg drew on the GIs as a valuable resource ("you got your information of Africa via America"). In expressing their awe of the GIs, people of his generation commonly cataloged which images associated with Black America left indelible impressions on them—images like the afro, which people commonly assigned an African significance. Displaced by their African fathers, young Black Liverpudlians accepted the invitation to universal belonging being issued from Black American quarters. But mutually imbricated ideologies of gender and locality—as mediated by the precipitous, sudden death of Black men's traditional livelihood—were also being transformed in the process, giving rise to a set of sanctions that would sharply circumscribe the ways Blacks could appropriate diasporic resources.

Despite the fact that young Black Liverpudlian men and women have shared the same pained relation to "Africa" as embodied in their relations to their fathers, their common retreat to "Black America" has actually resulted in the fracturing of local identity along distinctly gendered lines. Note the role Greg attributes to Black women in the fallout between the Liverpudlian and American Black men of the late 1960s and early 1970s:

> There was definitely a thing that, it's hard to generalize it too much, but Liverpool Black women were definitely interested in American men more so than Liverpool Black men, really. Now the knock-on effect was that Liverpool Black men resented that obviously and tended not to mix so much with the American Black men, really. That didn't stop the information coming through on a cultural basis about Black identity. That wasn't hindering that.

A similarly gendered view and experience of Black America was articulated by other men of Greg's generation who tended to trivialize women's attraction to the GIs, projecting onto women what seemed to be *their own* fascination with the Yanks' manifest Blackness. Another man put it this way:

> All the GIs were coming into the funk clubs. They had long coats and double-knit jumpers [sweaters] that you couldn't buy in England at the time, big afro combs and things like *Jet* magazine and Afro Sheen. And local girls wouldn't go out with local Black guys 'cause we were just scum. And their idea was [that] if they married a GI, they'd get back to the States where it was all happening.

Women's representations of their attraction to the GIs differed considerably. Karen, who married a GI, moved to the United States, and eventually moved back to Liverpool, described in quite different terms why Black America appealed to her in that era. Karen makes some of the same references to Black

American culture and thwarted African identity as did the men previously quoted. But she draws on Black America to position her racial identity within a feminist framework that challenges oppressive African and "homegrown" Black narratives concerning local Black womanhood. Unlike Greg, Karen constructs Black identity with scant reference to White domination:

> My consciousness . . . came from the Black movement in the States. At the Olympic games when those guys put their hands up in the air, it was a source of pride for me as a Black person. And because of the problems with Africans and what they termed us as ("half-castes"—the products of mixed marriages), I affiliated Black Americans as being more kin to me than Africa. I joined the Black women's liberation group and I joined the Angela Davis march in this country, and was very political in my sense as a Black person. *Anything* that emanated from there—from music to culture—was part of *my culture*!

In one forceful sweep, Karen critiques the pathologized category "half-caste" and chooses Black America as *her* culture—and indeed, her "kin"—over the ancestral Africa, which is implicated in the racialization of Blacks of mixed parentage. But the betrayal does not stop there; it is also the cherished seafaring history that she scorns. She spoke of the gendering of Liverpudlian Blackness in equally forceful terms:

> A woman like me was marginalized because I was seen as a feminist. A couple of Black men were good on the issue, but very few. So you would get that sort of commentary like, "Oh, they're all chasing after the American dream," and "They didn't want to know us." Black men in the city said it was a *historic* thing about White women; they say it was since the days when sailors came into town and they actually had relationships with White women because there were no Black women here. What happened when there *were* Black women here?! They *still* didn't want to know Black women. The hurtful things that actually happened to Black women here meant you could go after the American dream thing and feel some respect for yourself as a Black woman.

Karen critiques local Black men for invoking the proud seafaring narrative—the basis of Liverpudlian identity itself—to condone a contentious aspect of racialized sexual politics in the present day. Karen suggests that the manufacture of seafaring as tradition has compelled Black Liverpudlian women to access Black America as a counterhegemonic diasporic resource, one they could draw upon to feel some respect for themselves, as Black women. Black Liverpudlian men's idealized imaginings of Black America notwithstanding, the American dream for Karen did not have much to do with flash and glamour or class mobility. For Karen and other women who indicted Liverpool's racial-sexual politics, Black America represented a resource for attaining a form of self respect that was, according to them, unavailable locally. Crystal's earlier observation about what she and other Black women gained from the Black American presence in Liverpool is relevant here. She said, "We are so *proud* to be asked out by a Black man" (emphasis added). Lest it be understood that it was only as women that

Crystal and Karen appropriated Black America, it bears emphasis that they also spoke to Black America's contributions to the more general causes of anti-racism and Black empowerment. Crystal's narrative, quoted earlier, followed her (unquoted) discussion of the advances Black Americans have made in the struggle for affirmative action in the United States. Likewise, Karen made a laudatory reference to the two Black American athletes who, at the 1968 Olympics, put their gloved fists in the air in support of the struggle for Black liberation. Yet Crystal's and Karen's specific references to *pride* and *self-respect* went further, revealing the gendered and sexualized character of the radical Blackness they fashioned out of Black American raw materials.

The narratives presented thus far show that diasporic subjectivity among Black Liverpudlians was produced through a set of gendered antagonisms that mutually implicated Africa, Black America, and Black Liverpool, rendering each, in its own way, a highly contested resource for racial identity formation. These narratives illustrate how the racialized politics of kinship and desire have informed the construction of different categories of men (African, "homegrown," and American). Collectively, then, the ethnographic material and analyses presented here directly challenge contemporary theory, first, by complicating the place of "longing" in the formation of diasporas, and second, by problematizing the assumption that migration and "displacement" have been key to the formation of diasporic community and subjectivity in Liverpool. That is, in this case, migration did not result in diasporic longings; diasporic longings resulted in migration. This insight helps recontextualize Stuart Hall's sentiment, quoted in the epigraph and worth quoting again: "If the paper seems preoccupied with the diaspora experience and its narratives of displacement, it is worth remembering that all discourse is 'placed', and the heart has its reasons" (1990: 223). Arjun Appadurai's insight about the cultural politics of diaspora can be similarly reframed, if we dare to allow the ancestral tropes he implicitly invokes to refer us not to Africa but to *Liverpool*: "The politics of desire and imagination are always in contest with the politics of heritage and nostalgia" (1989: iii). In their appropriations of Black America, Black Liverpudlian women effectively contested both the hegemony of Liverpool as homeland and the rigidly racialized forms of desire and kinship that, some say, constitute its Black heritage.

DEPARTURES AND DISPLACEMENTS

The many instances of diasporic relation described above were shaped by a gendered politic of location that begins, at the very least, with the historical circumstances that brought different Blacks into various kinds of encounter. All the seafarers were men, as were the GIs, and thus the opportunity to emigrate was only open to women. In the foregoing narratives, then, we see the contentious but inspiring presence of the Yanks around Upper Parliament Street, where they were "flashing their money and sweet talking the women"; the masculinist inspiration they provided as they drove big cars down Granby Street; the migration of Black

Liverpudlian women in the mythical land called Black America, "the place where it was all happening"; and earlier, the cellar party milieu created by local Blacks and African seafarers, who dropped anchor with music in hand. The dynamics of presence and movement in these examples raise the question of how gender might be understood in relation to the production of diasporic space. In conceptualizing space itself, I use Neil Smith's eminently useful definition: space is a material realm, consisting of the arrangement of objects, events and relations (1992: 67). Space, he argues, is best understood as differentiated and hierarchical. Similarly, according to Doreen Massey, space is produced through material praxis and is productive and reflective of social relations; hence, space cannot be separated from power (1994: 249–272).

Seafaring is the logical starting point for a discussion of the gendering of diasporic space, considering that Black Liverpudlians, male and female, credit African seamen for giving birth to the Black community, even if not Black identity. Gilroy has identified seafaring as one of the concrete means through which noncontiguous places were joined, facilitating in turn the production of transnational Black cultures. Here he explains his use of the ship as a metaphor in *The Black Atlantic*:

> I have settled on the image of ships in motion across the spaces between Europe, America, Africa, and the Caribbean as a central organizing sumbol. . . . The image of the ship—a living, micro-cultural, micro-political system in motion—is especially important for historical and theoretical reasons. . . . Ships immediately focus attention on the middle passage, on the various projects for redemptive return to an African homeland, on the circulation of ideas and activists as well as the movement of key cultural and political artifacts: tracts, books, gramophone records and choirs (1993a: 4).

An argument against this model is that seafaring is too uniformly male to foster an understanding of women's agency in producing the Black Atlantic. For instance, "[Gilroy's] examples of how the unity of the black Atlantic is constituted . . . privilege a set of experiences historically inaccessible to women. The transatlantic experience on ships was available only to those politically and economically positioned in a male-dominated sphere" (Helmreich 1993: 245). I would argue, in contrast, that unequal access to mobility—and the gendering of presence, location, and travel that further result from differential mobility—provides a window onto the power asymmetries at the heart of diasporic relations, both across the Black Atlantic and within its constitutive locales. Put otherwise, the goal is to expose space-as-hierarchy rather than to search out a (nonexistent) material space produced in relations of equality.

In a similar critique, James Clifford notes that Gilroy's Black Atlantic history "leans toward the diasporic practices of men" (1994: 325). He suggests that

> [d]iasporic experiences are always gendered. But there is a tendency for theoretical accounts of diasporas and diaspora cultures to hide this fact, to talk of travel and displacement in unmarked ways, thus normalizing male experiences. . . . Retaining focus on specific histories of displacement and dwelling keeps the ambivalent politics of diaspora in view. Women's experiences are particularly revealing (313).

Again, notwithstanding the righteous spirit of the critique, I would urge diaspora studies to attend more to the politics of gender than to "women's experiences." That is, the asymmetries of power called "gender" are what constitute and normalize masculinity and femininity as categories of difference, producing in turn "women's experience" (J. Scott 1992). Hence, rather than reifying women's experiences and practices in the name of gender balance in diaspora studies, we should interrogate how particular practices, such as travel, and processes, such as community formation, come to be infused with gender ideologies (or "gendered"), and how such gendering effectively determines the different social and physical locations men and women can legitimately occupy. As well, examining the *meanings* of seafaring would reveal the formation of a decidedly gendered politics of staying, going, and returning. It is important not to conflate the *politics* of travel and *actual* travel. As the earlier testimonies of Clara and Karen have already suggested, the agency of women is evident in the ways they participate in making and contesting gendered inscriptions about seafaring. Studied from the vantage point of the port, then, seafaring shows the centrality of gender ideologies to the production of diasporic space.

Black Liverpudlian men's narratives show that gendered antagonisms, as mediated by class, shaped their ambivalent evaluation of the Yanks as producers of the diasporic space that Liverpool 8 constituted. Similar antagonisms operate in relation to the diasporic space produced by Black women's departure. Just as African seamen are credited with giving birth to this Black community, Black women's immigration to the United States expanded the space within which it presently exists. I scarcely knew a Black Liverpudlian who *did not* have *at least* one female relative in the United States. Despite men's rather neutral stance on their own sisters' migrations, when Black men commented upon the general phenomenon of Black women moving to the States, their remarks were drenched in disapproval. Men's narratives on the exclusively male migrations from Africa to Britain were completely devoid of critique. To wit, African seafarers are never placed in the category "immigrant". Yet, migration *is* the frame through which Black Liverpudlian women's movements are implicitly couched. Despite the possibility that African seafarers could have chosen to settle in Liverpool for reasons at least partially economic, this was never invoked as an analogously understandable rationale for Black women who may have also harbored economic reasons for immigrating to the United States. The gendered interpretations of these migrations are indeed quite sharp, for in contrast to women's representation of their mass exodus, Black men said things like "America is like a dream, a carrot. America is seen as an escape. It's seen as a place of prosperity."

The gendering of travel can be analyzed further by comparing the meanings attached to the return of Black seamen and Black women immigrants to Liverpool. Scott said earlier that Black seafarers' return to Liverpool was an event marked by parties "of an African style." By contrast, the tendency among women to drop their anchors back in the city's port is narrated with criticism—by men. On the matter of Black women's return, one man chided women for having pursued an American avenue of opportunity in the first place, representing their return as a failed defection. He remarked, " . . . [A]nd then there were the ones who got married, went to the States, couldn't handle it, and came back. The story's out now: it's not milk and honey, the grass is not any greener." In a more generous vein, Black men spoke of Black women as naive, suggesting that they were taken in by the apparent wealth of "the Yanks," as it was rather deceptively manifested in Liverpool, and by their big talk about having huge homes back in the States. Scott added another factor in their return: they came back to Liverpool because "they couldn't handle the racism in the southern states."

Kathleen was one of four Black women I knew who had married a GI, moved to the United States, and subsequently returned to Liverpool. She felt acutely the criticism leveled against Black women for leaving and the stigma attached to their return. Her father, an African, strongly disapproved of her marrying an American and moving to the United States. She left despite his wishes. When she bid him goodbye, he responded, "It's not like you're leaving; it's like you're dying." Kathleen's marriage dissolved not long after she settled in Pittsburgh. She considered returning to Liverpool but changed her mind after receiving a letter from her father in which he mentioned the daughter of a friend of his who had "gone to the States and married an American, and look at what happened to her! She's back in England now with her three babies, living off her father." She delayed visiting Liverpool for years so that she could save enough money to go back in style and escape the criticism for having left. On that first visit back she observed that "it felt as depressed as it was when I left, and in fact it felt even more depressed because now I had seen something different. So I made the conscious decision to remain in the United States because I felt I had more opportunities."[15] In stark contrast to most Black women I knew, those who went to the United States and later returned to Liverpool are now successful professionals. Kathleen said specifically that the survival skills she honed in the United States "made me the woman I am today."

Indeed, these women's difficulties adjusting to life in "Black America" began with their complete isolation. The demographic spread of these women's relocation, across the geographic expanse that is the United States, made it unlikely that they would be able to form community with other Black women from Britain. Of the four women I know who immigrated to the United States, one had lived in New York, one in Pennsylvania, another in Texas, and yet another in Utah. In their singularity, these women were absolute novelties, the charm of which quickly wore thin. And after two generations of Black American hegemony in Liverpool, these women were understandably shocked that Black Americans were so completely ignorant about the Black presence in England. Karen put it best, saying, "I think they thought England consisted only of White people in bowler hats sitting around drinking tea." Two women, independently of each other, said that when they told Black Americans that they were from Liverpool, they were met with the question, "Liverpool? What part of Africa is that?" Kathleen discussed the difficulty of befriending Black American women and the kinds of dialogues that would ensue when she finally did make friends: "They were shocked that there were Black people in England. In fact, a number of Black women that I befriended in the early years thought that I was putting on airs, and that I really didn't talk this way. So once I got over that hurdle it was like, 'Why did you marry a Black American? You could have married anybody!'"

Nascent American hegemony took a decidedly *Black* form in Liverpool—with ironic results. That hegemony allowed Black Americans to exert a class privilege in Liverpool that they would not have enjoyed in the United States during the postwar, civil rights, and Black Power eras. Hollywood images shown at the Rialto must have encouraged the view of the United States (and, by extension, the Black GIs) as glamorous and wealthy. Moreover, the myth unleashed by American hegemony was that there existed a place called "Black America" that would somehow resemble its various embodiments in Liverpool—a premise embedded in statements referring to the States as "the place where it was all happening." Despite their critique of the "Yanks" and of the women who appropriated the fabled land of Black America as a material resource, Liverpool's Black men were nonetheless able to draw on the GIs' presence, their relentless visibility, as a symbolic resource of their own—as proof that it *is* possible for a Black person to drive a big car down Granby Street, as Greg put it. As alternately embodied in people, place, and culture, diaspora's resources can be used to create liberatory possibilities for people who, for varied reasons, feel that they "are not fully positioned in any position," as Greg so nicely put it. Yet these resources scarcely free everyone completely, or in the same way.

Black Liverpool was produced through movements of many kinds, not just migration. Black seamen's decidedly fluid orientation in space is commonly heralded as a triumphant History. If it were not for the seamen, Liverpool Blacks would not have had access to certain foods and exciting music from Africa and the United States. Hence, Blacks' corner of Liverpool was created as a diasporic space through seamen's global travels. Like the seamen, the GI's brought another world into Liverpool 8, adding to the profound internationalism of this place. The GIs "opened things up," as Greg put it. The city was further transformed through young Black men's appropriation of Black American strategies of racial empowerment. They effectively pushed back the boundaries of where local Blackness could be lived. Speaking from an earlier generation, Caroline also recalled the era defined by the Black American presence joyfully: "Liverpool was a *smashing* place." Again, such nostalgic reminiscences offer occasion to rethink the ways that time and space figure in diasporic subjectivity, for in this case, "the past" is not a trope for Africa. Rather, it signifies the glory days of Black Liverpool, back when the local was global by definition. Blacks are not displaced from a home that is distant spatially but temporally. When Scott took me on his tour of invisible places, he asked me to picture people from around the world walking around in traditional dress. Liverpool is full of such ghosts. Here they took the form of GIs styling their afros and driving fancy cars. Now they're gone. Black women left with them. After the 1981 riots, discussed in the next chapter, more people left. Displacement, in Liverpool, is expressed most poignantly in reference to other people's departure—and with them, the departure of the real Liverpool. As Caroline *also* said, "All the smart ones got out."

1981

WHEN LONDON'S Notting Hill riots occurred in 1958, Britain's empire was dissolving, its economy was ailing, and its social fabric was unraveling. Black people, Stuart Hall famously argued, were the signifiers of this crisis (Hall 1978; Hall et al. 1978). Here I examine the rise of nationalism in an era of decline that culminates in the 1981 British Nationality Act and, also in 1981, a series of uprisings among Blacks and Whites across Britain. In the process, I pursue Hall's insight about the meaning of the Black presence by attending to contestations over place and *its* meaning.

Although many other riots occurred, if sporadically, in the years following the ones in Notting Hill, 1981 was a watershed. The St. Paul's riot in Bristol in April 1980 led the way for dozens that occurred a year later.

> In April, Brixton exploded in rebellion, in July, Southall—for blacks, Afro-Caribbean and Asian alike, all distinction between police and fascist had faded—and in the days following, Liverpool, Manchester, Coventry, Huddersfield, Bradford, Halifax, Blackburn, Preston, Birkenhead, Ellesmere Port, Chester, Stoke, Shrewsbury, Wolverhampton, Southampton, Newcastle, High Wycombe, Knaresborough, Leeds, Hull, Derby, Sheffield, Stockport, Nottingham, Leiscester, Luton, Maidstone, Aldershot and Portsmouth, black and white—rebellion in slum city—for the deprived, the state was the police. (Sivanandan 1982a: 48–49)

The press commonly described the rebellions as "race riots," but the term is misleading; it suggests that only Black people had accounts to settle. Rather, the racial divisions that the state, with the help of the press, worked tirelessly to produce through the 1960s and 1970s melted away as Blacks and Whites joined forces (Murray 1986).

The 1981 riots occurred in the midst of a longstanding economic recession. The British economy had suffered a precipitous decline in the decade leading up to that year. By the mid-1970s, 1.3 million fewer people had work—especially in the manufacturing sector—than ten years prior. Deindustrialization had begun in earnest. In late 1980, jobs in both the manufacturing and service sectors began declining by the tens of thousands per month (Massey 1982: 4). The jobs that young Whites once took for granted were replaced by "youth training schemes," which did not guarantee them jobs once "trained" (Roberts, Dench, and Richardson 1987). However, White youth of the 1970s were not disaffected from British society just because they were increasingly unemployed, but because they sensed an unprecedented degree of conservatism arising from new allegiances between the organs of the state and civil society (Gilroy 1987; Sivanandan 1987).[1] The government and the press, for example, launched a frontal assault on the welfare

state, which had hitherto assisted the working poor. Now the press branded them "scroungers" (Hall 1980). As well, workers who striked to demand better wages and working conditions were criminalized. Britain was becoming a "law and order society." As Stuart Hall noted at the time:

> Increasingly, it is the "public order" role which comes to the fore and this brings the police into the public eye in the role which most clearly aligns them with the interests of the state, the powers that be, and the status quo. It may be this which, for example, led Sir Robert Mark to itemize the pressures on the Metropolitan police force in 1973 as consisting of "72,750 burglaries, 2,680 robberies and 450 *demonstrations.*" (1980: 12, emphasis added)

The riots of 1981 did not represent a disruption of an otherwise peaceful milieu. That view, which was propagated in the press, conspired in the construction of Blacks as the source of Britain's problems. Throughout the 1970s, the activities of strikers and demonstrators, youth subcultures of resistance, as well as the Irish Republican Army were the stuff of everyday British life.[2] Integral to all of their battles was the one being fought over meaning. The state and the press explicitly defined demonstrations and pickets as subversive activity; they were policed accordingly (Hall 1980; Bunyan 1981/82). The discourse on such "political violence" represented protesting, striking citizens as threats to the nation (Bunyan 1981/82).[3]

Stuart Hall and others memorably crystallized the authoritarianism of the 1970s in the very title of their groundbreaking study of "mugging," *Policing the Crisis* (Hall et al. 1978). There was a war on "us," the good, law-abiding people of Britain. The police were given unprecedented powers to harass picketers, recalcitrant White youth, and Black people of all ages. "Special Patrol Groups" were formed within police authorities nationwide. Officers were retrained to wage military battles against the nation's various "enemies within." London's commissioner of police modeled his Special Patrol Group on tactics he observed in use by the British army in Northern Ireland: "He had his 200-strong SPG trained in 'snatch-squad' methods (to arrest ringleaders), flying wedges (to break up crowds) and random stop-and-search and roadblock techniques, 'based on the army's experience in Ulster'" (Bunyan 1981/82: 165). But the army proper still had a role to play, for if a particular strike was deemed too dangerous for the police to handle, troops were called in. State violence against people was sanctioned, while the people's political action against the state and against capitalist exploitation was criminalized. Britain's transformation into a police state was evident on the streets:

> Over a three-year period, every high street, bridge, railway, river, town and city in the country was surveyed by the military. Joint police-military exercises were also held. In 1974 Heathrow airport was occupied by the police and the army on four occasions, allegedly to counter terrorist threats; but in fact as a "public relations exercise to accustom the public to the reality of troops deploying through the high streets." (Bunyan 1981/82: 163)

The foregoing documents the development of a "law and order society" well before Margaret Thatcher was installed as prime minister in 1979. In her campaign, she endorsed authoritarianism as the answer to the crisis besetting Britain. As Frank Reeves writes,

> In a phone-in programme in November 1978, Mrs. Thatcher called for greater emphasis to be placed on the punishment of young criminals. She was tired of being told that it was not the youngsters' fault that they were in trouble and that society was to blame. "Instead of handing the problem over to social workers, we have got to provide the proper detention centres." The police force would have to be strengthened and tougher detention centres introduced. (1983: 139)

After she took office, the police's already growing use of their special powers under the "Sus laws" received further sanction. Under section 4 of the Suspected Person Loitering 1824 Vagrancy Act, the police were free to arrest "on suspicion" anyone who was thought, even without the least bit of proof, to be loitering with intent to commit a crime. Blacks became the prime suspects. The fact that Afro-Caribbean, African, and Asian settlers and their children had been terrorized by skinheads, as well as "ordinary" law-abiding Whites for years, and all over Britain, seemed not to inspire heavy-handed policing against the latter groups. Openly fascist groups such as the National Front (to be discussed more fully below) commonly marched through neighborhoods where Blacks lived, with the clear support of the police, who protected them.[4] Blacks who protested against National Front activities did so at their own risk. Several were killed by the police, including Blair Peach, an antiracist teacher and activist in Southall, London (Sivanandan 1982a).

If a rise in "political violence" was one aspect of the crisis, the entry and settlement of Asians and Afro-Caribbeans represented its most troublesome manifestation, as Hall has argued (1978). It bears noting that these were not the largest groups of immigrants; as of 1971, the Irish enjoyed that status (Holmes 1988: 271).[5] Despite their historical racialization, the Irish do not inspire panic in this period, although they certainly did in others (chapter 6). Immigration itself was not the problem; *Black* immigration was. To arrest it, Parliament imposed a series of measures in the 1960s, culminating in the 1971 Immigration Act. That law introduced a novel method of restricting the entry of people from the New Commonwealth (former colonies in Asia, Africa, and the Caribbean) into Britain. It decreed that as of 1973, only those with patrial connections to the United Kingdom would be granted unrestricted entry. This favored Whites from Australia or South Africa, for example, who could easily prove descent from a native-born— that is, White—Briton. Even though that measure effectively halted Blacks' immigration to Britain, the "problem" could still be invoked to great effect—and, indeed, without even referring to them explicitly. As Thatcher promised in 1978, "with the Conservatives, we shall finally see an end to immigration lest we feel rather swamped by people with an alien culture."[6] The press started filling in the details of Thatcher's general outline, finding (and perhaps fictionalizing) people who could testify that they indeed were feeling "swamped" (Barker 1981; Murray 1986).

Like her authoritarianism, Thatcher's nationalist political platform has roots in earlier discourses, ones that fearlessly invoked biological notions of race rather than cultural ones.[7] If one were to pick an arbitrary point at which to begin to trace, however briefly, the form that British nationalism took in the 1970s, the formation of the National Front (NF) in 1967 might be a reasonable choice. The NF is an ultra-right wing political party that openly espouses fascist solutions to social "problems." It has successfully seated numerable elected officials. Of course, fascist groups were in operation long before the formation of the NF. What the NF did was to bring together disparate groups that had hitherto been fractionalized and largely ineffectual (Holmes 1988: 264). Notably, one of the incorporated groups announced its indebtedness to the Nazis by calling itself the National Socialist Movement. Predictably, the NF program sought to preserve Britain's "racial stock" through the repatriation of Afro-Caribbeans and Asians.[8] Aside from organizing as a political party to push that agenda, it also operated at the grassroots, actively competing with groups like Rock Against Racism for the affection of White youth. The NF both preyed on their alienation from Britain— proffering, of course, some very different causes of it—and used some of the very same resources provided by youth culture as Rock Against Racism had developed (Gilroy 1987). Despite its various "successes" in the late 1960s and 1970s, the NF operated at something of a disadvantage. It had an image problem. For its blatant neo-nazism, it was easily spotted by ordinary White Britons as extremist (Gilroy 1987).[9]

The English nationalist of the same late 1960s/1970s period, Enoch Powell, minister of parliament from Wolverhampton and senior member of the Conservative Party, operated with no such disadvantage. In the late 1960s, Powell made a series of inflammatory speeches on the topic of Asian and Afro-Caribbean immigration. This is how he shot to fame. His appeal was founded on his claim to speak for the silent majority. His general tactic was to evoke images of powerless, voiceless Whites who were overcome by the presence of Black strangers on their streets. In a Birmingham speech in 1968, he referred to a letter an elderly White female constituent had allegedly written. She was being threatened and abused by Black immigrants to whom she refused to rent a room. "She is becoming afraid to go out. Windows are broken. She finds excreta pushed through her letterbox. When she goes to the shops she is followed by children, charming, wide-grinning piccaninnies. They cannot speak English, but one word they know. 'Racialist,' they chant. When the new Race Relations Bill is passed, this woman is convinced she will go to prison. And is she so wrong? I begin to wonder" (quoted in Collings 1981). No one else was speaking for these venerable, vulnerable citizens, so Powell stepped forward to do so. Another tactic was more incendiary. In the same speech, he warned that Black immigration unchecked would result in "rivers of blood" running through Britain. Violence was just around the corner—a self-fulfilling prophecy if ever there was one.[10] Unlike the NF, Enoch Powell enjoyed huge popular support and received much favorable press coverage. Arguably, the positive reportage on Powell's speeches produced more of a fervor over Blacks' settlement in Britain than there would have been otherwise.[11]

Another hallmark of Powell's nationalism was its pronounced focus on the children of Blacks as opposed to the immigrants themselves. As Colin Holmes observes, "At a time when primary immigration had already been strictly controlled Powell's emphasis turned to dependants [*sic*] and birth rates" (Holmes 1988: 265). Blacks' birth in England would scarcely make them English, he argued, and hence the "alien wedge" could only grow exponentially. The terms *Black* and *immigrant* became interchangeable, despite the fact that many Blacks were born on British soil. Social policy literature and academic studies of the period routinely used the term *second-generation immigrant* to refer to Blacks born in Britain. In 1981, the state responded to the fear Powell stirred up. Drawing on the novel terms of the 1971 Immigration Act, developed to halt the *entry* of Blacks into the United Kingdom, this Parliament, under Thatcher, passed the British Nationality Act, discussed in chapter 1. To be a British citizen, one had to have a parent born in Britain. The single year 1981, then, witnessed not only Black people's rebellion against their exclusion from the national community but also an unprecedented codification of that exclusion.

Paul Gilroy convincingly argued that all statements about nation in this moment were also, intrinsically, statements about race (1987). I would add that such jointly racist and nationalist rhetorics worked through place. The racist intent of the 1981 Nationality Act is scarcely disguised by its appeal to longstanding British traditions in which age-old genealogies in place (as opposed to just birth there) establish local community belonging. Nationalist discourse also exploited English phenomenologies of place by depicting urban locales in the idyllic, pastoral terms usually reserved for the countryside.[12] Asked to rescind her "swamping" comment or otherwise apologize for it, Thatcher held her ground: "Some people do feel swamped if streets they have lived in for the whole of their lives are really now quite, quite different" (quoted in Barker 1981: 1). Above, Powell posits that Blacks' physical occupation of such streets fundamentally offends; in their visuality, Blacks disturb the pleasant sense of place that defines English neighborhoods.[13] His White constituent is forced to confront that incongruity as she "goes to the shops." That seemingly innocuous phrase summons images of "the high street," the small, commercial hub that forms every neighborhood's center of gravity. In towns and cities across the country, the high street is the site of one's daily rounds. As Patrick Wright observes, the production of nationalist sentiment requires such quotidian reference points: "[The nation] works by raising a dislocated and threatened—but none the less locally experienced—everyday life up into redeeming contact with what it vaunts as its own Absolute Spirit. The rags and tatters of everyday life take on the luster of the idealized nation when they are touched by its symbolism" (1985: 24). Referring now to the dislocating effects of the Asian and West Indian presence in the sites of everyday urban life, Powell expresses a profound sense of national injury and, through that, defiance:

From these whole areas the indigenous population, the people of England, who fondly imagine that this is their country and these are their home-towns, have been dislodged. . . . I do not believe it is in human nature that a country, and a country such as ours, should passively watch the transformation of whole areas which lie at the heart of it into alien territory. (Quoted in Barker 1981: 39)

Nationalist rhetoric did more than exploit place ideologies and sentiments extant; it also spurred them on, making the struggle over race and nation one over territory.[14] That term calls attention to place as both a physical object to be fought for and a weapon used in the fight itself. *Territory* also announces the claiming of place by and for particular subjects and not others. Powell and Thatcher made such claims discursively, through their rhetoric, and materially, through both the legislative outcomes of that rhetoric and the racist violence it legitimated. As one Black man in the previous chapter remembered, "Going into town meant hand-to-hand combat. . . . There was a pub called The Boundary, and it actually was the boundary for Black people, as far as I was concerned. This was their home-land, not mine." Discursively and materially, then, place can be demarcated, claimed, occupied, and enjoyed—all through processes of racial exclusion.

How might the nationwide rebellions of 1981 be understood in view of this book's argument that place and localness shape all aspects of race in Liverpool/Britain? Barnor Hesse has argued that the common grouping of the riots into a neatly packaged semblance of national order and significance belies the great disparity among the ways these events have been lived and experienced across Britain (1993). In his examination of three riots that occurred in London, Michael Keith adds that close study of individual riots helpfully reveals "the manner in which struggles and conflict are deeply rooted in the local experiences of particular communities" while also introducing "historical depth and loca-tional specificity" into the examination of these actions (1993: 4). But this line of inquiry only equates the local with notions of specificity, rather than interrogat-ing the ideological content of the category. Ian Baucom's (1999) reading of Gilroy's (1987) analysis of the 1981 riots is helpful here. He observes that Gilroy attributed to Blacks a desire to protect their territory, having carved out a local, place-based community that did not have the nation as a reference point. Places marked *local* were antinational, then. But, Baucom continues,

That Gilroy, like most commentators, recollects the Brixton and Handsworth riots precisely as Brixton and Handsworth events . . . does not mean that they were not also English events. Rather they can be understood as recent interventions in a very long struggle to define what England is: a unitary, homogeneous, nation . . . or a var-iegated array of local communities. . . . In defending the right of the nation's subjects to define themselves as citizens whose primary loyalty is nevertheless to a "regional or local tradition," [Gilroy] re-create[s] one of the country's traditional ways of being English. (196–97)

The local both resists Englishness and defines it. As place emerges as both object and weapon, as it rises to the level of identity itself—expressing both Englishness and its alternative—all parties to racial contestation, not just the more powerful ones, put a premium on it. In sum, place, as a basis of power and hence subjectivity, has been very effectively harnessed to the nation. Yet place, being mobile, is by no means limited to its national(ist) significance.

"1981"

The attempted arrest of a young Black man, Leroy Cooper, on a street in Liverpool 8, formed the spark that would become the Liverpool riots.[15] Bystanders pulled Mr. Cooper from the police van, and a physical altercation between his defenders and the police ensued. Although this confrontation was settled that night, word about it spread by the next day and the rebellion began in earnest. The violence lasted for three days, during which time many buildings, including a bank and many shops, burned to the ground. The Rialto also went up in flames. A statue on Princes Avenue, depicting Huskisson, a reputed slave merchant, was destroyed.

A documentary about this rebellion, called *Riot*, aired in 1999. It begins with television news footage of the disturbances, as originally broadcast at their height. A reporter's voice is heard putting the event into context, "In two nights of the most violent demonstrations Britain has seen this century [now employing a haunting echo effect], this century, this century, this century . . . " Although the racialized riots in Liverpool are reputed to have been the most spectacular and devastating of the dozens that occurred in 1981, they share features with the others. Black people's pent-up anger over everyday forms of racism as well as their second-class citizenship was directed at the police, for being both perpetrators of racist abuses and visible embodiments of the state. And as in other demonstrations, here, too, Blacks and Whites joined in common cause against the police.

In the years before the riots, chief constable of the Merseyside Police Authority, Kenneth Oxford, had dramatically increased the use of its "stop and search" powers, which, as its name suggests, allowed the police to use their own discretion to detain someone on the street in order to inspect his or her person for possession of illegal material. Under Oxford, Liverpool 8 was under constant surveillance, and Blacks and Whites there were harassed on a daily basis. Margaret Simey, the community activist and longtime councillor of the Granby ward (the political district that includes Liverpool 8), described in her memoir the tensions that had been mounting for ten years prior to the riots: "Increasing demands for the police to assert their powers of control on the streets only added to the sense of alienation: Granby was habitually referred to by them as a criminal community and policed as such. For many it was then that the seeds of resentment were sown which were to bear such bitter fruit a decade later in 1981" (1996: 124). In *Riot*, Simey recounted having warned authorities in Liverpool that a riot was imminent. She said she could predict the exact day it would happen. The police, she remembered, had been closing down nightclubs in town where young Black people would go for a night out. One after the other, each one that Blacks frequented was mysteriously shut down. And then there was one. She warned that if the police closed that one, a riot would follow immediately. She turned out to be right.

In fact, it was not just young Blacks who felt the effects of Oxford's racist approach to policing. *Riot* featured a Black man from Liverpool 8 who told a story on his late mother's behalf:

> If my mother were alive today, she'd tell you the story of the day she was called "a breeder of mongrels" by Oxford's police force and how that changed her for life. She started to understand what was going on, because as a law-abiding citizen, who never had reason to talk to the police ever in her life, [she] was suddenly being abused on her own front doorstep not by one police person, but by ten or twenty of them.

No wonder, then, that "middle-aged white women helped make petrol bombs for the kids to throw" (CARF Collective 1981/82: 226). And as the riots unfolded, hundreds of Whites from outside of Liverpool 8 poured into the area to join in this epic battle against the police. A Black participant interviewed in *Riot* described the scene:

> Hundreds of White people started converging into the community at about five, six in the evening. And I'm talking hundreds. . . . And they were carrying sticks, iron bars, all kinds of weapons. . . . They come to join up with the Black youth, and what they were saying was that within their own communities, they suffer the same sort of brutality but the only [difference] is they don't get called niggers. (Channel Four)

The riots took place wholly within Liverpool 8 over the course of three days and nights. The demonstrators overpowered the police who, for their own part, worried that the violence would spill over into the city center, which is quite close to Liverpool 8. The police only managed to bring the riots to an end by resorting to military tactics, using CS gas to subdue their antagonists.[16] Prior to these riots, CS gas had been limited to military use in Northern Ireland (CARF Collective 1981/82: 226). According to one of my friends, Oxford phoned the home secretary in the middle of the night requesting permission to deploy the substance. She pictured him turning over and going back to sleep after approving its use. The way the police deployed this tear gas was also objectionable. The gas is contained in cartridges that are meant to be directed at walls and buildings, whereupon the gas is released. In Liverpool, the cartridges were aimed directly at people. The first casualty of police violence was a young White disabled man, David Moore. He was hit in his wheelchair by a speeding police van. Black writers in Liverpool have memorialized him in their work (Clay n.d.; Dennis 1988).

In the aftermath of the riots, two main issues absorbed Black political protest: the defense of the hundreds of people who had been arrested, and the effort to have the chief constable ousted. The drama of 1981 was not only in the riots, but in the protests they set in motion.

As transformative as the riots were, Black people I knew scarcely described them like they did other political actions (chapters 4 and 5). Rather, they focused on what happened as a result of the rebellions. They would pit the past against the future, articulating very different understandings of the transformations wrought by "1981." That year had become a signifier by 1991, even if there was no consensus on what, exactly, it signifies. Patrick Wright has observed that stories are remembered and narrated based on their endings (1985). Here we essentially have a story with no ending.[17] The continuing point of contention concerns the uses of place in 1981. As we see below, Blacks' deployment of a politic of place via their occupation of "town" was, to some, a breakthrough on the way to liberation. If Thatcher and Powell emphasized the incongruity of Blacks' presence in English towns, here we see Blacks exploiting that very perception, using it as a weapon. To others, though, "1981" represents an extremely tragic *misuse* of place, one that forestalled liberation.

My friend Cecelia, with whom I lived, stands on the first side of the divide. Cecelia was the only Black professional I knew who was not employed in the race relations or voluntary sector. She lives outside of Liverpool 8. She is Oxford educated, which makes her really unusual. Most Blacks in Liverpool do not make it to university, much less to such an elite one. Cecelia came of age in the era when people of mixed African or Afro-Caribbean and English or Irish parentage were claiming Black identity, en masse, for the first time. She participated in all the demonstrations of the formative late 1970s period (chapters 4 and 5). But the ones that followed the 1981 riots were special. Recalling them, Cecelia was at once sober and passionate, her intonations traveling between slow and measured speech and a rush to get it all said in what amounted to a soliloquy.

Time stood in abeyance as Cecelia relived a moment of unmitigated joy. She said she had recently had a conversation with two of her friends who said that they, too, had felt like her: that on one of the marches through town after the 1981 riots, they were actually redressing generations of Black women's oppression in Liverpool. That they were voicing the protest that their mothers and grandmothers before them could not. Cecelia said she had never felt that way before in her life and that she had not felt that way in the ten years that had elapsed since that moment. She wondered aloud whether it must have felt the same for Black Americans in the days of the first marches of the civil rights movement. Cecelia felt elated during those marches and for a long time afterward. People were focused on the emotional charge of events so cataclysmic as to touch everyone. She thought all things were possible now. Political change for Black people was occurring right there through the actual, physical presence of Black people in all their numbers. White people, Cecelia remembered, were standing on the sidelines confounded by the spectacle—"at a loss," in her words. "Blacks," she said, "were taking over the city." Previous marches had attracted a few hundred people, but this one, Cecelia said, drew hundreds of thousands of Black people—an impossible number, since the highest estimate ever posited for the city's Black population is 30,000.[18] Her embellishment conveys the monumental significance that she continues to assign to the event. The act of crossing Upper Parliament Street, going where they were always told "they couldn't go and shouldn't go," was tantamount to taking over the city. Blacks' physical occupation of the city center, in all their numbers, was as much a political statement as the demands that they went there to make.

In her soliloquy, Cecelia was not describing the riots but their reverberations, which centered on a hopefulness for the future. All things were possible. Others also focused on place—even if to describe utter destruction in Liverpool 8, some of which was positive, some distinctly negative. Participants burned down the building that had once housed the Rialto. By 1981 it had become a furniture store, Swainbanks. Note the different interpretations of that building in the accounts that follow. In one, a participant in the rebellion explains the rationale for the burning of each building, including the furniture store. "It was obvious why people went for the police, but there were exact reasons why each of those buildings was hit. The bank for obvious reasons, the Racquets Club because the judges use it, Swainbanks furniture store because people felt he was ripping off the community" (quoted in CARF Collective 1981/82: 226). For my friend Scott, though, Swainbanks stood for something else—something that also made it a legitimate target. For him, the building symbolized Black people's longstanding exclusion from Liverpool. I asked Scott how he felt to see it burn. He responded blankly, "I was happy." Yet, as Blacks suggested in the previous chapter, it was also a site of enormous pleasure for them. The Rialto is a main character in stories about Liverpool's glory days. It was the central point of romantic sociality. In my first visit to Liverpool in 1989, the building lived on despite its physical absence from the landscape. For example, in giving me directions on the street, people would happily refer to it as if it still existed. They instructed me to go past the Rialto, or turn left at the Rialto. That completely invisible building was still significant as the Rialto, despite its later incarnation as Swainbanks.

If Cecelia saw the protests sparked by the riots as a brand-new beginning, for others the riots were the beginning of the end. As Caroline said in the previous chapter, "Liverpool used to be a smashing place. All the smart ones got out." Caroline was among several women who emphasized that participants in the riots burned down stores in Liverpool 8. They pointedly emphasized that "they burned down the stores *where their mothers shopped!*" If the participants really wanted to make a statement, these informants asserted, they should have gone into town and set *those* shops aflame. Their actions, some argued, had a contradictory effect in that it did not cause any adversity to their antagonists. Rather they destroyed their own highly contained but in many respects joyful neighborhood (mitigated, obviously, by the constant police surveillance). In the different accounts about the Rialto/Swainbanks, the arsonists are not critiqued. But they are blamed for the burning of shops, which were never replaced.

The 1981 riots mark a critical break. In their aftermath, Liverpool 8 became more of an isolate. It was created as such, in the first instance, through the confinement of Black families there. In the 1970s, most Black people, along with much of the working poor, lived in housing owned by the local council. A council can place applicants wherever it chooses. Liverpool 8 is where the local authority concentrated Black people. Liverpool 8 became a dumping ground, as Margaret Simey wrote in her memoir: "Granby was a disinherited society . . . Granby was by now [the 1970s] notorious as a society of the unwanted, the left-behind, a population of rejects, the dustbin for the cast-offs of society that one planner assured me was a necessity in every big city" (1996: 132). After 1981, streets in Liverpool 8 were reconstructed so as to close them off, ensuring—or so it was hoped—that any future disturbances would be contained there.

The long-term effects of the riots, then, are contradictory. As we will see in the next two chapters, it further propelled Black people into the official political arena, centered in town. Yet it also destroyed their neighborhood. Furthermore, the riots resulted in the proliferation of race relations jobs which, on the one hand, provided employment for Black people but, on the other hand—and since these agencies became the official voice of the Black community—ushered in novel debates over political legitimacy (chapter 5). Undoubtedly, the most absurd outcome of the riots was that the British government, after carefully studying their root causes, decided that what Black people really needed was a more up-lifting environment. The government launched an initiative, as mentioned earlier, to have trees planted up and down Princes Avenue, a major street in Liverpool 8. But it also launched a second project: it spent fifty million pounds (then about US$121 million) on a Garden Festival Centre. If the trees were meant to mold Blacks into the likeness of law-abiding English people, then the happy introduction of flora seems to have had a similar goal: to transform the city itself into a proper English place, suitable for investment. Failing to bolster either the city's economy or its national image, the Garden Festival Centre died a natural death.

Genealogies: Place, Race, and Kinship

In the United States, race immediately evokes the grammars
of purity and mixing, compounding and differentiating, segre-
gating and bonding, lynching and marrying. Race, like nature
and sex, is replete with all the rituals of guilt and innocence in
the stories of the nation, family and species. Race, like nature,
is about roots, pollution, and origins. An inherently dubious
notion, race, like sex, is about the purity of lineage; the legitimacy of passage; and the drama of inheritance of bodies,
property, and stories.

—Haraway 1997: 213

DONNA HARAWAY suggests that in the United States race works fundamentally
through naturalized links between biology and kinship. She implicates kinship
more stridently here: "It is time to theorize an 'unfamiliar' unconscious, a different primal scene, where everything does not stem from the dramas of identity
and reproduction. Ties through blood . . . have been bloody enough already. I believe that there will be no racial or sexual peace, no livable nature, until we learn
to produce humanity through something more and less than kinship" (1997:
265). In a related context, Loic J. D. Wacquant emphasizes the specificity of
these fixations: "The idea that 'race' is a matter of 'physiology alone' bespeaks
the hegemony of U.S. folk notions premised on an obsessive concern with descent and blood admixture. . . . Only in the United States is 'race' defined solely on
the basis of descent and then, strictly so only in the case of African-Americans"
(1997: 224). Haraway and Wacquant pave the way for this chapter's concerns by
bracketing American cultural reference points. Ideologies such as the "one-drop
rule" and phrases like "of African descent" betray the importance of "blood" and
lineage not only to the American category called *Black* but also (contra
Wacquant) the one called *White*.

In Britain, descent has never attained hegemonic status as the premier determinant of Blackness—or of "race" more generally. Although eugenicists, their
sympathizers (like Muriel Fletcher), and the later National Front movement certainly drew on biology in arguing against interracial marriage and procreation, as
well as Black settlement itself, the formation of Black identity in that country

proceeded initially by supplanting the logics of nature with those of history and politics. In the 1970s and 1980s, more than in the ethnographic present of the 1990s, "Black" was explicitly defined as a "political" term that referred to Afro-Caribbeans, Asians, Chinese, Africans, Arabs, and other formerly colonized and currently racialized peoples, sometimes including the Irish. The radical contingents within these groups claimed a collective identity as *Black* based on their analogous experience of racial subjugation under White British rule, past and present.[1]

As an American, I was amazed and confounded to learn of this definition. So when I first visited Liverpool, I consulted a group of teenagers on the matter. In a group interview at the Caribbean Centre (see the preface) I asked them who the term *Black* applied to. One girl spoke right up, "If you're not White, you're Black." No one contradicted her. Some time later, Greg put more flesh on that formulation, rendering *Black* still political but much more narrow. In the context of describing his father, Greg indicated that West Africans are not Black. That term, he clarified,

[is] a political definition of what we have to do for ourselves living in a White environment. I see it more in terms of that. But my father was West African. . . . He was Nigerian and he didn't really have to find an identity within England. . . . He was pro–West African, pro–having children in Britain; he wouldn't define it as Black. . . . I know from being in Nigeria that my statements about being Black are predominantly not understood.

Greg frames the relationship between Black and African identities in terms of difference, not descent. Along similar lines, Greg earlier indicated that he became Black as a result of having gone beyond the family in search of answers to his questions about racism (chapter 2). Far from being a biological category, Blackness is a political practice, "what we have to do for ourselves living in a White environment." This chapter treats race as a kind of politic, one that includes but is by no means limited to a body politic.

Although scholars recognize race as a social construct, not a biological reality, it is still generally defined, even if for deconstructive purposes, in bodily terms. Michael Omi and Howard Winant define race as "a concept which signifies and symbolizes conflicts by referring to different types of human bodies" (1994: 55). Peter Wade urges that anthropologists produce more ethnographic analyses both of race's biological signifiers—genes, blood, and phenotype—and of the biologically weighted kinship idioms of descent and ancestry that are often (or only in the United States, Wacquant might add) at root in racial thinking (2002). In so urging, Wade, like Haraway, stages the encounter between race and kinship on biological ground. Might their relationship be understood on any other terms?[2] When race is analyzed primarily as a social category built on biological notions, this highly variegated phenomenon is reduced to one of its effects. Eschewing such narrow starting points, David Goldberg argues that race is "a fluid, fragile and more or less vacuous concept capable of alternative senses . . . a hybrid concept [that] assumes significance in terms of prevailing social and epistemological conditions at the time" (1993: 80–81).[3] To analyze race, as I do here, as an axis of power or as a kind of politic, is to proceed in the most open-ended terms possible, even while foregrounding power as the one undeniably essential component of racial processes and effects. It follows that in social practice kinship can be imagined and manipulated and adapted to the racial politic at hand in far more interesting and fluid ways than simply as chief repository of biological ideologies.

In the section that follows, we see that Liverpool-born Blacks (or, *LBBs* in common parlance) stage the encounter between race and kinship on political ground. There LBBs will describe the rise and initial successes of the social movement they inaugurated in the late 1970s, emphasizing that the particularity of Liverpool's Black families had to be reflected in their political discourses and activities. In this and other ways, the first section highlights LBBs' use of place and localness—as signs of "particularity" itself—to construct the relationship between race and kinship. The subsequent section shows the theme of family coming to bear in a variety of ways on LBBs' formulations about racial experience. Most crucially, we see LBBs using kinship to stake their claims on Liverpool as jointly local and racial subjects. In that regard, the kinship idioms that one might assume to be most salient to race—ancestry and descent—are shown to be more critical to place. Blacks "born here" trace their collective ancestry in order to situate themselves in Liverpool, while also representing their political agency there as a fundamental break from the racial politics of their parents and grandparents. As Greg's case has already shown, kinship may be invoked in order to announce one's racial difference from one's parents—with race understood in terms of political position and practice rather than as phenotype, "blood," or biological inheritance.

A few words about my modus operandi are in order. As will become increasingly clear, a major concern among LBBs is their longtime invisibility in Liverpool/Britain. Almost daily, Black people expressed to me their desires to have their historical presence documented and their contributions to society recognized. In particular, they yearned for public acknowledgment of Black men's military service in both world wars, when they were often conscripted as merchant seamen. Respecting their desires for historicity, I provide below and in the next chapter their accounts of their collective role in reshaping—perhaps revolutionizing—politics in Liverpool, yet without pretending to offer anything resembling History.[4] At once, I heed the oral historian's insight: every account of an event is also an interpretation (Portelli 1991). But I also see these narratives more in terms of genealogy, in Foucault's terms (1980: 78–92). History is invested with the conceited aura of truth. Genealogy, by contrast, is a self-conscious use of the past as a stratagem. Genealogy uses the pasts it recovers from marginal sources and in fragmented form toward unapologetically interested political purposes. I have just cited mine. Yet LBBs may be the real genealogists here; they often offered themselves up as sources of subjugated knowledge about the past with the goal, however implicit, of throwing aspects of the present into relief. LBBs' status as marginal subjects does not, of course, imply that they and the political movement described here stand outside of power. The politics of race, place, and kinship that LBBs describe and enact actually draws from dominant meanings and relations, even while refashioning them. More to the point, LBB positions have garnered tremendous local authority, enjoying hegemonic status. In both informal and official arenas of racial politics, LBB perspectives are the ones to beat. Here I present those positions as if they were stable, leaving the rest of the book to show the dilemmas, contestations, and ambivalences that the very category *LBB* has produced.

THE KINSHIP OF PLACE

In what follows, LBBs narrate their historic entry, in the late 1970s, into the world of public racial politics. It is historic, in their view, for forcing attention to the concerns of a local Black community, as opposed to a foreign-born one. Other sea-changes were already afoot. The *half-caste* category was giving way to radical Blackness. And many men who were in their twenties and thirties in the late 1970s knew life only in Liverpool. They were not the seafarers, the global wanderers. Many of these young men, along with their female counterparts, were launching what would become lifelong careers as activists. The variegated race relations field that flowered here as in much of Britain would replace the shipping industry as a reliable, if limited, source of employment for Black people. In resisting myriad forms of racism, Blacks were staking their claims on Liverpool, dropping anchor *here.*

Narratives on Liverpool-born Black politics commonly start with the founding in 1978 of a pressure group called the Liverpool Black Organization, or the LBO. The historical import that some LBBs assign the LBO is evident in the joyous ways they recall its rise, triumphs, and trials. By imbuing that organization with such significance, they also assert themselves as historical agents par excellence; their work results in the politicization of Black people and the fundamental transformation of Liverpool politics. One of the LBO's founding members, Howard, talked about the organization and what made it so much more valuable to him personally—and, in his view, to the community at large—than other existing organizations.

> It was the only organization I ever identified with in the seventies. A lot of so-called Black organizations developed and only lasted two or three days, or weeks. People kept coming up with "Black" this and "Black" that and expected people to join it. But the ideals and that weren't there or anything. It was basically people just forming these groups and usually it was the same people all the time, and they never got past the first stage.

Peter was another founding member of the LBO, and he, too, spoke of it nostalgically. "The organization was very dear to myself as a political platform in Liverpool, and I still don't believe we have one now like the LBO. That's why I remember it." Both informants represent kinship as central to Black political organizing. Peter recalled,

The LBO originated in 1978. The constitution itself went through hard times constituting itself because it was taking into consideration the makeup, the composition,
the historical nature of Liverpool's Black community, which was a multiracial
community, a Black and White community: White mothers, White fathers, Black
mothers, Black fathers, etcetera. So trying to do a constitution that would still keep
the power base in the hands—the very fact that it's called the Liverpool Black Organization suggests itself what group the group was addressing. But it wasn't just
addressing that group; it was race issues across the board and the welfare and development of the Black community, etcetera, which was demonstrated in the issues it
was involved in during its period. . . . So its constitution was important in terms of
the membership of the Liverpool Black Organization. So there was a type of affiliate
membership of people who were descendants of, related to, maybe through marriage,
to [Black people].

Howard's recollection of the LBO's beginnings is nearly identical:

When the LBO came we sat down and decided what the organization would be about
and the bone of contention was the identity of the Blackness, where we made our
constitution to fit around the LBO being a Liverpool-born Black organization, which
would involve families of the members. Which means that if anyone has a White
brother or sister or mother they could still be a part of the LBO because of the Black
brother, or mother. But no White man or White family could join it. It's the same
thing as I explained to you about the youth—that these people there have got a White
mother and [if] the White mother wants to come be a part of this she should be allowed to because she has brought up a Black. So the constitution was fitted around
that; it allowed Black members and White members of Black families. You had to be
a member of a Black family.

Without attending to the racial makeup of Black families, Howard suggests, the
LBO would have been like all the other organizations proliferating in the late
1970s: just "Black this and Black that." Although the criteria of LBO membership were debated, Howard echoes Peter in suggesting that the organization
could be defined in Black terms, while encouraging the participation of White
family members. Howard gives motherhood pride of place: "These people there
have got a White mother" and White women should belong because "they have
brought up a Black." Howard's description betrays a strict gendering of the
White presence in Black families, not only through his reference to White
women as mothers but through his silence on the possibility of White men as
fathers. "No White man could join it." Even without the benefit of population statistics, it is totally logical to assume that the White parent of most Black people,
since the beginnings of Black settlement in Liverpool, has been female. But that
does not mean that Blacks have not also had White fathers. Peter's account of the
LBO's beginnings suggests that Blacks did have White fathers and that they were
included.

Here in the context of political organizing, race and kinship are linked not
through biological tropes and idioms, but through place. The LBO constitution

reflected the perceived particularity of Blacks' kin ties *in Liverpool*. As Peter said, the LBO's constitution had to reflect "the historical nature of Liverpool's Black community," which is always a reference to its interracial beginnings (chapter 2).[5] The normativity of these relations lends weight to the conflation of dual racial parentage, on the one hand, and birth in the city, on the other. A "local-born Black" (an oft-used synonym for "Liverpool-born Black") becomes "mixed race" by default, even though some LBO founders (such as Howard himself) actually have Black mothers and African, Afro-Caribbean, or Black British fathers. As a sign of particularity itself, "Liverpool" inspires the particularity LBBs impute to Black families, which manifests here in relation to the normativity of White membership in them. By putting the "Liverpool" modifier in its name, members of this Black organization announced that certain "ideals" were in place.

In foregrounding the interracial character of Black families, LBBs are not making a case for the social recognition of two equally important identities based on the racial and ethnic backgrounds of each parent. They are not saying "we are Black *and* White," or "we are English/Irish *and* African/Afro-Caribbean." Rather, LBBs specify that "mixing" is about co-presence in the social arenas of the household and the neighborhood. Their families were composed of White and Black members. LBBs included White women in this organization in light of their political practice: "they have *brought up* a Black." LBBs such as Howard saw local Blackness quite specifically through an openness to White women who are connected to Blacks through family relationships. And not a few of these White women were active in LBB politics from their inception.

Lisa was one such woman. Of Irish Catholic background, Lisa grew up in a White area of the city and, after partnering a Black man, bearing a child with him, and moving to Liverpool 8, became a fixture of LBB political circles. In the early 1980s she worked as a teacher in a Black community institution in Liverpool 8. Her students were in their late teens and came of age under the still reverberating influence of the Black Power movement. But, she suggests, they were confounded by the kinship implications of the growing injunction that they self-identify as Black.

> I went to teach English in a Black college, and I forbade the use of "half-caste," "quarter-caste," and all those little derivatives. . . . And [the students] said, "If we don't say it, we're denying our White mother." I said, "No. You're not. When people shout after you, 'Nigger!' in the street, they're not thinking about your White mother! You are what they see, and they see you're Black. So you might as well say that you're Black and you're proud."
>
> And that was the big thing, you know. "I'm Black and I'm proud." "Black is beautiful." After that, there was no turning back. And that gave Black people in Liverpool, who were very very varied in skin tone, from very very pale like [names her grandson] to quite dark, the right to say, "I am Black; I define myself as Black." The right to say to White people, "I'm seen as Black, I'm seen as non-White." But I refuse to use the term *non-White* because it presumes that White is the norm. So I refuse to use

that word, and I'm going to use the word *Black*. And that's where you get the "LBB" from. You know, the Liverpool-born Black.

The students, according to Lisa, understood the term *half-caste* as an acknowledgment that they had White mothers, not White "blood." They perceived a contradiction between identification with their mothers and the call to identify as Black. Thus, explicit articulations about the meaning of White motherhood had to be central to the discursive practices producing, continually working on, the Black identity of this younger generation.

Black people's reference to "the Black community" includes White women who are partnered with Black men but even more explicitly those who are, like Lisa, mothers to Black children. There is no uniformity in the way Blacks position White women in their role as mothers. Generally, Liverpool-born Blacks heralded these women for having sacrificed their families of orientation to marry Black men. According to some LBBs, this sacrifice led to the acceptance of their White mothers as Black. For example, Abraham, an LBB in his sixties, explained to me that his mother was disowned by her family when she chose to marry his father, an African. He went on to assert, "She became Black. Her mother didn't want to know her, but her father snuck over to see her. She chose to be Black to marry him. She had a lot of hassle with seven kids. She is accepted as Black. Most people my age, or eight out of ten, [their] mothers are White and were accepted. She's part of us." Neither biological inheritance nor phenotype reckons racial identity. Indeed, Abraham here gives racial identity to his mother, rather than the reverse. Kinship, then, is a vehicle of racially transgressive practice, both on the part of White mothers and LBBs like Abraham who interpolate these women as Black. Abraham also articulated another very common position on White mothers, saying, "I never saw her [his mother] as White; I just saw her as me mum." Her kinship role is paramount and determining: it nullifies race altogether. White women's own views will be examined in chapters 7 and 8. The focus here is the positioning named *LBB*, and the key point is that kinship features centrally in LBBs' articulations of race-as-politics. Not only did LBBs account for the perceived particularity of Black families in the very constitution of the LBO, but they built the organization on the premise that the family was an important site of political mobilization around racial issues. And as Abraham's narrative on White motherhood just suggested, LBBs construct the racial identity called *Black* through politics, not phenotype.

Blacks are often distant from their White mothers' families of orientation. Some Blacks are cut off from what they see as the broadest possibilities of kinship owing to the racism of their mothers' families. Veronica, in her early thirties, indicated how racism affects kinship in the Black community. Veronica may be remembered from chapter 2, where she poignantly described her alienation from her African father. In the same interview from which I quoted earlier, Veronica contrasted the place-based roots available through each parent's line:

> I know where my mum comes from: here. The funny part is that I'm sorry that I don't know more about the White side, because my mum's family give her up for marrying a Black man. I have no White aunties and uncles. I've never known them.

I've only known the Black side, which you'll find quite, eh, a lot of that around here. You'll find it's all mostly one-sided. So you get a lot of the roots from the dad.

Veronica expressed a sense of loss for not knowing her mother's family, characterizing kinship in Liverpool 8 in those terms. She describes Liverpool 8's particularity in another way. In answer to my question about how she perceived her own identity growing up as someone of English and African parentage, she remarked, "I never really thought about it. I was brought up in a Black area, so, I didn't really think about the world out there because Liverpool 8 was just Black, really. You got a few people White and your mum White. But I never really looked at me mum as White. Well, that never really come into it." Like Abraham's mother, Veronica's was "just her mum." And the local space that creates this configuration of race is defined by its opposition to something else, which she did not have to think about: "the world out there." The common acknowledgment and invocation of White motherhood "around here" in Liverpool 8 effectively normalizes racially mixed familyhood through its spatiality. In that space, White mothers can become Black or can be positioned outside of race (as "just me mum") altogether.

LBBs generally suggested that anything classified as *Black* includes White people. The category LBB is a prime example. In order to reflect "the historical nature of Liverpool's Black community," the LBO constitution included the White members of Black families. But those families are still described as Black, not mixed or interracial. The category *Black* incorporates the very notion of mixedness. For example, a Black informant once described to me where she goes for nightlife: "Myself, I like to go to what you call a Black place, but it's mixed: it's Black and White." She constituted mixedness as a virtue. Broadly speaking, then, mixedness refers to the co-presence of Blacks and Whites in the family, the household, the neighborhood, the LBO, and nightclubs, rather than in the blood. The many ways and contexts in which *White* gets included within the category *Black* does not preclude clear distinctions between the two at other times, as I will discuss shortly. "Mixing" is not a free-for-all.

Because Black people and White women were linked through kinship, they were often mutually implicated in the racist discourse of the 1970s. The first public affront to the Black community to spark a response from the LBO drew on the ideologies of race, gender, kinship, and sexuality that Muriel Fletcher made famous. The premises of her famous report were articulated anew. All the concerns about the social inviability of mixed marriages and the children born of them, as articulated in the original document, were left completely intact. The catalyst to the first LBO action was the appearance in November 1978 of an article in the *Listener*, a publication of the British Broadcasting Corporation (BBC). The article profiled an upcoming television program about the difficulties of police work on Merseyside, the county that includes Liverpool. The copy I was given had the offending passage highlighted:

> It is a poignant scene, though that is not how the police of Merseyside would describe it! Less poignant, by far, is the other major social problem they face: the half-caste problem.

> Policemen in general, and detectives in particular, are not racialist, despite what many black groups believe. Like any individual who deals with a vast cross-section of society, they tend to recognise that good and evil exist, irrespective of colour or creed. Yet they are the first to define the problem of half-castes in Liverpool. Many are the product of liaisons between black seamen and white prostitutes in Liverpool 8, the red-light district. Naturally, they do not grow up with any kind of recognisable home life. Worse still, after they have done the round of homes and institutions, they gradually realise that they are nothing. The Negroes will not accept them as blacks, and the whites just assume they are coloureds. As a result, the half-caste community of Merseyside—or, more particularly, Liverpool—is well outside recognised society.[6]

Kinship, race, and place are inextricable in this passage. As a site defined by the transient presence of foreign Black seamen, the port of Liverpool is the object of a series of unquestionable and equally pathological associations. White women who have sex with African seamen must be prostitutes. Seaports do not have to be linked so indelibly to prostitution (which, also, does not have to be stigmatized), but the *Listener* article, like the *Fletcher Report* before it, proceeds seamlessly from one to the other.[7] The lascivious meanings attached to Black men and to the port became resources par excellence for the pathologization of Blacks of local birth: not only are they misfits for not having parents of their own "race"— they are neither Negro nor White—but even worse, in the quoted police officer's view, their mothers are prostitutes. Normal family life becomes impossible in "half-castes'" neighborhood of Liverpool 8, which is identified as the red-light district.

The *Fletcher Report*, published in 1930, was distributed to the media, social service agencies, and the police, as I noted earlier. The staying power of its premises cannot be overestimated, as indicated by their rearticulation here in 1978, forty-eight years after its original publication. And they still haunted 1990s Liverpool, as I discuss in chapter 8. The *Listener* article contained a new element, though. The premise of the BBC documentary, and the *Listener* article that promoted it, concerned the "difficulty of policing" on Merseyside. Liverpool 8 received special mention. When the *Listener* article appeared, authoritarianism was at its height all over Britain. The BBC was sympathetic to the plight of the police, charged as they were with bringing order to a place made unruly, in the first instance, by the perversion of racial norms and the consequent impossibility of familyhood.

In the landmark action precipitated by the publication of the *Listener* article, LBBs made resistance a matter not just of family life but of street life. The racialized discourse on their birth was a matter to be redressed publicly, since it was made so profoundly public by their antagonists. LBBs and White women formulated their plan in the bosom of Stanley House and executed it on the streets of town, garnering a lot of attention in the local press. Scott showed me documents from the now defunct Merseyside Anti-Racialist Alliance indicating that the organizational meetings drew about 250 people from a wide range of Black and trade union organizations. In what follows, Howard discusses LBO participation in the demonstration against the BBC. Both his outrage at the original offense and his elation at the outcome of the demonstration were palpable, though he related the story some thirteen years after the event.

> We took on a lot of issues regarding the local born Blacks. There was a demonstration—the first one was when a pig, some White bastard, turned around and said that we were the product of prostitutes and Black seamen. That was quoted by a policeman to someone from the *Listener*. We went down and organized a march. It was one of the first times I ever looked outside of Liverpool 8 in terms of the Black community. On that demonstration there was about one hundred or two hundred people from the start, but when we were going through town there were people who identified with Liverpool-born Blacks. I never seen it where people get off the bus and say, "There's something going on there; *I'm* Liverpool-born Black." And there were all different degrees of Blackness, if you know what I mean, that was in this march. But what was so sweet was that people said, "I'm Liverpool-born Black and I'm part of that."

Howard's allusion to skin color resonates with Lisa's above-quoted emphasis of the "very very" varied and often "very very" light skin color of Liverpool-born Blacks. Howard also affirms these shades as "just Black," refuting the "betweenness" that characterizes the entire half-caste discourse. Liverpool-born Black politics also redeemed interracial parentage, which, until now, people like Veronica had had the luxury of perceiving as unremarkable because of its spatiality—that is, through its enclosure in Liverpool 8, an area she described as "just Black."

These acts of redemption and affirmation were achieved, at least partially, through the forging of a very visible, very public set of racial politics that responded to the *Listener*. LBBs' response was public not only in the sense of capturing the attention of the media but also in their use of space. Howard continued,

> After that march, and when we had the meetings and that, and you sat down and started talking to people and you find out the man sitting next to you could come from out of the area and because you didn't know him, but he saw us walking and demonstrating and that he'd heard about through word of mouth and said, "Yeah, I'm Liverpool-born Black and I'm part of that."

Howard suggests that people were drawn into this movement by the sheer visibility of it, by Liverpool-born Blacks' recognizing themselves in a crowd of people "of all different degrees of Blackness." His narrative resonates with other LBBs' emphasis on the spatial dimension of protest, which we saw in Cecelia's soliloquy in the previous chapter. Resistance to these public politics would have to take Blacks to what Veronica termed "the world outside," particularly the city center or "town." Among Blacks I knew, "town" meant one thing: their total exclusion from mainstream Liverpool life, especially in terms of employment. To contest racial power, they *had to* enter town because that is where public offenses originated and where "mainstream" Liverpool and its institutions were located. Race became a body politic not only through the redemption of Blacks' characteristic phenotype *in Liverpool*, as it were, but also in placing their "just Black" bodies in the forbidden space called "town."

White women also made themselves visible there—yet as members of the Black community. They distributed fliers announcing that the demonstration would take place at the local BBC offices and at the police station where the quoted officer was based. One informant, Sean, remembered the tenor of the women's plea:

> I was walking in town and these two women, these two White women, came up to me, and they shoved this thing in front of me. It's like a petition it was. And I said, "What is this petition about," or something. They said, "It's about people calling us prostitutes because we slept with—our husbands are Black ex-seamen. There's a march on, and please support us." They were really, really upset. One woman was crying and she was saying, "Look, is your mum White?" and I said, "No. She's not. But she was born and bred in Liverpool." And she said, "Look lad, honestly, honestly we're not prostitutes. We're not what people are saying. Just because we love a Black man, we're being targeted. And we've got this march on and please come." And then they went off and they were getting to other people.

Black men generally referred to the place of White women in the community through their status as the mothers of Black children—not as the lovers of Black men, for example. Sean, though, makes a slip that he quickly corrects: he erases the explicit reference to sexuality, replacing it with the socially sanctioned marital bond ("because we slept with—our husbands are Black ex-seamen"). Yet there is the implication, even in his revised formulation, that White women's place in the Black community is based on their sexual relationship to Black men. The point is important because it goes unremarked in LBBs' narratives generally. As well, Sean's recollection suggests that the White women themselves were actually concerned about the assault on their sexuality.

In discussing the formation of the LBO, Howard gently argues for the inclusion of Whites, especially mothers, in this Black organization. But when he describes the BBC protest, he invokes Whiteness in a very different tone. "[T]he first [demonstration] was when a pig—some White bastard—turned around and said that we were the product of prostitutes and Black seamen. That was quoted by a policeman." Here the offending White is anonymous ("*some* White bastard"), except for being, crucially, a police officer—and male. He embodies institutional power, unlike the White mothers in their families, whose racial privilege is neutralized by that same institutional power (their respectability as Whites being negated through their inscription as prostitutes who consort with hypersexual African men). LBBs reconstruct these women's racial identity in view of their political practice: they have given up their own families by marrying and mothering Blacks. They have migrated into Liverpool 8 and Black *family* life. Howard's direct association of White men with power is consistent with his elision of White men as fathers in—albeit comparatively few—Black families of the 1970s. Along similar lines, Abraham had occasion to make disparaging remarks to me about the sexual practice of another LBB, Yvette, a woman with whom I lived for a while. She was living "out there" (deep in the neighborhood of Wavertree, a ten-minute walk to Liverpool 8) with "some White man." White men partnered with Black women remain White, according to Abraham, who is the same man who argued that eight out of ten Blacks have White mothers who are accepted as "part of us." For her radical choice to live in Wavertree, Yvette's partnering choice seems to have been, at once, out of "race" and out of place—in both senses of the phrase. LBBs, generally speaking, value mixedness, but not everyone may engage in it with impunity.[8]

Earlier I argued that LBBs' emphasis on place and its particularity explains the link they forge between race and kinship. One could further articulate those connections this way: If you are Black *and* were born in Liverpool, your parentage *probably* takes this form: White mother, Black father (whether African, Afro-Caribbean, or Black British).[9] Place politics consists in the institutionalization of that kinship relation as the anchor of race politics writ large. That relation, rooted in Liverpool's identity as a seaport, is also the reference point of phrases like "the historical nature of the Liverpool Black community."

In articulating links among race, place, and kinship in the 1978 founding of the LBO, members propelled the transformation of racial identity from *half-caste* to *Black*—a process that had already begun (chapter 2). But the more significant effect of their work was in the localization of that identity and, just as crucially, in the politicization of identity itself. White women in Liverpool 8 became, to different degrees, Black (chapter 8). And their children weren't "just" Black but Liverpool-born Black. That term, to my knowledge, has no analog in Britain. One is, for example, a Black Londoner, not a London-born Black. In Liverpool, one is never a Black Liverpudlian, but a Liverpool-born Black. Notwithstanding the prominence of *birth* in that term, the descriptor *Liverpool-born* does not refer simply to place of birth—although some LBBs themselves don't quite see it that way, as we shall see later. The more "Liverpool" rises to the top of the racial agenda, triumphing in the multiply fraught politics of difference (chapter 5), the more it gets naturalized. Place is an axis of power relations insofar as LBBs were constructed by it and insofar as they, in turn, used place to specify what kind of Blacks they were. And with that premise in place, they organized a political movement and went marching into the sites of mainstream Liverpool, where they drew others into the fold through the sheer force of their visibility in town.

THE PLACE OF KINSHIP

While the foregoing section showed LBBs asserting a local way of being Black—achieved by highlighting the particularity of kinship—below they assert a Black way of being local. In this case, LBBs draw on kinship idioms to emphasize their historical *presence* as Blacks in Liverpool. "We've been here for generations" or, alternatively, "for generations and generations," they often say. Such claims represent critical assertions of the time-depth of Blacks' *here-ness*. And in articulating those claims to me, a visiting scholar doing research about them, they advanced their longstanding political goals of making the history of the Black presence in Liverpool visible and of criticizing their also longstanding racial subjection there. What the generations idiom *re*produces is birth *here*; what their genealogies do is root LBBs, collectively, in place. What that kinship idiom requires, then, is a Black ancestral presence that can be traced infinitely back in time—the further back, the better.

But the assertion of Black *and* local ancestry *and* presence cannot rest on the form of parentage that most Blacks, by their own account, actually have. While LBBs could conceivably trace "birth here" through their White mothers, many of whom are originally from Liverpool, they cannot trace a Black presence in place through them. Many if not most LBBs have immigrant parents, one or both—but especially fathers—being from Africa or the Caribbean. Hence, the father's line cannot be used for the generational "birth here" narrative. Many adult LBBs do actually have Black Liverpudlian fathers. These men can provide local and Black ancestry, but not location within Liverpool's physical space. As seamen, LBBs' fathers were scarcely around, and thus they cannot serve the most critical function of the "generations" narrative: to provide witness to the everyday forms of racism that have, for years, defined the Black experience in the city. They can and do serve as symbols of Black heroism on behalf of the nation, for they commonly died as merchant seamen during both world wars. LBBs' fathers, even those born elsewhere, also form the basis of LBBs' claims to belonging in light of these men's participation in the local tradition of global seafaring. But, having died at sea, many Black men never had the chance to become elderly in Liverpool. In sum, Black fathers, like White mothers, are unavailable for the "generations and generations" narrative—a kinship idiom shaped, again, by LBBs' political goals as jointly local and racial subjects.

The "generations and generations" narrative requires a kinship relation that comparatively few Blacks can actually claim: Black Liverpudlian mothers. But that is immaterial. It is not one's own place-based lineage that is so important but that of LBBs as a whole. A collective place-based lineage asserts an age-old history of Black birth and presence here. And for that purpose locally born Black mothers work perfectly—and Black grandmothers even better. Black mothers loom large in LBBs' historical narratives. The trick, though, is to make Blacks' immemorial birth and presence *here* visible to Liverpool at large. Being confined to Liverpool 8 and Liverpool 1 (Pitt Street) before that, this settled (as opposed to transient) Black community was invisible to White people in town or "the world outside," as Veronica put it. Most important, the Black community was invisible to local politicians. Writing about the 1960s, Margaret Simey recalled that the city's minister of parliament "boasted that there was no racial prejudice in Liverpool, a boast which had never been challenged because the 'coloured', being largely seamen, accepted that their proper place was down by the docks and stayed in it" (1996: 108). Recounting her experience in a council committee formed in 1968 to examine racism's effects in Liverpool 8, she writes,

> Some of our suburban members did not even know the whereabouts of the area we were talking about and I was hard put to it to conceal my impatience. . . . Those of our members who had no first-hand knowledge of the inner areas found it hard to

accept that such evidence as we eventually assembled contradicted the habitual assumption that Liverpool was free from prejudice. . . . [T]here was no denying what we could each see for ourselves, that no black faces were to be seen behind the counters of the shops in the city centre, and few black customers. . . . We had identified a community in our midst whose existence we had never before noticed. Liverpool born and bred, surely they were entitled to a fair share of the rights of citizenship? (125)

With a profound sense of historical mission already well in play before I arrived, some LBBs participated in interviews happily, yet without the least care for what I might like to know. Rather, they told me what it was I just had to know, what I should be asking about.

Cecelia introduced me to her friend Jessie, a forty-one-year-old woman whose (Black) mother was born in Liverpool. Though she was perfectly amiable, Jessie was given to expressing herself rather curtly. She freely shared her sharp, often damning opinions on local racial politics, reserving special contempt for research on Blacks in Liverpool. Most of it is completely useless, she observed, then adding, "except the kind that you're doing." The implied contrast was between social policy-oriented research—which proliferated in Liverpool, as in the rest of Britain, during the 1980s—and research on local Blacks' precious history, one in perpetual danger of being lost because no one is writing it down, a lament I heard innumerable times. During the time of my fieldwork in 1991 and 1992, and on every subsequent visit, I was apprised of various efforts to record Blacks' history. This interest in history pertains to the group known as "the old Africans," the seafarers. There was a desire to know about these men's experiences as seamen, as well as about their cultural worlds, which the old Africans actually kept to themselves. But in regard to Black mothers and elderly Black Liverpudlian women in general, this desire for history is not about the cultural but the racial. Their lives and experiences were considered resources both for firsthand accounts of racism in early twentieth-century Liverpool and, just as crucially, for proof of the age-old existence of Blacks born here.

As Jessie sat down for an interview with me, she promptly proceeded to spout information without the benefit of a question. I was just a conduit. She began by suggesting that her mother would really be the one to talk to, but that she probably would not agree to be interviewed. The first details she offered about her mother were her age and her birthplace. She was seventy-six, and born in Liverpool. Jessie then added that her grandmother, also Black, was also born in Liverpool. If she were alive, she would be one hundred years old. Jessie went on to explain that her mother had managed to survive terrific racism in the city. In fact, a common theme in stories about Black mothers was their vulnerability to racism, which LBBs generally say produced these women's muted speech. Their depictions of their Black mothers and grandmothers emphasize that so much has happened to them and they had seen so much that they are still adversely affected. Hence the willingness of their children to speak about them and what they had lived through. Though still living, elderly Black women were scarcely available to tell their own stories—which was part of the story their children told about them.

Greg volunteered a gendered analysis of existing research on Blacks in Liverpool. It is overly focused on men, he observed. I told him in response about the trouble I was having in finding elderly Black Liverpudlian women to talk to; they were exceedingly elusive. Greg considered my difficulty to be symptomatic of elderly Black women's fear and consequent silence. He explained,

> Me friend told me a story. They're like fourth-generation Black settlers in the city, and certain family names go right back and me friend, whose grandmother was born here, she won't say anything. She's got a certain definition of things that makes them nondiscussible. . . . I think it's survival instincts, for women again. It's about what Black women have had to establish in order to survive. It's different from what Black men have established. And I think some of it is actually keeping quiet about it, leaving it alone. I think Black men, because of nature—testosterone [laughs] that comes through the bloodstream—I think that aggression takes them past that and that we can discuss this and not feel as all hell is going to break loose by opening up certain— and maybe Black women didn't have the support and questions weren't asked to prompt them.

Greg arranged for me to meet this fourth-generation Black family, the Ewings. This family featured briefly in chapter 2, where Clara traced her son Louis's lineage as a seaman through a long line of seafarers on both sides of the family. Interestingly, Clara's father (now deceased) was Black and born in Liverpool. But in her narrative about him, he did not play the part of a local, someone who could testify to racial events happening around Liverpool. As the seafarer, he was global. By contrast, her mother, also Black and also born in Liverpool, embodies the local. She tells stories about presence—or life as a colored person here. As the eldest living member of the Ewing family and as a woman, she is the one who tells the history of racial terror on the streets of Liverpool. She also becomes exemplary of its effects. Clara and her son Louis spoke of what she had witnessed. She survived much of what younger Blacks cite as their history. But she has declined many requests to share her memories in any kind of public context. She has even been offered money to go on television, but she is terrified and will not talk about the past. Louis described her as jittery and still completely convinced that "the powers that be," as he put it, would punish her if she spoke.

Two key events, the race riots of 1919 (described in chapter 1) and another that occurred in 1948, were scarcely detailed to me without reference to who saw and experienced them. These witnesses were always Black women. Since the riots of 1919 and 1948 are so legendary, it cannot be accidental that it is *these* stories that younger Blacks tell on behalf of their Black mothers and grandmothers. After Louis described his grandmother's jitteriness, Clara recalled one of the incidents that she and her now eighty-one-year old mother had witnessed during the riot of 1948.

> I must've been about 11. There was another riot. Me and my mother had gone to the cinema, the Rialto, and when we got out we saw crowds, hundreds of people, all running. And when we looked we could see this colored man in the front—we called

him "colored" in them days, but it's changed. We call them "Black" now. He ran to every door and they were throwing bricks at him and no one would open the door. And they were throwing big bricks at him. People were screaming, "Leave him alone," and a man said to me mum, "Take your children home." He didn't touch us. But because he's from another country, he might've been African or West Indian— alright, he might've been darker than us but we're all the same—they were stoning him. So you imagine how he felt! We were all crying, my brother and sister were crying. And someone said to my mother, "Get your children home." But no one opened their doors. I can still see that man running and banging on each door. There were dozens and dozens of people stoning him just because he's Black.

Likewise Jessie told of the terror her mother and grandmother experienced when she was young. Her grandmother witnessed the legendary figure, Charles Wootton, being chased into the River Mersey in 1919. In the riots of that year, the police took Blacks into "protective custody," allegedly to prevent them from being hurt in the ongoing violence. From Blacks' view, they were simply being criminalized. Jessie's mother (then three years old) and grandmother were among those held. These women also witnessed the riots of 1948. The enduring result of the terror that Clara's and Jessie's mothers faced is their fear and silence in the present day. At least these are the stories their children tell about them. Historical narratives are generational, gendered, and spatialized. Older Black women play the role of local witnesses and still-affected victims. These roles serve, at least narratively, to make their children's political action utterly defiant by dint of the contrast. They become the picture of racial resistance. The very vocal quality that LBBs attribute to their own generation manifests, at the very least, in their great eagerness to have this history told and their own willingness to tell it.

Scott's walking tour, described in chapter 1, included a generational narrative premised on his Black mother's presence. She lived in Liverpool (but was born in another city) and her husband was often away at sea. Scott attached great significance to his mother's identity as Black, saying that despite an appearance that could confuse her for White, she was before her time in adamantly asserting that she was Black—not colored, not half-caste. Having established the critical fact of her Blackness, Scott described his mother's approach to racial politics and credited his own political awareness to her teachings. An irrepressible storyteller, Scott here frames a childhood story in terms of its larger historical context. "In this city for quite a long time," he began, importantly,

Black people put a label on themselves, and the label they put on themselves was *half-caste*. It was a word which my family never ever used. My mother never used the word *half-caste*. My mother cringed when she heard others use that word. My mother from a very very early age told me and my brothers and my sisters: "You're Black." She used to sing a song to us, I think it was part of a Negro spiritual, I don't really know, but the words were, "I saw a picaninny crying down in Tennessee one night / His little heart was nearly breaking just because he wasn't white / Then his dear old mommy saw him and said son don't you cry / We know'd more of my [undecipherable] and she sang a lullaby." I forgot the rest of the words but part of it was, "You're your mommy's coal black rose." Now my mother used to tell us this and she used to sing it. My mother was lighter-skinned than you . . . lighter-skinned than [Cecelia]. But she said that she was Black and she was a Black woman. And this is what I'm trying to get across, you see?

Scott loved telling stories about his mother. And, indeed, there was so much in them. Scott drew heavily on those stories in constructing himself as a political actor. With his father away at sea for twelve or eighteen months at a time, Scott's mother was left behind "to deal with racism from landlords, schools, neighbors, from everywhere." Her strategy was to stay out of their way. Yet, the household was a safe haven for discussions of race. She often had her friends and sisters over to the house, on which occasions they would talk about politics. She would specifically instruct Scott to sit and listen quietly to adult discourse so that he might learn something. Another one of his stories about his mother—one that I often heard him share with others—went this way: the landlord of the flat where Scott's family lived did not realize that his mother was Black. On one of the landlord's visits to collect the rent, Scott's father, just home from sea, answered the door. The landlord demanded to know who he was, and his father responded bluntly, "I'm Mr. [gives his last name], who are you?!" The landlord responded, "You can't be Mr. _____; we don't allow niggers to live here." And so they had to move. Scott's story always had two messages, aside from the obvious racism of the landlord: his mother was easily mistaken for being, for example, Spanish or something else, but not Black, and that women, being at home while their husbands were at sea, were vulnerable to everyday forms of racism.

Scott has lived a different kind of life than his mother did. Although his stories about her are not about her fear, per se, they are about her attempts to stay out of the racists' way—which was hard, given their ubiquity. Scott could not strike more of a contrast to his mother. As an activist, he is perpetually "in the way" of racial power. He does not keep his head low. He refuses to give in to the still-pervasive forces that would keep him in Liverpool 8. He is quite proud to own property in a classy neighborhood. With great satisfaction, he described how he boldly applied for a mortgage—a story premised on the hostility and rejection that Blacks expect from White officials in banks. Scott has single-handedly waged antiracist crusades against his labor union. His mother's tendency to withdraw from just these kinds of conflicts has not been reproduced in her son. Scott's own life story depends on his stories about his mother. She enables the unfailing moral of his own autobiographical tales, which highlight his political agency.

Lucille, in her forties, tells a somewhat different story, but with a similar emphasis on her Black mother's and Black grandmother's presence. While Lucille's father, a Black man born in the city, was away at sea, these women were left to negotiate race relations with the other families in their neighborhood in the north end of Liverpool, near the Anfield football stadium. The "north end," a major site of Irish settlement since the mid-nineteenth century, will be described in some detail in chapter 6. Black people, living overwhelmingly in the south end, consider Anfield the nether end of Liverpool, a place so hostile to them that they would not want or dare to go there. I once expressed curiosity about it and was discouraged from venturing there. "It's the worst racism in Liverpool," Howard told me. Lucille and her family were the only Blacks in that neighborhood.

> Everybody knew us from one end of the road to the next. In fact all around the community everybody knew that we were this Black family, but that we'd been here sooo long, or should I say, they had been here so long that they were accepted. Obviously racism was in families. It was always, "It's all right, as long as they keep with their own kind." And that was probably one of the reasons we were accepted because obviously my mother married a Black man and she didn't trespass, although obviously growing up all her friends were White.

The theme of family recurs in LBBs' discussions of race and racism. Earlier, LBBs described the racism of their mothers' families. Lucille also locates racism in White kin circles: "Obviously, racism was in *families*." The local belonging of her family is, on the one hand, enabled by her mother's decision to marry a Black man. Yet it is also produced by her family's immemorial presence. Everyone, from one end of the road to the next, knew they were this "Black *family*" who had "been *here*" "*sooo* long." As with the other stories, racial experience—in this case, acceptance—is explained through a genealogical and female presence in place. Lucille's father was more of a newcomer, having lived in Liverpool 8 before marrying Lucille's mother. The "global men/local women" framework that colored Clara's narrative above is also evident in Lucille's. Both women's fathers played the role of seaman, always away. But while Clara's mother played the role of fearful witness, Lucille's mother and grandmother accounted for her family's safety and acceptance in just the kind of neighborhood that Blacks commonly referred to as utterly dangerous territory.

Family is such a theme in Blacks' descriptions and analyses of racial experience not because race and kinship are each, at root, biological ideologies that therefore belong together but because place gains much of its political force through genealogy. Notwithstanding its racial content and motivation, LBBs' common articulation of the link between place and kinship exemplifies national (and nationalist) ideologies. Cultures of place across the British Isles exalt the venerable qualities that are associated with time and history, resulting in the powerful imbalance between ancestry and mere birth here (chapter 1). Such is what it means "to live in an old country," to echo Patrick Wright's critical treatise on related matters (1985). The crucial aspect of lineage for Blacks in Liverpool, then, concerns place not race. The manifold implications of "the place of kinship" in Black community politics are discussed in chapter 5.

Although Blacks were clustered in Liverpool 8 and, before that, in the Pitt Street area of Liverpool 1, Black women still, by most accounts, had to "keep their heads low." In the present day, though, they are very visible; they are the linchpin of LBB genealogies. On my first visit to Liverpool, I was introduced to a thirty-something Black activist who voluntarily rehearsed the highlights of his family tree. The root of that tree and all the branches he named were Black and female. But best of all, these ancestors were each "born in Liverpool," as he said in refrain as he, impressively, went back yet another generation. He was not simply constructing a racial genealogy here, but a spatial one.

LBBs who cannot perform the same operation through their own genealogies assert historical presence through their knowledge of elderly Black women "born here." Most LBBs do not have a parent who is both Black *and* local; it is more commonly one of each. So, people freely cite the highlights of other Blacks' family trees. Though Greg does not identify as an LBB, for reasons to be discussed later, he nevertheless spotlights its central category of the "old Black family" that is so often traced through Black mothers. Above, he referred to his friend's family in the following terms: "They're like fourth-generation Black settlers *in the city*, and certain family names go right back and me friend, whose grandmother was *born here* . . ." (emphasis added). Abraham, in his early sixties, presents a similar case. He is the son of an African and a White English woman. His own age and birth in the city somehow seemed not impressive enough; he felt compelled to tell me of the very common existence of others even older. "I know Blacks eighty years old, born here," he told me. Jessie knew that I would be talking to Sean, who is a distant cousin of hers. This pleased her because, as she told me, his is one of the oldest Black families in Liverpool. The ultimate mark of authenticity and importance as Blacks worthy of being interviewed, it seems, is age-old birth in the city. I repeated Jessie's approving comment to Sean, whose own pride is palpable here:

> Well it's reputed that we're related to one of the oldest families, the [Halls] and apparently—I don't know how true this is—they were one of the oldest Black families in Liverpool, certainly one of the largest and this comes from me nanny (me mum's mum). She was a [Hall]. You're talking about . . . sixteen kids and her brothers and sisters and . . . then you've got their children and grandchildren and that's how it goes on. Apparently when me nanny died, the undertaker said, "One of the proudest things I've done is to bury your mum—he said to me mum—because she's the last of the [Halls]." And even he knew about it. And this is a White guy.

Even White Liverpudlians are impressed with old Black families, then. As Lucille suggested above, here again generational-depth in place triumphs over the racism Whites might otherwise express. Sean traces his place-lines through his Black grandmother.

Cecelia belongs to another old Black family. I knew it was old not because Cecelia would boast about it but because others would voluntarily recite Cecelia's genealogy for me. Her family also extends back in seemingly endless fashion and is always traced through her Black mother's line. Her father was from Sierra Leone, and he died at sea when Cecelia was young. Her mother and grandmother were both Black, and people I knew commonly professed having been acquainted with her late grandmother. Scott was only one among several LBBs who made a point of telling me where Cecelia's grandmother once lived. A reference to presence, the all-important *here-ness*, once again. A prominent middle-aged African community leader also found it worthwhile to mention that he knew where Cecelia's grandmother had lived. No one ever mentioned Cecelia's mother or where she lived, even though she outlived her mother (Cecelia's grandmother). Rather, Cecelia's grandmother, being older, was the more remarkable.

Cecelia, though, often talked about her late mother, whom she adored. Cecelia would occasionally launch into soliloquies about poignant moments in her past, as when she described the euphoria of the demonstrations after the 1981 riots. Her mother, by contrast, dared not step out of the prescribed boundaries for Black people. She regarded Cecelia's occasional ventures into town as journeys into a war zone and discouraged them fiercely. Similarly, her mother was—according to Cecelia—extremely concerned about the danger of her children's political activities and participation in demonstrations. The terror that had defined those spaces for Black people of Cecelia's generation, and even more so her mother's generation, provides the subtext for LBBs' descriptions of their participation in the demonstrations on the streets in downtown Liverpool, beginning with the march against the BBC. The passion of Cecelia's jubilant account of having broken through those barriers with a newfound political agency was matched, if not enabled by, the solemnity with which she described her mother's total resignation to stay within Liverpool 8.

LBBs describe the effects of historical racism in Liverpool on now elderly Black women; they commonly *witnessed* violence against other Blacks and now *they* are terrified. Although the actual subjects of this violence are duly noted and given sympathy, the real significance of such statements lies elsewhere. Stories about Black mothers and grandmothers—and, as we shall see soon, African fathers—help construct the political agency of the speaker. LBBs tell stories that emphasize their utter difference from their parents, defining themselves as political actors in the process.

Sean's mother was born in Liverpool. Her brothers died at sea, a fact that Sean parlays into an argument about his mother's political stance. "One thing that I think she tends to forget is she was born in Britain and her brothers were born in Britain, and they died for England. They died in a war fighting for Britain and [she's] got as much right to live in Britain as anybody—probably more than some." If, as the previous section showed, White women's loss of White family renders them Black in some LBBs' view, Black women's loss of Black male kin renders these women would-be Britons. Sean's mother lost all her brothers and in so emphasizing, Sean asserts her right to national citizenship. He goes on to indicate that she fails to seize these rights, opting instead for a restricted status in terms of local space and racial politics: "It's something to think about. I think she thinks, like the old school, that maybe Black people shouldn't go there, live here, and we should keep to our own. She accepts things without questioning them. Now whether that's because of her age or her upbringing that women shouldn't do this, that or the other, I don't know."

That outlook on race and gender defines "the old school." He breaks from that lineage. Here he contrasts his own racial politics to hers: "It probably could be her upbringing, but I think you shouldn't just accept things like that. You should

say I've got as much right to live here as anybody else—probably more." This is the second appeal he makes to her exceptional status, a quality of LBB political subjectivity pursued at length in the next chapter. Not only does she have a right, but she probably has more of a right than some others. His mother is passive, accepting the status quo. Other elderly Black women opt not to speak, while LBBs tell these women's stories with a sense of political urgency and historical importance. Black elderly women like Cecelia's mother did not step out of Liverpool 8, while Cecelia and her peers go marching right into town. Scott said that his mother would retreat from the racism that was everywhere. He, too, breaks from his mother's political lineage. He lives outside of Liverpool 8, and makes demands on banks, labor unions, and the like.

The ways that Black mothers feature in narratives on LBBs' emergent political activism resonate with Begona Aretxaga's analysis of the use of mothers as political symbols in Northern Ireland (1997). She argues that political discourses in Belfast link motherhood to victimhood, creating a "gendered politics of suffering" (105–21). In Liverpool, Black mothers, as local women, are also cast in the gendered role of victim. The global men are always brave if nationally unacknowledged heroes, dying for Britain—a point to which I return in chapter 9. Since at least the late 1970s, Blacks have been digging in their heels as locals. Hence, the premium on stories about here-ness leads to the feminization of racial oppression. Black mother and grandmother stories provide LBBs the ultimate narrative launch pad for their own bold emergence as political actors. This is not to argue that all of this is conscious on their part. It is to say that their investment in localizing racial experience seems to be mediating the kinds of stories they tell and the genealogies they trace through place.

LBBs also break from their African fathers' racial lineage. While they describe their Black mothers as largely silent and fearful, they depict their African fathers as indifferent or impervious to racism, owing to their mysterious yet secure cultural backgrounds. Earlier, Greg distinguished the categories *Black* and *African*, categories that he applied to himself and his father, respectively. He went on to describe his father as nonplussed by the politics of cultural difference in England: "If he didn't understand how you spoke, he wouldn't speak to you. If you didn't understand about his background, he wouldn't tell you about it." Peter said that Africans of his father's generation never felt part of Britishness or part of the indigenous Black population. "If my father was refused entry [to a pub, for example] on the grounds of the color of his skin, he'd leave. He didn't feel out of place anyhow, so there was no big investment. He didn't want trouble. My generation wouldn't take that." (Such a generational narrative about the birth of racial resistance, it bears note, is common among Blacks and Asians across Britain.) Africans' response to their exclusion, Peter continued, was just to set about building their own cultural centers and clubs (the Sierra Leone Club, the Nigerian, the Igbo, the Yoruba). Howard was more critical. He said of his own father that "he was completely colonialized. He had a respect for White people I couldn't understand." These perspectives obviously say less about their African fathers, per se, than about LBBs' own worldviews.[10] Yet there is some indication that older

African men realized that their children perceived them as apolitical in the face of racism.[11]

A Black freelance journalist and researcher, Ferdinand Dennis, traveled across what he calls "Afro-Britain" in the late 1980s. He recorded his "encounters, impressions and conversations" in a book titled *Behind the Frontlines* (1988). His chapter on Liverpool fascinates. Without setting out to do so, he wound up speaking to three pivotal figures in that city's Black history. One of these was Ludwig Hesse, who organized Black seamen into unions in the 1940s and who was also involved in the Pan-Africanist politics of that era.[12] Hesse's political work with "many notable black political figures" was carried on in Liverpool and beyond. London is mentioned specifically, but there may very well have been other sites. It is hard to imagine, for example, that Hesse would not have taken part in the important Pan-African Congress in 1945, held in nearby Manchester. The politicking that Hesse specifically mentions shows links with trade unions and White socialists, and also shows the profound internationalism that characterized the Pan-African movement generally. He and his colleagues went down to London, for example, to protest against a "famous rape case in the United States," the specifics of which are not mentioned (47). Yet Dennis also indicates that most of Hesse's political activities were focused on Liverpool where, for example, he and his comrades "fought tooth and nail" to have a community relations council established. "We got it only after a mass meeting in the town hall," Hesse explains (48). Hesse admitted to some political reticence on the part of African and Afro-Caribbean men. As Dennis indicates, Hesse's early political activities involved organizing street corner rallies in Liverpool 8: "The message of those rallies stressed the unity between the struggles of Afro-Americans, Afro-Caribbeans, and Africans. But it wasn't easy in a community of sailors: You had blacks who used to say, 'Oh, man I'm going home. As soon as I get a bit of money, man, I'm going home'" (46). Yet Hesse's critical comments below also refute the common LBB view that African men did not resist racism. Dennis writes: "With his long history of political involvement, Hesse was, perhaps understandably, annoyed with the younger generation of blacks who criticised his generation. 'They say we never fought back,' he said bitterly. 'But we were fighting back from day one. The accomoos in Ghana hoisted the red flag way before they knew anything about Marxism'" (48).

INVISIBILITY, EMBATTLEMENT, UNIQUENESS

The LBBs I knew who were in their thirties and forties described a break from the political lineages of race that they traced through their Black mothers and their African fathers. It remains now for LBBs to say what defines their own political subjectivity as local Blacks. I emphasize political subjectivity over identity because the latter is but an object of the former. Identity is indeed one of LBBs' concerns, but in order to understand why, one must appreciate the broader issues at stake. I also make the distinction in an effort to preempt questions that the narrow focus on identity would inevitably prompt: if a Nigerian marries an LBB what would their children be? Etcetera, ad infinitum. Such a line of questioning assumes that *LBB* derives straightforwardly from relations of descent, parentage, and ancestry—the cornerstones of American folk notions of race as well as ethnicity. The foregoing section has highlighted, for example, that Blacks' genealogies do not reproduce an *individual* Black's racial identity but the Black *community's* local identity.

Invisibility is the fundamental condition that LBB political subjectivity speaks to and against. As a theme, it refers to LBBs' intrinsically connected experiences as local and racial subjects. In so pointedly asserting that their "birth here" extends back for generations, they are decrying the fact that they are still, even now, not acknowledged to exist. The immemorial time-depth that LBBs so often invoke is intended to render their invisibility paradoxical. LBBs assert that people of Black and White racial parentage are indeed *Black* (not half-caste) and that many Black people (of mixed parentage or not) are not immigrants but locals, the latter predicated most fundamentally on birth here. The theme of invisibility bears profoundly, then, on their efforts to participate in public politics as a legitimate social group in their own right—the cultural identities of their parents, particularly fathers, aside. If invisibility is the centerpiece of what LBBs define as the unique plight of local Blacks, then uniqueness itself is a second grand theme in the same discourse. A third concerns LBBs' sense of being embattled. They catch hell from all sides, not just from mainstream, White-dominated society in Liverpool. These three themes, to different degrees, are captured in the formulations about identity that Peter articulates below.

"Identity," said Peter, "is something that I'm very interested in. I think it's a problem in Liverpool. It has been a problem and still is. . . . Coming to terms with our identity has involved a long process—*considering we're a longstanding community*—to feel proud." He highlights the historical continuity of identity as problem and suggests that such pride should not have taken so long in view of the time span of the community's existence. In what follows, Peter traces the evolution of LBB politics through a process that he called *politicization*. He narrates the process primarily through his own experience, which he then relates to the broader community of Blacks "born here." His personal experience included time served in prison.

> My experience is one with a view of the Home Office, prison officers, and the police.[13] How you're treated is determined by how you're identified. I was born in 1950. In 1970 I was a youth being told I was half-caste. My father was from Sierra Leone. My mother was from—was White. From Liverpool. I accepted the term *half-caste*. I more than accepted it. I wasn't claiming Whiteness, but I thought I must be half-caste because of the White parent. I wasn't politicized by '78, when the *Listener* article happened. I hadn't seen half-caste as a stigma. . . . Africans say they didn't see half-caste as derogatory. They wouldn't even question the term *quarter-caste*.

Identity, he suggests, is of singular political import: it determines how one is treated. Peter uses the passive voice, stressing the agency others have to define his identity—a theme throughout his narrative. Above, it is his African father and Africans generally, on the one hand, and implicitly, on the other hand, it is also the Home Office, prison officers, and the police. In what follows, he implicates additional White-dominated institutions. Peter recalled that when, in the early 1970s, people of mixed racial parentage first began to agitate for Black studies in the school system, they were met with this response from Whites: "But you're not Black." Their designation as *half-castes* rendered them invisible and illegitimate as Blacks. Their activism did eventually result in the establishment in 1974 of the Charles Wootton College for Adult Education, known affectionately as "the Charlie."

The foundation of LBB politics, from which many other political struggles and successes have sprung, was in the politicization of identity itself. As part of this critical process, new educational institutions like the Charles Wootton College had to be built, and mainstream ones had to be reformed. Peter's own politicization, he said, had come through books. "Before prison, I read Black Power stuff, books with images of Black people, the fist, Angela Davis, etcetera. I was becoming politicized but didn't realize it." He was also moved by reading about a girl trying to rub the color off of her skin. But there was a countervailing force circulating at the same time. Whites, Peter said, were under the spell of Enoch Powell.

"By the late 1970s," Peter continued, "I was well-conscious of what I was: Black. This was a difficult process, 'cause not everyone had come to terms with their identity." There is a linear process unfolding: he began as *half-caste*, and in the late 1970s became *Black*. Yet the process was not so linear: others had not yet "come to terms with their identity." This is how he explained that lag: "Here's a community that was a multiracial, multicultural whatever community. The variety is incomparable in any other part of the city." His use of the word *whatever* suggests that race and culture are unclear frameworks. Nevertheless, the community's variety renders it "incomparable," the mark of its "uniqueness." Nothing else exists like it "in any other part of the city." From there he reinvokes the linear history: "Yesterday we were half-caste. In the seventies we became Black. Today terms are put on us like *ethnic minority*. There's no negotiation on how you're described. No one came and consulted me whether I wanted to be called that." The term *ethnic minority* is objectionable for being forced on him. The British state and the Liverpool City Council are the unspoken antagonists here. The term *ethnic minority* features centrally in official discourse on identity and difference, legitimizing the claims any group might make on the state (a matter to be treated at length in the next chapter). In that discourse, the local—as opposed to the ethnic—has no legitimacy as a category relating to Blacks.

Peter suggests that there is a need for a definition, a term, that will legitimate local Blacks as a group. Now that people like himself are Black, Peter says, the question is how they might describe themselves with a legitimizing term of *cultural* identity analogous to those that describe other people—like the Somalis and the Chinese, he said specifically. The choice of these two groups is telling. Among Blacks I knew, these groups were almost uniformly used as examples of people with "their own culture," "strong families," and a "tight-knit community." More controversially, the Somalis are reputed to "keep to themselves." Peter suggested that he cannot consider himself culturally African "because of a few little things" like not being able to "talk African." "In retrospect," he explained, "I realize that my father kept African culture and language away from me. I had to remove myself from the room when my father would talk African. But I ate African food." Moreover, he says many Blacks with African fathers have not been to Africa, and those who have were not accepted as African while there. "They're looked at as being White English!" he says. LBBs' embattlement is marked by the variety of antagonists in play: the state and the Liverpool City Council, African fathers, and even Africans in Africa.

And with this he arrives at the significance of the category *LBB*, and he did so in response to my question about how he identified himself on the national census of 1991, which had recently been conducted. He said he checked the box marked "Black African." "But I'm Black," he added immediately. "[I'm] an African in terms identified and designed by Blacks born in Liverpool." This caveat trumps Africans' presumptions. Blacks born in Liverpool now define the terms of African cultural identity as it relates to themselves. From there, race goes on to trump culture as the single most critical underpinning of Liverpool-born Blackness and, similarly, Black Britishness. After all, the trajectory he is tracing is a racial one. It emphasizes the move from *half-caste* to *Black*. While "culture" is important, it turns out to be a pit stop. Its function was to critique African fathers and to throw the hegemony of ethnicity into relief. Race is the real issue. He says, "Terms like *Liverpool-born Black*, *Black British*—the Blackness is still in these terms. Those terms express that we were born here. The city we were born in happens to be Liverpool." This might be read as another appeal to uniqueness. While "the Blackness" remains stable in these terms, it is the fact of "birth here" that the terms *Liverpool-born Black* and *Black British* really highlight.

Unlike the cultural identities named African, Somali, and Chinese, *Liverpool-born Black* expresses the uniquely dire consequences of birth in the city, which LBB activism then targets directly. I began this section with Peter's observation that "Coming to terms with our identity has involved a long process—considering we're a longstanding community—to feel proud." He elaborated on that "long process" by commenting on its continuing psychological effects: "Identity problems of Blacks have continued to rise in [the form of] mental illness. . . . It's not a coincidence that the majority of Blacks suffering this were born in this city." The nation—which Peter, in the quotation above, invoked by likening the term *Black British* to *Liverpool-born Black*—disappears in this context. We are in Liverpool. He continues, "There's not a big number of people *not* born here who suffer from it. Mary Seacole House [a drop-in center for Blacks suffering from mental illness] to a large degree reinforces what I'm saying." Without wishing at all to divert attention from Peter's observation about mental illness, I want to highlight his appeal to the theme of uniqueness. It is Blacks "born in this city" who suffer from mental illness, which is an outgrowth of the painful psychological effects of racial identification, or reidentification processes. There is a continuing difficulty for Blacks of mixed parentage "born here" to feel proud of being Black. African and other immigrants apparently do not share this condition.

Indeed—and to harken back to the embattlement theme—they sometimes contribute to it.

Mary Seacole House deserves some comment. The efforts to establish such a center exemplify the kind of institution-building for which LBBs have successfully mobilized—although they are not the only ones who worked to establish it, and do not claim to be. A South African woman, Protasia Torkington, spearheaded the project. The center was named in honor of the Jamaican nurse who treated British soldiers wounded in the Crimean War. This symbolic gesture is one of myriad examples of how LBBs enact their concerns about invisibility, here using a diasporic resource in the form of a personage not widely known despite her heroism. Although Peter does not mention this, Mary Seacole was, in addition to being a heroic nurse, a sea traveler who had "wonderful adventures in many lands," as she put it in the title of her autobiography (Seacole 1988 [1857]). In naming this center after Seacole, it *is* the nation that is important. Blacks' historical relationship to Britain is being marked. Peter made the case explicitly, observing that Mary Seacole, because she was Black, is completely unrecognized for her selfless heroics for Britain. A White nurse, Florence Nightingale, occupies that role exclusively. Said Peter, "We can't expect that they're going to eradicate their history [British history], but they have to incorporate Black history, make some of it represented at some level." Even though this historical gesture redresses Blacks' invisibility within national historical narratives, the importance of Mary Seacole House is articulated in terms of distinctly local needs. The act of naming the center after Seacole is part of the consciousness-raising that continually has to take place in order to inculcate pride among Blacks "born here" because it is the lack of such pride, argued Peter, that contributes to the high incidence of mental illness among them in the first place. Ironically enough, though, Mary Seacole House is effectively invisible. It has no sign out front. Blacks fear that it would be the target of vandalism if it did, or that people frequenting the center would be stigmatized by being seen entering or leaving it.

"Identity is something the *local* Black population has been conscious of," Peter remarked. "A lot of work has been around consciousness raising." And the struggle continues. It must go on indefinitely because the forces that continue to create the need for consciousness raising and that still embattle the *local* Black population, resulting in the disproportionate incidence of mental illness among them, conspire to threaten his own son who, Peter intimated, is lighter-skinned than himself. "If I were to leave my son to his own devices, he'd go through pain. He must come to terms with the fact that he's Black. There's no use me trying to tell him anything else. I pick him up at school."

The themes of invisibility, embattlement, and uniqueness combine to form LBBs' inextricably racial and local political subjectivity. Peter traces a distinct trajectory through them. The great, longstanding time span of the Black presence in Liverpool, with which Peter opens, comes finally to relate most poignantly to his own son. Breaking from his African father's racially exclusionary parenting practice, Peter will actively shape an affirmative racial identity for his child. In addition to the above-listed themes, the temporal markers of generation, process, and history also color Peter's discussion of identity and its political and psychological significance. These markers bespeak the initial and continuing imperative of LBB activism. This chapter has already shown LBBs emphasizing matters of time-depth. Peter's narrative is thus exemplary of a cultural and highly political practice in which Blacks deploy the temporal as a key component of their uniqueness claims and as a means of rendering their invisibility paradoxical and therefore symptomatic of racial injustice. Peter's use of a temporal logic to relay the irony of local Blacks' marginality has the effect of rendering not just LBBs unique, but Liverpool also. In much of what follows, Britain will come into play in critical racial discourse only to situate Liverpool's exceptional status: it has the oldest Black community in the country, yet it is, according to LBBs, the most racist city in Britain. The embattlement theme also depends on the temporal, for local Blacks' disempowerment at the hands of myriad others has been continual and relentless, stretching as far back in time as their own generations-long presence in Liverpool. By 1991, as we see in the next chapter, LBBs were known as a collective of exceedingly vocal political actors with contemporary hegemony— which is to say with local authority on race matters.

Diaspora and Its Discontents: A Trilogy

Music dominates popular culture. It is central to this consideration of cultural identity because of its global reach, and because it is repeatedly identified as a special area of expressive culture that mysteriously embodies the inner essence of racial particularity. It supplies an ineffable antilanguage that provides ironic compensation for the exclusion of slaves and their descendants from literacy. It is also in music that the most intense legacy of the African past is concentrated, and though the significance of that legacy is open to dispute, the link itself is impossible to refute. It is important, then, that the area of cultural production which is most evidently identified with racial authenticity and Black particularity is also the most mutable and adaptive of forms.

—Gilroy 1995: 25

ON SATURDAY nights in south Liverpool, at about 1:30 in the morning, when the pubs in town close and the clubs shut their doors, many merrymakers make their way to Liverpool 8 to the African Community Centre and Social Club—better known as "the African."[1] In its former life, or so I was told, the African was a synagogue. Now, by day, it is the site of one group's ethnic organization. By night it is a popular after-hours spot frequented mostly by Africans, White women, and Liverpool-born Blacks, whether of African or Afro-Caribbean background. And like most leisure spaces in Liverpool 8, the African attracts young and old alike.

One enters after handing over the 50 pence (75 American cents) entry fee to the belligerent old African at the door. A friend of mine likened him to a Gestapo. Passing that gauntlet, one is greeted immediately by a dense cloud of cigarette smoke. The dancing takes place in a small hall that has a bar on one side and a stage on the other, where the disc jockey spins his tunes. The hall has the ambiance of a church basement. It is not done up in any way, save for the slightly peeling wallpaper that matches the rest of the room's darkish blue color scheme. The cigarette smoke is nearly all that functions as light. The African's complete lack of pretension is the essence of its appeal, for it almost undresses people, many of whom would have already made appearances in town with their good clothes on.

The music is sinfully good. As opposed to the hyper club/house beat that rocked the clubs in town, here at the African the beat slowed all the way down to a crawl—apropos of the late hour when people arrived there. Each beat made you pray for the next, which seemed a long time coming. Indeed, the halting beat consistently served up at the African was not African at all. It was as deep as it was hard as it was dirty as it was, thankfully, loud. The deejay spun a sublime, unpredictable mix of UK and American soul, reggae, and dub. Some songs were played faithfully every week, even months after they had disappeared from the charts. I never asked anyone else for their assessment of the music, but I was clearly not the only slave to this godforsaken beat. The dance floor was always full. After my first introduction to the African, I returned religiously on most Saturday nights.

Black musical styles—all hybrids—mix seamlessly at the African. But in terms of the mix of actual Black people in Liverpool, there *are* seams. As I stood in a corridor of the African one night, taking a break from the dance floor, my attention was suddenly directed to the next room, the one where food is served. An argument was in progress. I heard only one side of it—at that, only one sentence. Here was a Black woman, perhaps sixty years old, positively shrieking to a couple of younger African men: "I was *born* here!"

This chapter's goal is to analyze the contradictory racial positionings that Blacks in Liverpool occupy vis-à-vis each other. This chapter's burden is to explain, as sympathetically as possible, the political stances that those contradictions produce.[2] The pained outburst, "I was *born* here!" exemplifies the dilemmas at issue. Not knowing the speaker or any details about the argument in question, I draw from other LBBs' narratives in suggesting that a profound sense of invisibility brought her voice up to that shrill pitch. After all, in popular nationalist discourse, to be Black was to be an immigrant, an eternal non-belonger. So, with what manner of perceived presumption might these Africans have implied their own greater belonging to this sixty-something Black woman, born here? Crucially, this encounter unfolded in an African ethnic club, in a city that LBBs themselves characterize as the standard-bearer of African authenticity. What claims to status, privilege, and belonging does that institution, as the site of the argument, as well as LBBs' complicated relationship to African identity, bestow upon her antagonists? With all of these factors seemingly in play, she invokes an ideology of place via her birth here. Of course, nationalist forces had long since de-legitimated *ius soli*, or "law of the soil," as a basis of belonging precisely because people like her were increasingly being "born here." Nevertheless, place became the weapon of choice in her war of position against a couple of cocky Africans—*mere* immigrants, now not only to many White Britons but some would-be Black ones.

In this chapter, LBBs, Afro-Caribbeans, and ex-colonial West Africans engage in the difficult project of fashioning a political community out of the Black identity we saw produced in chapter 2. These groups have been differently racialized, here and abroad, under a variegated British colonialism. The group now known as LBBs has been positioned differently by the discourses of nation and ethnicity that attach to West Africans and Afro-Caribbeans. The latter groups have different histories of migration and settlement. They also claim distinct cultural heritages— from which *some* of them exclude their children. But here they all are, clustered for the most part in the small neighborhood known as Liverpool 8—a well-worn synonym for the apparent monolith known as "the Black community."

The analysis of these disjunctions requires another trip to diaspora—which, I argued earlier, is too often considered an existential state characterized by the displacement sensibilities arising from migration. Posing similar challenges, Gilroy focuses on "roots and routes," or the unpredictable and politically enabling travels and transformations of traditions and subjectivities (1993a; see also Clifford 1997). Like migration-oriented studies, though, that approach still takes movement as its point of departure. The accent is on the routes. In tracing the transnational, rhizomorphic paths of ideas, inspirations, and ideologies that wend their way into and out of Black cultural and intellectual productions, this model strikes a blow against the exclusivist and conservative politics of cultural authenticity unleashed by most appeals to roots. Analytically speaking, all those rhizomes and routes travel toward one destination: the triumph of cultural hybridity over an illusory purity. Here one might ask, is there anything that Black people do and debate *as diasporics* that might fall outside the scope of purity-as-problem and hybridity-as-solution?

David Scott theorizes the African diaspora in relation to the same apparently intractable predicament. He lays the blame at anthropology's door, criticizing its practitioners for presuming to pronounce upon or otherwise adjudicate Caribbean people's various claims to African cultural authenticity. Though one could take issue with his statement of the problem, his alternative is largely worthwhile: "Understood in [the] sense of a discursive tradition, the black diaspora constitutes an always *situated argument* over our relation to Africa and to plantation slavery, over the sense or senses in which we are 'African' and the children of slaves" (1999: 124–25, emphasis added). Usefully, Scott emphasizes the debates themselves rather than offering an all-purpose solution. Less usefully, Scott stipulates that a situated argument, for it to qualify as diasporic, must get routed through traditions, roots, and origins. That proposition actually depends on the same problem of authenticity that he and so many others critique, and continue to reify in so doing. Why must origins, African culture, and now slavery be the stuff of "authentic" diasporic debate?[3]

Chapter 2 showed Black Liverpudlians' complex positions on Black America. Even if we heard only Liverpudlians' points of view, the contestations over gender, sexuality, and class that they described exemplify diaspora as situated argument insofar as Blacks recognized each other as counterparts. Developing this line of analysis, I define diaspora here as a *counter/part* relation built on cultural and historical equivalences. To posit *equivalences* is to put meaningful differences (such as distinct colonial histories) on the same analytical plane at the

To access the appendices, go to www.westlegalstudies.com.

start, in order to then expose the ways they come to bear in social practice. The backslash in *counter/part* and the stress that may be put on either side of it index shifting relations of antagonism and affinity; these latter terms depend equally on *difference* while highlighting two possibilities for what people can do with it.[4] With this framework, I direct attention not to hybridity, as the ready-made solution to the singular problem of authenticity, nor to roots or routes, but to the roadblocks and pathways to political community right *here* in this place, and in view of place.[5] Diaspora is not solely a transnational relation.

Heterogeneous and mutually constituted relations of power such as gender, race, class, ethnicity, and nation all come into play as a variety of actors with contradictory stakes try to realize their agendas. Yet place, via "birth here," plays a mediating role in these efforts. Depending on the context, "here" refers either to Liverpool or to Britain more broadly. Below, for example, the state is the audience for LBBs' "birth here" claims. In that case, "here" is absolutely Britain. At other times, Blacks' own localism—or the authority they give to Liverpool above all else ("To understand Black people . . . ")—prompts a "birth here" claim that has the city, or even Liverpool 8, as a reference point. At still other times, the "here" in question remains ambiguous. These various possibilities are important to a larger understanding of place as a form of power. First, place is not reducible to any particular site; it is an ideological abstraction that commands authority and determines legitimacy in particular contexts. The social recognition of the importance of place to personhood or belonging or community makes "birth *here*" arguments work. Indeed, the more implicit this recognition the better for those born here, since the claim may go uncontested. Similarly, the various, even if ambiguous reference points of "here" imply that place is not reducible to either the local or the national as bases of community and identification. Rather, place—as an ideological abstraction that can take any number of forms, like "birth here"—can be mobilized to *produce* local and national communities. And "racial groups."[6]

Given the obsession with the authenticity question in Black diaspora studies— as opposed, for example, to the much fuller array of concerns covered in its Asian/American counterpart—one might assume that Blacks worldwide grapple mostly with matters of roots, traditions, and origins.[7] Those issues crop up here in Liverpool, but they are routed through people's larger concerns about racism, class difference, political leadership, and the discrepant forms of privilege and subordination that resulted from British colonialism, shaping postcolonial Black Liverpool in turn. My focus, therefore, is on the predicaments that my informants found most compelling. These dilemmas reveal the desire and difficulty of community, while also forcing the question: Who are we in relation to each other? "I was born here!" (and you were not) is one response. Such pathos are symptomatic of diaspora's discontents, by which I mean deeply felt, poignantly expressed senses of frustration or outrage or injustice. After all, if diaspora is a situated argument, it follows that it might just unfold in loud volumes.

Like their protagonists, the following three stories are distinct but related. They tell successively of LBBs' trajectory from invisibility to political hegemony.

With the moving time frame, I do not offer an authoritative History but a modest sense of process, showing the emergence of that hegemony. In the first section, Blacks born here participate in producing official testimony on race matters, with the state as their audience. Here we glimpse the now powerful positionality known as *LBB* at the moment when it seems to come into being. The second section pursues themes raised in the first. Through flashbacks, LBBs relay another moment (in addition to those presented in previous chapters) when they became a powerful, visible force—only now, their antagonists are a particular group of Afro-Caribbeans. The trilogy ends with ex-colonial African immigrants—the peers, so to speak, of the anonymous ones who opened this chapter. Their reflections on and positions in this community betray LBBs' political hegemony, their successful normalization of place as the preeminent basis for the legitimate political representation of a heterogeneous Black community.

WHEN AND WHERE THEY ENTER: LBBS AND THE STATE

> The time is coming when we, Liverpool Born Blacks, can no longer tolerate the situation we are forced to live in. The time is coming, in fact the time is very close, when more and more of us realise, and through the realisation act collectively to take that which is rightfully ours into our own hands. . . .
> [W]e will no longer be content to live in sub-standard properties in sub-standard areas. . . . [W]e will no longer put up with politicians and so-called Black West Indians put in places of authority above us. . . . We demand an equal opportunity and an equal equality alongside the working class White people of Great Britain.
> —Speech by activist Eric Lynch, 1980 (quoted in Lord Gifford, Brown, and Bundey 1989)

> I am very pleased to be able to introduce this book [*Equal Opportunities and the Employment of Black People and Ethnic Minorities on Merseyside*] as Chairman of the Merseyside County Council's Personnel Committee, founder member of Merseyside Association for Racial Equality in Employment, and someone who was brought up in the Liverpool 8 area. . . . Readers will not need reminding of the events which took place in July 1981. . . . It is clear from research carried out on Merseyside that one of the most significant causes is that employers and trade unions unintentionally practice discrimination.
> —Councillor Harry Kieran (Merseyside Area Profile Group 1983: 10)

> For a number of years the Commission [for Racial Equality, North West Region] has been concerned about the *particular* problems experienced by black Liverpudlians. In employment the problems are particularly acute in that black people appeared to be virtually absent from visible High Street jobs—such as in shops, stores, banks, building societies and Insurance offices—as well as from other important service sections of employment

such as the Local Authority, G.P.O. British Telecom, Passenger Transport,
Health Service etc. This is particularly disturbing in a City with a substantial
black/brown population settled for generations with the consequent absence
of problems related to language, dress, customs, traditions and culture faced
by many more recent immigrants to this country.
    —Merseyside Area Profile Group 1983: 111, emphasis added

These epigraphs are drawn from a firmly institutionalized genre of racial discourse: "reports." Reports are officialdom's vehicle of choice for disseminating
knowledge about what it calls "racial disadvantage" and "racial discrimination."
With varying degrees of enthusiasm and self-interest, the state and local authorities alike produce them. The nitty-gritty work falls to the myriad social welfare
and community relations councils, agencies, ministries, and departments under
governmental auspices. So common is this genre that I was occasionally asked if
that was what I was going to write—a report. Black people are tired of reports. I
was in Liverpool in 1989 when a new report about racism in the city had just
come out, *Loosen the Shackles: First Report of the Liverpool 8 Inquiry into Race
Relations in Liverpool* (Lord Gifford, Brown, and Bundey 1989), also known as
the *Gifford Report.* Just as I arrived at Peter's office at the Community Relations
Council for an interview, I heard him sighing about it on the phone: "Same old
shit," he said.[8]

The first epigraph is from a 1980 speech given by a Liverpool-born Black activist. Nine years later, the speech was reproduced as an appendix to *Loosen the
Shackles,* probably because his words turned out to be prophetic. He gave voice
to Liverpool-born Blacks' deep impatience with the status quo, warning of imminent collective action against the forces shutting them out of power structures
and, by extension, a better life. One dimension of the problem is that "so-called
Black West Indians" are being put in positions above "us." The stated desire for
equality with "the working class White people of Great Britain" appeals to the
national citizenship of Blacks born here and implicitly points up the immigrant
status of the West Indians. The second epigraph features a White official who is
so official that it takes him longer to recite his racial credentials—which include
having lived in Liverpool 8—than it does to make his statement about the unin-
tentional practice of discrimination. The third epigraph cites the results of a report of the North West division of the Commission for Racial Equality. It gives
straightforward testimony to Black Liverpudlians' invisibility in town. The *Liverpool Echo* (a daily tabloid) reported on that report with this clever headline:
"City Centre 'No Jobs Area' for Blacks" (Merseyside Area Profile Group 1983:
114). The headline makes a twist on the term "no-go area," a term that racializes
place by suggesting that Blacks make certain areas dangerous for Whites.

This section shows the premises of *Liverpool-born* Blackness just as they start to
become institutionalized. Toward that end, I analyze a report based on a wide-
ranging study published just before the 1981 riots, *Racial Disadvantage in Liverpool—An Area Profile* (1980). Blacks' impatience with reports notwithstanding, I
find this text invaluable as a point-blank and overwhelming description of racism

in the city, proffered at an exceedingly crucial moment in the formation of a public, mass Black politic. Black Britons from Liverpool participated in compiling,
analyzing, and presenting the data and in making policy recommendations. I
mark their Black Britishness here because that category is vital to the discourse
of the text, whose specific audience consisted of representatives of the British
state. Importantly, the term *Liverpool-born Black* crops up only now and again;
the category is in formation. To show how Blacks at that critical moment understood the effects of racism, I first give an extended overview of the report's content. I go on to analyze its discourse in order to show the construction of affinities across different experiences of racialization—or, a counter/*part* relation—as
well as the nascent suturing of Blackness and localness, and of both to "birth
here" in the context of official politics.

The authors of *Racial Disadvantage* note in their introduction that "three Parliamentary Race Relations Committees have visited Liverpool in the last eleven
years, and in our view have made regrettably little impact. We hope our submission
will help *this* Committee, in 1980, to set in train changes that will, at last, have a
radical impact on patterns of racial inequality, discrimination and disadvantage on
Merseyside" (Merseyside Area Profile Group 1980: 8, original emphasis). Their
book ended with this ominous statement: "But time is running out. A combination
of one of Britain's bleakest employment areas with one of Britain's most disadvan-
taged black communities could be disastrous" (114). Again, prophetic words.

The report proper is prefaced with a demographic profile of Liverpool that
notes the failure of large-scale surveys and censuses to identify "the largest racial
group in Liverpool: the Black British" (9). The report did note, however, that the
only national survey that attempted to count this group, the National Dwelling
and Household Survey, did so by including a "mixed-race" category. The authors
note that "[t]he number of black people interviewed [by that survey] was not
large enough to produce an accurate estimate of the size of the total black population, but it did show that the 'mixed race', or black British, sub-group was
clearly the largest racial group in the city, containing 35 percent to 40 percent of
the total black population" (9).

The crisis of unemployment is the report's first order of business. It distinguishes employment statistics and characterizes work conditions by group:

> The New Commonwealth born group in Liverpool consists mainly of Africans and
> West Indians: of these 25% were employed. . . . Over 40 percent of the Chinese pop-
> ulation worked in the restaurant business which involves long hours and low pay. . . .
> Asians, particularly Pakistanis, work mainly in unskilled or semi-skilled manufactur-
> ing jobs . . . [which] indicates the possible existence of a "sweatshop" sector . . .
> that continue[s] only through the exploitation of cheap non-unionized labor. (10)

The report indicates that unemployment is greatest in the inner city, where over
60 percent of the local Black population live. The unemployment rate there is as
high as 20 percent for male workers, while it stands at 9 percent elsewhere in
Liverpool (figures for women are not given). Unemployment for unskilled workers is 70 percent (11). Yet there is a built-in problem with the statistics, the report

suggests. The figures are prone to underestimating the figures on Black unemployment because Whites also live in inner-city areas. Hence, what employment inner-city Whites do enjoy causes an artificial lowering of the numbers for the area where most Blacks live. As the report makes clear elsewhere, the lack of racial or ethnic monitoring by some of the agencies that collected these and other figures makes it difficult for these studies to make comparisons by "race."

The report presents the results of other studies that did control for "race." These focused on unemployment among Black youth in Liverpool 8, which in 1971 stood at 32.5 percent compared with 19.5 percent for Whites (111). By 1976, according to one survey, 60 percent of Black eighteen-year-olds were without work. A smaller-scale survey conducted under the auspices of Liverpool University found that among sixteen- to twenty-year-olds, 45 percent were unemployed; without government schemes, that figure would be 60 percent (12). Racial discrimination accounts for these figures, the report argues. Citing a 1980 survey, the authors indicate that the Liverpool Careers Service had successfully placed 45 percent of its White applicants, compared with 27 percent of its Black ones. The report also cites a 1968 study that surveyed major employers in Liverpool:

> The I.A.S. [Inner Area Study] survey of 34 firms in Liverpool found that only 13 employed non-white workers, largely in unskilled jobs. The medium and large manufacturing firms were the most likely to employ black workers but only one had more than 2% employed and only 3 more than 15 black workers. A survey of 10,000 employees in 19 stores in Liverpool revealed that only 75 were black. Of these only 10–12 were serving at counters and in 7 stores no black workers were employed at all; others employed black people in stock rooms, transport or canteens. (13)

These figures, it has apparently been argued, reflect that Black youth do not look for jobs, and do not use available resources to find work. The report disputes this point, citing another study that surveyed "all school leavers in the Granby triangle area," 50 percent of whom were White and 50 percent of whom were Black. Of the Black school leavers 68 percent had made weekly visits to the local Job Centre, compared with 55 percent of the White ones; and 52 percent sought work through advertisements, compared with 27 percent of the White ones (14).

Although the report gives penetrating attention to racial discrimination in the business sector, other sites of racism are not minimized. Indeed, the report often emphasizes the interplay between unemployment, underemployment, and poverty, on the one hand, and such issues as housing, health, policing, and education on the other. "The residential concentration of black people in Liverpool," the section on housing begins, "is one of the most visible features of their structurally distinct position. The black population, despite a period of over a century of residence in the city, has been drawn into the worst areas of housing and there are signs that this situation is deteriorating" (31). In 1976 (when the latest figures were available for use in the report), all racial minorities were concentrated in the Granby ward, where 30 percent of the total population consisted of these groups (31). Significant—but unknown—numbers of Africans, Asians, West Indians, and locally born Blacks, the report notes, also live in the surrounding areas. In either case, these groups occupied "inner-deprived" council estates (property owned and operated by the Liverpool City Council), rooming houses, or privately rented flats or houses. The privately rented accommodations are neglected by absentee owners who make "a short speculative profit on a deteriorated housing stock" (34). The report prefaces its description of racism in the allocation of council housing by relaying the injustice in temporal terms: "Black households in Liverpool should have achieved a fair degree of access to Council housing by 1971 as there has been a local population of over 5,000 since 1919" (35). But instead, the council estates where Blacks live are the ones that most commonly fall into disrepair and suffer from malign neglect. As well, Blacks are waitlisted indefinitely for better council housing outside of Liverpool 8. Whites have a 31 percent success rate in attaining council housing outside of Granby, compared with 11 percent for Blacks. Seventy-eight percent of Black applicants fail even to be admitted onto the housing queue, compared with 32 percent of Whites (39).

The authors are also critically concerned with the sex trade that was settling into Granby. Prostitutes, they complained, come from out of the area into Liverpool 8, where their clients, also from outside, seek them out. The 1980 report testified to the ordeal this presented to female residents of Liverpool 8, who could not walk through their neighborhood unmolested. The report criticizes the police for their lack of attention to this issue.

The authors had a more grave concern about policing. One researcher cited in the report found that police in Liverpool did not use the "Sus" law (see chapter 3) as much as did police forces elsewhere in Britain. Rather they drew more on the specific "stop and search" powers that had been given to the Liverpool police under the Corporation Act of 1922. These powers allowed the police "to search any person who may be reasonably suspected of having or conveying in any manner anything stolen or unlawfully obtained" (74). This had the effect, the report argues, of sanctioning the surveillance and control of people in Liverpool 8, especially young Black men. This surveillance received further sanction from the British state, which had instituted a nationwide scheme of "community policing." Its ostensible purpose was to improve relations between communities and the police, but the increased presence of the police in Black neighborhoods was tantamount, the report argues, to simple spying. So, under the friendly guise of "community policing," the police would "stop and search" the people of the area. The study found that "young unemployed men from the inner city can be expected to be searched a minimum of three times during the course of a year" (74). Moreover, it is a particular group of Black males who tend to be criminalized—the "Liverpool-born" ones, "the majority of whom come from stable and supportive homes" (73). Their criminalization results from abusive treatment at the hands of the police. For example,

[T]he police frequently utter racial remarks; they are prone to arresting black people for subjectively evaluated street offences (e.g. abusive behaviour, resisting arrest) which are police-defined and in fact frequently occur as an outcome of a racial slur to which the black person reacts; legal rights on arrest are sometimes denied;

allegations of physical threats by the police and actual assaults are frequently made; the police are said to plant weapons or drugs on black people; finally charges may be conflated so that the person is faced with a number of subjective and unnecessary charges. (72)

The obvious domino effect of this criminalization is that young Black men have great difficulty finding work because they so often have police records. They become ineligible for social work positions that provide services to the Black community, the report says (47). Also obviously, the outright hatred that Blacks have for the police means that they are scarcely inclined to, perhaps, resolve the problem of bad community-police relations by joining its forces. The report reasons that Blacks would be even more hostile to Black police officers, whom they would likely consider sellouts (78).

Antiracist groups, ethnic establishments, and individuals have also been subjected to racial harassment. The report provides the following litany: "fascist daubings on community centre doors, and assaults on individual homes, desecration of graves, threatening or abusive phone calls or letters to known anti-racists, smashing in of windows of ethnic minority restaurants [Asian ones are later specified] or of bookshops known to distribute anti-racist or anti-fascist materials, and physical attacks on individuals in the street" (79). The police say these are just random attacks, though.

From beginning to end, the authors express exhaustion over having to present evidence, yet again, about racism in Liverpool. This is the fourth time the Parliamentary Home Affairs Committee has visited Liverpool to hear such evidence. Rather forcefully, this report criticizes all governmental authorities for not recognizing when and where Blacks enter *as Britons*. And rather subtly, I think, the report suggests that Africans and Afro-Caribbeans—even if through no fault of their own—are blocking the state's view of Blacks born here, rendering the latter invisible. As I argue below, that invisibility is the source of the discontent, or the inescapably frustrated tone, that finds expression in LBBs' perhaps unwitting deployment of nationalist logics *via place*.

As I noted earlier, the authors reserve sharp criticism for social surveys that failed to identify and count the Black British, and for obvious reasons: demographic data is used by policymakers. The only survey that managed to identify this group, the authors note cautiously, did so by counting people of "mixed race." To repeat, "The number of black people interviewed [by that survey] was not large enough to produce an accurate estimate of the size of the total black population, but it did show *that the 'mixed race', or black British*, sub-group was clearly the largest racial group in the city, containing 35 percent to 40 percent of the total black population" (9, emphasis added). The original survey, it bears note, did not use a "Black British" category.[9]

Place of birth, not parentage, emerges as the most relevant determinant of racial categorization in the report. The authors' conflation of *mixed race* and *Black British* implies that if one is mixed race, one was born here and is therefore British. The authors index their ambivalence about the mixed-race category by putting it in scare quotes and then supplanting it with the term *Black* British. Place, though, renders the Black British "racial group" highly significant: they are clearly the largest one. This group's plight includes their invisibility, despite representing 35–40 percent of the total Black population. For all intents and purposes, then, place distinguishes two groups within "the total black population": those born here and those born elsewhere. In a section that details the ways various racial groups experience discrimination in employment, the authors state that "The New Commonwealth born group in Liverpool consists mostly of Africans and West Indians." The phraseology, "____-born", is quite common in Britain. Its prevalence may shape the authors' occasional appropriation of it, both in reference to the New Commonwealth groups and to Blacks born in Liverpool. But even more to the point, the politics of birth unfolding in Britain must have influenced the authors' deployment of it as a distinguishing feature among these various racial groups. Put otherwise, the authors do not object to the use of birthplace as a legitimate distinction; their concern, rather, is that some Blacks are not recognized for having been born in Britain. In sum, Black Britons are situating themselves in a counter/*part* relation vis-à-vis the other Blacks who make up the total. But, as we see below, they also reproduce the ideological function of place by suturing Blackness itself to "birth here."

Having established in the opening pages that "mixed-race/Black British" people are a large part of the "total black population," the authors go on to edge the immigrants out from under that umbrella by referring to them in the language of ethnicity. Citing a 1971 statistical study that aimed to devise "a set of indicators" for "strategic and local planning" purposes, the authors critique its reliance on data that only concerns the New Commonwealth–born group: "At this point ethnic minorities were identified as an important indicator of 'vulnerability'" (65). That study, then, equated the New Commonwealth–born group with ethnic minorities. The authors of the 1980 report proceed to criticize ethnicity discourse for evading questions of race: "This is well justified considering the mass of national and local evidence that has examined racial discrimination . . . etc. But such racist practices operate on the basis of colour of skin, not on nationality or ethnic origin, although this [*sic*] may be a contributory factor." This critical point could be the centerpiece of an argument *against* the very distinctions *by birth* that operate in the 1971 study. Instead, the 1980 report replicates the mistake it aptly identifies in the former. For, we have already seen the critical reference to the "mixed race/Black British" in Liverpool as a large and unique "racial group." The report continues: "Therefore *a large section* of the indigenous black population has not been identified" (65, emphasis added). This statement is ambiguous; it implies that the "New Commonwealth born" group might also count as "indigenous." Previously, largeness referred to the "mixed-race/Black British" group. But the real emphasis here, it seems to me, is on the occlusion of Blacks' indigenousness in the 1971 study, which conflated New Commonwealth birth and ethnic minority status. Indeed, New Commonwealth immigrants become, by this point in the report, the sole reference point of ethnicity discourse. Race, meanwhile, is reserved for Blacks born here. For example, the authors note,

"Many local ethnic minority community centres have been (or are being) developed with local authority support (Caribbean, Pakistan,[10] Chinese, Rialto) and several local agencies engaged in work with the locally-born black community are being partially funded (Charles Wootton Centre, South Liverpool Personnel, Elimu Wa Nane)" (63). Ethnic minority institutions are designated *local*, but the term *locally born* is linked to the term *black community*. The report continues, "These initiatives, however, barely scratch the surface of what is required to combat serious under-achievement of the black and ethnic minority communities in employment, housing education and social welfare" (64). The report relies on the distinction throughout, often using the phrase *local black and ethnic minority*. The phrase "black and ethnic minority" was common in Britain as a whole in the period under discussion, and into the early 1990s. Although the term *Black* has often been used to include people of Asian, African, and Chinese background alike (especially in the 1980s), that usage has never been uncontested by members of those same groups. The phrase *ethnic minority* accounted for those not wishing to be "Black."[11] Note that in Liverpool, though, the phrase becomes "*local* black and ethnic minority." And local means "born here."

Above, the authors argue that the culture and ethnic origins of immigrants are only minimally important factors in the discrimination they face. Race is the issue. That argument calls crucial attention to the racism of Whites, not the "culture" of Blacks—wherever they may have been born. Yet that fine point has a brief shelf life in the text. In what follows, the authors quote approvingly from the official findings of a group commissioned to gather population data in Liverpool for policy purposes. That commission critiqued the failure of the 1971 National Census of the United Kingdom to count Blacks born here. The authors introduce a quotation from those research findings with this statement: "The lack of an adequate data base and the use of an 'immigrant' indicator in an area of black British concentration has led to the failure to identify a further category" (65). Now quoting those research findings, it continues, "The *special* needs of the Liverpool-born Black population, whose problems are not linked at all to the problems of newness and culture—i.e. 'immigrant' problems. They are the *specific* result of racist structures of discrimination and disadvantage" (65, emphasis added). This passage gives credence to the view they just criticized. The premise that immigrants face disadvantage because of their newness and culture returns through the back door. The sarcastic tone with which they refer to "immigrant problems" betrays their frustration. The authors may not have seriously considered newness and culture to be the real source of immigrants' problems. Fifty pages prior, they carefully outlined the positioning of Africans, West Indians, Pakistanis, and Chinese within the city's racialized political-economic structure. But by this point in the text, those groups have melded into immigrant-ethnics, allowing the Liverpool-born Black population to emerge as the ones whose subordination is "the *specific* result of racist structures of discrimination and disadvantage."

Without question, much energy was expended in emphasizing that this particular group of Blacks must never be confused with immigrants. LBBs' utter frustration with their invisibility leaps out in one remarkably provocative quotation that the authors provide with seeming relish. The quotation, which is from a local community worker, follows a discussion about a conference on education that had recently been mounted.

> The conference was called to consider the effectiveness of the service provided by the [Liverpool Education Authority] for ethnic minority groups at the further and higher education level. A good deal of time was spent discussing the language and cultural needs of ethnic minority groups, and it seemed that many of the representatives from the colleges had little understanding of why it is that black people are under-represented in colleges. Those contributors with local experience strongly expressed the view that the needs of the Liverpool born black people were not being met by the Authority's colleges. The problem was not one of language or culture but "race" and "racial discrimination," a view clearly stated by the following quotation: "We only know one language, that's Liverpudlian. We only know one culture, that's the English culture. Come into Liverpool 8 instead of talking about Liverpool as having a big immigration problem. What it has is a race problem." (27)

This passage forges the implicit distinction between "ethnic minority groups" and "black people" that suffuses the entire text. "Language and cultural needs" belong to the conflated discourse of ethnicity and immigration. The term *black*, by contrast, is subsumed inexorably into the discourse of the local. This move is effected spatially, by the invocation of Liverpool 8, which has a race problem not an immigration one, and linguistically, by the reference to "Liverpudlian" as a language—not to be confused, that is, with "English."[12] The imagined gulf between things Liverpudlian and things English is the topic of the next chapter.

Several critical points arise from the foregoing analysis of the 1980 report. For the first of these, we must remember that immigration in Britain was constituted as a Black phenomenon. The "problem" of "swamping" owed to the "influx" of Blacks. They, per Thatcher, had a threateningly different culture. The terms *Black* and *immigrant* became absolutely synonymous. Yet here in Liverpool those terms are being radically separated. Liverpool-born Blacks could be saying that "we Blacks are not immigrants." But the frustration that invariably underwrites this declaration actually produces the inverse of that formulation: immigrants are not Black.

A second crucial point follows from the first. For years, people of mixed racial parentage were constituted as half-castes, not Black or Negro (the term used in the 1930 *Fletcher Report*, for example). This was a key obstacle when, in the 1970s, people of mixed African/Afro-Caribbean and English/Irish parentage started organizing for such things as Black studies. They were met with the response, "But you're not Black." The 1980 report announces that they are Black. But not only that; now, they monopolize the category. Afro-Caribbeans and Africans are immigrants or ethnic minorities, not Blacks.[13] Of course, there is no reason why they should be *Black;* that category is as malleable as any other. However, the narrowing scope of Blackness has implications. In this very moment, the tides are turning toward race as the organizing principle of grassroots and radical politics. The report itself is taking a step in that direction. Again, the

authors are very sympathetic to the way these groups are affected by racism. Nevertheless, their presence directs undue focus, in policymaking circles, to the issue of culture at the expense of race. When race is the issue, we must attend to the "specific" needs of what is "clearly" the "largest" of the "racial groups."[14]

The 1980 report might seem to reflect the coherence and recognition of LBBs as a social group. It is better understood as an artifact of LBB politics in formation.[15] Yet the premise that will become key to LBBs' eventual political hegemony is very pronounced in the report. It operates with a logic so transparent, it seems to require no elaboration. That premise concerns place.

Across Britain, local belonging is reckoned through rhetorics of continual, generations-long presence in a place. The 1981 Nationality Act, I earlier argued, drew on that seemingly innocent place-based genealogical principle toward racist ends. The 1980 report deploys the same logic for the purpose of racial critique. It argues, for example, that "The Black population, *despite* a period of over a century of residence in the city, has been drawn into the worst areas of housing" (31). A few pages later it makes the point again: "Black households in Liverpool *should have* achieved a fair degree of access to Council housing by 1971 as there has been a local population of over 5,000 *since* 1919" (35). References to the time-depth of Blacks' presence in Liverpool is a feature of *all* critical racial discourse in and about that city. Here is a variation on the theme: "Two major planning documents [of 1979] . . . contained no explicit reference to the special needs and problems of what is in fact one of the most long-standing black communities in Britain, whose disadvantages have by now received sufficient documentation to merit specific attention" (60).

I do not mean to detract from the critique of racism here but to pinpoint the place-based roots of LBB racial discourse. On the one hand, it depends on the innocent, impartial logic of time, which is always—I do not mean sometimes—marshaled to dramatize the gravity of the forces of racism. Words and phrases like "despite," "should have," and "since" highlight racial injustice by couching it in terms of Blacks' historical presence in that city and suggest what would have automatically happened (better housing, for example) were it not for racism. Through place, time proves a racial point. On the other hand, this logic depends on the same premise of British nationalism—Blacks, though "born here," are still not British—that it is ostensibly resisting. Blacks' deployment of this logic could have a dangerous, if unintended effect. It could conspire with the racism of White landlords and the Liverpool City Council in rationalizing the assignment of poor housing to immigrants, since they have not been here very long. More broadly, this line of argument suggests that the temporal is necessary to make the case that racism is wrong. That is, if LBBs did not have time on their side, as it were, would racism be justifiable? Ironically, though, the statements "Blacks have been here so long" and "there has been a local population of over 5,000 since 1919" absolutely depend on the presence of immigrants, even as it subtly renders them invisible by here—and only here—calling them Black rather than African or Afro-Caribbean, and by rendering them part of the "*local* population."

The attention that this and other reports have showered upon Blacks has not mitigated the racism that affects, however differently, the counter/*parts* who make up the "total black population."[16] Yet the analytical value of the 1980 report is, first, that it shows how Blacks in Liverpool understood racism and its effects, which in turn motivated the activism not only of LBBs but people of all racial positionings in the city. Second, it shows LBBs' sense of frustration with their invisibility. If that condition was both symptom and source of their powerlessness, then the boldness with which they announced their existence was important to their eventual hegemony. In addition to the 1981 riots and the *Listener* protest, the political action described in the next section was formative. The last section reflects the ultimate political legitimacy that LBBs had won by the early 1990s.

The Caribbean

In this section, LBBs and Afro-Caribbeans debate, rather publicly, LBBs' status as a distinct "racial group." Told from the standpoint of the victors, this is an account of a landmark political action that the LBO undertook in 1981, just before the riots. Ethnographically speaking, though, the time frame is really the early 1990s, when the episode in question was, on numerous occasions and with great enthusiasm, recounted to me—by LBBs.

A few years after the *Listener* controversy another explosive article appeared in a Liverpool tabloid, the *Daily Star*. Dated May 7, 1981, the article was titled "When Blacks and Browns Fall Out" and focused on the views of Frederick Reese, then director of the Merseyside Caribbean Community Centre. Mr. Reese opined that the real race problem in Liverpool was not to be found in the relations between Blacks and Whites but between Blacks and "browns," by which he meant people of mixed Black and White parentage. Reese argued that "the far greater threat comes from the Liverpool born blacks, the products of mixed marriages. The half caste population is well over 50 percent of the non-white population of Liverpool. They are concentrated in Liverpool 8 and if they ever come together, they would swarm over everybody else." The LBO organized a takeover of the Caribbean Centre (better known as the Caribbean) in protest of the article and other longstanding grievances against the Centre.

Scott read the article to me on the occasion of our first meeting. He had come to see me at Cecelia's house, carrying his folder marked "Anti National Front." In chapter 1, I suggested that some of its contents exceeded that topical boundary. But the article from the *Daily Star* fit right in. The NF argued that the whiteness of Britain was in grave danger. As well, Thatcher was swept into office in 1979, at least in part, through her promise that under the Conservatives "we shall finally see an end to immigration, lest this country become rather swamped by people of an alien culture." In 1981, Frederick Reese used Thatcher's own language (which implicated the likes of Reese himself) to argue that Blacks are being "swarmed over" by "browns." Further, his statement carried the same ominous overtones that were the mark of NF, Powellite, and Conservative Party discourses about "race."

In chapter 4, I described the main lesson that Scott learned from his mother: the terms *colored* and even more so *half-caste* were demeaning to Black people.

From there he told me about the Reese affair. Scott's back-to-back narration might be interpreted as a chain of events in and of itself: his mother's views, in Scott's account, enable his participation in the political action organized in response to Reese's remarks.

> Now listen to what I'm saying here. . . . This is on May 7, 1981. Three reporters from the *Daily Star*: "When Blacks and Browns Fall Out" [reads the text of the article aloud]. There was murder over this article!! We had meetings. We had demonstrations. This Reese had to leave Liverpool because he's a West Indian who has this slave mentality. The slave mentality that if you're not seen with a dark black skin that you're colored, and if you're not colored you're half-caste. If you're not half-caste you're octoroon, high yellow. This is sickening.

Not wishing to offend, I laughingly questioned the slight against West Indians implied by his "slave mentality" analysis. Oh, no, I was quite wrong, he shot right back. Scott implored me to listen to him carefully: I should not think that he is anti–West Indian. After all, his father was from the Caribbean and he might have a holiday there sometime or even consider living there. "But," he went on, "someone born and brought up here in Liverpool would look on the lightest-skinned Black person as Black. Here, as in London, the White racist will not make a distinction between one who's light-skinned and one who is darker: you're both equally Black." To illustrate the point, he compared our skin colors, putting his dark arm next to my much lighter one. He looked me seriously in the eye and intoned, "You're as Black as me." No matter the shade of skin, then, we are all equally Black—and following from his mother's teachings, we are "just" Black. Not partially Black. And certainly not "brown." It is uniquely Blacks born and bred in Liverpool who understand this, he argues. West Indians, accordingly, undermine the counter/*part* relation that should connect Blacks across phenotypic difference. To explain their position, Scott draws on West Indians' unique history vis-à-vis other Blacks in Liverpool: Afro-Caribbeans alone hailed from societies where slavery was institutionalized.

Cecelia and Yvette volunteered another account of the Reese affair. I was sitting in Cecelia's kitchen when Yvette popped in for a visit. Saturday afternoon chitchat soon gave way to a dramatic reenactment of LBO history. For a good hour and a half, Cecelia and Yvette happily regaled me with stories about the glory days of Black politics. In this context, I asked what they seemed to consider a strange question: Did the LBO response to Reese's remarks create LBB identity?

> CECELIA: What it did was highlighted and focused Liverpool Blacks. But it didn't—
> that needed to be done in light of what was happening with the Caribbean [Centre].
> You see, because the [Liverpool City] Council was only down the road of negotiating with all the ethnics, and ignoring us. And they thought we were included in that, but in fact the Caribbean were also excluding us—
> YVETTE: Physically excluding us from the building.

CECELIA: Because when the Pakistan Centre got built and the Caribbean Centre, there was never no Liverpool Black Centre. So they just assumed that all Blacks were using the Caribbean Centre and that wasn't the case because the Caribbean structure and makeup was from the islands, and if you're not from an island, you can't go. And so the action was taken because they had no one on their committee representing Liverpool-born Blacks. Nobody at all. They had this policy to say that you're not an islander so you can't be on the committee. So after the action [in which the LBO occupied the center for a few weeks], the committee got together, and they offered us two places.

YVETTE: Which we ceremoniously declined!

CECELIA: And they kept having these meetings and meetings and meetings, just to make a decision to take two Liverpool Blacks on their committee. And these meetings were raucous 'cause every time they'd break up.

YVETTE: [Names one of the executive committee members] was good, he was on our side. But God, these bloody old West Indian men. Ohhhh, for Christ's sake! And they're still in there today!

CECELIA: But the thing is, they never ever bothered to do anything. They'll die eventually. But they knew they couldn't carry on anymore like the way they used to. They're back to their old mode but they're wary of their actions. It brought in [names two LBBs] to do the Carnival.

Cecelia's immediate response to a question about the creation of LBB identity is to imply its prior existence: the action against the Caribbean Centre "highlighted and focused Liverpool Blacks." There is no telling how she might have finished the thought she started here: "But it didn't . . . " Perhaps she would have said that it did not "create" Liverpool-born Black identity, since those were the verbatim terms of my question. Such an answer would also be consistent with her opening statement suggesting that "Liverpool Blacks" already existed. The identity *LBB* is as eternal as their longtime presence in Liverpool. It does not have a beginning any more than "African" or "West Indian" would.

By contrast, Black identity is not naturalized. Its beginnings are pinpointed. In the previous chapter, Peter narrated the move from *half-caste* to *Black* quite definitively. Thus, if *Black* is a relatively recent innovation—one that sedimented in fits and starts, as Peter also suggested—*Liverpool-born Black* must have emerged afterward. Nevertheless, questions about LBB identity are met with indirection and, indeed, some surprise. I once asked Scott how the term *Liverpool-born Black* originated. Never stumped by a question, he was taken aback by this one. He thought for a minute, and finally decided that he could not recall when he first became conscious of it. Failing for a definitive answer, he speculated—only partially in jest—that it may have been he who first coined it. I asked another LBB of Scott's age to explain how the term originated. He looked at me askance. What kind of question was this? By way of a polite answer, he offered that it merely distinguishes Liverpool-born Blacks from, for example, "Manchester-born Blacks and London-born Blacks." LBBs' propensity to cast their existence endlessly back in time may color their vaguely anxious responses to questions premised on the category as a social creation. In making these points, my concern is not with the history of the term itself but with the place-power upon which it depends, and which is further naturalized through it.

Yet Africans, Afro-Caribbeans, and even some Blacks born here are quick to highlight the social construction of *LBB*. A middle-aged Nigerian proffered a precise time line for it: "*Half-caste* is becoming obsolete in the city. Instead a lot of people are calling themselves 'Black.' After the riots, it became 'Liverpool-born Black,'" he explained. Another Nigerian, this one in his thirties, was less matter-of-fact: "Liverpool-born Blacks are between Blacks and Whites. They don't know what they are yet. It takes an event to tell them what they are." With an unabashed presumption of authority, he denigrated Liverpool-born Blacks for lacking an identity that is as natural as his own. A natural identity does not need to be produced by events like the one presently under discussion. Finally, some people who would qualify as Liverpool-born Black are suspicious of the category on several counts. Greg was among a few Blacks I knew who criticized the overly local focus that it lends to Black politics at the expense both of a global perspective and a more explicitly Afrocentric one.[17] Other Blacks born here suspect that the category was fabricated by academics at Liverpool University and the social policy establishment connected to it. A few derided the term as a euphemism for *mixed race*.

These various detractions show how hegemonic the category *LBB* had become by 1991. It was *the* way of referring to Blacks born in Liverpool, showing up casually in everyday speech, newspapers, bureaucratic reports, and the like. These detractions also betray the great ideological labor that was required to imbue that category with legitimacy in the first instance. Liverpool-born Blackness, as a phenomenon, is built in part on the premise that in the grand scheme of race, racism, racial identity, and racial policy—in short, in whatever way race is made salient—"birth here" matters. By implication, so too does birth there, wherever that might be.

Like the furor over the *Listener* article, the Fred Reese affair occurred just as people of mixed racial parentage were staking their political claims, as Blacks, on the city's institutions and businesses. Unhelpfully, another Black person came forth ever so publicly to redefine the struggle. LBO members were impelled to respond in like fashion. So they took over the Caribbean Centre. As Peter explained,

> When the meeting [about the Fred Reese remarks] disbanded . . . [we] went to the Caribbean Centre—which was only five hundred yards down the road from Stanley House—*aaaaaand* we took it over! Got the people *off* the premises, locked the gates, and took it over—but took it over with a plan, i.e., that we provide things for the children. We provided things for the kids: inflatables, etcetera. We'd open it during the day until all the demands were met.

The LBO alleged that the center excluded the community's youth, and so provisions for children were an important component of the political action. In her own description of the event, Cecelia claimed that one of the men at the Centre said that "the problem is all these half-castes and we don't want them in here." "They wanted nothing to do with them, and that kind of thing. And it was occupied the next afternoon!" The triumphant tone in her telling of the story resounds with Peter's own. Peter continues the story here, developing the plot:

> Then the direction of the action changed because as far as I was concerned, it was an LBO action. It was an LBO meeting, and LBO members, and the LBO that went down there to take it over. And now people were saying, "Well, this is 'the community' what's done this, that it was 'the community' that was in here making these demands." So now we got this vague "community" thing so all statements that went out to the press—particularly to the Black press, the *Caribbean Times*, etcetera—particular spokespersons were elected to talk on behalf of this imaginary "community" and, like, I myself made it personally clear that I was angry about it . . . Now at the time, you're not even going to go against that. You're going to say, "Okay, let it be a community action" with the understanding that you're not going to make a big point of it. But maybe we should have.

The conflation of the LBO with "the community" betrays the paradox of LBBs' burgeoning and very public activism. The *Listener* article argued that "local-born Blacks" were without family and community. They were even outside of "recognized society." Now there is "a community," but it bursts into existence with a potency that shocks: it is angry, militant, and violent. Their targets are not just White institutions but Black (or "ethnic") ones. The LBO demanded attention and they got it. Peter remarked on the importance of this historical moment, commenting that "they said that it was 'a community action.' Now *at the time* [in 1981], you're not even going to go against that." Since the press followed LBO members' lead in using the legitimizing idiom of "community," Peter argues, it would have been counterproductive to question that term. His concerns were well-founded. The LBO left itself vulnerable to the charge that it did not actually represent the community—which is exactly what the press claimed when the LBO (albeit in reconstituted form) turned its attention away from the Caribbean Centre and onto the institutions of local government in the aftermath of the 1981 riots (Merseyside Area Profile Group 1983).[18]

As suggested earlier, members of this heterogeneous Black community contest the category *Liverpool-born Black* on several grounds. My first clue of its contentiousness came when I invoked it in casual conversation with an Afro-Caribbean man who worked at the Centre. He immediately interrupted me, suggesting that I instead adopt phraseology like "Africans, Afro-Caribbeans, and their descendants." Such would never fly among LBBs, who would fault it for subsuming them into the discourse of ethnicity over race, for defining them in terms of their ancestors born elsewhere, and for denying them the right to name themselves. My informant warned me that some people would object to my use of *Liverpool-born Black.* And *he* certainly did. He continued, saying that "there are a lot of self-appointed leaders around here. When I need representing I will go and represent myself." Ten years after the takeover of the Caribbean Centre, the wounds were still fresh. To situate this diasporic debate more completely, it is necessary to elaborate further on its roots and stakes.

The British state must be implicated for turning racial subjects into ethnic ones. As the foregoing section showed, government institutions relied on the language of ethnicity and culture to explain (or explain away) *racial* disadvantage. As well, the state put a premium on birth here even while de-legitimating it, which may have encouraged Black Liverpudlians to seize it as a means to correct their invisibility. Along similar lines, the state made ethnicity the centerpiece of its project of managing racial difference and quelling antiracist political action. For example, under section 11 of the Local Government Act of 1966, organizations representing people from the New Commonwealth and Pakistan were eligible for state funding to develop community-based institutions. This provision and similar, ostensibly liberal state programs stipulated that government support would only go to avowedly nonpolitical organizations.[19] Ethnically oriented ones like the Caribbean Centre were almost guaranteed a degree of official sanction not accorded to those built on an explicit racial politic—ensuring, as well, that organizations run along these disparate axes would not always be compatible (Jacobs 1986, Simey 1996). Cecelia marked that difference as she rehearsed the highlights of LBO history, commenting that the Liverpool City Council "was only down the road of negotiating with all the ethnics." LBBs' many complaints about the lack of a "Liverpool Black Centre" that would match all the ethnic ones indexed not only their invisibility but their lack of an officially recognized platform, on par with the Caribbean Centre, from which to air their points of view.

The stakes of these debates go even deeper. Reese and the above-quoted man at the Caribbean Centre shared a certain anxiety about LBB activism, even if they defined Liverpool-born Blackness differently. Reese constituted LBBs as a distinct racial group owing to their parentage: "the far greater threat comes from the Liverpool-born blacks, the products of mixed marriages." Ten years later, my informant at the center defined them as a political group. His instantaneous response to my use of the term *Liverpool-born Black* was this: "There are a lot of self-appointed leaders around here." His words reflect the political hegemony that LBBs had achieved by 1991. To halt its forward march, he advocates a terminological shift to "Africans, Afro-Caribbeans, and their descendants." Such would not only rein LBBs back in, but redefine "the Black community" in terms that position Africans and Afro-Caribbeans at its center.

Ironically, the LBO's response to Reese's remarks confirmed his worse fear: LBBs *did* get together. But what might explain Reese's fears in the first place? In search of a tentative answer we might briefly consult constructions of race in the colonial Caribbean, which differed starkly from the ones trying to operate in postcolonial Liverpool. In full acknowledgment of the many factors that might compromise the validity and wisdom of the forthcoming attempt at contextualization, I find it useful to draw on historical and ethnographic material about the Caribbean.

As a first step, we might consider the function of mixed-race categories under slavery. Across the eighteenth-century colonial Caribbean, people of mixed origin, known as *coloreds*, increased in number and occupied a great variety of statuses (R. Smith 1988). Brackette Williams shows that in British Guyana free mulattos served as a buffer group, even to the point of putting down slave rebellions. And after slavery, their identity "placed them in a category apart from the newly emancipated non-Mulatto slaves" (1991: 141). With slavery's abolition in British territories, the divergences among color-based statuses did not result in a polarized system, but remained full of ambiguities. Classes were composed in terms of race, and the racial system itself allowed for "minor inconsistencies" such that the "colored middle class" consisted of "some blacks and some Jews as well as people of mixed racial origin" (R. Smith 1988: 93).

For the purpose of diasporic analysis, such history is no more interesting than what contemporary people do with it. Colonial Jamaica provides a crucial, if suggestive case study of how slavery is put to use in the construction of racial identities and political allegiances in the present day, revealing in turn why diasporic subjects in Liverpool were at such cross-purposes. In a series of ethnographic articles, Jack Alexander set out to explain the "culture of race" through kinship and notions of legitimacy among middle-class Jamaicans (1977, 1984). He conducted fieldwork in Kingston from 1967 to 1969, a period of continuing immigration to Britain. In that period, Jamaicans derived their understandings of racial solidarity and group interest from the history of slavery, he argues. They saw themselves, as a whole, to be "mixed up" racially, dating back to slavery—and, indeed, because of it. Alexander's informants invariably traced their genealogies back to an original ancestral pair, consisting of a dominated (Black) female slave and a dominating (White) slave master. This is an origin myth, for no one was able to name these figures with any certainty; people just assumed that this was their family's past. His informants perceived themselves as all equally "mixed up"—a view that precludes an ideology of bounded racial categories. They also understood the great variation in phenotype to characterize Jamaican society. Along the same lines,

> The vast majority of racial descriptions are of physical appearance. However, these elements of physical appearance are significant because they are taken to be outward signs of race. . . . At the same time, physical appearance is considered a somewhat unreliable indicator of race. For instance, it is freely acknowledged that siblings who have the same racial composition can have a very different physical appearance. (1984: 163)

Contemporary interracial unions have "an air of illegitimacy" around them due to people's critical origin stories, which begin with the "illegal union of a white male master and a black female slave and their illegal mulatto offspring" (168). Finally, "In the cultural definition, the solidarity that arises out of racial sameness is an intrinsic property of that racial sameness. People stick together because they have the same blood, and there is no more explanation necessary" (168).

Several key differences are notable between the Kingston and Liverpool cases. Perhaps most important, interracial procreation in Liverpool is very contemporary as opposed to historical. The category *Liverpool-born Black* accounts for the normativity of interracial procreation. In Jamaica, that normativity was part of a violent, if vague past that everyone was nonetheless understood to share. They were all equally "mixed up." But the crucial point is this: in Jamaica, to be of actual, identifiable mixed racial *parentage*—as opposed to ancestry or descent— was perceived as a threat to racial sameness and therefore racial solidarity.[20] This view recalls Reese's remarks, in which "Blacks" were one racial group and "browns" another. Blacks and "browns" do not even seem to be *counter*/parts. Moreover, the "racial sameness" of the "browns" was threatening precisely because it could fuel *their* racial solidarity.

Arguably, the roots of the Reese affair also lay in the World War II era. In 1941, at the invitation of the Ministry of Labour, 345 skilled workers from Jamaica were brought into Liverpool to work in the munitions factories. At the time, "local" Blacks were locked into low-paying, unskilled jobs, while the West Indians were conspicuously better-educated and better-paid. A fair amount of tension developed between the two groups (and between West Indians and Africans). Black Liverpudlians described West Indians as "arrogant and smart," while some West Indians were loath to socialize with the locals (C. Wilson 1992: 415). As one stated, "One of the problems about Liverpool is that all classes of colored people have to mix together—ones you wouldn't look at at home. The better type of Jamaican does not want to associate with the type of person who goes to [Stanley House]" (Richmond 1954: 94). Some were also scandalized by the choice to locate Stanley House in the lowly south end of the city, where all Blacks lived at the time. Black Liverpudlians also detected a rise in racial tensions, which they attributed to Whites' consternation at having to compete with better-skilled West Indians for jobs. Yet class difference did not totally prevent West Indians and Black Liverpudlians from finding common political cause. West Indians were fed the same diet of racial indignities: they found it difficult to find decent accomodations, were given jobs beneath their credentials, and were ignored by their labor unions. So they established the Liverpool Branch of the League of Coloured People (LCP), which made dedicated efforts to link the struggles of West Indians, Africans, and Black Liverpudlians.[21]

Tina Campt argues that memory is the essential vehicle of diasporic identification:

> The direct and inherited memories of diaspora define and sustain a sense of relation . . . among communities separated spatially in diaspora. As both remembrance and commemoration, this memory technology engages strategic forms of forgetting imposed institutionally from without as well as individually and collectively within specific communities. Memory provides the source of the defining tension of diaspora (2004: 180).

While the present analysis emphasizes "*this* place" over transnational formations of diaspora—indeed, LBBs and Afro-Caribbeans are anything *but* spatially separated—Campt's suggestion about memory is pregnant. Some pasts are remembered, others forgotten. That the "situated argument" of the Reese affair lives on in memory is evidenced not only by its continuing narration but its function as a frame of reference. It structures the *counter*/part relation in the present.

My informant at the Caribbean Centre, for example, contested the legitimacy of LBBs as representatives of Blacks' interests in the political arena. LBBs also seem to carry the memory of West Indian workers' class privilege as they entered Britain. At the start of this chapter, I quoted an LBB activist who said, again publicly, that "We will no longer put up with . . . so-called Black West Indians being put in places of authority above us." Moments like the formation of the LCP, fleeting though they may have been, seem rather forgotten.

However objectionably, Reese gave voice to a major predicament: the racial battle lines were more cross-cutting than those dividing Blacks and Whites. Getting to the bottom of the relationship between LBBs and Afro-Caribbeans is not my goal.[22] But at the very least, this case suggests that colliding histories of racial subjugation, class formation, and identity construction are as much the stuff of diaspora as intercultural exchanges and political linkages—as historically transformative as those inspiring phenomena have been. As well, the histories and memories at issue referred to recent pasts, not ancestral ones. When the Reese affair occurred, LBBs had scant legitimacy as Blacks, much less as Liverpool-born ones. Through their bold, public political actions (the *Listener* protest, the riots and the demonstrations that followed, the takeover of the Caribbean), LBBs announced their presence, articulated their racial politic, and began to take over the stewardship of a heterogeneous Black community.

The recognition of that heterogeneity is a major issue in official racial politics, affecting the ways Blacks' needs, desires, and interests are represented. Situated debates may traverse the well-worn roads of racial purity and authenticity, but these are not the matters that actors really sought to settle. Above, LBBs were concerned that all children could access the Centre's (rather considerable) grounds and facilities; this goal had been achieved by 1989, when I made the mistake of asking a group of young people at the Centre whether they were of Caribbean background (see the preface). And in the 1990s, it was a venue for youth-initated events, like one commemorating the anniversary of Malcolm X's assassination. LBBs' sights were also set on redressing a racial situation that could only be called dire. Reese made his infamous remarks in the same historical moment represented in the 1980 report analyzed above.

The point of this section is not simply to highlight LBBs' outrage over their slight at the hands of the Caribbean Centre, but to show that outrage as a mobilizing force on the road to somewhere else. The triumphant tone that animates LBBs' narration of this story reflects more than the satisfaction of comeuppance, then. The Reese affair was compelling to the narrators because it exemplifies a formative moment in the rise of a very powerful and, according to *some* memories, unprecedented set of Black politics. LBBs cherish these memories, like the ones from the era when they became Black (chapter 2), because these were the days when Black Liverpool, as a political entity, came into being—again, according to *their* memories. For the visibility it afforded LBBs, the LBO is a touchstone of that past. Peter mourned it thus: "The organization was very dear to myself as a political platform in Liverpool, and I still don't believe we have one now like the LBO. That's why I remember it. It was an organization of action not talk." By the

PREFACE

The Congress shall have power to promote the progress of science and useful arts, by securing for limited times to authors and inventors the exclusive right to their respective writings and discoveries.

U.S. Const. art. 1, § 8, cl. 8

The field of intellectual property (sometimes referred to as IP) is one that continues its rapid growth. Just a few years ago, individuals who identified themselves as practitioners in the field of intellectual property were met with blank stares. Now IP professionals are in constant demand, and it is a rare issue of any legal periodical that does not include advertisements for IP practitioners. Many experts believe this rapid growth can be attributed to the spread of computer and communications technologies throughout the world. Reflecting this, more technology-related legislation was introduced in the 105th Congress than in any previous Congress. Trademark and patent applications filed at the U.S. Patent and Trademark Office have doubled in just the past five years. Similarly, there is increased emphasis on the need to enhance protection of written materials, including computer software, through copyright registration.

Today's competitive businesses recognize that nearly 80 percent of their value can lie in their intellectual property. With increased technology and global communication come greater challenges to protect intellectual property. Misappropriation or infringement of valuable proprietary information is a keystroke away. Thus, companies and law firms value the expertise of IP professionals who can assist in adopting strategies to ensure IP assets are fully protected.

IP practice groups make extensive use of paralegals. Paralegals are involved in nearly every stage of trademark and patent prosecution and maintenance practice and in the area of copyright registrations and IP audits. The field offers significant opportunities for client contact, challenging issues, and personal and intellectual growth. The specialized nature of IP practice produces highly capable and efficient paralegals whose contributions are valued by both other legal professionals and clients. Expertise in the field is recognized by salaries that are often higher than those for other paralegals. In addition to law firm IP practice, many paralegals are employed in-house at companies with significant IP assets. These paralegals work closely with in-house counsel to meet the company's needs. In brief, the field provides significant and rewarding opportunities for career satisfaction.

The recent increased interest in intellectual property coupled with nearly daily changes in IP law has caused a relative scarcity in texts that provide both sound foundational concepts together with the practical advice needed to ensure success for IP paralegals.

This text provides a comprehensive guide to each field within the umbrella of intellectual property, namely, trademarks, copyrights, patents, trade secrets, and unfair competition. The methods by which each is created, procedures to register or protect each, duration of rights, protection from infringement, and time I first met Peter in 1989, he had joined the ranks of the talkers. He occupied the hallowed halls of officialdom. I earlier quoted his "official" assessment of the *Gifford Report*: "same old shit."

"THE POSTCOLONIAL BOURGEOISIE"

The title of this section avoids another term, *new niggers*. With it, LBBs refer to West Africans who occupy or compete for jobs in the post-1981 race relations field. These are not the seafaring Africans of old, but a professional class. These Africans came of age at the tail end of the colonial era and began immigrating to Britain in the 1960s. They arrived as students, refugees, business people, skilled workers, or through a host of other circumstances that LBBs distinguish from the local tradition of seafaring. These Africans came on airplanes, not ships. They came from well-to-do families, Yvette told me. They had the ability to drop anchor and set sail at will. Some of them did not go "back home" after graduating from university, but chose instead to set things up in and around Liverpool 8. Others pursued careers in Liverpool's expanding but still highly limited race relations industry, which effectively replaced shipping as a source of employment for Black people. From LBBs' point of view, those jobs were born of the violence that burned the streets of Liverpool 8.

In this section, "1981" is the historical reference point of situated, diasporic debate. LBBs' contentious relationship with the postcolonial bourgeoisie is exemplified in the words of Jessie: "They don't have a *clue* about community. Where were they *before* 1981?" she asked me rhetorically. "Where were they back when I was the only one involved in Stanley House, with four White workers who weren't even from here?" These newcomers represent a further threat: hailing from West Africa, they have perspectives on racism that differ greatly from those of LBBs. And, as Yvette's comment betrays, LBBs perceive them as privileged. They strike a stark contrast to the local Black population, she went on to tell me, and they are rarely committed to helping the community's youth attain similar achievements as they have. But this critique is double-edged. To help Black youth in any numbers, Africans have to enter the very field that LBBs claim as their preserve.

The travails of Nigel, a thirty-five-year-old Igbo from eastern Nigeria, offer a window onto that double edge. Nigel arrived in England in 1979 with the intention of attending a university in London. But he was told that his qualifications were not acceptable. Although he passed the necessary examinations in Nigeria, he was told to redo them because British standards were higher. Nigel redid them and went on to study business administration, and then earned a master's of public affairs in finance at Liverpool University.

Africans are not strangers to that institution. One of the ways that Liverpool became home to such an old Black population (in addition to the role played by the shipping industry) has been through its university. *Staying Power*, a public exhibition on Blacks' history, mounted at the city's Labour History Museum, noted that "Liverpool merchants, keen to cement trade relations, encouraged West African chiefs to send their children for a taste of English education. They boarded with local families and some may have stayed on" (van Helmond and Palmer 1990: 14). In the mid-1960s, some Nigerians escaped the civil war that followed independence and attended Liverpool University. Because of its solid reputation, that institution attracts many international and British students. But it has been home to very few Black Liverpudlians, most of whom live within walking distance of it. The earlier-mentioned *Gifford Report* noted that a researcher who sought to study Liverpool-born Blacks in higher education could only find sixty-three people who qualified for the study (Lord Gifford, Brown, and Bundey 1986: 116). Black people have had difficulties graduating with the qualifications from secondary school that would even allow them to get to university, as the 1980 report and the *Gifford Report* show. I was told on several occasions that the city of Liverpool has produced only one Liverpool-born Black Ph.D. A White professor at Liverpool University told him that he lacked the ability to earn a doctorate, so he set sail for the United States. Since then, another LBB whom I know has earned a Ph.D., also from an American university. A few of my other LBB friends, like Cecelia, attended university—mostly outside of the city. Yet African nationals have historically had a significant presence at Liverpool University. Education is both enabler and marker of the higher class status of ex-colonial Africans vis-à-vis LBBs.

Nigel went on narrating his own trajectory in Liverpool. After receiving his master's degree, he sought work in the business sector in town. Despite his qualifications, he was unsuccessful. His accent marked him as a foreigner, and hence the first half hour of any interview was inevitably absorbed by inquiries into his residence status. He was asked to produce every possible permit and document confirming his right to be in Britain before any discussion took place about his résumé. Failing to find work in the field of finance, he got a job selling insurance. Again, his accent marked him as different, he told me, and he was doomed to failure. Finally, he pursued another strategy to advance himself professionally. He sought work in the voluntary sector. He got himself onto management committees in community organizations and sought to help represent Black people's interests in the fields of education and social services. But Nigel was disturbed by what he observed. Below he comments on the hegemony that LBBs had, by now, achieved as the primary representatives of Blacks' interests in official spheres. LBBs have become eminently visible, at least around the tables where policy is made.

I went to meetings which were called and I saw no presentations from the African community here. Only the presentations were from Liverpool-born Blacks. I've been to several meetings of the [Liverpool City] Council, and I haven't seen any representations except the Liverpool-born Blacks. I've had some meetings with the Black Race Units officers; they're all Liverpool-born Blacks. But parentally they are linked to Africa. But because they are born here, with the accent, [and] even though we [Africans] are well-qualified to work in public services due to our backgrounds, we are not able to get the jobs.

I see a two-part prejudice there. We have the White man being racist to a Black person. And we have the Black person being prejudiced against a Black person because of the national—where you come from. So there's an identity clash between the Black community, which is still happening now. But you have to lead yourself, you have to work twice as hard as the Liverpool-born Black to get yourself—you have to work three times as hard to get yourself as high up as the White community. So that's the kind of disadvantage and suffering that we have, we who are from Africa, not from here—not started here.

Jeff, a Liverpool-born Black man, spoke just as passionately on the very same issues. Jeff worked in town as a race relations officer. He corroborated Nigel's view: there is a trend in pushing Liverpool-born Blacks forward as candidates for race relations jobs. He was sympathetic to credentialed Africans, but added, "But you know Black people have been here—*born* here—for three hundred years, and it's not before time. I mean there's a *huge* lag to be made up for" (all original emphasis). He indicated that a new race relations position was being created in the Liverpool City Council and that several educated Africans, some of whom held jobs well beneath their credentials, were applying for it. "Yet," he continued, "there is a Liverpool-born Black man who is also applying, and although his academic credentials may not be stellar, he is well-known and respected throughout the community and people will have confidence in his ability to do the job."

Although he did not mention the identity of the LBB applicant, I knew it to be Peter. His "front line" education and longtime participation in community politics rendered his credentials beyond reproach in LBB circles. And not only was he a founding member of the LBO, but he also showed the kind of selfless risk and militancy that LBBs still celebrate, particularly in reference to the young Black men who adopted a Black Panther stance in their fights with the Skinheads. These Black men pushed back the boundaries of where Blacks could safely live and travel. As one member of this group said in chapter 2, "We couldn't understand why we couldn't go here, there, or the other place. . . . So we organized." Peter was among them.

He did wind up getting the position. How the White officers of the Liverpool City Council evaluated and ultimately approved his qualifications, especially over that of well-educated—or, perhaps, *differently* educated—Africans, I do not know. But in LBBs' view, Africans just do not have Peter's credentials, garnered through lifelong work on behalf of the community and not, as the cynics say, "on the backs of it." Indeed, Africans are sometimes confounded by LBB political practices and perspectives on racism, a point I pursue later. In the meantime, Jeff corroborates Yvette's view of the Africans as a privileged group vis-à-vis LBBs:

> There's a bit of a snobbery I would say on the part of one or two of the Africans. And there's certainly a lot of snobbery on the part of some of the Asians. There's also the class dimension. I would say that every Liverpool-born Black person is a working-class person, essentially. But then I think Africans and Asians, when they come here, bring with them their own sort of class and caste system which they've been brought up with.

Nigel's background in Nigeria shows the colonial roots of class difference between recent African immigrants and LBBs. In the previous chapter I suggested that young LBBs ascribe a conservative politic to their African fathers due to the colonial context of their upbringing. Ironically, that very context contributed to the albeit limited privilege of Liverpool's more recent African immigrants. Nigel provides an exquisite outline of this postcolonial politic of location:

> Some [Liverpool-born Blacks] who have got better jobs are not qualified [like] those ones who come from Africa and West Indies who have studied, who have qualifications. But, rather, they [Liverpool-born Blacks] have got community experience. They can speak the language of racism. Drawing back again to Africa, we didn't know racism. Myself, I didn't know racism until I came here. . . . [T]he type of history we learned was that the White man is superior. But since I came here and walked on the street and saw a White man picking up a cigarette on the floor—that was the first time I saw it, and it was an eye-opener to me! I was at Heathrow Airport. It was full up with Whites, and I saw a White man sitting there picking up cigarettes on the floor and I said, "What is happening?" So I went and offered him one. And he took it and said, "Thank you." Right then I changed my mind and said, "These people are not superior to us."

As in the Reese affair and the controversy over "these bloody old West Indian men," post/colonial histories of race are colliding here in Liverpool. In Nigeria, Nigel received a British education (even if he had to repeat it in England) and was routinely exposed to Black professionalism, even under colonialism. Nigel "didn't know racism" until he got to England where, upon landing at Heathrow— that is, within minutes of his arrival—he immediately realized that "these people are not superior to us." LBBs, with some exceptions, have lived their entire lives in England, "knowing racism" and its effects very intimately. The above-discussed report as well as Peter's discussion of mental illness (chapter 4) might be recalled here. The White man at Heathrow defied Nigel's imagination, given the ideological content of his education. Of course, Nigel's efforts at gaining the meaningful employment worthy of his education were thwarted by racist and nationalist politics. But he also finds himself in the unlikely position of competing with uneducated Blacks. Liverpool-born Blacks do not have to produce any residency documents. Plus "they have the accent."

Yvette arranged for me to meet a friend of hers, Kofi, another Nigerian, then thirty-eight years old. In 1973, Kofi immigrated to England to study, originally settling in Wolverhampton. Two years later he relocated to Liverpool. Unlike Nigel, he has no family in the city. A complete self-starter, he now managed a job-training program in Liverpool 8. When I arrived at his office, Yvette happened to be around. In making the introduction, she represented my research interests to Kofi. She informed him, in chatty jest, that I was in Liverpool to study ghetto people. Turning to me she said, also with a smile, that Kofi represents the Black bourgeoisie. Any Black person with a job, she explained, is the bourgeoisie. In so noting, she marked Kofi's difference from local Blacks. She went on to tell me, in Kofi's presence, that since he was not "from here," he would not be able to tell me too much about Liverpool. Then she qualified her comment, "Well, you've been here since you were a teenager, haven't you? Well, then you could tell her *some* things." Kofi's pleasant smile belied his acute awareness of what Yvette was intimating about his legitimacy.

Kofi has come under fire from the Liverpool-born Black establishment for being an outsider who now occupies a good, eminently visible job in Liverpool 8. He echoed Nigel's words in saying he did not understand racism until he arrived in Britain.

> I came here when I was eighteen or nineteen with a totally different outlook on Black people and their lot, if I can put it that way. . . . I first came into this community not really understanding why Black people behaved in certain ways. Like, one thing was when I first came to the U.K., I used to see Black people marching and all that for equal rights, and I couldn't understand it. I thought, "Why don't people just go to college and get themselves an education and do what I've done?" I'm here now and there's racism but it's not diverting me from getting my qualifications [academic credentials] and so on. And I couldn't understand how if you've been under the pressure of racism for a very very long time, it's very difficult because you're customized into thinking in a particular way. Opportunities are limited for you. And people don't have the role models I had.

Kofi's relationship to the LBB power structure was much more amiable than was Nigel's. Kofi has worked hard to make friends with LBBs like Yvette. But he had a difficult time adjusting to the meanings of Blackness that obtained in Liverpool and to the "visible" signifiers of that category. The journey between Lagos and Liverpool, via Wolverhampton, was as long as it was eye-opening. He tripped over his words in describing it:

> I also found that when I came from Wolverhampton, which has—Liverpool has the highest percentage of people from mixed marriages and if you go to a place like Wolverhampton, and most of the Black people are Jamaicans—I mean both parents are Jamaicans or Africans. I mean, Black people are more visible. So when you drive into Wolverhampton or Birmingham or into Nottingham, you see [he points to his eyes] Black people, and they're visible. That's the thing that struck me in Liverpool: you couldn't see Black people in town, or anywhere else. Okay, it's down to people who are from mixed marriages tend to have lighter skin and I suppose coming from somewhere where everybody is predominantly "black" [his intonation implied these quotation marks] with dark skin, when you come into Liverpool it's the lighter skin that you tend to see. And again in those days, with my background, to be Black you had to be "black" like me [delivers a thud to his chest]. So I didn't see that. I was wondering, "Where are all the Black people?" . . . But the thing that is also predominant is that when you then go into town as well, even what I would call "light-skinned Blacks" you didn't see them. I now have an understanding of why that happens, which is the racism in town and all of that. Those are the things that struck me.

"So how did you come to view Black people of mixed origin?" I asked him.

Well, to start with, growing up in Nigeria it was acceptable to call people of mixed race "half-caste" because to a lot of Nigerians it was not an abusive term. It was purely a biological description of somebody who comes from a mixed race. And that was part of the problem I had because I used to talk a lot about people being half-caste and I realized very quickly people of mixed origin didn't like it because they would attack you the minute you call them half-caste. So you have to bear in mind my own perceptions of things in those days. That gave me the impression that the Black people in Liverpool were actually aggressive as well because you'd go up to somebody and say, "Oh, have you seen that half-caste person" and the next thing they're on your—[cuts himself off]. It's an abusive term, which I didn't know at the time. And I thought, "What's the matter with those people?" You know, I try to be friendly and the first thing you say they bite your head off! But it was the way in which I saw it in those days.

Kofi's words bear the mark of LBBs' influence. Coming from Nigeria and then Wolverhampton, he was unable to "see" Blacks in Liverpool at first, but then learned to do so. In that singular respect, Kofi gives the lie to understandings of race that depend on or otherwise reify bodily signifiers. Although the body is a racial signifier of major proportions in the West, the bodily markers themselves are cultural and historical rather than being plain to the naked eye. Kofi has learned to "see" race through LBB eyes. Testifying further to the completely cultural character of race, Kofi voices LBB explanations about why Blacks are invisible in town. That is, he has assimilated to a local political culture that centers on the racism that he once minimized. He has revised his thoughts on the term *half-caste*, courtesy of LBBs' venomous responses to his use of it. He can recite all LBB narratives about race—a mark of LBB hegemony itself.

Although it has been difficult, Kofi suggested, he has managed to win local Blacks' trust. Yet they still remind him that he does not really know what it means to be Black in Liverpool because he has not been there since birth, as Yvette stated explicitly. He defends himself against this charge by joking with people that he *is* an LBB: a Lagos-born Black. More soberly, Kofi said he is still occasionally called "a new nigger" even after he thought he had won people's acceptance. I asked him whether he thought this label was a critical comment on his class status. He closed his eyes, said, "Yes," and let his head drop.

Unlike Kofi, Nigel has not been given the LBB embrace. Nigel has family connections in Liverpool through an uncle who settled in the city. His uncle's wife, a White English woman, and her friends, Black and White, form part of Nigel's social network. One of these friends is Claire, a middle-aged Black woman born in Liverpool. Claire has been his passport to community activism. Significantly, Claire identified herself to me not as a "Liverpool-born Black" but as a "Liverpool-born African." She was the only person I knew who used this term, which she reported using on every form that asks for her racial or ethnic identity. She does not distinguish between the old Africans and the new ones, for she does not consider the latter illegitimate community members. Accordingly, she has facilitated Nigel's work, which consisted of establishing a multiculturalist organization, by serving as a bridge between Nigel and the LBB power structure. Other LBBs I knew described a vouching system whereby a would-be but unknown LBB (who may live far from Liverpool 8, for example) is rendered "safe" (local slang) by an LBB who *is* known. Yvette described the usual method, which consisted of just saying, "He's alright, he's an LBB." Claire could not, of course, claim that Nigel was an LBB; he was obviously Nigerian. Rather, she vouched for him simply by showing up with him at political meetings. She described all of this to me with a tone of incredulity, with words like, "Can you believe, I actually had to accompany him?" Even though Claire does not identify as an LBB, the basis of her legitimacy is that she is known to others in Liverpool 8. All she had to do to help Nigel's cause was to show up with him as a recognized LBB personage herself.

The irony of LBB politics is that they have a distinctly anti-immigrant tenor that resembles that of White British nationalism. Their own "birth here" politic plays directly, if inadvertently, into the racial premises that served to exclude them from rightful belonging to the nation insofar as, to repeat, "birth here" colludes with the ideology that it ostensibly resists: that *Black* and *immigrant* are synonymous terms. LBBs also couch their critique of immigrants in the same political-economic terms voiced by the White working classes: "Immigrants are taking away our jobs." And some Blacks who are not immigrants are essentially treated as such.

It has been fairly common for African fathers and White British mothers to relocate their children to the father's country, where their adolescent children could receive the fine British education that racism in Britain made unavailable. Or, the entire family relocated. A good friend of mine, Gordon, was sent, on his own, to his paternal uncle's home in Nigeria, where he spent his adolescence and young adulthood. On returning to England, Gordon attained a degree in business administration from Manchester University. When he returned to Liverpool to occupy a leadership position in the community, LBB power brokers did not receive him well. He seemed to come out of nowhere. Compelled to prove his "birth here," he produced his passport. But that was not enough. In a casual conversation with Cecelia, I referred to Gordon as an LBB. I thought she might choke. Befuddled, I clarified that he was born in Liverpool. Her response: "Well! You'd never see *him* on any march!" Nor did Gordon see himself as an LBB. He knew that his class status was a bone of very serious contention. He was proud that he spoke without a scintilla of Liverpool in his voice. He also drove an attention-getting foreign car around the fairly poor environs of Liverpool 8 (although he lived miles away) and dressed in "flashy suits," as Gordon himself called them. And, as he also admitted, he was not one to demonstrate and march into town.

African immigrants, and even Blacks like Gordon who grew up in West Africa, claim the outsider position as an advantage, for it allows them to offer youth an alternative understanding of society. Gordon was quite proud that his organization, which catered to youth, had a capitalist ethos and (so he thought) no political content to speak of. And therein lies the source of LBBs' concern, for they do not want avowedly apolitical perspectives to become institutionalized, as they fear they would be if Africans run "local" and "Black" organizations. Perhaps, then, the critical issue in debates about immigrants is not just that they are not born here but that, somehow, on the matters of LBBs' "unique," dire, deeply rooted, historical racial oppression, Africans and Afro-Caribbeans "just don't get it." Gordon has lived a formative part of his life in Nigeria, contributing to his relative privilege now. Like Kofi, who at first did not see why Blacks in Britain did not just forget all this racism stuff and pursue an education, Gordon was mystified by LBBs' lack of education. He could not fathom why young Blacks were not taking advantage of the opportunities available to them. Up until the late 1980s, for example, British citizens automatically received grants to pay for their education. Black youth should have been flooding Liverpool University. He made it all sound ridiculously easy: he did it, and so could they. But it is precisely the racism of the school system that compels Africans, like Gordon's own father, to send their children off to Nigeria to be educated.

Unlike Nigel and Gordon, Kofi came to see things LBBs' way. He told me of arguments he has had with LBBs on the matter of policing in Liverpool 8: he once believed that more of a police presence would make the neighborhood safer. Nigel, on the other hand, reduced the authority of LBBs' critical discourse on race to their accents. He never indicated what it was they actually *said* with these accents, just that LBBs had them while Africans and West Indians did not. LBBs also have an advantage, he suggested, because of their fluency in "the language of racism"—a rather cynical phrase. Similarly, Nigel believed that LBBs' sole objection to his organization was his immigrant status. Nigel's organization had an explicitly multicultural approach—one that LBBs like Yvette found completely inappropriate. The issue is race, she argued, not culture.

CONCLUSION

West Africans, Afro-Caribbeans, and LBBs were produced as racial subjects through related but distinct colonial histories that include, at the very least, indirect rule, slavery-inspired racial ideologies, and the *Fletcher Report*, respectively. Each of these forms of subordination now privileges some Blacks in relation to other Blacks, a contradiction that defines Black Liverpool as an irreducibly postcolonial formation of diaspora. Africans bring their British education—one of the "benefits" of colonialism—with them to Liverpool, where higher education for Blacks born here is a tragic rarity. Africans and Afro-Caribbeans fancy themselves the possessors of stable racial identities, unlike Blacks born here whose claims to Blackness have been challenged by those same groups. In a fascinating twist of plot, LBBs wind up monopolizing the category *Black*. They also use the birth here idiom to their advantage, despite its attachment to nationalist ideologies meant to exclude them. These groups' distinct histories under British rule, whether here or abroad, come together and collide. Diaspora refers as much, then, to antagonisms and power asymmetries as to the links that people make in the hope of overriding these. That all of these discontents and desires unfold in (or in the name of) one little neighborhood called *Liverpool 8* shows that diaspora does not require an ocean to be in full effect.

On my last visit to Liverpool in 1999, I asked my friend Joseph to read the published version of chapter 2. Years earlier, Joseph used the word *diaspora* in conversation with me, saying that people of the African diaspora—of "black blood," he clarified—were all connected. Joseph was speaking in global terms and that vision was consistent with his poignant testimony, quoted at length earlier, about Black America's influence on him. Since, for Joseph, diaspora is all about the links, my attention to conflict took him aback. "You didn't focus on Black unity," he said, obviously disappointed. He thought I overstated the frictions between Liverpudlian men and the Yanks, and between Liverpool's Black men and women. I came up short on two counts: in neglecting to show unity both across and within Black communities, I undermined it. Or at least failed to contribute to it.

Diaspora must never be made synonymous with the project of unity—nor with origins, authenticity, difference, roots, routes, or hybridity. These terms just give voice to the discrepant desires and discontents of counter/*parts*.

My City, My Self: A Folk Phenomenology

Having only seen pictures of the white cliffs of Dover, I was
greatly looking forward to seeing them with my own eyes. . . .
I stand on deck and watch the captain. He is staring at the
white cliffs of Dover, and then beyond them to the hills
whose smooth rounded shoulders easily bear the weight of the
toy-like cars which snake up and down them. . . . Beyond the
captain is Britain. On this bleak late winter's morning, I am
happy to be home. As I look at the white cliffs of Dover I realize
that I do not feel the nervous anticipation that almost forty
years ago characterized my parents' arrival, and that of their
entire generation. I have not travelled towards Britain with a
sense of hope or expectation. I have travelled towards Britain
with a sense of knowledge and propriety.
—Phillips 2000: 20–22.

THIS QUOTATION is from *The Atlantic Sound*, by Caryl Phillips, who was born in
the Caribbean and immigrated to Britain with his parents when he was a child.
His book describes his sojourn to three places important to the history of slavery:
Accra, Charleston, and Liverpool. Above, Phillips has crossed the Atlantic on the
first leg of his journey. Britain is finally sailing into view. His sensual longing for
the white cliffs of Dover, and the womanly hills that lay beyond them, evoke his
claim on Britain, where he travels with a sense of (patriarchal) ownership. Just
beholding those white cliffs renders him British. With that privileged position in
place, he later travels up north, by train, to Liverpool.

As the train pulls in to Liverpool's Lime Street Station, I am struck by the satanic
quality of the station. Pigeons fly overhead, darting in and out of broken windows.
The station is a throwback to an era of Victorian expansionism when huge arches and
long black platforms were the norm. Somehow Lime Street's crumbling grandeur
seems appropriate for a city which has long recognized itself as being in a state of
decline. (Phillips 2000: 94)

given the situation of the students discussed above. And many faculty members do try to assist the students by helping them understand what constitutes the minimum requirements for a thesis or dissertation.

What is an acceptable thesis/dissertation?

The purposes and the requirements for a thesis or dissertation are usually stated in the official document describing your particular degree program. Those statements, however, only give you some general principles to follow. For example, as a doctoral student you may read from your program manual that the purpose of the dissertation is to undertake a substantial research project which results in a significant advancement of knowledge in your field. It has to demonstrate originality, analytical integrity, a high degree of scholarship, and sound research methodology (cited from the UCLA Doctoral Program in Social Welfare Manual, 1994-95). If you are not satisfied with such general statements, you may go further to check out other documents and thesis/dissertation guides. However, it is unlikely that you will find the specific and detailed answers you seek as to what constitutes an acceptable thesis or dissertation. Rather, you will be encouraged to discuss your questions with faculty members, especially your academic advisor. But the advisor, again, will not find it easy to describe to you the minimum requirements for the thesis or dissertation.

If you are just trying to get some rough idea about what a thesis or dissertation looks like, you are better off to simply borrow from the library a copy of the successful work of a recent graduate of your program and take a close look at it. If you insist on obtaining some very specific measures of the minimum requirements for a thesis or dissertation, you will probably never get them. It is not that such statements are not helpful, but that they are nearly impossible. Given the variety of the substantive topics you can choose from and the diversity of the approaches you can use, any uniform statement about the requirements in a more specific language would appear to be inappropriate.

This, of course, leaves you with a question as to what role faculty subjectivity would play in judging your thesis/dissertation work. You may have heard a fable about writing dissertations, i.e., a rabbit getting a diploma from a lion not for a good thesis but for pleasing the lion. And the moral: "It's not the contents of your thesis that are important -- it's your PhD advisor that really counts" (cited from a computer-generated page posted on the door of a Ph.D. students office, n.a.,

16

new and international developments will be addressed for each of these fields of intellectual property.

Each chapter begins with an introduction to the topics covered therein and concludes with a brief overview of the material presented. Information is arranged in a building-block approach so the reader is presented with comprehensive coverage of each topic. Discussions of each field of intellectual property conclude with a section on the new and emerging issues in that field and then an overview of international implications, such as the methods by which intellectual property can be protected in other countries.

The substantive overview of each topic is complemented by the use of forms, sample agreements, checklists, and other practical guides. References to useful resources and web sites are provided in each chapter and online in Appendix C so readers can gather additional information. The specific tasks in which IP professionals are involved are fully addressed. Finally, discussion questions are provided to ensure thorough understanding of each topic. A glossary highlights critical terms, and selected trademark, copyright, and patent statutes are provided.

The field of intellectual property is one of the most dynamic and challenging of all legal specialties. Many of the issues are cutting edge: How can a domain name be protected? How can a company ensure its trade secrets are not misappropriated by an employee? What is the best way to protect a computer program that may be obsolete in three years? How can a business be sure its web site does not infringe that of a third party? How can intellectual property be protected in a global economy?

Providing assistance to IP owners thus provides unique opportunities for learning and growth. Moreover, the field of intellectual property is inherently interesting. All of us see and recognize trademarks each day. All of us read books, watch movies, and use inventions. Thus, readers bring a wealth of practical and firsthand knowledge to the study of IP law. This text allows readers to link their experience as consumers with the substantive information presented to ensure IP owners are provided a full range of strategies and methods to protect their valuable assets.

ADDITIONS AND ENHANCEMENTS TO SECOND EDITION

Each chapter ends with the following new features:

- Trivia (a "fun" section pointing out interesting IP facts, statistics, and trivia; for example, one of the chapters on patents notes that the youngest patentee in the United States is a four-year-old);
- Case Illustration (a short "brief" of a case that illustrates some of the principles discussed in that chapter);
- Case Study and Activities (a factual scenario involving a fictional company, Watson Inc., a Disney-like company that operates an amusement park, is given in each chapter, requiring students to identify various IP problems Watson is encountering and suggest strategies to solve those

Phillips draws a straight line between the apparently unmediated visuality of place, "Lime Street's crumbling grandeur," and an equally transparent social phenomenon, a city in decline. In the tradition of the British travel narrative, Phillips relates his first impressions of the strange and foreign place.[1] On arrival at Lime Street Station, he takes a taxi ride, whence he meets his first native. The native makes a joke. With an air of upper-crust English superiority, Phillips dryly notes, "This encounter is, I presume, an example of the famous Liverpool humour" (94). He is surprised when he exits the cab at his hotel. He cannot see the River Mersey. "I . . . find myself looking for the sea. I half-expected to step out of Lime Street Station and on to a seashore promenade, so closely do I associate Liverpool with the sea" (94). When he finds it, he is disappointed. It is "singularly uninspiring" (94). In the hotel, he meets a clerk who has "a noticeably different" accent, and he is puzzled. It is not what he expected of a northern accent (94).

To his own surprise, Phillips then realizes that "I . . . am actually looking forward to my time in Liverpool" (94). Since he was eleven years old, he has sensed that there was something "disturbing" about the place. He attended a football match in the northern city of Leeds, when Leeds United was playing Everton, one of Liverpool's two football teams. Phillips was standing near a half dozen Everton fans. "One of them asked a question about a Leeds United footballer that the others could not answer. I answered the question. Almost as one, they turned in my direction. 'Fuck off! We're scousers and we don't talk to niggers.'" Here is what Phillips takes from this encounter: "For many years afterwards, I was always careful to distinguish Liverpool from Manchester, or any of the other northern industrial cities. In my mind, Liverpool was a place to be avoided. A dangerous place" (96).

Phillips details Liverpool's other excesses, a litany of what makes the place so disturbing. The damage of the 1981 riots was so extensive that "the government appointed a special minister to deal with the problems of Liverpool alone" (96). When the Liverpool Football Club finally signed a Black player, John Barnes, Whites hurled racist abuses at him from the stands. As well, "Liverpool found it difficult to stay out of the news." Liverpool football fans were "contributing" to deadly violence in Belgium, while still others were killed at Hillsborough, in Sheffield. For years, Liverpool had been succumbing to "violence, unemployment, poverty and depression at a rate that was far in excess of other British cities" (97).

Liverpool, for Phillips, is excess itself. The individual marks of that excess combine to render the city not only off the scale of any other English city—in the South *or* in the North, as he explicitly tells us. Liverpool is also beyond the pale of any known civilization. Perhaps the people of Liverpool do not live in a city after all. Rather, they seem to live in one elaborate signifier. In contrast to Britain, evoked through the magical white cliffs of Dover, Liverpool's physicality is satanic (perhaps like its people?). Liverpool is a place apart. It has nothing to do with Britain, the North, or Phillips himself.

UNDERSTANDING "LIVERPOOL"

In the spirit of Scott's thesis, this chapter argues that to understand Black Liverpool, you've got to understand the historical production of "Liverpool," the signifier. Toward that end, I study the city's mainstream White majority. Failure to do so would render Whites an anonymous mass. They would be invisible apart from their role as Blacks' collective antagonists. If Blacks are always more and less than what Whites make them out to be, then the reverse must also be true. More seriously, failure to study Whites' Liverpool would effectively render Blacks' Liverpool a place apart, having nothing to do with the rest of Liverpool, never mind Britain. To understand "Liverpool," I ultimately argue, one has to understand the city's postcolonial displacement, its dislocation from the would-be embodiment of British modernity to a signifier of all that is wrong with Britain.

In pursuit of these issues I study four "Liverpool autobiographies," each written by a White man of working-class Irish background.[2] Since the 1960s, when a nostalgia industry sprouted in the city, publishing companies have produced a fair number of "local interest" books. Overwhelmingly about the past, these tracts generally concern history, autobiography, or architecture. The name I have given the autobiographical versions of the genre suggests that these texts concern the life of persons only by extension; "Liverpool" is the real subject. Place is anthropomorphized on nearly every page. To different degrees, the authors ascribe powerful human effects in the realms of consciousness, experience, and identity to place—whether that place be the city itself or its constituent locales. In so doing, these authors enact English cultural premises—what I will call a folk phenomenology—that regard place not only as the producer of identity but *as* identity (Baucom 1999). My city *is* my self. The fact that these are Irish selves does not disturb the point that they enact English culture.[3] The real irony is that these Liverpool-Irish authors use English premises about place-as-personhood to produce a "Liverpool" that, as far as they are concerned, hasn't a thing to do with England. And the importance of that connection is this: the exquisitely reified Liverpool that they produce has everything to do with the suturing of place and race both in the term *Liverpool-born Black* and in LBBs' political practice, as detailed in the previous chapter and as it comes to a head in the next. In fact, these odes to Liverpool exemplify the form of documentation that Blacks long to produce for themselves. As I suggested in previous chapters, Black people yearn for textual preservation of their own memories, their own important history, their own relationship to the sea and the port, and to the Liverpool places synonymous with all of these: Pitt Street and the early Granby. As I sit writing about Whites' Liverpool autobiographies, two LBBs I know are penning their own.[4]

The earliest text in the genre is *Autobiography of a Liverpool Irish Slummy*, by Pat O'Mara. Published in 1933, well before the nostalgia industry came into full bloom, this book is commonly cited in standard Liverpool scholarship. His autobiography is also distinguished by its New York publisher; the others were issued by either a local or regional firm. O'Mara clearly anticipated a wide British and

American readership, while the other authors write mostly for other Liverpudlians. For example, *Reflections on the Mersey: Memoirs of the Twenties and Thirties* by Frank Unwin (1983) grew out of the author's hugely popular radio program, *Music and Memories*, on BBC Radio Merseyside. By 1983, when his book was published, his program had been running for fourteen years, during which time the author received thousands of letters of appreciation. These inspired him to write *Reflections*. The jacket cover of another autobiography, *Growin' Up: One Scouser's Social History, 1925–42*, by John Woods, says that this "hugely enjoyable book . . . will appeal to Liverpudlians of all ages" (1989). Finally, in *My Liverpool*, author Frank Shaw (1971) clearly hoped for a non-Liverpudlian audience as well as a Scouse one: he happily translates Scouse terminology and inside jokes for the rest of us. Of these books, Shaw's most defies categorization. It is not strictly an autobiography, although he does reflect more than occasionally on his own life. And although his text is not strictly historical, it does engage in time travel.

Among the shared features of these texts, one stands out: they each constitute selfhood through place. Their titles forge the connection explicitly, with *My Liverpool* as perhaps the most obvious example. In the title *Autobiography of a Liverpool Irish Slummy*, "Liverpool" specifies what kind of Irish person O'Mara was. His personhood is further shaped by another kind of place, a slum. *Reflections on the Mersey: Memoirs of the Twenties and Thirties* maps the sea, via the River Mersey, onto a kind of life narrative. Finally, *Growin' Up: One Scouser's Social History* situates the self within the social and, through the term *Scouser*, places both within Liverpool. Another shared element among the texts lies in the ordinariness of the lives they narrate, which forms the basis of their appeal. One Scouser's social history, for example, or the autobiography of one "Liverpool Irish slummy" bespeaks the collective experience of the group to which he belongs. The author's life is an extension of that of his readers, who will enjoy the book because their own lives, memories, and culture are celebrated in its pages. To various degrees, the texts also position Liverpool outside of England. Their city is a place apart. Since Liverpool is so unique, living an ordinary life there is reason enough to write an autobiography. And what makes Liverpool so special is its glorious relationship to the sea. Of course, shipping is dead now, so a distinctly mournful tone suffuses the texts published after O'Mara's 1933 *Autobiography*.

In order to situate the following cultural analysis of Liverpool's trajectory, it is necessary to first consider the position that the local normally occupies within globalist theories and visions. The much-remarked decline of national boundaries as sites of political efficacy has created a discourse on the local as an entry point of global forces and flows. In anthropology, the global never appears without the local. After all, those flows have to land somewhere.[5] Why do flows not land in regions or countries? Because—however problematically—the local connotes smallness, "*here*-ness" and, with these, the density of detail that is, now more than ever, the anthropologist's stock in trade.[6] Despite the partnership implied in the "local/global" dyad, the two exist in gendered relation.[7] The local plays the role of a recipient, albeit not necessarily a passive one. In fact, her agency is located in her ability to refuse or otherwise resist global penetrations. Some argue, for example, that local identities have emerged as a critical response to globalization (Hall 1999; Harvey 1989, 2000; Gupta and Ferguson 1992). In other versions, the local provides the "cultural context" that renders the global graspable. She domesticates the global, becoming a mere trope for ethnographic specificity in the process. For example, anthropologists argue against the view that we are all headed for Mc-World by demonstrating ethnographically and through the lens of culture that external forces can never determine the meanings or effects that any particular idea or commodity will come to have in a "local setting," for such is always a complex social arena in which any number of mediating factors come to bear.[8] In sum, the local is treated as the theater where global dramas are worked out.

In contrast to these views, I treat the local as a discursive construct that results from the impulse to map processes, practices, and phenomena. It has no a priori spatial or social form. The local is the outcome of power-laden processes through which the social gets defined and differentiated spatially. Viewed thus, it can be any size and can articulate with any other spatial or social categories.[9]

The local in Liverpool is not epiphenomenal to the global. It does not provide "cultural context" but produces the very idea of it. The local is an artifact of discourses that map notions of "cultural particularity" onto the city.[10] The local is a profoundly political positioning, one that emerged out of the still-unfolding history of British modernity. In Liverpool, the local gives expression to the city's ostensible cultural difference vis-à-vis England and/or Britain, depending on the context. And the premier signifier of that difference is Liverpool's relationship to the sea, as embodied in men and ships dropping anchor and setting sail. The global is used—within the city and without—as the starting point of discourses that set Liverpool apart from its national context, notwithstanding the shipping industry's death. And although Liverpudlians invoke the city's irreducible globalness in glowing terms, it is also a lightning rod for jointly racialized and gendered anxieties. Yet the ultimate irony of the local's globalness lay in the fact that Liverpool once inserted itself into out-of-the-way places only to become one itself. The fact that an international port can become remote bespeaks more than the vicissitudes of economics and politics in the fate of the city's shipping industry; it suggests the importance of place as an axis of power relations. Why does place matter? What is Liverpool remote from? Liverpool's marginality owes not to its geographic location—for example, as a seaport that lost its competitive edge to other ports. Rather, that marginality owes to Liverpool's *historical* dislocation. The postcolonial subjectivity expressed in Liverpool autobiographies refers to the insuperable loss of the city's stature as the producer of global, nay imperial, economic relationships.

The section that follows isolates O'Mara's text because it was the only one written in the colonial era. The subsequent section historicizes the concomitant declines of Britain's empire and Liverpool's fortunes. It shows Liverpool's abrupt transformation from a "gateway of empire" (Lane 1987) to an "out-of-the-way place" whose population finds itself displaced "by powerful discourses on civilization and progress" to draw on Anna Tsing's formulation about another national context (1993: 7–8). The final section treats the fall of shipping as the central motif in what are essentially tales of postcolonial Liverpool selfhood—as Whites experience it. That section also draws links between the "Liverpool culture" they gather almost exclusively around themselves, on the one hand, and the eminent "Liverpoolness" of Blacks' own cultural practices on the other.

A Tale of Two Liverpools: Chapter One

Pat O'Mara, author of *Autobiography of a Liverpool Irish Slummy*, does not provide a clear sense of when his story begins, but a few benchmarks, along with the book's 1933 publication date, suggest that we enter Liverpool at the dawn of the twentieth century. The book's first order of business is to give place a distinct, indelible personality—the better to explain the self that later comes into focus. Liverpool, he tells us in the opening paragraph, is "the greatest seaport in the world" (3). If this sounds vainglorious, one need only read on to the next paragraph, where a distinct ambivalence rushes in. O'Mara proposes to take us on a walking tour of the city, much like Scott did in introducing me to Liverpool. "But before we look at Liverpool," he instructs us to

> glance swiftly across the Mersey to Birkenhead, biggest city in lovely Cheshire . . . beautiful rural-seaside Cheshire. Strange people over here, very quiet and very English—as the few of us sensitive Irish slummy children knew whenever our periodic "Bank Holiday" excursions to such delightful places as Egremont, Seacombe, and New Brighton would be made. This was the land of the "One-eyed" people—a sarcastic nickname given them by less shrewd Liverpudlians. The Mersey separated us. It was an effective separation. Now if we look to the left [to Liverpool], as our overhead train drones peacefully along, we see an entirely different picture. It, also, is England, but how different from that across in Cheshire! That low-lying structure in the immediate foreground is the Sailors' Home. Here, sailormen of every color and race commingle, sign on, get paid off. Usually . . . they take their entire pay-off and march across the way to the "Flag of all Nations," that big alehouse . . . so named because of the diverse flags bedecking its interior. Here they meet the pimps and, after the pimps, the whores from Brassey Street in the South-End and Scotland Road in the North-End, or the semi-whores and semi-pimps (out o' workers), or the numerous begging children, the progeny of the last-named. Then begins a brief and torrid festival, ending sometimes fatally and nearly always tragically. (3–4)

The Englishness of those strange, quiet people over there in the "lovely Cheshire" throws the "Irish slumminess" of children like himself into blunt relief. It does not seem like one finds many English people in Liverpool, which is not quiet, never mind delightful. Yet, O'Mara points out, Liverpool *is* actually part of England—even if only technically or ironically so. Otherwise, why make such a point of the fact that this, too, is England? After so clarifying, he paints an ugly little picture of the goings-on over at the Flag of all Nations alehouse. O'Mara makes the name of that pub so conspicuous that its welcoming overtones of international brotherhood become ironic. The Flag of all Nations is a reference point in a narrative meant to clarify that Liverpool is, in fact, England. Yet the description of its carnivalesque sociality ensures that the reader will never confuse Liverpool for an ordinary English locale.

In the next passage, he takes us up to the city's famous north end, to Scotland Road, which is the site of the authentic Liverpool for Whites past and present. The Irishness of that place is interrupted only by the presence of global-colonial seamen who buy from the women at its world-renowned market:

> Over there, meandering northward, lies that acme of all British slums, the internationally famous Scotland Road. Midway in this thoroughfare stands Paddy's Market, also internationally known, where the refuse of the Empire is bought and sold. Old clothes, old boots, bits of oilcloth, turbans, frayed domestic and foreign underthings—to sell such stuff brazen female hawkers seated on the flag-floor lure Coolies, Chinamen, African Negroes and other Empire Builders with [a] consumptive cackle. (4–5)

From there, O'Mara's narrative morphs into a quasi-sociological treatise. Here he shows the spiraling effect of these female hawkers' poverty:

> Just across from Paddy's Market stands Richmond Row, where, in its squalid shacks—sleeping sometimes ten in a single room for threepence a night—live most of these transient women hawkers. The majority of these young women, after peddling their wares in or outside the Market, sally forth at night toward Lime Street, there to barter anew—this time with their bodies, up alleys, for a mere pittance and to anyone, regardless of color or race. After such nocturnal forays they meander homeward, get drunk on methylated spirits, engage in internecine warfare, and usually end the night in that stumpy little structure up the road, the Rose Hill lock-up. (5)

O'Mara goes on to describe the Working Boy's Home, where the city's destitute children could get some tea, bread, a pair of boots, and "a bed, to sustain them while they scour the city for work" (5). From there, it is on to the Brownlow Hill Workhouse, where impoverished men, women, and children do the city's most demeaning work for no pay, living in borrowed clothing that must be returned after they have completed the sentence they have served for being hungry. The workhouse, writes O'Mara, is occupied "mostly by wretches tired of battling for existence on the outside, who have come here to stop worrying, to work and to die. It is a lost city" (7). I risk the cliché by suggesting that O'Mara's portrait is something out of Dickens, who was not long since gone by the time this book was published. Unfortunately, though, O'Mara is not writing fiction. Alive to the importance of his ethnographic account, he writes,

> Perhaps, haphazardly, the better class of people around whom most English literature centers, have heard of the Workhouse, the Test House, "Cob" Hall and the other landmarks of Liverpool. But they have no actual contact with them. These institutions are part and parcel of the sinewy arteries that branch off from these seven miles of docks and comprise the slums—a bit of Ireland united, save in religion. (10)

This is a Liverpool one would want to enter only in the comforts of a text—and even then, only barely so. With its edgy, cynical tone and sober content, this introduction braces the reader for the many awful details to come. And if, by the end of the first chapter, the faintest trace of Englishness—which O'Mara associates with the forms of class privilege, elitism, and respectability characteristic of the quaint and quiet Cheshire—might still be detectable in Liverpool, the next chapter's depiction of the Brick Street environs wipes it out. That neighborhood is foreign in every conceivable way.

> Such is a brief outline of the significant places in Liverpool that I knew best. . . . Most of my early life was spent on Brick Street, a street of abominably overcrowded shacks near by. Negroes, Chinese, Mulattos, Filipinos, almost every nationality under the sun, most of them boasting white wives and large half-caste families. . . . Not only were these ugly tribal-scarred fellows from the West Coast of Africa accepted by white women as equals; many times they were considered the white man's superior. (11)

A later passage shows O'Mara actually enjoying the presence of such variously colored men. They lend a global character to Liverpool. Capturing the Pier Head milieu he writes of "the [River] Mersey containing ships in from all parts of the world and boasting men of every nationality—Madagascans, Lascars, Liverpudlians, Negroes, Indians, coolies, Cockneys leaning over the different ships' sides counselling us in their variant languages" (84). The internationalism of the city, marked by the language of these men, invites O'Mara to treat Liverpudlians as one nation and Cockneys as another.

In O'Mara's autobiography, the global comes to life as a meaningful cultural category. Internationalism is constitutive of Liverpool, rather than entering it from the outside. Yet the city's globalness was also paradoxical. He defines the city not through a generic internationalism but through a racial one. At any given moment, an unlimited array of the world's men would have been docked in Liverpool. But O'Mara focuses on the empire builders. In the very process of being marked by race, the global is also gendered and sexualized. He renders the presence of colonial men acceptable everywhere except around Brick Street. At the Sailors' Home, the Flag of all Nations, Paddy's Market, and the docks, their presence is fleeting. In these places, they remain seamen. They're just passing through. Brick Street, by contrast, introduces the problem of semen. They are here to stay. They produce "large" half-caste families. White women's practices recast Liverpool's globalness. Before we arrived at Brick Street, the women were only bartering their bodies with these men, which seemed acceptable in view of the women's poverty. In now marrying these colored men, White women invert imperial hierarchies and cement Liverpool's un-Englishness. The global does not refer us to the spread or scale of social phenomena but to the racial and gender politics of movement within and beyond Liverpool.

In other respects, O'Mara implies that this place is the very picture of English society, even if not Englishness. Liverpool's landmarks are workhouses and boys' homes. Since these sites testify to the grave effects of class subordination—so basic to English society—they should be better known. Likewise, he writes of

"that *acme* of all British slums, the internationally famous Scotland Road."
Liverpool is exceptional for being so very characteristic of England/Britain. It
also has many claims to world fame. The whole world knows about Paddy's
Market and the slums of Scotland Road.

As he continues, the positioning of Liverpool and Liverpudlians vis-à-vis
Englishness and Britishness becomes more fluid and contradictory. O'Mara
proudly declares himself British, despite the dissonance entailed in being an Irish
slummy in England. He describes Liverpool as the most Irish city outside of
Ireland—which is quite enough to render it beyond the pale of Englishness in
this period (19). But Britishness is another matter. Recalling his years at "an
English school filled mainly with Irish-Catholic boys," he says this:

> The British always won wars—not the English, but the British—giving the impres-
> sion that we were all more or less brothers under the skin, the Irish, the English, the
> Welsh and Scotch. . . . We were the kingpins; and we were always in the right—these
> are the straight, patriotic impressions that remain. And then came religion—and ah!
> that was something else again. . . . The best I can say is that what I derived from my
> elementary English-Irish schooling was an intense love for the British Empire and an
> equally intense hatred for England as opposed to Ireland. . . . But we children at
> school, despite the intense religious atmosphere of the Catholic school, were rather
> patriotized and Britishized—until we got back to our shacks, where we were sternly
> Irishized. . . . The paradox has remained in my make-up for years. (75)

Two key factors distinguish Liverpool from England in O'Mara's view. First,
Liverpool is unavoidably an international space and second, it is a site of defiant
and proud, if subordinated, Irishness.[11] In their encounters with international
sailors, Liverpudlians become one national group among others. Language dif-
ferentiates them from Cockneys, while religion is the key signifier of Irish difference from the English. Britishness, while important, belongs to the larger sphere
of world politics, in relation to which the Liverpool Irish are invited to stick their
chests out. Otherwise, O'Mara uses Britain to highlight Liverpool's exceptional
status. The city's slums are the acme of the general British variety.

The end of O'Mara's autobiography sees him in Baltimore, where he had been
working as a taxi driver for some twelve years. The detail he leaves us with, on
the very last page of a three-hundred-page volume, is of him enjoying Conrad's
colonial classic, *Heart of Darkness*.

FROM GATEWAY TO OUT-OF-THE-WAY

Scholarly stories of globalization tell of places worldwide being transformed by
mobile capital, commodities, people, and cultural influences. Liverpool's history,
or stories about it, moves in reverse.[12] After having enjoyed an illustrious career as
the enabler of global mobility, it becomes an out-of-the-way place, the constitutive outside of British discourses on civilization and progress. Liverpool's current
marginality vis-à-vis Britain provides a case study in what Lisa Rofel describes as

"[t]he active processes by which projects of power and knowledge crafted in the name of modernity . . . both encompass and abandon the subalterns they create, leaving them to maneuver along the boundaries of inclusion and exclusion" (1999: 13).

In what follows, I historicize the shipping industry with an eye toward analyzing its place in the making and unmaking of "Liverpool." The local emerges as a powerful, if contradictory, cultural positioning forged not in response or reaction to the global, but in the context of national contestations that date at least as far back as the late eighteenth century and continue to unfold in the present. On the one hand, the local was born of elite desires to construct a lofty, respectable image for Liverpool, given a larger national context in which the status of being "not London" marked a place as provincial. No matter how "global" it was, Liverpool was always already a faraway outpost of the metropole, subject to the capital's status as the standard-bearer of civilization. On the other hand, the bourgeoisie did such a good job elevating Liverpool's self-image that the local ultimately came to mark a proud position of cultural difference not only from London but from the nation as a whole.

Liverpool's economy was built on a single industry, but it was quite a complex and variegated one. Its most spectacular growth occurred in the mid-nineteenth century, and owed to the rationalization and coordination of its many parts: shipping, shipbuilding, banking, warehousing, docking, as well as regional transportation and dock administration to name a few. Liverpool was a nerve center, a "global city" in Saskia Sassen's terms (1991). Liverpool manufactured next-to-nothing. But it provided transportation for everything: piece-goods (one trillion items in 1857 alone), coal, iron bars, rails, hoops, rods, and pigs; linen, manufactured goods, pottery, copper, metals, cotton yarns, and machinery (Hyde 1971: 40–41). The railway network it built and controlled in the north of England allowed commodities to flow within Lancashire and out of it to the rest of the world. In addition to manufactured goods, the region's main exports were coal and salt. The circulation of those two materials set off a technological chain reaction: they were used for the manufacture of chemicals, causing advances in the production of textiles and soda, which led to innovations in the making of glass and soap, the latter requiring fats, which were procured from West Africa in the form of palm oil, a commodity that gave direct rise to the presence and eventual settlement of West African seamen in nineteenth-century Liverpool.[13] At the height of its powers, just prior to World War I, Liverpool's port handled 36 percent of Britain's export trade, and 22 to 24 percent of its imports (Hyde 1971: 128).[14]

Interestingly, all accounts of the city's shipping industry of which I am aware—even the popular ones—make some attempt to set the record straight on slavery. For generations, Britons from within the city and without have called upon Liverpool historians to explain or otherwise acknowledge the city's role in the slave trade (chapter 7). But scarcely do critics or scholars problematize the concrete role that British shippers played in colonialism.[15] Of course, as I suggested in chapter 1, early twentieth-century Britain provides myriad examples of the inextricable links between colony and metropole, wherein the imperial interests in places like Sierra Leone demanded the peaceful negotiation of race relations in Liverpool and other ports. But there is a lot more to this story, as the following sentence betrays: "The dream of opening up West Africa to Liverpool had continued to influence the thoughts and actions of McGregor Laird." He was one of the city's most important shipping magnates. Historian Frank Hyde, author of the sentence, goes on to say this:

> In 1852 he, together with other Liverpool and London men, formed the African Steam Ship Company with a direct service between Britain and ports on the West African coast. The small steamships for this company were built by Lairds. A Charter was granted giving the directors rights and privileges in the development of their trading connections and a mail contract was also negotiated. At first, the company achieved a moderate success, the prospects were excellent, so much so that in 1869 there seemed to be good grounds for the creation of a competitive line. Accordingly, in that year, the British & African Steam Navigation Company was formed. Although the firm originated in Glasgow, its vessels sailed from Liverpool from the start. Liverpool once again became involved directly in the organization of West African trade and, through this, indirectly in the political and economic policies of the region as a whole. (1971: 61)

This passage is the height of nonchalance. The impending colonial control to which the author alludes should arouse no particular concern. "Opening up West Africa" appears here as one capitalist's dream. Perhaps his sexual fantasy. Indeed, according to Hyde, Laird does not seek satisfaction for himself, but for Liverpool. Or maybe Laird *is* Liverpool. Hyde evokes the geopolitics of business through the image of masculine figures. We see the desires and concrete actions of *London* men and *Liverpool* men. But he also imbues place with agency: "Liverpool" is doing at least as much as McGregor Laird.

Hyde's language makes place and person inextricable. That relation reflects a spatial division of labor that dates back to the industrial era. Urban areas were commonly built, if not on single industries like shipping, then on a select few of them. Such specialization made their economies interdependent—as the coal-and-salt narrative above suggests—as well as competitive.[16] In Hyde's account above, London and Liverpool are partners, but elsewhere (as we see later) these ports compete. Hyde subtly evokes this place-versus-place relation in his mention of Glasgow, whose ultimate role in "opening up West Africa" is rendered minimal in comparison to Liverpool's. In the present day, Manchester remains one of Liverpool's main rivals (the other being London), even if their competition manifests most importantly in relation to football. P. J. Waller explains their historic relationship thus: "Manchester men, Liverpool gentlemen: this familiar tag represented the antagonism between the mercantile and manufacturing functions of the cities. Mancunians alleged that they suffered from a client condition. Liverpudlians controlled both the inward movement of raw materials for Manchester industries and the outward flow of finished goods" (1983: 86). In British economic history, places feature like characters in a novel.

Mid-nineteenth-century Liverpool was populated by a growing number of Celtic groups—Scottish, Welsh, Manx, and, most problematically, Irish. As John Belchem problems. As an entertainment conglomerate, Watson has a host of trademarks, copyrighted books, songs, movies, and patented inventions for its amusement park); and

- Internet Resources (a short section is given at the end of each chapter with Internet web sites specific to the information previously discussed in that chapter).

This edition also includes a discussion of domain names as trademarks, an enhanced discussion in Chapter 3 on trademark searching, and new charts, lists, and timelines, including the following:

- timeline in Chapter 4 for intent-to-use marks;
- checklist in Chapter 4 for trademark applications;
- chart showing due dates for documents required to maintain a trademark in force;
- list of do's and don'ts for trademark use;
- chart analyzing a trademark infringement case;
- chart showing infringement remedies in trademark cybersquatting cases;
- chart showing copyright notice requirements; and
- list of copyright infringement myths.

Readers will also find new information on electronic systems at the U.S. Patent and Trademark Offices for filing trademark and patent applications, and discussion of new legislation, including the following:

- Anticybersquatting Consumer Protection Act (relating to trademarks);
- Digital Millennium Copyright Act (relating to copyrights);
- American Inventors Protection Act of 1999 (relating to patents);
- Madrid Protocol (relating to trademarks);
- Patent Law Treaty (relating to patents); and
- WIPO Internet Treaties (relating to worldwide protection of digital content).

Finally, this second edition contains enhanced discussions of piracy in the music recording industry, including updates on Napster, Kazaa, and Grokster; a discussion of new copyright protection now available for the design of vessel hulls; and a discussion of the use of the International Trade Commission as an alternative to patent infringement litigation in federal court.

Note to readers. Throughout this text, helpful web sites, fees, and addresses are given. Due to the transitory nature of some web sites and frequent changes in fees and other similar information, it is possible that such information may not be current at the time you read this text. The web site of the U.S. Patent and Trademark Office, www.uspto.gov, provides current fee and address information. Similarly, the web site of the Copyright Office, www.copyright.gov, provides up-to-date information for frequently changing topics and fees.

writes, "The Liverpool-Irish . . . have always suffered the prejudice and negative reputation which now blight the city itself" (2000: xiv). Beginning in the late eighteenth century, the Irish immigrated in the hope of escaping colonial economic exploitation in Ireland, only to confront it again within England itself. The proximity of the Irish among English people sparked fears of degeneration.[17] Despite English people's anxieties about their growing presence, Sir Robert Peel argued against "condemn[ing] too precipitately the incursion of Irish labourers into England. We must . . . consider well the advantages as well as the disadvantages of cheap labour" (quoted in Gallagher 1985: 109). With the potato famine of the late 1840s, their numbers grew exponentially into the hundreds of thousands (Gilley and Swift 1985). In the first half of 1847 alone, 300,000 Irish people immigrated to England, with many remaining in their port of arrival, Liverpool (Gallagher 1985: 107). In all their numbers and in their complete impoverishment, they overwhelmed the social resources of the city, especially in terms of housing and health care. They suffered from poverty-related diseases including typhus (dubbed "Irish fever"), which rationalized their segregation into the already overcrowded slums, where they were said to drink excessively. Many Irish settlers had the additional misfortune of being Catholic in Protestant England. There were some English Roman Catholics in Liverpool, though, and some tended to the medical care of their Irish counterparts. But generally "the divisions of class, culture and nationality proved greater than the bonds of shared religion" (Gallagher 1985: 108). Conversely, the intractable religious divide between Irish Protestants and Irish Catholics proved greater than any cultural and national bonds they might have shared. The politics of class and religion that defined the Irish Catholic presence in Liverpool has had precipitous and far-reaching effects that extend into the present day.[18]

Liverpool's bourgeoisie, for its part, was ethnically diverse. Many were born in Ireland, Wales, and Scotland. The English among them hailed from points beyond Liverpool. The finance, insurance, and shipping moguls who steered the city's economy in the latter half of the nineteenth century were lured from "the farms and fields of their ancestors" (Hyde 1971: 46). Not only were these elites born outside the city, but they scarcely resided there. As importers and exporters, they were no less the travelers than the seamen they hired. Liverpool was merely a convenient base, the occasional port of call for their thoroughly global operations. Their children, who were expected to maintain the family's high station, were educated outside of Liverpool in the prestigious British and continental universities where they could make business connections (Lane 1987: 65).

Over the course of the nineteenth century, these mobile capitalists were criticized for failing to invest in Liverpool and for showing no interest in its settled and largely impoverished population. In response, they fashioned themselves into "old families," a designation that carried an air of aristocratic indigenousness and social legitimacy. The importance of these elite families' assertions of rootedness, says sociologist Tony Lane, is still evident: "By the 1950s none were left to wield significant economic or political power, although their influence has in other ways proved remarkably durable: the proud rhetoric they used to insist the stature of Liverpool as a world class city sent down deep roots amongst all classes of the people" (1987: 54). Through various projects sketched below, they crafted a distinct identity for themselves and the city.

Members of Liverpool's bourgeoisie distinguished themselves from the grit and grime of manufacturing, associated with the rest of northern England, by styling themselves as gentlemanly capitalists. Still their wealth did not in itself secure their respectability. To become acceptably bourgeois in a city of such misery, the old families were put upon to engage in myriad and sundry philanthropic efforts (Simey 1951). Some were more disingenuous than others, as observers of the time noted (Walton and Wilcox 1991). For the impoverished people on whom it was showered, this aid came at a high price, for philanthropists in the Victorian era represented the poor as the problem. They and their intractable social ills were pushing available resources past their limits. The bourgeoisie also contributed to a racializing discourse about "darkest England," a term that William Booth, founder of the Salvation Army, used to describe the working classes of London and Liverpool. They were no more civilized, he opined, than Africans. Philanthropic organizations were also hotbeds of eugenicist thought. All told, the ideologies espoused by these "friends" of the poor rationalized their subordination.

By the mid-nineteenth century, Liverpool was nationally known as a city built on slave trading. The mercantile elite responded by blaming outsiders for this trade (Arline Wilson 1998: 61). As part of a more long-term strategy, they elevated the city's most passionate abolitionist, William Roscoe, to the status of Liverpool icon. Roscoe was even more useful for having authored a biography of Lorenzo de'Medici, the Florentine who was as famous for his patronage of the arts as for his commercial prowess. De'Medici was an inspiration to Liverpool shippers and merchants, who had already been pressured to invest their wealth in more socially beneficial ways. And so they brought Culture to Liverpool, hoping to counter the view that their cares were limited to commodities and profits—a view that had been circulating around England for some fifty years. In 1795 one observer noted that

> Arts and sciences are inimical to the spot, absorbed in the nautical vortex, the only pursuit of the inhabitants is COMMERCE. . . . Liverpool is the only town in England of any pre-eminency that has not one single erection or endowment, for the advancement of science, the cultivation of the arts, or promotion of useful knowledge . . . the liberal arts are a species of merchandize in which few of the inhabitants are desirous to deal, unless for exportation. (Quoted in Arline Wilson 1998: 56)

Institutions concerned with arts and letters sprang up in this moment and flowered through the nineteenth century. Literary and philosophical societies promoted intellectual debates and the dissemination of scientific knowledge in the interest of modernity, which they understood as continual future-oriented progress. Architecture, also a measure of civilization, provided further topics for discussion in these circles. All of these developments were meant to enhance Liverpool's national image. London was commonly the reference point through which professional elites assessed the modernity of their own city and selves. At once, they sought to attract London's attention while also superseding that city's achievements and, therein, ensuring its future irrelevance. In 1890, one Liverpool writer offered up this spectacular vision in an article titled "The Future Supremacy of Liverpool":

> From Liverpool to Manchester will run continuous quays, on which will be discharged and loaded merchandise from all parts of the world. Around these quays will spring up streets, squares, manufactories, mills, offices—all that goes to make a great city. . . . This vast city will be the greatest and richest ever known to the world. . . . London, compared to it is out of the way. . . . [W]hoever lives long enough will find the great city on the banks of the Mersey will be the commercial city of the future. (Quoted in Belchem 2000: 4)

As Liverpool entered the twentieth century, its educated citizens worried that this world city still lacked a comprehensive, authoritative History worthy of it. In preparation for the upcoming seven hundredth anniversary of Liverpool's founding, such a History was supplied. Liverpool's modernity was constituted in the pages of Ramsay Muir's 1907 account, *A History of Liverpool*. Belchem argues that Muir rendered most of Liverpool's past inconsequential in order to throw into relief the remarkable progress of the modern city (2000). Just as important, Muir wrote for a popular Liverpudlian audience as well as a scholarly one, portending future trends.[19] Prior to the publication of Muir's account, the only Liverpudlians who were producing histories were those who saw modernity as a threat. The middle classes (as opposed to the commercial elite) were anxious about the progress enveloping them. Antiquarian societies sought to produce what they called "local history," which would proudly distinguish Liverpudlians from metropolitan, aristocratic culture by capturing the pristine glory of the region surrounding Liverpool before the onslaught of industrialization (Kidd 1998).

The projects outlined above provide a sampling of the labors that went into the making of "Liverpool," the idea. Historians, the middle classes, moguls, and would-be aristocrats responded in their own, often self-interested ways to critiques of the city and themselves emanating from within Liverpool and without. A specter of grand proportions, "London" provided a major impetus for these projects. Another lay in the quest for legitimacy among a wealthy, tiny, and mobile elite. The origins of Liverpudlians' notorious exceptionalism, what Belchem aptly calls "Merseypride" (2000), lay in these nineteenth-century efforts to boost or otherwise craft an image of the city in the national eye and the local imagination.

The beginning of the end of Liverpool's shipping industry coincides with that of the British Empire.[20] Early signs of Britain's imperial decline are visible at the turn of the century. Much of the difficulty was political. The Boer War of 1899–1903 proved costly in human and monetary terms and lasted much longer than Britain ever expected. The independence of South Africa in 1910 further exposed the difficulty of territorial expansion. Likewise, the difficulty of maintaining colonial rule in so many far-flung colonies was exposed in the single year 1919 when nationalist movements and uprisings occurred across a host of British colonies (May and Cohen 1974). Even in the era of high imperialism (the late

1880s and 1890s), Britain's economic strategies betrayed its tenuous hold over foreign markets. In what follows, Hobsbawm traces the roots of Britain's ultimate decline to that earlier period:

> Britain exported her immense accumulated historic advantages in the underdeveloped world, as the greatest commercial power, and as the greatest source of international loan capital; and had in reserve the exploitation of the "natural protection" of the home market and if need be the "artificial protection" of political control over a large empire. When faced with a challenge, it was easier and cheaper to retreat into an as yet unexploited part of one of these favoured zones rather than meet competition face to face. (1969: 191)

In his 1933 autobiography, Pat O'Mara wrote that "the British always won the wars." The Suez Canal crisis of 1956 ushered in a new era. Opened in 1870, the Suez Canal was central to Britain's mercantile economy. It provided a shorter route to India and the Far East, and was much more cost efficient, owing to the ease of passage it provided for the steamships that had, since the 1860s, become the cutting edge of shipping technology. Under British control, the Suez Canal provided British shippers near-exclusive access, which disrupted the balance of trade previously existing among other commercial partners.[21] In the 1950s, Britain's attempt to maintain control of the Suez Canal by illegitimate, covert means had to be aborted in full view of the world. Much to Britain's humiliation, newly independent India played a key role in the United Nations negotiations that resulted in this totally unprecedented check on British military power. Decolonization and cold war politics produced a new world order. Britain lost more than its control over a vital conduit of trade; it lost its powerful aura of independence and invincibility. The shipping industry, for its part, held on in this transitional period, engaging in a robust trade with Britain's present and former colonies. But dependence on that trade was part of Britain's problem, as Hobsbawm suggests above.

Like the British Empire that it helped to constitute, Liverpool's shipping industry declined in fits and starts. During its boom period, the 1850s through 1914, shipping and finance magnates sat in local government or held other positions of great influence (Hyde 1971: 210). Under their stewardship, the city's economy developed in almost completely commercial terms. Since there was little impetus to build or invest in enterprises unrelated to Liverpool's phenomenal cash cow, its economy was left completely vulnerable to national and global forces.

The city's fortunes had always depended on world peace, as the onset of World War I made plainer than ever. Merchant ships became war ships, and the ports gave in, if not to outright state control then to the military's formidable demands. Meanwhile, the merchant fleets of Japan, France, and the United States emerged as powerful competitors, serving Britain's domestic and foreign markets. Liverpool shipping lost its edge by the war's end. The years that followed brought a major decline in worldwide trade and record-high unemployment rates.[22] In port cities, the recession was felt on the streets. Although Black and White men did wartime service together, back in Britain the presence of Black men became an irritant to their unemployed White counterparts. A series of race riots occurred across the country and the world in the single year 1919 (May and Cohen 1974). As I mentioned in chapter 1, a West Indian seaman, Charles Wootton, was mobbed and chased into the River Mersey to the chant of "let him drown."[23]

Foreign competition grew in strength in the 1920s and 1930s, a period also marked by worldwide depression. Liverpool's economy was further devastated by industrial capital's mobility within England. In the late 1930s, northern manufacturing concerns realized that their foreign markets were better accessed through the ports of London and Southampton, and so they moved their operations out of Lancashire and down to the Midlands to be closer to them (Lane 1987: 36). A few decades later, with the rise of the European Common Market, British trade with the continent grew in importance, a development that left Liverpool "marooned on the wrong side of the country" (45).

The decline of Liverpool shipping was steady, but erratic. In the 1950s, the industry bounced back, only to face its ultimate demise in the 1980s.[24] Indeed, since shipping itself was so variegated, the decline was felt differently within its various sectors. There were numerous kinds of ships (containers, trailers, cargo liners, passenger liners, and so on), each of which underwent shifts in usage and availability. As Lane notes,

> Throughout the postwar years the number of British ships and the number of seamen have consistently fallen. In 1950 there were over 3,300 ships but by the end of 1984 only 940 or so. This huge reduction in fleet size embraces a number of other changes [including] . . . the decline of empire, the expansion of trade with Europe, changes in types of ship, in voyage patterns, company ownership, size of crew and division of labour. (1986: 7)

Elsewhere Lane states that "at any time after the Second World War until the mid-1970s there were only the odd months when a seaman would find it hard to get a job. . . . With a ready availability of ships and a complete spectrum of trades and world regions to choose from, it was an entirely normal thing to move around and be apparently footloose" (22).

The steady decline in Liverpool's economic viability since the 1930s is reflected most dramatically in the migration of its citizens. Pat O'Mara wrote *Autobiography of a Liverpool Irish Slummy* as an immigrant. Every successive national census of the United Kingdom since 1931 has shown a continual and at times precipitous drop in Liverpool's population, from a high of 856,000 in 1931 to a low of 481,000 in 1991. The biggest declines occurred between 1961 and 1971, with a decrease of 131,000 people, and between 1971 and 1981, with a decrease of 93,000 (Laverty 2003: 33). Given a national culture in which place is equated with personhood, and given the love of Liverpool so successfully cultivated over all these years, what can such drastic population loss mean?

In the study from which I have drawn so heavily, Francis Hyde traces the rise of Liverpool's port over the impressive time span of almost three hundred years. Despite his attempts at optimism, his conclusion offers what amounts to an obituary of the shipping industry. Ten years later, a journalist was moved to offer another (and oft-quoted) postmortem—not for the shipping industry but for the city itself: "They should build a fence around Liverpool and charge admission, for sadly it has become a 'showcase' of everything that has gone wrong in Britain's major cities" (quoted in Lane 1987: 13). In the earlier-quoted passage from *The Atlantic Sound*, Caryl Phillips updated that view, writing in 2000 that the city had long been succumbing to "violence, unemployment, poverty and depression at a rate far in excess of other British cities." And, in point of fact, Liverpool's unemployment rate, as of 2001, stood at 7.1 percent, which is more than twice the national average (Liverpool City Council 2002: 11). The facts themselves are not necessarily in dispute; rather, it is the point of the facts chosen that I find significant. Those facts, more often than not, refer us to Liverpool as "the worst of Britain." The origins of Liverpudlians' uniqueness claims may very well lie in the nineteenth century. But Britons from places other than Liverpool seem to rehearse the Liverpool-is-unique argument as much as Liverpudlians themselves, albeit toward different ends and with different effects.[25]

The marginalization of northern England, described briefly in chapter 1, came to a head in the era of British decline. Before the fall, the North was associated with the industrial worker. In the period of deindustrialization, the North was associated with the unemployed worker (Rawnsley 2000). Always the sign of excess, Liverpool is associated with the unemployable worker. In search of reasons why, one continually confronts the ready-made and eminently place-y explanation that Britons of all stripes (academics, politicians, journalists, business people) bring to bear, indeed, whenever "Liverpool" bears explaining. The shipping industry, and its docking concerns in particular, were notoriously exploitative. Dockers made up a casual labor force hired on a day-to-day basis. Those dynamics are marshaled in order to explain the recalcitrance of Liverpool workers. "Long after the decline of the docks, shipping and casualism," Belchem writes, "Liverpool workers continued to protest against workplace impositions and innovations—national agreements, bureaucratic structures and new work practices—which denied their residual independence and democratic local autonomy" (2000: 213).[26] Backed by strong, paternalistic labor unions, dockers were given to frequent striking, which remains the image of Liverpool workers. For that reason, businesses have refrained from building or investing in the city (Massey 1994).

Liverpool represents, in excess, everything that is wrong with Britain. It gets singled out for excessive striking because that practice stems from the "peculiarities" of the shipping industry which, along with the sea itself, pass as the undisputed foundations of the city's "unique" culture. John Belchem suggests, "To unsympathetic observers 'militant' Merseyside represented the 'British disease' at its worst" (2000: 214).[27] The national malady in question consists of chronically high inflation, low industrial productivity, slow or no growth in the number of jobs or in the gross national product—in short, the barely working capitalism of the 1960s and 1970s (see chapter 3) that Margaret Thatcher pledged to fix.

Liverpool's culture of work is not the only example of its waywardness. In the early 1980s, Liverpudlians voted a radical left wing party, Militant Tendency, into local government. Militant was way too left for the Labour Party, especially given the times. In the early 1990s, the Labour Party was struggling to reconstitute its national image from that of "loony leftism" (a Conservative Party caricature of all progressive or even slightly liberal-leaning political agendas) to the centrism that would make the party viable in national elections. Liverpool became a whipping boy. Political commentary in the national press became absorbed with the question of whether Militant was really out of the city for good.[28] Bad Liverpool.

Nationwide, Scousers are stereotyped as criminals, an inscription that begins in the seaport days. Since people were so poor, incoming foreign seamen became the hapless targets of the locals. Of course, seaport or no seaport, wherever there is poverty there is crime. Perhaps Liverpool's association with crime has stuck because the victims were associated with the sea and because Liverpool never escapes the marking "seaport." In 1999 Jack Straw, the home secretary, visited Liverpool, whereupon some officials apprised him of a crime prevention program they had developed, one that might serve as a national model. Visiting the upstanding citizens of Milton Keynes a few days later, Straw told some journalists about his meetings in Liverpool, offering these remarks: "I thought: 'What the devil is this? You know what Scousers are like, they are always up to something.'" He then added, "Please do not repeat that to anyone from Liverpool." These remarks caused a furor. Liverpool officials' attempt to contribute something worthwhile for Britain as a whole is "humorously" discredited. In this context it is worth noting a link between the categories "Scouser" and "Black." Both are indelibly associated with criminality and are hence disqualified from dominant notions of Englishness. To be English is to be law-abiding. The principle of law is the cornerstone of English civilization (Gilroy 1987: 72–79).[29] The 1981 racialized riots in Liverpool are also a sign of criminal, indeed violent, excess. Not only were they worst among the dozens that occurred that year but, as the film *Riot* clarified, they were the worst riots, racial or otherwise, in twentieth-century Britain.

Localism characterizes British communities as a whole. But Liverpool has too much of it. Indeed, Liverpudlians' community pride can actually be used against them. When, in 1993, two ten-year-old boys killed a two-year-old, James Bulger, the tragedy provoked questions about what is wrong with Liverpool, not Britain. The national press demanded to know: Where is all that community spirit that Liverpudlians are so boastful of? In response to Liverpudlians' own emotional responses to the event, one famous journalist dubbed Liverpool "the self pity city." The physicality of place featured in explanations of the crime. In chapter 1, I quoted a writer for the *New Yorker* who explained in a "Letter from Liverpool" how these murders could have happened. The city's degraded landscape is, if not the cause, then at least a significant factor in the production of the city's unique society, its utter difference from England.

The roofs of houses stretch to the horizon: pebble-dash semis, low prefabs, dirt-encrusted red brick row houses, mock-Tudors, a handful of high-rises, boarded-up shops. A large, squat pub called the Mons—"short for the Monstrosity," say the locals—stands, in its bleak anonymity, *as the inverse* of whatever cozy virtue English pubs once had. This is a landscape emptied of energy and innovation—a city that no longer knows what to do with itself." (Emphasis added)[30]

Football is the national sport, of course, and English fandom in international competitions has been known to reach a violent pitch. Within England, though, it is Liverpool where fandom runs afoul. In the wake of the Hillsborough disaster of 1991, in which ninety-five visiting fans of the Liverpool Football Club were crushed to death, the press accused Liverpudlians of being, first, to blame for the tragedy and, second, disingenuous in their grief—the "self pity city" again. The national tabloid, the *Sun*, actually likened the fans to animals. The song that serves as the Liverpool Football Club's anthem, "You'll Never Walk Alone," expresses their sense of a common identity forged in marginality: no matter what, we have each other. Some detractors of those sensibilities have produced a Web site that parodies Liverpool pride. Its address features the line, "You'll Never Work Again."

Liverpool never occupies a middle position on any scale through which British society is understood. The precise means through which Liverpool is made to exemplify Britain also sets the city apart from it. Since the decline of its shipping empire, this city has fallen from any semblance of whatever grace it once had. Formerly a symbol and enabler of Britain's own globalness as a maritime empire, Liverpool has been reconstituted as a site of, again, intractable localism—and this, in a country that is world renowned for its own insularity. To wit, if Liverpudlians, at least since the days of O'Mara, have drawn on the city's status as an international seaport to construct Liverpool as "not England," many Britons use their country's island geography to render Britain "not Europe." Since the formation of the European Economic Community (later the European Union), various British governments—most notoriously, Thatcher's—have refrained from joining fully for fear of compromising Britain's political and economic autonomy and its "unique" heritage and culture. Yet Liverpool's insularity is excessive. And the worst part of it is, those recalcitrant Scousers refuse to try to redeem themselves! They remain impervious to Britain's erstwhile attempts at its own reinvention, socially, politically, and economically—or so the argument goes.[31]

Liverpool's fundamental outsider status manifests palpably in the autobiographies written after the concomitant fall of the British Empire and Liverpool's shipping industry. The authors struggle to rehabilitate Liverpool. Their pages wreak of a postcolonial dislocation defined, in the first instance, by the profound sense of loss they express for the era when Liverpool was a thriving seaport—important to Britain and the world—and, in the second instance, by Liverpool's descent into complete marginality.

A TALE OF TWO LIVERPOOLS: CHAPTER TWO

LBBs have constituted themselves as a group by arguing that the local is just as legitimate a basis of identity for Blacks as ethnicity. But the residual authority of ethnicity discourse leaves some LBBs to ponder, What is our culture? Do we have one? They point out that their West African and Afro-Caribbean parents, as well as the Somalis and Chinese of south Liverpool, all have their distinct customs, foods, and languages. LBBs, meanwhile, speak just like White Liverpudlians. Many LBBs grew up eating the African foods prepared by their fathers but are otherwise critical of these men for withholding African culture from them. The culture question betrays the downside of the uniqueness idiom. Cecelia argued strenuously to me that to be LBB was fundamentally to *lack* culture because LBBs do not speak a distinct language. Caroline said the same; Somalis, she told me, "have their own culture," while LBBs do not. Claire derided young people for not being able to cook "cultural food," a reference to African dishes.

White Liverpudlians claim to have lots of culture. They have culture to spare. They can and do pinpoint its unique content, and they name all of it *Scouse*. That term originally referred to a seamen's stew based on the Scandinavian one, "lob-scouse," which consisted of stewed meat, biscuits, and vegetables. When meat was too costly, it was excluded; in those cases it was "blind scouse." Currently, *Scouse* refers to the totality of working-class Liverpudlian culture. Working-class people are Scousers. Their accent is Scouse. They live in Scousetown. The humor to be found there is Scouse humor. Although the stew called *scouse* was popular in the first half of the twentieth century, the term *Scouser* dates only to the 1960s. Its emergence coincides with the beginning of the end for Liverpool shipping. Belchem attests to the importance of this moment in the invention of Liverpudlian tradition by noting that Pat O'Mara never uses the term *Scouser* in his 1933 autobiography (2000). The work of nineteenth-century elites who busily wrote histories of the modern city for popular consumption—interpolating readers as Liverpudlians, not Britons—and who asserted the supremacy of their city over the likes of London, and who fashioned an image of Liverpool as irreducibly global, set the stage for Scousers to assert their cultural difference. For their own part, Scousers named themselves after a seamen's stew from Scandinavia, not England.

As O'Mara sat in Baltimore reading *Heart of Darkness*, the authors of the other Liverpool autobiographies were children playing around the slums of Scotland Road. *Reflections on the Mersey*, by Frank Unwin, provides a stunning contrast to O'Mara's text and best introduces some of the prevalent themes in the others. Loss is chief among these. Unwin's memories are framed against substantial out-migration from Liverpool: many Scottie Roaders have "pulled up their roots and made their homes in other countries and other climes" (1983: 60). The possibility that Scottie Roaders might have gone to other parts of Britain goes unremarked. Indeed, Unwin uses terms that usually describe nationals to refer to Liverpudlians. He is fond of phrases like "expatriated Liverpudlians" and "Scottie Road exiles." Their emigration, and hence displacement, is from Liverpool, not Britain. And so too, he argues, has Liverpool been displaced. Unwin laments its "rapid decline as one of the world's great seaports." "Those were the days," he says, "when Liverpool seemed to be the centre of the world" (161).

The 1920s and 1930s were the best of times and the worst of times. Liverpudlians' humor, especially under duress, receives a good deal of comment. Unwin makes difficult topics easier to digest, like so: "Our neighbours were

always hard-up, hungry and deprived. But they were warm-hearted and friendly"
(10). In later describing a fascist march, Unwin writes, "That was one of the
grimmer episodes in Liverpool's history. But there was plenty of humour as
well" (145). Unwin's many references to that humor bespeak an oft-ascribed
quality of Liverpudlians: they have lived through extremely difficult times, but
their humor and strength of spirit eased their pain. Unwin, a Protestant, discusses
sectarian violence humorously, too.

> As children, we were victims of religious intolerance. Walking home alone from
> school, I was often seized by a gang of boys . . . demanding: "I or O?". Now we all
> knew what that meant—"Irish or Orange" . . . If you were a Roman Catholic you
> were assumed to be Irish, for some strange reason, and if you were a Protestant, you
> were automatically labelled "Orange". The trouble was I never knew to which group
> my captors belonged. So I had to tread very warily and try to weigh up the opposi-
> tion in an effort to give the answer that pleased them. Invariably I failed lamentably
> and gave the wrong one. Next morning I'd arrive at school sporting two black eyes
> and a squashed nose. (76–77)

The passage goes on to describe the "complete delight" he felt as a youngster observing the beautiful pageantry that attended both Roman Catholic holidays and
Protestants' celebration of Orangemen's Day.

Unwin's Liverpool is incredibly full. It is crowded with people, objects, say-
ings, food—all from long ago. With equal relish, Unwin treats events big and
small—from the three-day bombing blitz of the city in May 1941 to the day the
Liverpool Zoological Gardens were opened. The weather of 1938 is detailed ex-
haustively. With love and deepest admiration he treats every single happening
and every interesting character of the 1920s and 1930s. Yet none of these appears
without place. Be they streets, neighborhoods, music halls, or the little shop on
West Derby Road, the individual places that make up Liverpool testify to its
magic. Unwin cheerily interpolates his readers as locals by challenging them to
remember this place or that one: "One of the most picturesque areas of Liverpool
was Pitt Street, commonly called 'Chinatown'" (73); "I feel sure that there are
quite a few Merseysiders who enjoyed a cup of tea in Ma Anderson's cafe in
Dale Street" (71); "And how many Liverpudlians retain happy memories of
Hutchinson Hall, at the south end of Mill Street, Toxteth?" (74); "There used to
be plenty of good-humoured heckling at the 'Smith Street Lamp'" (75); "And
what of Dock Road?" (79); "With typical 'scouse' humour, Liverpudlians very
quickly found nicknames for many of the city's well-known places" (78); "There
are many colourful characters around Scotland Road" (82). And so on. Place,
Unwin suggests, produces very powerful forms of recall—for Liverpudlians.
"For most expatriated Liverpudlians the mere mention of a familiar place or thoroughfare brings an instant sigh of nostalgia and an excuse for a heart-warming
chat about old times" (60). He describes a letter he received from a soldier
stationed in a foreign land: "In his mind's eye, he told me, he'd walk back to
Liverpool seeing places that once seemed squalid and ugly, but were now shining
and beautiful" (61). Crucially, tracts like the one under discussion, or radio

SUPPLEMENTAL TEACHING MATERIALS

- The **Instructor's Manual with Test Bank** is available on-line at www.westlegalstudies.com in the Instructor's Lounge under Resource. Written by the author of the text, the *Instructor's Manual* contains suggested syllabi, lecture notes, answers to the text questions, useful web sites, and a test bank.

- **Online Companion™**—The Online Companion™ web site can be found at www.westlegalstudies.com in the Resource section of the web site. The Online Companion™ contains the following:
  Chapter Summaries
  Trivia
  Internet Resources
  Appendices

- **Web Page**—Come visit our web site at www.westlegalstudies.com, where you will find valuable information specific to this book such as hot links and sample materials to download, as well as other West Legal Studies products.

- **Westlaw®**—West's on-line computerized legal research system offers students "hands-on" experience with a system commonly used in law offices. Qualified adopters can receive ten free hours of Westlaw®. Westlaw® can be accessed with Macintosh and IBM PC and compatibles. A modem is required.

- **Survival Guide for Paralegal Students,** a pamphlet by Kathleen Mercer Reed and Bradene Moore, covers practical and basic information to help students make the most of their paralegal courses. Topics covered include choosing courses of study and note-taking skills.

- **West's Paralegal Video Library**—West Legal Studies is pleased to offer the following videos at no charge to qualified adopters:

  The Drama of the Law II: Paralegal Issues Video
    ISBN 0-314-07088-5

  The Making of a Case Video
    ISBN 0-314-07300-0

  ABA Mock Trial Video—Product Liability
    ISBN 0-314-07342-6

  Arguments to the United States Supreme Court Video
    ISBN 0-314-07070-2

programs like the one that inspired it, seem not to produce nostalgia. These media just reflect what, in phenomenological fashion, is always already there. In this case, it is a place to be perceived—if even in the mind's eye. A place that embodies transcendental truths of the self (if only the clutter of preconception can be cleared away), and a place that acts. What place does is produce human consciousness, experience, and action both in the form of events of long ago and the mournful recollection of them. If place can do all of that, then place must be the current that sustains life itself.

In an earlier chapter, I indicated that the 1981 riots were sparked by the attempted arrest of a young Black man, one Mr. Leroy Cooper, on a street in Liverpool 8. A few years later, journalist Ferdinand Dennis interviewed Mr. Cooper, paying special attention to his art. He was a poet, photographer, dancer, musician, and graffiti artist. Writes Dennis: "Crossing over Parliament Street, into [Princes] Road, he showed me more evidence of his handiwork. A graffiti read: 'Love life, love Liverpool'. It had been his entry in a newspaper competition for a city slogan. The readers voted it top, but the judges settled for something with a more commercial appeal" (1988: 65). The same person who, however unwittingly, became the spark of such spectacular rebellion participated in the city's effort at self-promotion and created a lovely slogan that appealed to the voting public. When the slogan was passed over, Mr. Cooper chose another way to spread his message. Dennis's references to Upper Parliament Street and Princes Road clarify that the graffiti, "Love life, love Liverpool," appears in the interracial neighborhood of Liverpool 8. This makes the slogan all the more poignant, for these streets were the site of a very violent uprising enacted in the name of racial justice. The slogan now implores racial Others of various description to love the city as much as they love life itself. And the slogan clearly struck a chord with the voting readers, many of whom were probably White. For Whites as well as Blacks such as Mr. Cooper, city and self are one and the same. To celebrate one is to affirm the other—even if race divides. People may very well imbue place with human qualities including the capacity for action, but clearly actions such as writing Liverpool autobiographies and spray-painting signs reading "Love life, love Liverpool" perform the lion's share of the work of producing place-y selves.

Unwin's own tribute to this love-worthy Liverpool is sprinkled with pregnant little references to another place, London. Its overstated appeal renders Liverpool's important achievements invisible. Unwin writes, "Tourists visiting London always make a point of visiting Madame Tussaud's famous artworks." Note the painful attempt at braggadocio here: "Once upon a time, Liverpool also boasted its waxworks" (70). Unwin's text is full of other sources of Liverpool pride, always framed in comparative perspective: "The outstanding sportsmen produced in [Merseyside] are probably more numerous than in any other part of the country" (85); "Incidentally, I wonder how many people remember that great attraction at Eastham—the Maze, which almost equalled the more famous one at Hampton Court?" (111); "Shopping in the city was a real pleasure in the 30s. Outside of London, Liverpool, arguably, had the best shopping centre in England"

(136); "Outside London, the great ballroom dancing era made the most lasting impact on Merseyside [which] boasted some of the finest ballrooms in the country, dozens of highly-talented orchestras, and many of the best dancers in the land" (200).

Any claims Liverpudlians might make about the great stature of their city in national terms, and on absolutely any score, must inevitably and grudgingly bow to London. Phrases such as "London apart" or "excepting London" or "outside London" absolutely cannot be avoided upon entering either texts about Liverpool or the place called Liverpool. My friends put me constantly to the test. "How do you feel about London?" I would be asked, expectantly. I disappointed people by confessing that I actually like the city. On one occasion, Scott met me at the train station upon my return from there. We went across the street to a pub and had a few pints with a friend of his, a middle-aged man who treated me to a long list of London jokes—to Scott's complete delight. These jokes flew with such rapid fire that I could remember only one: "What's the best thing about London? The first train out."[32] Other English places do not escape unscathed, however. Writing in 1933, O'Mara defined Liverpool against Cheshire and other "delightful" places. "Less shrewd" Liverpudlians had derisive names for the people who lived there. In Unwin's memoir, Manchester is also the object of Liverpool's one-upmanship game. Whatever Manchester did, Liverpool could do better. Liverpool is embattled.

The world beyond England is essential to Liverpool's identity. The city's engagements with that world are now the stuff of memory, history, and lore. And, unlike England, that world can be counted on, at least narratively, to substantiate Liverpool's claims to greatness—claims that again refer us to uniquely Liverpool places. O'Mara conveyed the importance of Cammel Lairds, just across the River Mersey, by calling it "an internationally known shipyard" (1933: 4). Scotland Road, he tells us, "was internationally famous," and Paddy's Market was "also internationally known" (4). Now, with the death of shipping, Liverpool's world renown speaks back to the city's incomprehensible invisibility and drastically diminished national relevance, even if only for the benefit of these texts' undoubtedly local readers. "Mention Paddy's Market to seamen in almost every port in the world and they'd immediately know where it was and how to get to it when their ships docked in Liverpool" (Unwin 1983: 61). Like O'Mara, Unwin claims that Scotland Road "is known all over the world" (60). Scott, in his walking tour, claimed that any sailor in the world of his own age could tell me about Park Lane. The author to be considered shortly, Frank Shaw, relays how Liverpool's status should properly be understood nationally: "[O]ur city is not just a provincial seaport but a second metropolis" (1971: 15). But, of course, the first metropolis is London, Liverpool's most formidable, unforgiving antagonist.

John Woods, author of *Growin' Up: One Scouser's Social History*, is not nostalgic. His tone is intense and critical, apropos of his focus on the shamelessly rough edges that define the Scouse persona. Scousers' defiant stance originated in the deplorable poverty and squalor in which they were forced to live in the 1930s. Thousands of families were affected not only by the casualism of dock labor but by the irresponsible ways that seamen's wages were distributed. Hunger was commonplace:

> Children seemed to be permanently hungry; sometimes kids would wait for carters
> or dockers or any man coming home from work and beg for left-overs from their
> 'carrying out.' . . . Poverty was permanent but destitution was intermittent; we all
> knew the difference. I can recall the times when my father's allotment from sea was
> not paid on time; sometimes it could be up to a month late. Such times could defy
> description. (27)

In the same passage, Woods provides a similar list of memory-packed "little corner shops" as Unwin had before him. But Woods does not recall them with admiration. Rather, we learn that these shops actually cheated people, forcing them to incur debts they could scarcely repay, raising prices when people were most vulnerable, and using scales that overweighed food items. In place of typical humor, we get typical—and, he suggests, justifiable—criminality. He describes the Christmas of 1936, when his father was at sea and his mother was at home, penniless. Miraculously, they had a huge Christmas dinner, supplied by a couple of lads who knocked off a butcher shop and played Robin Hood with the spoils (27). In his description of leisure spaces we also feel the sharp edges of class difference. Rather than painting a quaint little picture of the pubs around Scotland Road, he describes the arbitrary rules of the managers, who occupied a higher class position than most customers. There was always a special room in the back for high-paying patrons, while the rest were confined to the lowly front, where they, as riffraff, could be controlled. The police were often called in to discipline poor people who, Woods intimates, were treated like children.

Woods treats religious divisions very seriously as well. Bitterness, ignorance, and bigotry bred amid poverty. Scotland Road was divided along sectarian lines, Catholics living on the top end and the Protestants (mostly Anglicans) living at the bottom. Only their mutual love for football lessened the animosity. Liverpudlians have, for decades, given the city's two football teams religious affiliations. Everton was designated Catholic, and Liverpool was proclaimed Protestant. Rather than engendering hatred, these religious associations infused the sport with a humorous angle that only enhanced the competition between the teams' respective supporters. Football brought people together, he argued. "Even the geographical positions of the grounds helped, as people had to walk up the Valley together; this encouraged conversations, not only about football but many other topics. Then came the singing, sometimes religious, mostly witty" (76). One could question why the "geographical positions of the grounds" did not instead produce antagonisms. Nevertheless, it is relevant that Woods assigns place the role of producing, even if for a moment, a common identity.

In all of the texts under discussion, Liverpool comes off as a tough town. Small gangs of boys terrorized other children on the basis of religious difference, as Unwin shows. Only football, Woods suggests, relieved these hostilities. Fights between men and women—and between both and the police—were legion. O'Mara's earlier description of the sordid goings-on at Flag of all Nations alludes to violence. Unwin indicates that certain parts of the city, including Scotland Road, were so tough that policemen patrolled in groups, assuring their safety through their numbers. On Saturday nights, drunken brawls outside of pubs were common "and some of the women could throw a left hook as well as any man. Many a policeman woke up in hospital on Sunday morning" (1983: 63–64). Yet the tenor of Unwin's descriptions of such incidents is "typically" humorous, which jibes with the quality he and others ascribe to Liverpudlians' approach to life generally. Woods prefers to emphasize Liverpool people's grittiness, their "rough dignity" (1989: iv), their refusal to submit to authority, their impertinence. He makes the point most emphatically here, betraying some of the Liverpool pride that is, again, mediated by local critiques of Liverpool's national image:

> Nowadays Liverpool, perhaps for political reasons, seems to attract more than its share of bad media publicity. They all choose to forget the city's positive contributions throughout this century. During the war, for instance, towns competed to raise cash for the war effort, Liverpool coming top with eleven and a half million pounds. We supplied more than enough servicemen and women, many of whom never returned. Maybe our quick wits and sharp articulation frighten outsiders, although most comment on the hospitality and humour they encounter on their visits. I think what puts a lot of politicians off us is that we don't suffer fools gladly and tell them so! (99)

On that note he ends the book. With vigor, Woods argues that Liverpool is invisible. It is also embattled: "They all" conveniently forget Liverpool's contributions to the nation. "They all," then, seem to be Britons generally, not just those of London and Manchester. And "they all" are threatened by Liverpool, even though they admit to enjoying their stay in the city. With no less vigor, Liverpool-born Blacks argue that they, too, are invisible, but within Liverpool. They, too, often base that claim on the tremendous loss of life their families suffered in World War II, and charge that White veterans' societies in the city never invite Black participation in ceremonies honoring war heroes. Moreover, Whites and Blacks alike critique Liverpool-born Black activists for the vehemence with which they engage in political battle. They are given to settling matters in their own ranks through violence. They speak rudely and crudely, all in the name of justice for the Black community, so the critique goes. Their quick tongues spew venom over in town, at meetings of the Liverpool City Council. How different is that from the quality Woods ascribes to Liverpudlians, generally: "Our sharp articulation frighten[s] outsiders. . . . We don't suffer fools gladly and tell them so!" The following anecdote shows a Black person's mastery of this reputed centerpiece of Scouse culture. Days after the 1981 riots in Liverpool—as smoke was still rising up from the ashes, to the tune of a few million pounds sterling worth of damage—Margaret Thatcher arranged a fast and furious trip up to the city. Her functionaries were to round up the usual suspects of local officials, whom she proceeded to scold on arrival for failing to nip the riots in the bud. The 1999 documentary *Riot* featured several parties to that event, which was held at the Town Hall. One was a Black community worker. After ripping local officialdom into little shreds, Thatcher glared over at him and asked, with no small degree of condescension,

"And who are you?" He preempted her question. He had this to say: "Yo, Maggie, we're not here about jobs and unemployment. We're here about the race issue." His manner of address to the prime minister (however well-deserved) would make a fine addition to the Hall of Fame of Scouse Impertinence.

Frank Shaw's *My Liverpool* does not sit still. It is impertinent. It refuses to be read in conventional, linear fashion. Shaw seems to invite the reader to begin anywhere and to skip around at whim. At one moment we might be reading auto-biographical material and then, without a bit of notice, we get a few songs. Lengthy examples of Scouse humor, relayed in Scouse phonetics, are scattered throughout the book. This text is a celebration of the first order. In sharp contrast to O'Mara's autobiography, Shaw's text creates a Liverpool one might actually want to enter. But it is not easy. It is so dense with Scouse idioms and inside jokes—totally impenetrable to the outsider—that some of Shaw's pages are oc-cupied more by explanatory footnotes than by expository prose.

Shaw died shortly after finishing this book, published in 1971. He had enjoyed an illustrious career as a chronicler of things Scouse. The biographical material reveals that he received an honorary M.Sc. (Master of Scouse) from Warwick University, where he presented a thesis "proving that Shakespeare was a Scouser" (239). A student of linguistics, Shaw coauthored several books, includ-ing *Lern Yerself Scouse*, which is available at all bookshops (except at Source Books, a Black bookseller) and the gift shops of all tourist sites. Shaw also pub-lished widely in British periodicals and a few American ones. He intended *My Liverpool* to be the definitive book on the city.

One remarkable feature separates Shaw's autobiography from the others: he in-vites Black readers. A Black person appears on the cover art, and the opening page features a story about Toxteth: "They [*sic*] were these men putting up flats in Toxteth—and that's really one of the tough areas of Liverpool. They'd got a big dog and they put up a notice 'Guard Dog—Beware' inside a wire fence. Well, a gang of 10 year olds just come and stole the dog!" (11). As any of Shaw's readers would know, "Toxteth" (like Liverpool 8) is a functioning synonym for "Black people." His prominent placement of this story announces that Blacks will feature nonchalantly in his generally cheerful discourse on Liverpool culture. As well, the punch line of the story does not depict Blacks as criminals, but pranksters. By de-picting Toxteth through toughness and humor, Shaw positions Blacks as Scousers. Now let's examine the solitary and none-too-subtle reference to Black people from Unwin's text:

> I often read today of the many and varied excuses offered in mitigation of children falling foul of the law. They are deprived. They come from poor social backgrounds. . . . While there may be a grain of truth in this, I have little sympathy for such excuses. Many of my generation were desperately deprived. We came from poor back-grounds. . . . [W]e didn't go round smashing things up or mugging old ladies. (1983: 17)

We have already encountered O'Mara's meditations on the Black presence in Liverpool. John Woods, for his part, actually has a Black man in his "social history"—one who, by Woods's own account, was admired around Scotland Road.

But he fails to mention that he was Black. An elderly Black man I knew once told me about his father, Jim Clark, a well-known swimmer who lived in the Scottie Road area. This informant emphasized where his father lived a few times precisely because it was so unusual for a Black person to live there. Because of that rarity, the reader cannot infer from place, in this case Scottie Road, that this well-respected person was Black. Here is how Jim Clark features in Woods's memoir:

> The canals were used by all the local kids; sometimes one would go missing and then a search by local men would ensue. If unsuccessful, the police were informed and when finally Jim Clark arrived, we feared the worst. He was, beyond doubt, the best underwater swimmer in Liverpool. He would sometimes find a drowned child, trapped by weeds or rubbish tipped by the irresponsible. (1989: 42)

While Woods renders this Black person invisible, Shaw makes a point of treating Black people as just another part of the happy Scottie Road milieu. The following rhetorical query begins a paragraph devoted to how lively his neighborhood was: "Who would want to run home to telly when the Negro still had a puppet show in Scotland Road with his famed buttermilk rhyme?" (1971: 34). Shaw implies that lots of people enjoyed this Negro's puppet show. And just before this passage, Shaw made a quick but no less fascinating reference to racism: "Once I ran home to tell my aunt I had seen 'two ladies fighting!' After the Lusitania riots and the 1919 anti-Negro riots no sight should have surprised" (33). Shaw implies that the anti-Negro riots were the height of absurdity. He says no more about the matter. Indeed, his reference to these riots is out of place in the context in which it appears. Perhaps he is being strategic, slipping in a quick critique of racism amid otherwise humorous memories. Perhaps he means to remind his readers that not all Scousers recall these times quite the same way.

The Beatles play a part in this tale of postcolonial Liverpool. Predictably, their success is historicized differently by Blacks and Whites, but toward similar ends. Both groups highlight Liverpool's cultural fullness as evidenced in the vibrant music scene that the city has historically enjoyed. Unwin's autobiography dedicates a chapter to the music halls in town. Earlier, I quoted Black people as they recalled all kinds of music—African folk, jazz, Black American soul—being played in all manner of venues around south Liverpool (cellar parties, the Rialto, nightclubs). As a Black informant once told me, "Who needed London when you lived in Liverpool?" To that, Shaw adds this comment, "To the world the Beatles may have seemed a unique phenomenon. Not to us. It's the Irish and the Welsh in us. We are all singers in Liverpool" (1971: 63). The Beatles, then, were not the exception but the rule. The Liverpool milieu and its roots in Irish and now Welsh culture—but certainly not English culture—would have, of course, produced the Beatles. Blacks locate the Beatles' cultural roots elsewhere, decrying their invisibility in so doing. My own friends positively recoiled at any reference to the Beatles, as does one of Ferdinand Dennis's informants:

> The Beatles? We got no time for the Beatles 'round here. They're just another example of the white music industry ripping off black music. Where do you think the Beatles

learnt their craft? They come from up Penny Lane way [which is in Allerton, in the south end, maybe a mile or two from Liverpool 8]. There are no nightclubs up there. They learnt it round here, in Liverpool 8. John and Paul were taught to play the guitar by a Trinidadian guy, Woodvine. He used to own a nightclub that played Stateside music. He was a musician himself. John and Paul used to hang around him. That's where they picked up their style from. But nobody ever mentions Woodvine. Nobody! When Woodvine opened another nightclub he invited them to the opening. They didn't go, they were too big to know him then. So we round here don't have any time for the bloody Beatles. (1988: 57–58)

Dennis, who is not from Liverpool, then makes this interesting observation: "This angry response, delivered in a thick Liverpudlian accent, was my second reminder of *where I was*. His ferocity startled me" (58, emphasis added). Dennis admitted to his informant that he was unaware of the Beatles' connection to Liverpool 8, to which his informant replied: "That's the way they, white people, want it" (58). Whites' and Blacks' distinct accounts of the Beatles' cultural roots share a critical concern about invisibility.

Thick Scouse is ferocious. Dennis's response to his informant's vehemence jibes with Woods's earlier attribution of ferocity to Scousers: "Our sharp articulation frightens outsiders. . . . We don't suffer fools gladly." The fact that Scousers and non-Scousers are here agreeing on Liverpudlians' special intensity—as conveyed quite ably through their accent—says less about Liverpool, per se, than about how "Liverpool" is produced through localism, its alleged cultural difference from the rest of Britain.

Frank Shaw is undoubtedly as proud a Scouser as there has ever been. But he was not a born and bred one himself. He died at age sixty having lived half of his life in Liverpool. He does not specify which years he spent in the city, but he implies that his family took up residence there during World War I, following some previous visits by his father, who was from Ireland. Hence Shaw was between four and seven when he came to live in the city. He missed the opportunity to be born in the city by a couple of years. These points are important, first, because Shaw makes them so, notwithstanding the vague time line he offers. Second, as I argued at length in the previous chapter, "birth here" renders one a *local* subject—only a national one when the British state is involved. "Birth here" is the primary basis of political legitimacy in official circles. In Shaw's case, birth here seems a requirement for one wishing to write the definitive book on Liverpool.

Shaw's love for Liverpool leaps from every page. Anyone can become a Scouser, he claims, offering himself up as the first example of this truth. His commitment to this view might explain the inclusion of Black people in his "definitive" text. In the same spirit, he translates countless Scouse expressions, unlocking eternal cultural mysteries for the uninitiated among his readers. Chief among these is "why we talk this way," or what has been folklorized in Liverpool as "an accent exceedingly rare" (Belchem 2000). Other English people, of course, have local and regional accents, but as far as Scousers are concerned, their variety tops out. (Recall in the previous chapter a Black person's excited comment, "We know only one language, that's Liverpudlian"—as opposed to English.) It does not stop at being merely rare; it must be exceedingly so. If, for Unwin, place has the transcendental power to produce exceptionally strong longings among "Liverpool expatriates," for Shaw, the magical powers of the Scouse accent assimilates outsiders into the culture of this place. "When strangers live among us long enough—I've spent over half my life here—they get to like us. When they have learnt the language. Soon enough their own noses will be stuffed up. 'Coming from Liverpool', said actor Norman Rossington, 'is like belonging to a worldwide club, an exclusive clan'" (1971: 19).

Of course, Shaw's intervention is to argue that this clan does not have to be so exclusive. Strangers are welcome to join in. There is one group, though, that Shaw excludes quite decisively. Shaw warns the possible visitor that not everyone to be encountered in Liverpool is a Scouser. He lists a highly class-inscribed set of behaviors, sharply delineating which are Scouse and which are most certainly not. Unlike Woods, Shaw critiques Liverpool's middle class not for their political and economic privilege but for their links with places elsewhere, especially England. He alludes to Englishness through the essentialist idiom of gentility: "And there is still a good deal of genteel . . . snobbery centred on our [Reparatory Theatre] (vastly inferior these days to the average amateur theatre) and the [Philharmonic] (good music, I suppose, but nothing really to do with Liverpool—it could be any city)" (1971: 15). Liverpool, then, must never be confused with any English place. For something to be of relevance to Liverpool culture it must be radically different from what one might find elsewhere. Middle-class culture in the city is slavish imitation. The upper-crust in Liverpool are "such as you could meet everywhere; they say, through their noses, just what you would hear in Southampton or New York. Their minds keep in the ready-made rut, their customs are copies, their life a mimicry" (1971: 15). To seal the differentiation between Scousers, on the one hand, and Liverpool's middle class, on the other, Shaw traces the latter's racial genealogy: "The whole of this group . . . see themselves as descendants from the slave-trading merchants of the 18th century" (15). Accordingly, he scorns the places associated with middle-class life, adding with a phenomenological flourish that it is uniquely from "those vile slum houses stretched along the waterfront, ugly warrens facing our lovely Mersey [that] comes a strange and lovely quality, of courage and humour and friendliness, which I find ever-refreshing. I hate our soul-killing garden suburbs" (14).

Shaw issues a friendly invitation to his non-Liverpudlian readers to join in the many pleasures of Scouse culture. But should one decline, this can only be taken as an offense. He says as much in a lead-up to the above-quoted remarks about the Beatles: "Unless you realise that we are all minstrel boys, or girls, in the 'Pool you cannot understand us. And if you say you don't want to understand us I have to take me coat off to you" (1971: 63). "Take me coat off to you" suggests that fighting words have been spoken. Nowhere is there any indication that Scousers might, in a spirit of reciprocal engagement, want to admire or otherwise experience the virtues of other English people's ostensibly different cultures.

Instead, when the Scouser travels within England, he or she becomes all the more staunchly committed to Liverpool. Shaw informs us that "[w]hen two men from Liverpool meet in other parts—as they are likely to, for we are a much-travelled community—one does not ask the other what school he went to or whether he is from Rose Hill or Mossley Hill. They are as one against the 'enemy.' . . . This standing-up for our city, wherever we may be, tends, I fear, to make us disliked" (1971: 19). As Woods indicates, British outsiders find Liverpudlians off-putting, but nevertheless seem to find Liverpool hospitable. Now we learn that Liverpudlians toughen up when they go to that other world called "England," perhaps refusing others' hospitality. Shaw seems proud to constitute English people as the enemy. He, like Woods before him, is proud to claim that Liverpudlians are disliked nationally. In fairness, Shaw was speaking of a friendly football rivalry that unfolded in a pub in Harwich. Shaw and another Liverpudlian who happened to be there formed an alliance in support of Liverpool Football Club against the supporters of Arsenal, a London team. Yet and still, the light-heartedness of his example cannot mask the seriousness of the point it illustrated: Liverpudlians travel through the rest of England with an "us against them" subjectivity that engenders animosity wherever they go.

On the matter of Scousers' English journeys, it is instructive to consider the following incident, not because it supports the above authors' charge that other Britons dislike Scousers but because it is indicative of a *national* culture and politic of place. These are, in this case, mediated by economic and, in a round-about way, racial inequality. In September 1991 a small scandal erupted when Liverpool people who had moved to the southern town of Bournemouth for work were accused of being criminals and low-lifes. One of the national newspapers, the *Independent*, ran the headline, "Scouse Equals Louse in Genteel Bournemouth" (1991: 5). The paper reported that "'Liverpudlian' has entered the local vocabulary as a simile for all that is bad in people. In one local newspaper report, the owner of a takeaway food shop experiencing trouble from local youths likened their behaviour to a bunch of Liverpudlians'" (5). In the same story, a white Liverpudlian offered the interesting analysis that "[it's] white racism. There is no black community here and the scousers do all the jobs nobody else will tackle. We get blamed for everything" (5).

Here people from two places, Bournemouth and Liverpool, debate the nature of Liverpudlianness. The nation itself is a subtext, for it is through such national media vehicles like the *Independent* that this image of Liverpool travels across Britain. The local tabloid, the *Liverpool Echo*, covered the story, as it generally does when the city's image gets tarnished. Letters to the editor in this newspaper routinely speak back to what its readers perceive as Liverpool's denigration in the national media. In this case, the *Echo* directed as much anger to the national press as it did to the people of Bournemouth, for it blamed the *Independent* for representing "Liverpudlians as being behind drugs, crime and prostitution in Bournemouth" (*Liverpool Echo* 1991: 8). What the *Echo* missed, though, was that Bournemouth was being chided, if subtly, for its "genteel" pretensions. Another unspoken dynamic in this exchange is that Bournemouth residents, the newspapers, and Liverpudlians themselves were all describing Scousers as immigrants without the proper papers, as trespassers in a place perceived to belong not commonly to the people of Britain but exclusively to the people of Bournemouth. And, not to be left out, race emerged as a very potent idiom, one that White Liverpudlians used to mark and resist their subordination. With ease, the discourse on race could be grafted right onto place.

MY CITY, MY SELF

The sense of loss that pervades the narratives of both Blacks and Whites underscores an inseparable city/self relation. The places that both groups use to define their respective "Liverpools" are gone. Pitt Street was blitzed in 1941 and razed ten years later. Granby Street served as a reasonable facsimile for a while, largely until the death of the shipping industry (chapter 9). People describe Granby Street as dead. Scotland Road still exists, but the authors discussed above do not describe its contemporary life. Rather, the emphasis is on invisible places, which include buildings, houses, shops, and streets around Scotland Road. The loss of place is matched, crucially, by the loss of population. O'Mara's autobiography is full of people; the later authors dwell on their exodus. Unwin spoke of the migration of "Scottie Road exiles." Liverpudlians, Black and White, have left Liverpool because it has long been economically depressed. If the essential Liverpool produced an essential soul to go with it, then people's concern about population decline has to produce their yearning to bring Scottie Road back to life. Woods and Unwin, for example, take great care to provide as many names of actual people from the old neighborhood as they can possibly recall. In so doing, they put all those Liverpudlians who have left back where they once were. Back where they *really* belong.

Liverpool's culture consists not in its unique attributes but in the attribution of uniqueness to the city and its selves. LBBs, I noted earlier, were confounded by my suggestion that the term *Liverpool-born Black* might have a history. This chapter has shown that by the late 1970s, when the term first appeared, "Liverpool" was so reified that the "Liverpool-born" aspect of Blacks' transformed racial subjectivity fell imperceptibly into place. Liverpool-born Blackness arose out of a structure of feeling about "Liverpool" that was in formation at least one hundred years before the rise of Black identity. Without in any way wishing to explain away the content of LBBs' claims in the public arena, the idioms in which they couch those claims—invisibility, embattlement, and uniqueness—go a long way in suggesting that place shapes race fundamentally.

That thesis applies to Britain as a whole. In his earlier-quoted remarks from *The Atlantic Sound*, Caryl Phillips confessed that he had long considered Liverpool a dangerous place, one to be avoided. He wrote of his encounter with Liverpudlians who said, "We're Scousers. We don't talk to niggers." Phillips and those Whites are participating jointly in a troubling discourse on uniqueness that effectively naturalizes place-as-explanation. First—and this is where ethnography helps us—Blacks

Please note the Internet resources are of a time-sensitive nature and
URL addresses may often change or be deleted.

Contact us at westlegalstudies@delmar.com

and Whites in Liverpool tend to couch every single thing they do in terms of its irreducible Liverpoolness. All four authors studied here engaged in that practice.
I once heard a Black woman characterize as "Scouse" the fact that "we take taxis
to travel two blocks." No matter what a Liverpool person does, he or she lovingly
marks it *Scouse*—even a proud declaration that "we don't talk to niggers." Second,
Phillips conspires in this localization of racism. What makes the statement abhor-
rent to him is less the fact that they were so proud to be racist than the fact that they
happily declared themselves Scousers in that critical moment. Phillips conspires in
their construction of their ostensible difference. To him, they were not "racist
Whites" but "racist Scousers."

Scousers' renegade subjectivities are not produced whole cloth within
Liverpool but are rather productions of English cultural notions about place, as
produced within a preeminent site of English otherness, in a general climate of
Liverpool/British postcolonial transformation. The next chapter shows how critical racial discourse sutures localness—or, Liverpool's ostensible cultural difference from England/Britain—to whiteness.

A Slave to History: Local Whiteness
in a Black Atlantic Port

I want to draw a map, so to speak, of a critical geography and
use that map to open as much space for discovery, intellectual
adventure, and close exploration as did the original charting of
the New World—without the mandate for conquest.

—Toni Morrison

DENOUNCING HIS BONDAGE and narrating his runaway plot to freedom, Frederick
Douglass wrote, "Every slaveholder seeks to impress his slave with a belief in
the boundlessness of slave territory, and of his own almost illimitable power. We
all had vague and indistinct notions of the geography of the country" (1994a
[1855]: 310). Because Douglass's enslavement was effected, in part, through the
control of his conception of space, his runaway plot depended on his ability to
imagine a point geographically and politically beyond his master's reach but
within his own. Years after his escape, as an abolitionist on the lecture circuit in
Britain, Douglass spoke further to the importance of space—this time, transnational. Here he explains why he was bringing his cause to the British public:

> [T]he distance between London and Boston is now reduced to some twelve or four-
> teen days, so that the denunciations against slavery, uttered in London this week, may
> be heard in a fortnight in the streets of Boston. . . . There is nothing said here against
> slavery that will not be recorded in the United States. I am here also because the slave-
> holders do not want me to be here. . . . The slaveholders would much rather have me,
> if I will denounce slavery, denounce it in the northern states, where their friends and
> supports are, who will stand by and mob me for denouncing it. . . . [M]y influence
> now is just in proportion to the distance that I am from the United States. (407–8)

The nineteenth-century politics of slavery, in which narratives like Douglass's
played a significant role, show how crucially space figured in the exercise and
experience, the formation and transformation of racial power.

In this chapter, LBBs and their White supporters narrate and denounce
Liverpool's role in the history that forever linked Africa, Europe, and the Americas.
And like Douglass, they differentially implicate local, national, and transnational
spaces in racial subordination, while also strategically appropriating them in opposition to it. In narrating slavery, they effectively suture locality and race—
whiteness in this case—first by placing Liverpool at the center of that excruciating

history and then by drawing boundaries around city space as they map that history's continuing effects.[1] Collectively, these actions show the fallacy of treating the local as a subordinate to the global, or as a mere outpost of it. In contemporary narratives about Liverpool and slavery, the local comes to life as a pivotal agent, whose importance in creating the hemispheric space called the Black Atlantic is considered second to none. In turn, the effects of the agency imputed to Liverpool lie in the racialization of space in Britain as a whole.

Curiously, although slavery implicates Whites in the subjugation of Blacks, the anthropology of slavery (to the degree that one exists) focuses on the latter group, occluding the possibility that Whites' subjectivities have also taken shape in relation to that past.[2] In a related context, Gilroy states the case powerfully. Citing White scholars of Western modernity, he observes that "if it is perceived to be relevant at all, the history of slavery is somehow assigned to blacks; it becomes our special property rather than a part of the ethical and intellectual heritage of the West as a whole" (1993a: 49). This fallacy is evident in an otherwise elegant article by David Scott, in which he critiques anthropologists for inquiring into the authentic historical consciousness of New World Blacks. But for a few caveats, his critical questions guide the present analysis:

> What are the varying ways in which . . . slavery [is] employed by New World peoples of African descent in the narrative construction of relations among pasts, presents and futures? What [is] the rhetorical or, if you like, ideological work that [it] is made to perform in the varied instances and occasions in which [it] is brought into play? What space [does] . . . slavery occupy in the political economy of local discourse? How [does this] figure . . . participate in those techniques by means of which the construction of appropriate bodies and selves are effected? (1991: 278)

These questions merit expansion not only racially, as I suggested above, but spatially. Much of the history of slavery—including resistance to it—took place in Europe, which in the United States is the forgotten node of the Atlantic triangle.[3] More important, the present analysis is not about "local discourse," a phrase that flattens out a dynamic spatial category by limiting its purview to questions of context and detail. Instead, I emphasize the production of a discourse on the local. I also ask, How does the mapping of racial histories reflect and further shape a nationwide politic that produces "the local" as such. To frame these issues in terms of "mapping" is to attend, quite literally, to geography—the writing of the earth, the active production of spatial knowledges. In that respect, this analysis highlights Black people's agency in transforming a hemispheric history—one that forged "the New World," "the Black Atlantic," and "the African diaspora"—into a brutally local, excruciatingly White affair. Indeed, Liverpool-born Blacks' relentless localization of that history enables their implicit argument: slavery is *not* "our special property."

Liverpool-born Blacks study their city's past in an effort to locate the origin of racial processes and to explain their continuance over time, as I show in the first section of this chapter. Their will to knowledge is animated by the belief that theirs is the most racist city in Britain. In constituting Liverpool's identity through a singularly poignant history, these actors fashion slavery into the ultimate signifier of local whiteness. This inscription marks Liverpool's *difference*, rendering its White population beyond the reach of civilizing discourses on racial progress—that is, liberal antiracism—understood to obtain in the rest of Britain. To Liverpool-born Blacks and many Whites, the city's history has an inescapable power to explain the putatively unique racism there. Hence narrating slavery through place is key to antiracist practice in the city. And those narrations have a tremendous effect: they produce mutually exclusive moral geographies of race that shape Whites' subjectivities within *and* beyond this once imperial but now marginal port city.

Narrating slavery was also a key stratagem for Frederick Douglass and other Black abolitionists in the context of their own freedom struggles. Indeed, there is an uncanny kinship between the politics of representing the peculiar institution in the antebellum Black Atlantic world, on the one hand, and in contemporary Britain, on the other hand. In both cases, the efficacy of these narrations derives not only from the content of their critiques but from their deployment of a politic of place—one that is itself refracted through the other mobile discourses of gender, sexuality, and race. In the penultimate section of this chapter, I briefly discuss the antebellum slave narrative and then go on to analyze contemporary negotiations in and about the former slave port of Liverpool as latter-day varieties of it. The point of this exercise is not simply to show the likenesses between these two sets of slave narratives. Rather, it is to use the difference between them to make a critical comment about the way that race matters get spatialized—or, more particularly, localized—not just in Liverpool, but in Britain.

WITNESSING SLAVERY

A strategically brief overview of Liverpool's role in the Atlantic slave trade must suffice to set the scene, for it is the contested narrations of that history that I analyze here.[4] The financial infrastructure of the British slave trade was located in Liverpool. Slave ships were built in Birkenhead, just across the River Mersey. From Liverpool's port, slavers set sail to Africa, and to its port they returned after their American run. The exact date in which Liverpool merchants began slave trading is unknown, for they commonly bribed customs officials or falsified documents concerning the destinations of their ships in order to avoid paying export duties on their cargos (Fryer 1984: 32–36). The first documented voyage of a Liverpool slave ship is dated 1700. Years before, however, the slave ports of Bristol and London were already in high gear. Of the thirteen British slave ports, Liverpool, Bristol, and London were the most important, often vying for dominance. In the late eighteenth century, Liverpool overtook its rivals for good, wresting control of 60 percent of the British slave trade, which was legally abolished in 1807 (Fryer 1984).

When Blacks invoke that history, they focus on the immoral role Liverpool played in the slave trade. With equal horror, they decry the widespread ignorance about that participation and about slavery in general. One of my informants, a White teacher in the British equivalent of a junior high school, testified to this ignorance. Here he tells of a twelve-year-old Chinese Liverpudlian boy's rude discovery:

> He was going through one of our history textbooks, looking ahead . . . and he came across some pictures of slavery. I think there were some supposed examples of first-hand evidence, like posters about slavery. And he couldn't believe it! And this kid is twelve. He couldn't believe it! He was absolutely aghast. The thing that I was quite taken aback about was his blatant surprise. I said, "What are you doing?" And he said, "Look at this! People used to sell Negroes!" That's exactly what he said. I said, "yeah, it was called slavery." And he didn't know that! He was looking at this and his eyes got wider and wider. He said, "God!" And he was just flabbergasted by it.

This boy's racial positioning beyond the Black/White binary around which slavery gets narrated is not what fascinates here.[5] Rather, it is his age. His shock substantiates LBBs' view that slavery is shrouded in silence. Yet his innocent, visceral response also fascinates, for here he was confronting an unfathomable violation of the very cornerstone of contemporary Western morality: human beings are "free," as opposed to chattel. Yet his teacher takes that morality very much for granted—notwithstanding the fact that it came about fairly recently and in the face of great resistance. His immediate response to the student's horror is not to share his outrage over the selling of Negroes but to feel blatant surprise that the boy was so incredulous and aghast. Thus, does he offer this flat explanation: "Yeah, it was called slavery."

Slavery's specter envelops Liverpool. In the course of my fieldwork, I scarcely inquired into that topic. Rather, I asked about the variety of race matters that gripped Black people's lives, and they routinely referred to it in their replies. With striking frequency, they would make totally unsolicited references to where slave merchants used to live, the buildings erected with their money, the secrecy surrounding their sinister activities around town, and the streets bearing their names. Places known as the one-time haunts of slave merchants were called upon to testify against them and their historic crimes. That slavery constructs whiteness is evidenced in Black people's focus not on the enslaved but on the enslavers.

In the act of placing their historical memory, mapping it onto city sites, Liverpool-born Blacks recall a highly specific, experiential past related to slavery: the moment they learned about their city's role in the Atlantic slave trade. And their racial subjectivities were often transformed in those moments. Yvette recalled her own epiphany for me. We were walking one day through a park and cemetery in Liverpool 8, when she interrupted our conversation to tell me that it was right here that she, at twenty-three years of age, first learned that Liverpool was once a slave port. In 1977 a White community worker who taught Black studies showed her headstones belonging to slave merchants. That discovery, she said, explained the racism she had always known, inspiring her to become a political activist. Slavery's physical remains moved her. Or did the community worker do that? We can never know her actual thought process back in 1977. Yet the sight of those headstones in the present inspired her to share a memory that stressed the effects of place upon her consciousness and actions.

The premier signifier of slavery is the central dock area, or the Pier Head. The iconic buildings clustered there give Liverpool its magnificent waterfront skyline. The modernist exemplar of the city's architecture consists of a set of squatty structures known as the Albert Dock. Opened in 1846, it was once a cutting-edge docking and warehouse facility. A series of changes in shipping technology rendered the Albert Dock obsolete by the mid-1970s, and so it laid derelict until the 1980s, when it was reincarnated as a shopping, arts, and entertainment complex geared toward British tourists. Black people and some Whites assign a different history to the place. They say that slave ships landed where the Albert Dock now sits and further claim that slave merchants stored human cargo in a set of tunnels near the site.[6] Sixty-something Abraham spoke soberly of having spent his childhood playing around those tunnels. He expressed such sorrow about having used that site as his personal playground, saying in a pained whisper, "I didn't even realize what it was." LBB historical memory speaks with as much horror about the delay in acquiring such knowledge as its content. Alluding to the fact that Blacks cannot get jobs in the touristy shops and attractions there now, Abraham continued: "Now they don't want Blacks around there. And that's the *irony* of the Albert Dock."

When I first arrived in Liverpool, Cecelia gave me a city tour, the climax of which was the Albert Dock. And she was only the first person to tell me, "These buildings were built on the blood of slaves." Her tour included the Cunard Building, also located at the Pier Head. She pointed out the casts molded in the image of Africans that adorn the upper reaches of the building's façade. Their visages symbolized the wealth generated from the slave trade. Scott gave me still other lessons on race and architecture. With Liverpool's history as one of his hobbies, and Black history in Britain and the United States another, Scott would spend his leisure time reading about the slave trade. He showed me the notes he had compiled based on his library research. One passage read, "In a ten year period 12 million slaves were shipped to the Americas. As a result you have Saint George's Hall, the Town Hall and the [other] buildings in the city." Reading over my shoulder, Scott emphasized to me that "it cost *a lot* of money to put up those buildings!"

Blacks' sense of place is animated by their sense of race, or the meaning and power they assign to a particular brand of whiteness defined by the city's past. Akeem, in his early twenties, here describes how he feels historical whiteness, evoking the palpable, if ghostly, presence of slave merchants in downtown Liverpool:

You can see the whole place is built up on the money of the slave trade. Definitely. Liverpool's like that in general. You should visit these type of places, you know like the *old* buildings and the Bluecoat. Even, like, your Barclay's Bank, especially Dale Street, Castle Street. That was the center of it. You can just go into those places, and you just *feel* it.

He let out a slow, deep groan after making that comment. By contrast, two Black men gleefully pointed out the irony of the fact that the respective antiracist organizations they run are housed in the former domiciles of slave merchants. "They must be turning in their graves to see this!" one mused.

Despite how frequently people such as Cecelia, Abraham, Akeem, and Scott told me about these buildings and the slave merchants who built them, they also routinely insisted that no one knows that this city was once a slave port. As Akeem put it, "There's a lot more to be uncovered about Liverpool. You know, like, the Town Hall with all the Black faces. People don't even look for that. Liverpool's got a lot hidden." Though they speak urgently of this hiddenness, their own knowing eyes grant place an agentive role: witness. The brick of this building and the mortar of that one together give evidence, just as did the embodied presence of ex-slaves who, many generations ago, traveled to Britain with their stories of bondage. Now that no living person can give witness, it is place that speaks. Or, at other times, places are themselves indicted. Among the most noteworthy of these indicted places, seen as a symbolic link between the slave-trading past and the racist present, is Granby Street. Many LBBs speak of it nostalgically as the once hub of community life—before the riots and back when shipping was king. Since then it has become a sign of Black impoverishment, disempowerment, and criminality. Granby, I was told, was a slave merchant.

LBBs' positioning vis-à-vis other Blacks in the city was described in chapter 5, while White Liverpudlians' relationship to the rest of the country was the topic of chapter 6. For present purposes, it becomes important to specify Black Liverpool's place in relation to the national Black community. LBBs often quipped that theirs is the most thoroughly researched Black community in Britain—and still the most oppressed. They direct their ire at the voluminous reports discussed previously, including *Loosen the Shackles*. That study detailed the discrimination Blacks face in all institutional contexts, concluding that racism in the city is "uniquely horrific" (Lord Gifford, Brown, and Bundey 1989). The ambiguity of the slavery allusion was not lost on one Black informant, who said that the shackles need to be ripped off and burned, not "loosened." While the *Gifford Report* stresses Liverpool's uniqueness within Britain, other scholarly texts render Black Liverpool invisible—precisely for its uniqueness. Writing of Black British historiography, Barnor Hesse explains, "Liverpool is not simply the region of an earlier (temporalized) settlement, it is a settlement *elsewhere* (spatialized)" (1993: 163). Note how Kobena Mercer narrates Black Britain's history: "*Born in the great migrations of the 1940s, fifties and sixties*, and coming of age in the 1970s, eighties and nineties, entire generations of black Britons have had the complex and contradictory vicissitudes of late modernity as our conditions of existence" (1994: 2, emphasis added). Some historical narratives give a nod to older Black communities in the port cities of London, Bristol, Liverpool, and Cardiff, Wales, as Paul Gilroy does in *The Black Atlantic*: "Black settlement in that country goes back many centuries, and affirming its continuity has become an important part of the politics that strive to answer contemporary British racism" (1993a: 81). Yet the power of that statement is undone by the one that follows: "However, the bulk of today's black communities are of relatively recent origin, dating only from the post-World War II period" (81). Sociologist Steven Small, who is from Liverpool, focuses more attention on the city. Describing its Black population as a "contemporary anomaly," though, he appeals directly to Liverpool exceptionalism (1991). He writes, "The pattern of inequality and disadvantage is far more severe than elsewhere in the country. . . . The contrast is heightened when we take into account the fact that blacks have been elsewhere for *decades*, but in Liverpool for *centuries*" (516–17, original emphasis).[7]

In relation to Black Britain, LBBs I knew spoke bitterly of what they perceive as the greater racism they suffer. They observed that Blacks in London, whom they generally characterize as immigrants, work in the ritziest, glitziest shops in the very center of that city, whereas they, despite their "generations and generations" in Britain, remain invisible in downtown Liverpool. One young woman asked me pointedly, "How many Black faces have you seen working in town?" I told her that I had seen one. "They're keeping us in the background. . . . I've yet to see Black people in George Henry Lee's and Marks and Spencers. As I say, they've got to employ them, but they don't put them in the public view. They put you in the stock room or to clean toilets." Another Black woman, Clara, described what she observed when she worked in London, years ago. She expressed unmitigated shock that Black people were working in the "high fashion shops," as she put it. "London *has* progressed. It's *amazing* what I saw! Why can't it be like that in Liverpool? We're not all *stupid*!" Here her voice hit a high pitch and it cracked on the word *stupid*. She continued, "They're very good down there in London, with Black people. Even though they say it's getting a bit better in Liverpool, it is still bloody wrong." Cecelia noted that Liverpool Blacks cannot even get jobs in McDonald's—an example that so many other people seized upon as dramatic testimony to the "uniquely horrific" racism in Liverpool. Despite the reputation these restaurants have for hiring Black youth, here in Liverpool, she explained, they are run by White Liverpudlians, who just do not hire Blacks. Clara and Cecelia argued that only the city's slave-trading past could explain racism *this* vile.

When LBBs speak about Liverpool's "uniquely horrific" racism, their fleeting, ostensibly explanatory references to slavery could easily be missed. When they do make explicit connections, their theories articulate a profoundly material—not just symbolic—relationship between place and race. The tunnels around the Albert Dock that Abraham mentioned are key here; some people argue that they allowed slave trafficking to continue well after the trade was legally abolished. Because it lasted so long, the "mentality" (as Blacks sometimes say) it required is still in the recent past and formed part of White people's upbringing. White Liverpudlians teach racism to their children, who teach it to their own children. The transparency of this logic, appealing as it does to straightforward socialization processes, belies its deeper roots in the culture and ideology of place in Britain.[8] Their explanations participate subtly in the discursive process through which Liverpool gets cut off from the rest of the nation.

In chapter 1, I suggested that belonging to a "local" community is often construed through a generations-old presence in place (Strathern 1982; A. Cohen

1982b). Later, Liverpool-born Blacks traced their own venerable place-based genealogies (chapter 4). More indirectly, chapter 6 showed White Scousers' articulation of a generational theme. They mourned the loss, via migration, of tens of
thousands of their fellow Scottie Roaders. Such an up*root*ing of population implies a disruption of place itself insofar as generations lend British places—with
Britain chief among them—an eternal quality (Wright 1985). Because place is
thought to root people, folk theories of continuity (or change) in a place rely on the
category of personhood most associated with social reproduction—generation—
whether they draw on its kinship version or not. Tellingly, Frank Shaw charged in
the previous chapter that middle-class White Liverpudlians see themselves as the
descendants of slave traders; I am less concerned about the truth value of that
statement than in the logic that underpins it. The foregoing points suggest that
racial discourse in Liverpool cannot be understood apart from the salience of
place in Britain. For example, above all other possible societal influences there
might be in Liverpool (such as the deeply translocal phenomenon of mass media),
it is families rooted in place and in perpetuity who are thought to determine the
course of racism. The city seems to be hermetically sealed. It is apparently unaffected by social processes occurring elsewhere in Britain—a view that is encouraged by the individuation of place (and all the uniqueness claims enabled therein),
the conflation of place with personhood, the ascription of material capacities to
place, and not least of all by the marginalization processes already discussed.
As Liverpool is shoved off the national map, White Liverpudlians—or *local*
Whites—get constituted as a breed apart from the collective of White Britons.

   The politics of interracial parenting and partnering bears discussion in this context, for the status of White women in the Black community again raises the question of kinship, somewhat complicating the racial polarization Blacks otherwise
describe. Most generally, LBBs spoke of the White women of their community as
exceptions to the city's racist norm. Black men and women alike often heralded
them, particularly their own mothers, for having sacrificed their families of orientation to marry Black men. Many Blacks saw these women in nonracial terms, as
"just me mum." My Black friends who were in their thirties volunteered childhood stories that credited their mothers for teaching them how to deal with
racism. Yet they also noted the lack of discussion in their households about how
their mothers felt as White women in an otherwise Black family. Other people described a growing divide between White mothers and their young adult Black
children who, in developing a heightened racial consciousness, would summarily
place their mothers in the adversarial category *White* that critical discourse on
racism constructs (chapter 8). Middle-aged Black men who were married to
White women said that they do not talk about racial politics with their wives,
whom they perceive as too sensitive to their implications.

   White women I knew who were part of the Black community were very vocal
about slavery in their conversations with me. Without any prompting on my part,
one woman historicized racism through the slave trade, and another spoke angrily about Liverpool's shameful role, which she said included the selling of
slaves at the Pier Head. Another, Barbara, indicated how she learned about that

history. She was merrily making her way home after being down at the docks for the Columbus Quincentenary celebration that the city had mounted, an event that horrified Blacks I knew. As she walked down Granby Street, some young Black men asked her where she had been and then expressed alarm at her innocent response. They informed her about the connection between Columbus and the slave trade, arguing that Liverpool was built on slavery, and that this commemoration was therefore an affront to Black people. Like Abraham, who had played innocently around the Albert Dock, Barbara expressed real sorrow about where she had spent her day out.

Slavery has become an especially poignant moral narrative about race in Liverpool—yet within a national context generally absorbed by the crisis that has surrounded race, and in a hemispheric context where slavery has attained great moral authority. Events relating to racism or the Black presence in Liverpool routinely begin with a narrative about and a denunciation of the city's role in the triangular trade. And these representations of slavery, bound as they are to representations of Liverpool, are often met with volatile responses by actors of various racial and spatial positionings. Liverpudlians, Black *and* White, make race a spatial issue by debating what did or did not happen *here*, in Liverpool. Place is important in these debates because, ultimately, it *explains*. (To understand Black people, you've got to understand Liverpool.) Materially and symbolically, city sites mediate racial conflicts by providing evidence. As I show in the contemporary "slave narratives," when Whites and Blacks contest the accuracy of details about Liverpool's past, they seem more concerned with the necessity of dredging them up. These contentions reveal people's investment in either clinging to or shattering the precious illusion of racial harmony extant in small corners and tenuous relations.

Blacks complain of not learning about the slave trade until scandalously late in life, and for them this betrays a concerted effort among Whites to conceal the immorality on which Liverpool was built. Scott, for example, predicted that I would encounter denials that slaves were actually sold in Liverpool, for his own notes document the selling of as many as fifteen slaves on its waterfront. Indeed, I did witness the invocation of a related point in a tour of the Town Hall, organized by the Liverpool City Council. For two weeks every year, the council offers these tours, which accommodate about twenty people each and require advance reservations. I saw only White people at the two tours I attended. The tour guide, a Mr. Bins, works for the council's public relations office. Mr. Bins weaved a stunningly detailed narrative of global, national, and local history, without the benefit of notes. His mastery of this material was matched only by the utter joy he took in presenting it. He made his only reference to slavery in specifying what luxury items seventeenth-century Liverpool merchants sold from the cellars of the Town Hall: ". . . and the goods which came from the West Indies as a result of the slave trade, which brought huge amounts of money into Liverpool—although slaves, in fact, *never* were brought here." The emphasis on *never* was his. The second time I took the tour, he did not mention slavery at all. Since Blacks charge White Liverpudlians with erasing the city's slave-trading past, it is worth asking people like Mr. Bins how they select material for their narratives.

Mr. Bins is from Liverpool, as I learned in interviewing him after my second tour. He described his interest in history as "obsessive," but lamented that the people who take his tours only want to hear Liverpool's history rather than British and world history. He also finds that people believe history consists most importantly in "what they can remember." He labors to disabuse them of that notion. With the benefit of this introduction to his pedagogy, I asked Mr. Bins about the veracity of his point regarding the sale of slaves in Liverpool. I withheld my question until I thought I had established some amiable relationship with him, so desperate was I to avoid provoking him. He responded to my query by saying that he welcomes challenge. He also responded nonverbally, changing his body posture completely on hearing my question. Until this moment, he had been leaning forward in his chair, his forearms resting comfortably on his knees. Literally, and I do believe figuratively, his back then went straight up. He proceeded to indicate, rather forcefully, that "the slave trade is controversial—and rightly so." Mr. Bins said he argues with his colleagues about whether the Town Hall was built with "slave money"; he takes the position that it was. Getting increasingly emphatic, he continued, "History is bad enough without being made to seem worse. It's very emotional. Anyone who attempts to lessen the suffering is accused of distorting the facts. It's not science—history—is it?"

Clearly it is not, for Mr. Bins acknowledged throughout the interview that he presents his material with certain aims in mind. In that regard it is worth asking, *whose* suffering is he attempting to lessen? If power can be diagnosed from the forms of resistance it generates (Foucault 1978; Abu-Lughod 1990), Mr. Bins's tour of the Town Hall might be aimed at countering the moral power vested in the discourse on antiracism enveloping Britain generally and Liverpool in particular. For decades, race and antiracism have been the subjects of sustained debate, taking the various forms of riots and other kinds of violence, as well as legislation and policy initiatives. A nationally publicized state-sponsored inquiry had recently focused on Liverpool's "uniquely horrific" racism, conjuring slavery in its very title, *Loosen the Shackles*. Mr. Bins's narrative practice shows just how efficacious spatialized critiques of racial power have been in Liverpool. That is, he seems to be resisting the growing, morally loaded contention that Liverpool played host to the selling of slaves: "They *never* were brought here." His desire to "lessen the suffering" might best be read as an attempt to mitigate the effects of highly racialized knowledges on White Liverpudlians. For such knowledges unequivocally position them—as inextricably White *and* Liverpudlian—as Black people's oppressors. In the resultant "official" narrative, he refrains from dispensing knowledge he admits to having at his disposal (that the Town Hall was built with slave money). And while he rather breezily mentions the source of Liverpool's one-time wealth ("and the goods that came from the West Indies"), he went on to dispute, emphatically, a point about what happened, or did not, *here*, in Liverpool's physical space.

There are two opposed but intimately connected sets of racial inscriptions circulating within that space. Blacks inscribe racial interpretations of Liverpool's history onto its landmarks, while White Liverpudlians in powerful positions follow them around erasing these marks. Antiracist practices in Liverpool—and the forms of resistance they generate—hence represent "spatial practices" (D. Moore 1998; de Certeau 1984). In its deployment in and *about* Liverpool, discourse on racism—routinely narrated through slavery—serves as a way of localizing white-ness, differentiating Whites across the national landscape according to their presumably distinct moralities.

THE ANTEBELLUM SLAVE NARRATIVES

The jointly spatial and racial practices enacted in twentieth-century Liverpool beg to be linked to nineteenth-century abolitionism, for that movement also con-structed moral geographies of race: individual Southern states, the South writ large, the North, the United States, Britain. But my ultimate aim is not merely to show the likenesses between the antebellum slave narratives and those of con-temporary Liverpool. Nor is it to posit the ruptures wrought by slavery as the ori-gin of an African diaspora or of diasporic subjectivities per se; nor is it to suggest that slavery is the object of Blacks' "true" historical consciousness.[9] One simple fact motivates this brief return to the antebellum Black Atlantic world (*not* merely to the United States).[10] When contemporary Blacks and their White sup-porters condemn racism by narrating and denouncing slavery, they draw actively, if implicitly, on the once insurgent but now hegemonic moral authority that their antebellum predecessors so righteously worked to produce. What follows, then, is a history of the present (Foucault 1978), a genealogical frame for understand-ing the contemporary moral authority of slavery. And it is for the very sake of this present that we should undertake this study, for the antebellum politics of narrating slavery offer invaluable cautionary tales for contemporary antiracists in Liverpool, in Britain more broadly, and, indeed, in other societies where historic crimes are narrated through place.

The antebellum slave narrative is the only genre in the history of Western let-ters addressed solely to the politics of race—so that liberty may speak from a text, in the words of slave narrator George White (Sekora 1987: 491). As first-person accounts of enslavement, they made the author's life paramount; others among the enslaved were brought to bear only to illuminate the drama and poignancy of the protagonist's singular experience. The narratives sought to in-duce moral indignation among White readers in the American North and abroad, garnering their support for abolitionism in so doing. As didactic writings, they constructed moral positionings for their Black authors—and, crucially, for their White publishers and readers. As John Sekora argues,

> Clearly the meaning of the slave writing did not inhere exclusively in the text of a narrative alone. Meaning flowed into and out of a narrative in a series of acts of power. The primary abolitionists respected language as an instrument of power, to be used with care to influence behavior. As sponsors they saw themselves as guardians of the common weal; authors they viewed as molders of civic morality; and readers,

as corrigible citizens. . . . All are actors in the impending drama of reformation. At issue is the action, not the writing that induced it. (1987: 500)[11]

Abolitionists' efforts targeted the South, but the racialized terrain extended farther, for the Northern White abolitionist machinery trafficked in the same ideologies that justified slavery. As Frederick Douglass was moved to comment, "Opposing slavery and hating its victims has come to be a very common form of abolitionism" (quoted in Davis and Gates 1985: xviii). Even the eminent White abolitionists of the time, William Lloyd Garrison and Wendell Phillips, who symbolized the putatively antislavery North, admitted that their chief concern was to produce a genuinely Christian morality for Whites. Again Sekora writes: "Garrison said his ultimate intention was not to end slavery but to compel men to do their duty, and Phillips announced proudly, 'If we never free a slave, we have at least freed ourselves in the effort to emancipate our brother man'" (1987: 504). White abolitionist sponsors expected slave narrators to present simple but sensational facts, both in their books and their lectures, while leaving the moral and political pronouncements to those of supposedly superior intellect. Frederick Douglass described this racial division of labor in characteristic elegance:

> "Tell your story, Frederick," would whisper my then revered friend, Mr. Garrison, as I stepped upon the platform. I could not always follow the injunction, for I was now reading and thinking. New views of the subject were being presented to my mind. It did not entirely satisfy me to *narrate* wrongs; I felt like *denouncing* them. I could not always curb my moral indignation for the perpetrators of slaveholding villainy long enough for a circumstantial statement of the facts which I felt almost sure everybody must know. Besides, I was growing and needed room. (1994b [1893]: 662, original emphasis)

Those newly escaped from bondage sought nothing less than the total overthrow of a morally bankrupt social order. But slave narrators' tactics were, by necessity, attuned to the vulnerabilities of potentially sympathetic Whites. Garrison was always primarily concerned with how they would respond to the narratives. Thus were the narrators charged to depict slavery's horrors vividly enough to stir the senses without being too graphic—lest they offend more polite sensibilities. They had to employ persuasive rhetoric without seeming too literate—lest either the status of author or ex-slave be doubted. They were to move an audience by the power of the "autobiographical truth of their message," while focusing attention "upon [their] race rather than upon [their] own individuality" (Foster 1994: 4). They were to condemn slavery fiercely without implicating their White audience and without raising the specter of racial equality. Not only did the narratives speak about racial brutality, then, but they also spoke from within a veritable minefield of "racialized relations" (Small 1994)—less brutal to be sure but vexing nonetheless.

While the White abolitionists seemed concerned about the narrators' capacity to challenge a stubbornly entrenched ideology, the slaveholders seemed entirely convinced of it. And so, they bitterly contested the narratives' authorship and the veracity of the narrated details. Here, again, resistance—in this case, that of slaveholders—is diagnostic of the content and form of power extant. Certainly, if anything can complicate "the romance of resistance," as Lila Abu-Lughod's so-titled article urges (1990), it is the imputation of it to slaveholders. Their resistance to abolitionism betrayed the power potentially unleashed by the slave's use of the word. Douglass's case serves well as an exemplar. In his first narrative he quotes his once master admonishing his wife about the dangers of slave literacy: "If you teach that nigger (speaking of myself) how to read, there would be no keeping him. It would forever unfit him to be a slave" (1986 [1845]: 78). This insight was fortuitous, for as Douglass wrote, "The more I read, the more I was led to abhor and detest my enslavers. . . . I loathed them as being the meanest as well as the most wicked of men" (84). Narratives like Douglass's proliferated during the antebellum period, enjoying a wide distribution and readership.[12] These moralistic condemnations bitterly contradicted slave owners' own representations of the enslaved as being content with their lot. In this regard, the real effect of abolitionist discourse on what Sekora called "the impending drama of reformation" (1987: 500) was not in creating White sympathies in the North, but in forcing the South into the impossible position of justifying their system (Ellis and Wildavsky 1990). Failing to do that, proslavery forces charged that Douglass was a fake, and his narrative a fabrication of White abolitionists. Many narratives did betray the heavy hand of White abolitionist editors, while others were indeed authored by ex-slaves, who often stressed this fact by titling their narratives with the tag, "written by himself." Less common were slave narratives "written by *her*self." The most famous of these was Harriet Jacobs's *Incidents in the Life of a Slave Girl* (1861).[13]

Antebellum slave narrators also forced attention on the South by titling their works in a way that constructed "a moral geography of slavery" (Sekora 1987): a dossier of Southern slave states and the methods of slave labor exploitation contained therein, as in "Narratives of the Sufferings of Lewis and Milton Clarke, Sons of a Soldier of the Revolution; during a Captivity of More than Twenty years among the Slaveholders of Kentucky, One of the So-Called Christian States of North America." Yet narrators' goals also required that *national* borders be constituted as moral ones. Slave narrators often went abroad, so that their message would gain the widest possible reach. The Black abolitionists were a major attraction in Britain, enthralling the audiences they packed into large and small venues across the country, in big city and tiny village alike. As R.J.M. Blackett (1983) argues, Black abolitionists in Britain sought to erect what Douglass called "a moral cordon" not just around the South but around the United States itself. Their goal was to forge international revulsion of that nation as long as it held Blacks in captivity. Douglass, for example, titled his own tract "Narrative of the Life of Frederick Douglass, an *American* Slave" (1986 [1845], emphasis added). Not only did slave narrators' work center on morality; it created moral centers.

Space was key to the antislavery stratagem, not least in realizing one's dream of escape from bondage but also in titling one's narrative and telling one's story on the lecture circuit in Britain, thus expanding the territory of antislavery feeling and abolitionist mobilization. And in yet another turn, they created the hostile space that any slaveholder would enter in traveling internationally so that, in Douglass's words, "wherever a slaveholder went, he might hear nothing but denunciation of slavery, that he may be looked down upon as a man-stealing, cradle-robbing, and woman-stripping monster, and that he might see reproof and detestation on every hand" (quoted in Blackett 1983: 6).

Arguably, however, in appealing to Britain's moral authority, the Black American abolitionists were also creating it.[14] In drawing a moral cordon around the United States and aiding hence in its reformation, Britain could not help but emerge as the moral vanguard—if only by default, and despite its pivotal role in orchestrating the Atlantic slave trade in the first place and, in the second, enslaving Africans in the Caribbean for generations. This contradiction was duly noted by proslavery forces, who sought to challenge Britain's growing importance in the abolitionist movement (Blackett 1983). Black Americans nevertheless saw hope there because it had abolished the slave trade in 1807 and, in 1833, abolished slavery in its territories (Blackett 1983; Ware 1992). The spatial stratagem of abolitionists also derived from the fact that White Americans, "[i]n spite of their strong nationalism . . . still deferred to Great Britain as a model for cultural and social living" (Foster 1994: 17). In their own activist work, White British women likewise appealed to what they considered Britain's advanced state of civilization in arguing that British society should condemn U.S. slavery outright (Ware 1992).

Despite how immoral slavery seems now, abolitionists' strategies show that cultural preconditions were necessary for Blacks' narratives to move White people to action. In Britain, it was White women who were so moved, for slave narratives appealed to a firmly entrenched morality of gender that was not racialized there as it was in the United States.[15] That is, the sanctity of the woman's body, no matter what color, and the sacrosanct, nonracial value placed upon motherhood together formed fertile ground for the male slave narrators to cultivate. Douglass's famous portrait of his grandmother, lonely now that all her kin are gone (either fled, dead, or sold away), dramatizes the havoc slavery wreaked upon Blacks by casting it in terms of motherhood.[16] Such gendered appeals to White women's morals formed a crucial part of Blacks' lectures in Britain. Black abolitionist J.W.C. Pennington, for example, exhorted a public meeting of the Edinburgh Ladies Emancipation Society in 1849 this way: "Ladies of Scotland! Mothers and sisters, slave children are saleable at eight years old. Can the mothers of Scotland let their children go from them at the tender age of eight years?" (quoted in Blackett 1983: 31). The narratives also appealed to sexual morality. Foster writes: "In narrative after narrative by male slaves, graphic portrayals of sexual abuse of slave women by white men abound" (1994: xxxii). While their narratives condemned plantation society for making the rape of Black women lawful, they also betrayed a masculinist subjectivity that constituted the rape of Black women as one of the burdens of Black men's own enslavement.

By narrating slavery from the standpoint of the slave, Black abolitionists sought to produce a radically different social order. The twentieth-century slave narratives reveal a similar effort but in a way consistent with the way place has come to serve as witness in Liverpool. Here again slavery is narrated, only now it is from the standpoint of the port. The appeals Liverpool-born Blacks make to the moral authority of slavery reveal their own attempts to forge a radically different future. Yet the tactics of abolitionism—and, crucially, the spatiality of them—are important not as simple corollaries to contemporary discourse in and about Liverpool. Rather, those tactics form the basis upon which that discourse can be most fruitfully and critically analyzed.

Three Slave Narratives from Twentieth-Century Liverpool

One: "The Interesting Narrative of a Liverpool-born Black Schoolteacher, Written by Herself"

The silences surrounding slavery are produced not only in the rarefied environs of the Town Hall but also in the everyday context of schools. As a prelude to the first "slave narrative," I provide below an ethnographic account of this silencing, showing why the local citizenry learns about slavery so late in life.

For several weeks, I conducted fieldwork in a school located just outside of Liverpool 8. The students are between the ages of nine and twelve. After explaining to the head teacher of the Integrated Humanities Program that I was studying national history and identity, I asked to observe how history is taught there. He happily obliged and summarily read off a list of topics in progress. When he arrived at one titled "Liverpool in the eighteenth and nineteenth centuries" he thought aloud that I would not be interested in that—as if that had nothing to do with British history. Indeed, I was. I casually noted so, masking my excitement.

An utterly remarkable event occurred on the first day of my observations. The teacher for this unit of lessons, a middle-aged White man, asked his students, most of whom were White, questions about the wealthy merchants of Liverpool, whose activities they had already read about. As I did not have a copy of the material, I was shocked to hear the students relay its contents. In response to the teacher's question about what these merchants were trading, one student said, "Wine," an answer that met with approval. Another answer soon followed: "Tea." In retrospect I am struck by how thoroughly my informants had trained me to think about slavery in spatial terms. On hearing these "correct" answers, I wrote in my field notes, "There are casts of African heads on the Cunard Building, and the answer is WINE?!" Some time later I mentioned to the head teacher my concern that in this lesson, one that I thought warranted at *least* a passing reference to slavery, there was no mention of it. His verbatim response: "This was not meant as a Black history lesson." He explained that to incorporate slave-trading into this unit "would have meant extending the amount of the material beyond a level where [the students] could really handle it. . . . As it is, a great many kids have difficulty handling that material and interpreting it in a fairly intelligent way." Ever conscious of the response of Whites to narratives on slavery and careful to "lessen their suffering," not upsetting their delicate sensibilities, the supervisor sanctions the teacher's silence about the past.

This same school is in the dubious position to boast of having one of the three Liverpool-born Black schoolteachers in the entire city, a woman I call Ms. Battle. In an interview with her, I asked what she teaches her students about the relationship between Black people and British society. She responded that "race is a very important issue," one she cannot confront without first filling in what she called two "gaps" in her students' "general knowledge." The second gap she noted concerned slavery. She seemed genuinely surprised that her students arrive at school knowing nothing about it. But it was the *first* gap she described that reveals more about the salience of localness to cultural constructions of slavery. Ms. Battle spoke of the first gap thus: "You have to begin with the basics. You have to tell them about their city—even little things, like when they're writing, [they're] referring to Liverpool as a country as opposed to a city. And first-year students not knowing that London is our capital city, and where it is. 'London is another country' and things like that. And that's where we're starting from." Ms. Battle here suggests that her students conceive Liverpool as a world unto itself—off the map of Britain.

It was my special pleasure to observe Ms. Battle teaching a lesson on empire. The first half of her lesson involved colonialism and the latter detailed the workings of the slave trade. From memory, she wrote the following (excerpted) narrative onto the blackboard. Here she steadfastly tries to fill in the second gap, the one about slavery—even as she leaves the first gap dangerously untouched. Or perhaps her narrative served to widen it.

The British Empire provided Britain's industry (and therefore its owners) with a source of vast cheap raw materials. These materials came from all over the world. . . . All this added to the growth of wealth within Britain, *with Liverpool as the second most important port*, nearest to the Atlantic Ocean and the passage to the Americas where the slave trade found its dropping off point. The trade worked like a triangle and indeed historians called it the Slave Triangle. *Ships ("slavers") left Liverpool for Africa. . . . If you look at the docks of Liverpool many of them have their connections to this trade, for example Huskisson Dock, named after a man who owned many slave ships. The Tate Gallery in the Albert Dock is so named because that particular warehouse belonged to Tate and Lyle, the sugar manufacturer. From all over the world commodities were brought into Liverpool's docks* to supply the growth of the industries throughout the Northwest. The towns we know of in this area, for example Manchester, Birkenhead, Preston, Chester, and even Leeds in West Yorkshire, all prospered by the import of cheap raw materials. When the British East India company set up shop in India, the Asian people had an enormous trade in cloth manufacturing. Eventually when India became part of the British Empire this trade was dismantled *and the raw silk and cotton was sent, via Liverpool, to the cotton towns of Lancashire. In the mills it was woven into cloth then, via Liverpool, returned to India for sale."*

The issue here is not historical accuracy, but historical emphasis and the ideological work it might unwittingly accomplish. The italics I have added to her narrative show Ms. Battle placing Liverpool at the center of imperial history for these unsuspecting twelve-year-olds. With this in mind, this sentence becomes crucial: "All this added to the growth of wealth within Britain, with Liverpool *as the second most important port.*" Stating that Liverpool was the second most important slave port might convincingly relay its significance. But which was the first? Arguably, in a lesson on empire and slavery, the fact that the nation's capital was *the* most important slave port (as seems to be the implication here) warrants a mention. In Ms. Battle's narrative no other slave ports are mentioned; Liverpool alone is culpable. In singling out Liverpool, she betrays the same proclivities toward localism that she attributes to her students. To wit, London might as well be another country considering the negligible role it plays in Ms. Battle's narrative on British imperial history. Yet her narrative helps underscore the point that Liverpool, as a site defined in "local" terms, is also global—and problematically so. The world does not fold into the local, transforming it into a global site. Rather, the local travels outward, orchestrating the imperial linkages among British places and foreign ones. The local is very "extroverted," in Doreen Massey's terms, even if Liverpool's globalism does not manifest here as a "progressive sense of place" (1993).

Above, Ms. Battle deployed the local in an effort to shape the racial perspectives of her students. Her broad, antiracist objectives in representing slavery may be gleaned from her discussion of another lesson, which she described to me in an interview. In that lesson, she showed examples of propaganda used to justify slavery. For instance, she held up pictures of one bishop and then read a quotation in which he referred to Black people as chattel. At the end she said, "If you're offended, I'm sorry you're offended . . . and if you don't want to say it to me, say it to your parents, and by all means, let's get your parents in, and we'll talk about it." She continued,

> I think I had four parents in. They were lovely. They were very very nice to me. They just said to me, "Miss [Battle], I've always taught them that we're all the same, and that we shouldn't treat Black people badly." And I said, "Yes, I understand that, but you must understand that you're teaching them *your* point of view; what *I've* got to make your children understand is that even if *they* treat me as equal to their White teachers that there are people outside and there are people—their mates—that won't do that." And they were great! They were very understanding and very sympathetic.

Ms. Battle's strategy has a precedent in antebellum politics. She anticipates that her blunt discourse will cause offense. When it does, she calms the waters by telling these White parents that it is not they and their children who are being indicted but "their mates." Negotiating a similarly racialized minefield as did her antebellum predecessors, she de-essentializes whiteness, colluding in the parents' desire to be exempted from the immorality that her discourse exposes, earning their support.

The institutional parameters in which Ms. Battle operates cannot be overlooked. She is the lone Black teacher in a school where slavery is a matter of Black history—a taboo topic that the students "can't handle." How, then, do she and her message attain legitimacy? Just as the slave narratives and their authors did: with the visible support of a retinue of White sponsors. In what follows, Ms. Battle alludes to the presence of a White colleague during her confrontation with the parents, suggesting its role in her success: "I think because [she names a White teacher] was with me . . . we got them to the point where they didn't have a leg to stand on because they knew what was going on in the country and in the world, and they realized what we had to do in making their children aware." As Sekora notes, the real power of the antebellum slave narrative lay in the action induced by the text—not the text itself. And like the authors, publishers, and audiences of those slave narratives, in the contemporary one, it is teachers, students, and parents who are all drawn in as "actors in the impending drama of reformation" (1987: 500).

In Ms. Battle's narrative, slavery has a lot of work to do. Despite her aim to fill the second "gap" in her students' "general knowledge," she, like Douglass before her, wanted to do more than simply provide "a circumstantial statement of the facts." Her narrative was meant to induce moral indignation—and not just about slavery but racism itself, and not only as it affects her as a Black teacher in Liverpool but also as it manifests in Britain and the world. In the tradition of the slave narrative, Ms. Battle's tactics are meant to accomplish nothing less than the abolition of a social order overdetermined by racism. Despite its moral intent, her narrative bears critical analysis.

Just as ex-slaves invoked the experience of other slaves only to illuminate the singular experience of the protagonist, so too does her narrative. While she explicitly connects Liverpool to other national locations, she does so only to assert Liverpool's centrality; Manchester, a city larger than Liverpool, is described as a "town." Articulated relentlessly from the standpoint of the port, her narrative brings other places to bear only insofar as they illuminate the drama and poignancy of Liverpool's singular role in the slave trade. Crucially, though, her ostensibly radical practice is enacted in a context where London and the rest of Britain are scarcely imagined, as evidenced by the fact that her own students have a "vague and indistinct notion," to hark back to Douglass, "of the geography of the country." Unlike the antebellum narratives, then, which sought to represent the whole through the singular, her narrative effectively *dis*connects Liverpool from Britain by dint of its silence about other sites important to the nation's role in the slave trade. Indeed I never once heard anyone mention that London was also a slave port. London existed either as Liverpool's eternal nemesis or as the vanguard of racial politics, the site where civilizing, liberal, antiracist discourses had triumphed. Ms. Battle, for her part, does disrupt this view by calling attention at once to local, national, and global issues of race ("they didn't have a leg to stand on because they knew what was going on in the country and in the world"). But most slavery discourse shows London forging boldly ahead, while Liverpool remains hopelessly out of step, mired in the backward, "traditional" ideology inherited from its "unique" slave-trading past.

Two: "To Erect a Moral Cordon"

Some people say that Liverpool's architecture, for its grandeur, is without rival in Britain (London apart). The next slave narrative takes place in town, at the Walker Art Gallery, one of the city's exemplary buildings. In the summer of 1991, it mounted an exhibit called *Exotic Europeans*, featuring the art of nineteenth- and twentieth-century Chinese, Indian, and African people on the topic of (White) Europeans. Intrigued by the ironic title, I visited the exhibit when its curator was scheduled to give a gallery talk. Roger works for a prestigious arts organization in London. He came to Liverpool to discuss the aims of the exhibit, how the objects were selected, and some problems of interpretation. The audience consisted of ten people, all women and all White except for me and another Black woman. One of the White women was a museum administrator.

Roger is a soft-spoken, academically oriented White man who seemed to be in his early forties. His talk was chock-full of pithy quotations from art historians and other scholars, all carefully written on note cards. In his closing remarks, Roger departed from his prepared text to offer a personal observation. He said he was pleased that the last stop in the four-city tour of *Exotic Europeans* was Liverpool, explaining that it could contribute to what should be a continuous dialogue about history. He decried the silence around how Black people got to Britain, saying that Whites rarely discuss the Black presence in terms of colonialism. He critiqued empire for the megalomaniacal mentality it required, and pointed up the irony of the fact that the White British have been all over the world—as we see in this very exhibit—yet are in such a panic about Blacks now settled in Britain. As a climax to these remarks, he proffered a wholesale condemnation of Liverpool as a particularly racist city, owing to its role in the slave trade. He closed with an injunction that White Liverpudlians take a long hard look at that past.

At this point a White male security guard, probably in his sixties, came into the gallery after standing outside listening to what he obviously considered inflammatory statements. On storming into the gallery to offer his rebuttal, he made a very important reference to Roger's origins: "I don't know where *you're* from, but . . ." With this implicit reference to Roger's distinctly non-Liverpudlian accent in his own unmistakably Scouse one, the guard went on to defend the city by saying that the Labour History Museum had just featured an exhibit that, as he phrased it, "Liverpool 8 people" put on and that there had also been a Chinese exhibit. Outraged and offended, he shouted his points across the room to Roger, pointing his finger angrily, his face becoming more and more red as he continued exhibiting some very unlikely behavior for a security guard in a stuffy art museum.

Roger's comments and the security guard's rebuttal opened up a discussion about racial politics in Liverpool. Two elderly, seemingly middle-class White women chimed in with their views. One said confidently that at least there is no

ACKNOWLEDGMENTS

No text is the product solely of its author. Many individuals contributed significantly to the development of this text. As always, my first thoughts go to Susan M. Sullivan, Program Director of the Lawyer's Assistant Program at the University of San Diego. Sue gave me my first opportunity to teach and has always provided support and encouragement. She is a respected colleague and valued friend.

My current Program Director, Gloria Silvers of the Legal Assistant Program at Georgetown University in Washington, DC continues to display enthusiasm and passion for education. She has been of invaluable assistance and a tremendous source of encouragement.

Special thanks to the reviewers who evaluated the manuscript on behalf of the publisher and provided clear and concise analysis. Their comments and suggestions were of great assistance.

Vicki Brown
Carl Sandburg College

David Moser
Belmont University

Adam Epstein
Central Michigan University

Kent Thomas
Southeastern Career College

Konnie Kustrom
Eastern Michigan University

Finally, my most sincere appreciation to the following individuals at Delmar Publishers who provided guidance and support throughout the development of this text: Pamela Fuller, Acquisitions Editor; Sarah Duncan, Editorial Assistant; and Betty Dickson, Production Editor. Additionally, Barbara Coster provided excellent suggestions and comments as she edited the entire text. Thanks also to Argosy Publishing for its typesetting and production of the text, as well as their input for graphical displays within the text.

Last, but of course, not least, deepest thanks and love to my husband, Don, and our children, Meaghan, Elizabeth, Patrick, and Robert, for their amazing patience and understanding while I worked on this text.

I would also like to acknowledge the following companies and publishers who permitted me to reproduce trademarks or copyrighted material for this text:

The American Red Cross granted permission to use its AMERICAN RED CROSS DESIGN® mark.

Black and Decker Corporation granted permission to use its BLACK & DECKER® mark.

Dayton-Hudson Brands, Inc. granted permission to use the TARGET (& BULLSEYE DESIGN)® mark.

Dell, Inc. granted permission to use the DELL (STYLIZED)® mark.

General Mills, Inc. granted permission to use its CHEERIOS® and BETTY CROCKER (& SPOON DESIGN)® marks.

racism against the Chinese, to which another White woman responded, "That is absolutely *not* the case!" The first woman's friend later made the happy point, "We accept *our* minorities. Everyone knows there's a Black element in Liverpool 8. I lived there, and Whites got on fine with Blacks." Roger called her comment patronizing and suggested she talk to some Black people from the area because the ones he knows have a wholly different view. The other Black woman in the audience then contributed to the discussion. She thanked Roger for his point about Liverpool's history, adding that around the docks there are iron bars to which slaves were chained, as well as tunnels where they were kept while slavers were in port. Pursuing that point, a young White woman complained that there was far too much celebratory history of the docks and that there could be a whole museum on Liverpool and slavery. Another White woman added that the importance of imperialism to Liverpool's former wealth is evinced by the currently depressed state of the city's economy. After a few such exchanges, the museum administrator asked a question relating to, of all things, the exhibit. In a seemingly calculated move, she steered the conversation away from slavery, imperialism, and contemporary racial politics in Liverpool by asking Roger a question about the representation of Mary Kingsley in one of the artworks. That thwarted a discussion inspired by a comment about the need for precisely this kind of dialogue.

When the program ended and people began to mill about, the museum administrator swiftly approached the Black woman. She told her pointedly that she was mistaken about the bars and the tunnel. She said this was a local myth about Liverpool and that slavers with human cargo in tow never docked in the city. Overhearing these remarks, Roger intervened, saying quite to the contrary that they docked there all the time. He then rattled off bibliographic references in which this historical data was documented. This silenced the museum administrator, who was then told by the Black woman that her knowledge and understanding of history were part and parcel of a White supremacist worldview. The security guard, meanwhile, was pacing around outside the gallery, fuming. As I exited the gallery, he approached me to make some more disparaging remarks about Roger who, he reiterated, had "the cheek" to come here from wherever and tell them about Liverpool! Roger's misbegotten view of the city was, to the guard, painfully obvious by dint of his ignorance about the *Staying Power* exhibit at the Labour History Museum, an exhibit that chronicled the history of the Black community in Liverpool. That the guard approached *me* to make these points is, I think, curious. Might he have thought that I was, to use his phraseology, a "Liverpool 8 person" and that I would thus sympathize more with his defense of Liverpool, than with a non-Scouser's antiracist call to arms?

The guard's primary concern was to defend Liverpool against the most damning critique imaginable, for here the city was singled out quite explicitly from other places in Britain as having an especially shameful past and was charged with being especially racist for that reason. Worse still, these charges were brought by an educated White middle-class man, whose accent would immediately place his origins in southern England. Roger's status as an outsider seemed a major source of the guard's ire, as evidenced by his opening: "I don't know where *you're* from . . ." And in contrast to Ms. Battle's students, who betray a shaky understanding of Liverpool's relation to the rest of the nation, the guard operated with firm knowledge of the city's embattled status. The privileged position from which Roger launched his views are significant here. His association with "modern," "liberal" London, the moral vanguard, lent him the authority to make a radical critique of Liverpool. These, again ostensibly, radical critiques merit scrutiny.

The geopolitics that frame this slave narrative are akin to those of their antebellum forebears. These texts, constructing a dossier of Southern slave exploitation, allow the North to emerge, if only by the insidious logic of default, as a moral geography. The title of Douglass's narrative implicates the North as well, but in so doing it positions Britain as America's more righteous brother; hence, Britain must lead the way despite its own role in the slave trade. Similarly, pronouncements that erect a moral cordon around Liverpool render the rest of Britain authoritative on race matters. Liverpool becomes Britain's symbol, par excellence, of racial backwardness. What William Pinar wrote about the contemporary North/South divide in the United States—derived from cultural mappings of slavery in that country—is applicable here in Britain. He argues that "the North constructs the South as other, as a racist primitive place, a splitting off of its own racism and cultural development" (1993: 64). Likewise, ostensibly radical critiques of Liverpool that rely on the now well-established moral authority of slavery serve to trap and grind the British slave trade into Liverpool soil, absolving other places on the national map. In yet another turn, they imbue their respective, ostensibly bounded White communities with a more moral form of whiteness.

With all due respect to Roger's intentions, it remains crucial to analyze the moralistic tenor of his critique. His injunction that Whites take a long, hard look at the city's history betrays an attempt to construct a morality for White Liverpudlians—one best enabled by confronting the clear evils of slavery. Yet the motives of White abolitionists Garrison and Phillips shows that morality was not enough; for them it was an end in itself, bearing precious little relationship to the actual humanity, never mind equality, of Blacks. The fatal flaw of moralistic discourse was that it invited too much self-absorbed, self-referential soul-searching to constitute a concrete program for overturning the vicious racial order that characterized American (not just Southern) society. And likewise for Liverpool in its own national context.

Three: "Incident in the Life of a Slave Port"

The ubiquitous slave-trading Whites in Liverpool strike a rather masculine pose. Interestingly, it is White women whose romantic, sexual, marital, and procreative activities so thoroughly violate the proscriptions of those presumed to be their own forebears.

When there is a special event, the Black community of Liverpool gathers at the African, the social club described in chapter 5. On one autumn Sunday, it hosted a celebration for a newly founded ethnic organization, the announcement for which was posted all around Liverpool 8. It specifically invited all "Africans, African descendants, and their friends." As is common in any public or private function in Liverpool 8, many White women were there, including a few elderly ones dressed in African garb, serving sandwiches and performing other hosting duties. As is also common at these events, the bar was open. Seated in one of the back rows were two middle-aged Black women in the company of a couple of White women. These women caused quite a disturbance, providing continuous, disruptive commentary throughout the various presentations. A distinguished African community leader introduced one of the first speakers, a Black woman who was once an important political figure in Liverpool but now lived elsewhere. In his introduction, he noted that she was born in Liverpool. One of the Black women in the back was unimpressed. She retorted, "Pphh. So were we!"

The day's festivities also included a presentation by Paul, a Black man from Manchester in his thirties. A self-described "Afrikan Educationalist," he is, according to one blurb, "highly involved in the dissemination of positive information about the Afrikan phenotype which is then distributed 'by any means necessary' under the banner of Kemetic Educational Guidance." His lecture concerned the miseducation about Africa to which people are subjected in Western educational institutions and the effect of such distortions on African identity. For example, he critiqued the terms commonly used to define Black people. The term *Black*, he said, is problematic because it does not link so-named people to their land or their origins. By way of illustration, he asked the rhetorical question, "After all, where is 'Blackland'?" No sooner did Paul utter the question than did a quick retort come shooting through the audience from the back of the room: 'Granby Street!' With that the hecklers laughed uproariously. Indeed, these women were relentless in their heckling. Every point Paul made was met with their comical critique.

To worsen matters, there was an intoxicated White woman, perhaps in her forties, who walked up to Paul several times as he was speaking. She would pick up his maps and the other materials carefully arranged on the table in front of him and leaf through them. She stumbled around in the space between Paul and his audience, trying to make her way to the bar. On that journey she would try desperately, but in vain, to get a light for a cigarette she was holding with none-too-steady a grasp. As much as people moaned and whispered about this woman, she was not removed from the hall—as some people thought was appropriate. Instead, one man or another took turns pleading with her to sit down, guiding her gently back to her seat.

Trying so hard to maintain his composure, Paul continued. After formulating his general critique of Western knowledges about Africans, he related it to a personal experience. He spoke of a lecture series he attended in Manchester called "Understanding Africa," featuring the historian Basil Davidson. Unhappy with Davidson's approach to the subject of slavery, Paul challenged him by asking him who *his* grandfathers were. Paul recounted for us the question he asked of Davidson, "If we were slaves, you were slave owners, no?" He then described Davidson's defensiveness at this charge and noted that Whites must deal with the fact that they are descendants of slave owners.

This premise inspired a critique that was shouted in the form of a question by one of the White women belonging to the cheerful group of hecklers—only now they were less cheerful. She seemed concerned about the embodiment of these historical roles in distinct "races," nominated as *Black* and *White*. Thus she posed the defiant question, "Well then what about mixed-race people?!" I thought this was a brilliant question. While Paul was explicitly arguing that slavery is not the "special property" of Blacks, this woman's question highlighted the problem of dragging that volatile Black/White dichotomy of the past into twentieth-century Liverpool, a time and place defined as much by interracial kinship, sociality and community as by virulent racism. Paul paid no attention to her poignant query. As he continued his lecture, another White woman formulated a critique. She seemed to detect a threat lurking in his discourse on "race" and History, and thus interrupted him seeking affirmation for her excited disclaimer, "Yeah, but there's nothing wrong with Black marrying White!" She repeatedly offered this point as a refrain to several successive statements Paul made. Though his statements did not refer to the topic of marriage, interracial or otherwise, Paul's invocation of racialized descent (through reference to contemporary Whites as the descendants of slave owners) may have sparked this woman's defense of interracial partnering. Unlike the comments the hecklers had hurled to the front of the room hitherto, this point seemed of desperate importance. Lacking affirmation from Paul, she sought it from her neighbors, whispering to them: "It's alright for Black to marry White. . . . It's alright for Black to marry White."

When the exasperated Paul finished his presentation, several Black teenage boys crowded around him, initiating discussion of the material he had tried to present, against all odds. He commented to them about what had just transpired, focusing on the drunken woman who had been stumbling around during his presentation. He told these boys that they should be glad that she is not mother to any of them.

Later on I chatted with Paul, who was still seething. He disapproved of the way the entire event was structured. Another room should have been used. The bar should have been closed. The drunken woman should have been removed. He regretted accepting the invitation in the first place, vowing never to repeat his mistake. As for the hecklers, he commented, "I know how Liverpool people are; they do not want someone coming in from outside to tell them anything." The chaotic scenario that had just unfolded is typical in Liverpool, he said, "and this is exactly why people in Manchester do not like this city." (Later that evening, Cecelia expressed relief that "no one important from out of town" was there.) Paul also criticized Liverpool-born Blacks because they do not travel outside of Liverpool for important "Black" events, such as the lecture series "Understanding Africa." "Manchester is just up the road," he said.

As the festivities wound to a close, I introduced myself to the two Black hecklers, Caroline and Jean. As we stood chatting in the corridors of the African, Caroline said she was absolutely appalled by Paul's discussion of slavery. She said it was completely unnecessary for him to harp on about that, with White people right there. "How were *they* supposed to feel?!" Caroline demanded to know. She insisted that he had gone "way over the top." Then she and Jean started speaking to me at once, saying how embarrassed they were and how uncomfortable he made them all feel by talking about slavery. Caroline also took this opportunity to chide Black men for what she perceived as a glaring contradiction in their racial politics. She asked me rhetorically, "If they want to keep everything Black, why do they marry out?"

The thesis that slavery is the preeminent signifier of whiteness was most excruciatingly illustrated here at the African. A Black man's invocation of slavery immediately summoned up a potent, if latent, racial tension: the precarious status of White women in the Black community. The Black women's investment in protecting the White women from embarrassment—or "lessening their suffering"—reveals how effectively slavery discourse has come to produce narrow, immoral racial positionings for contemporary Whites. Paul constructed a brute, irreducible distinction between Blacks and Whites that allowed for no middle ground, which is where White women are usually positioned in this, "the most racist city in Britain." The dichotomy at the heart of Paul's discourse inspired two White women to hone in on issues of home, one asking, "What about mixed-race people?" and the other rising to the defense of interracial marriage. To wit, Paul's statement to the young Black boys ("be glad she's not your mother") castigated White women through the familiar. As mothers to Black children, these women are not only valued and revered *as Whites* but also, potentially, judged and condemned. The antebellum slave narratives sought to engage the morality of White women by showing how slavery debased even this most cherished and supposedly "most human" of all bonds. Likewise, some Liverpool-born Blacks remove their mothers from the category "White" by saying that they never perceived them in racial terms. Yet here at the African, motherhood was indelibly racialized—whitened—by the invocation of slavery.

In reference to gender and sexuality, the White women at the African may have defied the proscriptions of slave traders, but they actually followed the somewhat problematic lead of nineteenth-century Black male abolitionists. These men, it will be remembered, understood the sexual abuse of Black women as one of the burdens of their own enslavement. The White women who posed their pointed questions to Paul were similarly relating to others' bondage in terms of how it affects themselves. They intrinsically localized what was, in Paul's discourse, a placeless representation of slavery. His discourse, though, was proffered in a Black space, and White women in the audience correspondingly referred it to their own complex, tenuous positioning there and, indeed, in the home (chapter 8). Yet and still, it could be argued that these same women were *courageously* challenging the dichotomous relation between Black and White whose invocation in this context— by an outsider nonetheless—carried at least the implied threat against their status. Hence, it was the hecklers who authored this slave narrative, for it was they who challenged slavery's ideology of irreducible racial difference which, as Blacks strenuously argue, continues in the present day.

CONCLUSION

The sobering evidence of "uniquely horrific" racism in Liverpool must ground these final remarks. My chief concern, after all, is that Liverpool-born Blacks come to enjoy full citizenship, with all the rights and privileges it entails. While the silences that surround slavery are also sobering, I have argued that antiracist efforts may be misplaced by enslaving that history—holding it in captivity within the city limits. Perhaps Liverpool's shameful history would not matter nearly as much if Blacks were fully incorporated into the city's mainstream social and economic life. Indeed, the slave-trading past of London (where Blacks have jobs in "high fashion shops") is far more "hidden" than is that of Liverpool.

My critiques of the twentieth-century slave narratives are ultimately intended to push antiracist politics in more productive—indeed, less dangerous—directions. Antiracism in Liverpool requires a radically different spatial politic, one that breaks the moral cordon that has been erected around it. The Black abolitionists, for example, recognized American Northerners' moralist pretensions and struggled to call attention to the concrete links among local, translocal, and transnational forms of racial power. Hence, rather than allowing London to stand as the moral vanguard, we might ask how the brutal racial practices enacted in Liverpool are connected to, or even enabled, by translocal processes across Britain. This question relates directly to Douglass's critical insight about the complicity of the North in the brutality of slavery institutionalized in the South. We might further ask how London is complicit in the marginalization of Liverpool, and how this marginalization—in political, economic, and social terms—affects racist practice in the latter. Although this complicated question cannot be answered here, let it be read as a call for critical attention to "local absolutism," analogous to what Gilroy aptly calls ethnic absolutism: "a reductive, essentialist understanding of . . . difference which operates through an absolute sense of culture so powerful that it is capable of separating people off from each other and diverting them into social and historical locations that are understood to be mutually impermeable and incommensurable" (1993b: 64).

Local absolutism is perpetuated in Liverpool itself. Liverpudlians, Black and White, consider that city a world unto itself. I share Ms. Battle's concern about her students' ignorance about slavery. But that ignorance may owe to the ways Liverpudlians divorce themselves from the national collective of Britons, imagining themselves an alternative nation—as we also saw in the previous chapter. Her own narrative unwittingly reentrenches Liverpool's individuality. Indeed her own supervisor implied that a unit of lessons about "Liverpool in the eighteenth and nineteenth centuries" was not a matter of British history. And the people who line up for Mr. Bins's tours of the Town Hall expect to hear Liverpool's "unique" history. The hegemony of localist thinking is most baldly evidenced by the fact that Ms. Battle's students think Liverpool is a country. Sadly, this appeal to localism also informs the historiography of Black Britain, where Liverpool is invisible or where its Black population is rendered an exceptional case. Remarkably, the only actor in all of the foregoing discussions to specifically cite and resist Liverpool's marginality was the security guard. He referred to Roger's ignorance of what *had* actually been happening in Liverpool. Unfortunately, these happenings only concerned exhibitions about the Chinese and Black communities. Exhibitions on ethnic history and the history of slavery are important, but they are not nearly enough for the task at hand: dismantling racism.

In 1994 the National Museums and Galleries on Merseyside installed a permanent exhibit, *Transatlantic Slavery: Against Human Dignity*, housing it in the Maritime Museum at the Albert Dock—a popular attraction among British tourists.[17] While Blacks I knew were elated with this development, I remain ambivalent. The exhibit's placement in already marginalized Liverpool suggests that this "out-of-the-way-place" is where Britons should properly go to learn about slavery. For his purposes in *The Atlantic Sound*, for example, Phillips had thirteen British slave ports from which to choose. Why Liverpool?[18] Such narratives and commemorations all but invite the rest of White Britain to visit Liverpool not simply to access a "circumstantial statement of the facts" but to denounce White *Liverpool* while there. This is an inversion of Douglass's spatial politic, which sought to expand the territory of antislavery feeling, forging international revulsion of the United States. Here, the territory of liberal antiracist feeling is not being expanded but contracted so that White Britons, in their own travels to Liverpool, may conveniently absolve themselves of any complicity in racism against Blacks in Britain as a whole—in their own communities *and* in Liverpool. Such would not be possible if the slave-trading past were ritually and institutionally narrated and denounced not only in the other twelve British slave ports but everywhere. To its credit, the exhibit treats the history of slavery in hemispheric rather than local terms. But situated where it is, the exhibit may work to further lodge Liverpool's identity in the eighteenth century, rendering it—now permanently—a place apart. A national aberration. A slave to history.

On a visit to Liverpool in 1997, I spent time with a close friend who makes part-time work out of giving tours of the city thematized around its history as a slave port. His clients include students of all ages, as well as groups of British and international tourists. I accompanied my friend as he gave his tour for a group of international scholars, including many Black Americans. His narrative, while passionate, was devoid of the sentimentality that characterizes tours of African slave castles (Ebron 2002; Holsey 2003). As with the annual tours of the Town Hall, this one impressively recreated the social milieu of slave traders and abolitionists, showing, for example, sites where matters of slavery were debated. As with Mr. Bins's account, this one was also notable for its seamless interweaving of American and British histories. But here, as in Ms. Battle's narrative, no other slave ports ever got a mention. After considering the national implications of Liverpool's racial identity, I took up the point with my friend when I saw him again in 1999. I rehearsed the main arguments I made above. He fought back with indisputable historical facts, all relating to the dominance of Liverpool traders. After going back and forth for a few minutes, he relented. He agreed to list Britain's twelve other slave ports in his future tours. Then he added, chuckling: "You know, Jackie, it's all down to the Liverpool psyche." I asked him what he meant. "It's all about boasting," he said.

The Ghost of Muriel Fletcher

> In the white world the man of color encounters difficulties in
> the development of his bodily schema. Consciousness of the
> body is a solely negating activity. . . . Below the corporeal
> schema I had sketched a historico-racial schema. The ele-
> ments that I used had been provided for me not by "residual
> sensations and perceptions primarily of a tactile, vestibular,
> kinesthetic, and visual character," but by the other, the white
> man, who had woven me out of a thousand details, anecdotes,
> stories.
> —Franz Fanon

> My wound is geography. It is also my anchorage,
> my port of call.
> —Pat Conroy

IN A NATIONALLY televised documentary about race, a host of Black people from
around Britain were surveyed on the topic of identity. Two of the interviewees,
from Liverpool, were a brother and sister of mixed racial parentage. Asked how
they identified themselves, the brother said that he is Black, while his sister said
(I am paraphrasing here), "Sometimes I say I'm Black, and sometimes I just say
I'm half and half." A friend of mine had watched the program in a pub with his
friends and later recounted to me how they all cringed at her failure to assert,
simply and without qualification, that she is Black. But they were more horrified
that a respondent from Liverpool spoke in such ambiguous terms. She was, to
them, representing the city. At the moment that "Liverpool" was called upon to
speak, it conjured up the very terms that construct it as Other. Although we can
never know this young woman's perspective on halves, the mortification that her
words provoked is more revealing for present purposes. My friend's response
signals a form of double consciousness, or what W.E.B. Du Bois described as
Blacks' tendency to perceive themselves through the eyes of Whites, who look
on in pity and contempt. Here, though, the others looking on are not Whites,
per se, but the rest of Britain.

The racialization of Liverpool proceeds through a seemingly transparent geographic fact: this city is home to a racially mixed Black community. Of course, there are Blacks of mixed parentage all over Britain (and the world). The national census of 1991 showed that 39 percent of Blacks have a White parent, for example (Modood 1997).[1] But the difference here is that Liverpool is always already "different." Hence the "racial" makeup of "its" Black community features prominently within the repertoire of "details, anecdotes, and stories" out of which "Liverpool" is woven. The city's indelible association with interraciality sets it apart. And as in the cases previously discussed, the irrefutability of Liverpool's uniqueness derives from its historical beginnings as an international seaport. In British periodical literature, for example, this kind of statement is typical:

> The riot streets—"Toxteth" only to strangers, "Granby" to Liverpudlians—are as unwelcoming to outsiders such as me as they ever were. The census records indicate that Liverpool *is the only British city* where "a group of mixed heritage" outnumbers every other non-white community (if you leave aside the Chinese). The descendants, mostly, of African seamen from the port's great days, they have intermarried with white Liverpudlians for years, and still do. But you never see *Granby people* in the city centre. It is one of the few neighbourhoods in Britain that feels like a ghetto. (Emphasis added)[2]

The author's goal in this article is to analyze both the downturn in Liverpool's economic situation and the mixed results of the city's attempt to commodify itself by marketing nostalgia. Blacks' absence from the city center—I presume that he means as workers—is a symptom of racism and a cause of their disproportionate poverty. The effects of their invisibility in town are visible around Granby, where Blacks live. Yet these important points are neither illuminated nor advanced by his historical account of Liverpool's racial makeup. Indeed, in providing that very account he writes himself into a corner; he seems at a loss for how to name the subjects of his remarks in "racial" terms. Identifying Blacks as "Granby people" allows him to sidestep the complexity that he himself has constructed. This presumed "complexity," I would suggest, is integral to the racial identity of the city itself.[3]

Interraciality is by no means unique to Liverpool. The point bears repetition precisely because "Liverpool" is at once a sign of that multidimensional phenomenon *and* of uniqueness. A few brief anecdotes, culled from beyond the city, should illustrate the point. The first anecdote: At a conference years ago I had the pleasure of meeting a prominent scholar of race in Britain. I introduced myself by saying that I was doing research on identity politics in Liverpool. She mused in response, "Oh, well, as you know, they have a lot of identity politics *there!*" I take this "wink-wink" comment as a reference to interracial birth, sexuality, procreation, parentage, and marriage. The second anecdote: A good friend of mine, a Black Londoner, once relayed to me a comment made by a friend of hers who was just back from a visit to Liverpool. On surveying the racial landscape represented by Blacks' comparatively light skin color, she thought to herself that there had surely been a lot of (wink-wink) mixing going on. That she subsequently shared this observation with her friend in London exemplifies the circulation of stories that produce "Liverpool." The third anecdote (and my favorite): In conducting her own research on White mothers of Black children in Leicester, a city in the English Midlands, France Winddance Twine noted that her informants commonly puzzled over why she would pursue this topic there. They told her, "You should be doing this research in Liverpool!"[4]

By what means has Liverpool come to represent the British capital of interracial birth, marriage, sexuality, and procreation? The answer lies not simply in the race-thinking that renders these as "phenomena" in the first instance, but in place-thinking. Interraciality can only define the city if geography—or spatial knowledge—is made to appear innocent. The journalist above, for example, informed us that "*census records* indicate that Liverpool *is the only British city* where 'a group of mixed heritage' outnumbers every other non-white community." This normative mapping actively creates Liverpool's difference, even if it pretends to be a mere description of it. Through such localizing practices, the racial demographics of the country as a whole (39 percent of Blacks have a White parent) become completely invisible—even if, ironically, the rest of the country is needed in order to render Liverpool so particular. Such associations and evasions contextualize my friend's horrified response to his counterpart's nationally televised "half and half" answer. His mortification reflects a double consciousness shaped fundamentally by place, or the insuperable identification of Liverpool—never Leicester—with unusually and overwhelmingly complex racial histories, constructions, and positionalities. With this deconstruction of Liverpool's "complexity" in place, let me offer another prelude to this chapter's main concern, which is to show that LBB politics have either created or left unanswered certain ambivalences and ambiguities concerning race. The ethical conundrum of my enterprise must be spelled out before proceeding, as it is symptomatic of the dilemmas later described.

Previous chapters showed that LBBs have been quick to mobilize against publicly articulated affronts to their racial identity and community. This chapter may very well be considered the latest in a long line of such offenses, which begin with Muriel Fletcher's *Report on an Investigation into the Colour Problem in Liverpool and Other Ports* (1930). Fletcher is remembered for betraying her informants' trust and for presenting a twisted depiction of interracial families, which she argued were not viable. Yet the material to follow highlights community members' own contrary and ambivalent positions about the very practices that LBB politics have stridently defended. In some cases, people discussed the difficulty of speaking to each other, much less to a researcher, about these issues. The trope I have chosen for this chapter, "the ghost of Muriel Fletcher," names my desire to hold these important tensions both in view and at bay. The battle against Muriel's ghost would not be served by erring in the opposite direction, which would entail the creation of a patronizing portrayal that papers over contradictions in deference to the still-reverberating effects of prior damage.[5] Such a portrayal would actually render invisible both the enormous political agency LBBs have seized and the tangible results of that agency. The battles they waged in the struggle over racial meaning were crucial to their work in the spheres of rights, jobs,

Hallmark Cards, Inc. granted permission to use its HALLMARK (& CROWN DESIGN)® mark.

Kellogg Company granted permission to use its KELLOGS®, KELLOGG'S CORN FLAKES®, and EGGO® marks. KELLOGS®, KELLOGG'S CORN FLAKES®, and EGGO® are trademarks of Kellogg Company. All rights reserved. Used with permission.

Nabisco, Inc. granted permission to use the MR. PEANUT DESIGN®, OREO®, and RITZ® marks

Starbucks Corporation granted permission to use the STARBUCKS (& DESIGN)® mark.

Texaco Inc. granted permission to use the TEXACO (& STAR DESIGN)® mark. Courtesy of Texaco Inc.

Much of the basic information in this text relating to trademarks, copyrights, and patents is from the websites of the U.S. Patent and Trademark Office and the U.S. Copyright Office, and the author wishes to acknowledge these agencies. No copyright is claimed in any of the materials or forms of these agencies, including but not limited to Exhibits 4–6, 5–4, 6–1, 12–1, 13–2, 18–1, 18–2, 18–4, and 19–1.

education, and political representation. Moreover, the power of LBB constructions of race is evident, at the very least, in the contentions they have produced. An even better response to the demons that Muriel's name summons up would be to think ever so critically *about* the local and *beyond* it. By opening the category up for another inspection, we might come to appreciate that all of us—not just Liverpudlians and other Britons, but even writers and readers of ethnographies—are implicated in the process through which localization becomes racialization.[6] We can also see how the local creates a set of anxieties for the racial subjects that produce it and are produced by it, even as this selfsame space of difference provides certain comforts, a safe harbor. Geography is a wound *and* a port of call.

As with any hegemony, LBB tenets, if they are to hold, must respond to the realignment of social forces, including those that stem from LBBs' own successes in the localized politics of race. As a result of LBBs' multipronged antiracist critique, many people became fluent in what Nigel, in chapter 5, derided as "the language of racism"—so fluent indeed that one prominent LBB warned me not to distinguish between activists such as herself and Blacks generally. "We are paid for being Black," she told me. Hence, in her view, all Blacks would be able to function in jobs like hers because every Black person has an experiential understanding of racism and a critique of it. This apparent fluency in the language of racism was predicated on another force produced by LBB activism: the premium now placed on an unequivocal racial identity named *Black*. LBBs displaced skin color as a basis for determining Blackness, even if not banishing it completely. No matter how light the skin, the argument goes, everyone of African, Afro-Caribbean, or Black British parentage was Black. Furthermore, one's Blackness was located in one's politics—like those of LBBs as opposed to those of their African fathers—not in the shade of one's skin. Ethnicity was rejected as was, more significantly, any reference to "halves." The category *Black*, through its attachment to place (*Liverpool*-born), accounted for White parentage, especially motherhood. And White women, for their racially transgressive kinship choices in the domains of marriage and motherhood, were included in this radicalized community, also defined as Black. This chapter argues that these two forces—fluency in the language of racism and the premium on Blackness—clash in the period succeeding the LBB revolution. Privately, some express ambivalence about the increasing visibility among Blacks of a phenotype associated with Whites. A related quandary, raised in the third "slave narrative" in the previous chapter, concerns White women's positioning vis-à-vis critical discourses on race and racial identity. The two sections that follow treat these matters in turn.

IN/VISIBILITY

Within a few days of beginning this research, I made a huge gaffe. Luckily, I only made it to Cecelia who, from the start, was a great friend to me and supporter of my work. In conversation with her, I referred to a high-profile activist as White. Cecelia was shocked, if somewhat amused. She nearly burst a vein trying to make me realize that he was actually Black. I felt embarrassed to have made such a horrible mistake. It did not occur to me at the time, though, to ponder why the mistake was so horrible. Instead, I just submitted to the lesson that Cecelia promptly set upon teaching me. Cecelia thought that I would not get very far in my work if I could not recognize a Black person when I saw one. She pulled out pictures of a friend's children, a girl and a boy. They had straight blond hair and a skin color that I could only barely identify as hinting of Black parentage. Their mother is Black, and so, Cecelia stressed, "They are *Black!*" I got the point. I was a much easier sell, however, than some members of her own community.

After I first made the acquaintance of Caroline and Jean at the affair at the African, discussed in the previous chapter, I met with them a few times at Caroline's home. On my first visit, Caroline repeated the question she had rhetorically posed to me at the African: "If they want to keep everything Black, why do they marry out?" Her critique, which I heard her articulate in exactly the same terms on a few occasions, was targeted at Blacks like Paul whose discourse, according to Caroline, implied an absolutist view toward Whites. In this context, Jean proffered that a lot of the children of Black and White unions—whom she described as "mixed race"—have "white skins." "They are not Black. I've always thought so," she said. Jean's comment only makes sense in the context of the dominant LBB view, which argues precisely the opposite: even if children of mixed unions have "white skins," the fact of Black parentage renders them Black.

The significance of parentage is evident in all the terms that describe it and the phenotype perceived to result from it. The term *mixed race* was one among a plethora of circulating terms that described people who were not, to use another phrase I heard several times, "full Black." By strict definition in Liverpool, the term *mixed race* applies to a person who has parents belonging to what are understood as distinct racial categories, as I indicated in chapter 4. The term *full Black* was a shorthand reference for people with two Black (whether African, Afro-Caribbean, or Black British) parents. It cropped up in contexts in which young people—never beyond the early thirties—sought to differentiate the circumstances and experiences of racial identity formation associated with the two major forms of racialized parentage recognized in Liverpool: having two Black parents versus having one Black and one White. I only heard Blacks of mixed racial parentage use this term—one that would positively repulse older LBBs like Cecelia and Scott. Only one person who used the term, Greg, put a qualifier around it to mark its danger. Greg was speaking about how the cultural diversity of Liverpool 8 played out in his friendships growing up:

Yeah, you become aware of who has West African parents or *a* [West African] parent and who had West Indian parents and who had White parents. So I had lots of friends, but they were all in mixed areas [that is, of mixed racial parentage]. . . . It may be a situation of me having different questions than someone who was West Indian, 'cause their culture is—you could well have two parents who were West Indian 'cause of the nature of how West Indian settlement in England [took place]. Male and female came over. But with West Africa, it was predominantly male, so if anything they [children of two West Indians] were, em, [thinks for a few seconds] "full Black" in a sense—careful with the word!—but full Black in a sense, and I was mixed race, so their questions might have been different from mine, questions around searching for their identity.

In Greg's formulation, the progeny of both types of unions search for identity.[7] But their questions are different. For now, the significance of parentage lies in the ways that Blacks grapple with its meanings among themselves, in this period succeeding LBBs' unprecedented struggles against its racialization by Whites in town, by "those bloody old West Indian men" at the Caribbean Centre, by "those old Africans what come from back home" (as Veronica termed the seafaring Africans, in chapter 2), and by "the postcolonial bourgeoisie," or recent African immigrants. The danger of the term *full Black*, obviously, is that it implies that people of mixed racial parentage are not *really* Black.

And then there's the term *light-skinned*, which is a euphemism for the contested term *mixed race*. But, of course, a lot of people are light-skinned without being "mixed race." I am a perfect example. By my informants' standards, I was "light-skinned," which meant I might also be "mixed race." Many people assumed that I was. They would tell me, "You look like a local girl." With that, they would ask which of my parents was White. My response was always the same: "Neither. Both of my parents are Black." That, then, always settled the matter for them; I was not "mixed race."[8] Nor were they surprised at my answer, for many people with two Black parents are "light-skinned." A twenty-nine-year-old LBB I knew, Gary, articulated a variation on the theme. He said that I would be perceived as a "homegirl" around Granby Street, even if people did not know me. In a different context, he was moved to explain the distinction among the terms *mixed race, light-skinned,* and *Black* because he caught himself using the controversial term *mixed race*. The "real" Black perspective, he was busily opining, was located on Granby Street where most people are "mixed race—well, Black." To say *mixed race*, he clarified, is to refer to "someone who is light-skinned, not someone who is not Black." Finally, he added, "When I say Black, I don't mean skin color but attitudes, ways of thinking. Basically, what's inside." Gary has two Black parents and for this reason, he said, he did not experience the "identity crisis," as he put it, that Blacks with White parents have undergone. In describing his own "inside," he named the plethora of diasporic influences upon him: Bob Marley, Afrocentric thinkers such as Molefi Asante, and, of course, the Black Power movement.

LBB political activists, whose mobilization on racial issues has been so consequential, would agree with Gary that people called *mixed race* and *light-skinned* are indeed Black; but they would prefer that those terms just go away, lest they turn into identities and detract from the political force that accrues to the strength in Black numbers. Sean put the case succinctly:

What's made the Black community as a whole powerless to do anything about their position—the bad housing, the lack of jobs, bad education—is because they've split themselves and they've done it themselves. The problem is a lot of Black people in Liverpool have married White women or the other way around. So the term *mixed race* is out at the moment, so then the child then becomes "mixed race." Or, that's what they say. I'm in the same position. My wife is White. And we have a little lad, and so they would say that he's mixed race. I mean, you could then go on to say, "Well, what happens when he gets married and has kids?" It just goes on and on and on. The term *Black* always used to be deemed as offensive [to Blacks]. . . . But once the community sees itself as Black—that's it, full stop and there's no "half-caste" or "light-skinned" or "mixed race"—then we'll get somewhere. [He adopts the voice of Blacks in the political sphere.] "This Black community wants this,"—not *part* of the Black community because the other half is saying, "We're mixed race."

The fact that these terms circulate at all suggests that Black people still grapple with the meanings of parentage and phenotype, despite their own erstwhile attempts to render them socially insignificant. That is, White parentage, as well as the physical features that are perceived to signify it, are not supposed to matter as criteria for belonging in the Black community. Now, the terms of debate seem to be shifting. Jean, who is of mixed racial parentage, earlier implied that having a Black parent does not necessarily make one Black; rather, one's physical appearance does it. Sean's parents are both Black, but he married a White woman. He is concerned that his little lad does not get construed as anything but Black. Crucially, Sean's narrative reaches into the next generation through the assumption that his son will marry a White woman: "What happens when he gets married and has kids? It just goes on and on and on." He obviously meant the last statement to refer to the proliferation of categories. Yet it also aptly applies to interracial procreation itself: Sean projects it into the future through his son, which then prompts Caroline to ask, "If they want to keep everything Black [which seems to be Sean's goal], why do they marry out?"

Sean's critical concern about the power of racial categories based on color distinctions stems from his firsthand knowledge of Apartheid. He sailed to South Africa as a seaman and was traumatized to observe Blacks' subjugation by Cape Coloreds in the shipping industry, and the way both were subjugated by Whites. Bringing the issue back home, he says that Black people have participated in the production of an analogous system of racial hierarchy, first by accepting the term *half-caste* and, second, by continuing to subdivide themselves according to parentage and skin color. In the past, the term *Black* offended. Now, if the community is to get anywhere, everyone with a Black parent must identify as just Black, without qualification. When, in another generation, Sean's grandchildren are born, they should be regarded as Black. And he will certainly "see" them as such, no matter what they look like. But Jean will not.

My good friend Veronica had a perspective on the term *half-caste* that differs from the dominant LBB view. At thirty-two years old, her life has been shaped by LBB politics, not as a participant but, as older LBBs might argue, a beneficiary. She worked in an institution in Liverpool 8 that not only served young Blacks like her but also employed them. LBB activism made her very existence, her local-cum-national citizenship, visible to officialdom in town and it did so in unequivocally Black terms. In a previous chapter, I quoted Veronica on the matter of how her own parentage affected her growing up: "I never really thought about it. I was brought up in a Black area, so I didn't really think about the world out there because Liverpool 8 was just Black, really. You got a few people White, and your mum White, but I never really looked at me mum as White. Well, that never really come into it." She lamented not knowing her White aunts and uncles. Because her mother was "given up" by her family, all her "roots," she said, come from her Nigerian father. She regrets that she cannot access roots from her mother as well. Veronica very much sees herself as Black. She has had to be convinced, though, to stop using the term *half-caste*:

> I liked it in the old days when you could say, when you're talking about someone in the old days and you could just say, if someone—I didn't mind using the word *half-caste*. It didn't offend me, but nowadays it will offend. Especially my sisters, it will offend. They ring me about it, you know. [Names her sister] would be able to talk to you about it because she's lived in a White area for about twelve years as a Black woman married to a White man. And they went to live in an area, [she names it]. Have you heard of it? It's posh. She's probably had *her* experiences as a Black woman! She's a bit darker than me, I think. She hates the word *half-caste*, you know.

Veronica does not hate the word. Here she explains why she "liked it in the old days":

> When I'm talking to a friend, and you're trying to find out who they're talking about and they say, "You know that girl, that half-caste one, the one with the loose, curly hair"—that was the way to explain who a certain person was. And I'd say, "I know her, but I don't know her name." But now you can't do that now because people won't have the term *half-caste* used. So you'd have to either know the name or, you know, just think of—you know, the brown-skinned one. But when you mention the word *brown*, you're not sure whether it's going to be me, you, our [mentions a sister]. . . . But mind you, you could say, "[describes her sister's features more minutely]." But . . . your hair is looser than mine isn't it? But to differentiate between me and you, they'd have to find something different. So naturally, you're going to look. Whereas, people are getting offended by it now. Everybody seems to be taking offense. It's getting very [struggles for a word], whereas no one wants to speak these certain words so it's getting very difficult to communicate!

Veronica longs for the simplicity of an earlier era, before these stringent pressures on speech. In her view, the term *half-caste* was just an innocuous descriptor. Now she is supposed to join her sisters and other Blacks in railing against it—evidence of the success of LBB critiques. However, the paradox of LBB hegemony is that the very thing that was not supposed to matter—White parentage—has been reinscribed. In what follows, Veronica engages me in a meeting of minds because my own skin color was similar to hers.

> VERONICA: How do you feel if somebody says, have you got a White parent? What are your parents? How do you feel about that assumption? It doesn't affect you in any way?
> JACKIE: No, because it's not an insult.

VERONICA: You don't take it as an insult? Some people would, you know? Like with my son you might think he's got a White parent, but his dad is Black but I am light (I'm Black as well). But people—like my son is just where he could have two just light-skinned parents, or colored. But I bet when he's older he'll get people asking, "Have you got a White mother?" or, you know, "What's your mum?" I've found, like, myself even, it *is* cheeky asking! It is a cheeky question [laughs], when you think about it, you know? But everything is cheeky in this day and age, you know! But I'm thinking people will be asking—like, I wanted to ask a girl once ('cause she was like my son's complexion where you couldn't tell whether he was full black or not, you know?) "What is your parent, three-quarter caste or half-caste or, just plain . . ." You know?! And I don't know why I wanted to ask this question, you know! But I wanted to ask it you know! But I thought, "I'm getting worse. All this color thing is making me ask to know what they really are or where they're from, you know?"

The most important thing to notice in this quotation is Veronica's humor. Amid the dead seriousness that surrounds her, she finds the profound turn in the racial climate funny. Everything is cheeky now. As a harbinger of that turn, the assumption of White parentage has become to some degree insulting in this now proud-to-be-Black community. That pride—another LBB success story—is starting to tarnish White parentage, particularly as it concerns the next generation rather than the current one. The "insult" of it, for example, is not evident in Veronica's subjectivity as the daughter of a White woman; her mother was "just her mum." But in speaking about her son, Veronica positions herself as a decidedly Black mum. The father of Veronica's son is Black. Using Veronica's own terminology, that would make him "full Black." But his skin color, in her "view," is ambiguous. He might be mistaken as "mixed race." He will be asked questions. Will they know what he "really" is? Color is an unreliable marker, she suggests.[9] To know for sure, one has to make cheeky inquiries about the parents, which could very well offend him. Apparently, then, parentage now matters to Blacks despite LBBs' attempts to make it not matter to Whites. What I should have asked Veronica is how she would feel if her son were to be so mistaken. At the very least, we know that she does wonder whether her son's color—or, better, the perception of it—will cause *her* to be imagined as White. Given the normativity of White motherhood, and what has become, for some, the insult of it, is she anxious that such inquiries will render her, as a Black mother, invisible?

In chapter 4, I used Peter's genealogical narrative as an exemplar of LBB political subjectivity. Back in the early days of Black community formation, Whites in town argued against funding Black studies because "half-castes" were not regarded as Black. Peter also discussed the implications of his son's skin color, which he described in conversation with me as very light. Peter is inculcating a Black identity in his son: "There's no use me teaching him anything else. I pick him up at school." The appearance, then, of the father—both in phenotypic terms and in locational ones (at school)—assures that the son will be regarded as Black. This future-oriented generational process contrasts sharply to what happened in the past. The LBBs I knew who were, like Peter, in their thirties and early forties all remarked that their African fathers were obstacles to their own formation of African cultural identity. Now that LBBs are parents themselves, they actively produce the Black racial identity of their children. But the question still burning is, Does Black parentage and, now, *parenting practice* suffice to render a person Black—in the eyes of other Blacks?[10]

Veronica laughed about the craziness of "this color thing," which has produced more anxieties than there have ever been before. On the one hand, she frames the issues rather differently than LBBs have articulated them, at least in their political work. For them, the issue is race, not "color." They were concerned, for example, about the racialization of their kinship relations. They were concerned about the notions of absolute pathology that underwrote the *half-caste* category, justifying the subordinate positions of Africans, Afro-Caribbeans, the White women married to them, and their children within society. On the other hand, the significance of color, and phenotype more broadly, is still unresolved.

Earlier, Veronica suggested that the term *half-caste* was a harmless phenotypic descriptor. Phenotype itself became more problematical in the quotation that followed, where she discussed the "insult" of assumed White parentage. Some people, she implied, would take offense at the implication that they are not "full Black." As she continued, phenotype emerged as a site of pronounced vulnerability. Veronica puzzles over her sister's dedicated efforts to get her family, as well as the people in the predominantly White neighborhood where she now lives, to recognize her children as Black. This is what Veronica says about her sister and her sister's children:

> You got, 'em, like my sister's kids. I'm a bit mixed up with that because she's the same color as me, and her husband's White—and her kids come out White to me! And she's always on "My kids are Black! They're Black!" But I thought, "Oh, they're White!" And the kids are always going on about "They're Black, They're Black." You know, if they were to go into another town and say they're Black, they're going to get laughed at because they got blondy brown hair, but they're "Black" you know! So I keep saying to her, "You can't tell the children they're Black, when they're White." They look White, but they may be Black inside. But I won't argue with her on that because I know it'll end up in a big fight because she's very very defensive about it, you know.

Veronica's sister's efforts have been successful insofar as, by Veronica's account, the children are proudly and unambiguously declaring themselves to be Black. But she also makes the fascinating suggestion that Liverpool is where these children make sense *as Blacks*, implying that there are no other places in Britain where Blacks with blondy brown hair would be accepted. The implication of her statement about "going into another town" jibes with her representation of her own upbringing in Liverpool 8. She never had to think about "the world out there."[11] As chapter 4 made clear, Whites "out there" racialized Liverpool 8 indelibly. But within it, Veronica had the luxury of being surrounded by other families just like hers. Geography is a port of call.

Blackness, Veronica suggests, can be found inside the body when the outside confounds: "They look White, but they may be Black inside." In my mind, if not quite in Veronica's, that formulation separates race from its key signifier, phenotype, thereby denaturalizing them both. Clearly, the child's "inside" has to get produced—which is what Veronica's sister, Sean, and Peter are doing with their children. On a larger scale, LBBs built a social movement that produced the "inside" of people like Veronica. The irony, though, is that some of the very people thus transformed remain skeptical about whether the inside is enough. They associate Blackness with phenotype as much as with politics, or "attitudes" as Gary put it earlier. Indeed, phenotype gets read through the lens of politics—that is, through the very act of producing the "inside." Configurations of skin and hair betray a person's (presumed) racial parentage, further implying how he or she came to be Black. Such persons are assumed to have been politically indoctrinated, a process that would have induced an "identity crisis." I only heard Blacks with two Black parents use that phrase. And for them, there was no apparent process at all. They were the ones who would tell me "we were *always* Black in our family." Along very similar lines, Sean, who is not "mixed race," critiqued people who are for having willfully participated in the half-caste discourse. They should have known better, he implied.

Considering how fundamentally race is constructed through phenotype in Western societies, I would suggest that one of Black Britain's most radical moves has been to decouple race and the body. In chapter 4, I outlined that process through reference to the historical rather than biological construction of the term *Black*. That chapter also argued that LBBs have complicated the relationship between Blackness and phenotype by articulating race-as-politics. In that vein, they have insisted on the equal Blackness of people who fell outside of what had been the traditional, visually defined boundaries of that term—boundaries erected, as mentioned above, by Africans, Whites, and Afro-Caribbeans. My own appreciation for these moves informed my answer to the nested questions Veronica posed to me:

VERONICA: What do you think about that? What do you think the child should be taught, like? To look at them you wouldn't—I don't think they look colored, really. You wouldn't think he's got a colored mother. The daughter, I wouldn't know she was colored because she's got long hair, straight, you know? And she's telling them to say they're Black in school.

JACKIE: It's probably healthy for them to grow up thinking and knowing that they're Black.

VERONICA: You think so? I don't know. I suppose it's good for them to know that they're Black, not that if someone says to them, "Oh you've got a colored mum. Fair enough, are you Black or White then?" What would you say? I think their case is confusing, for them that don't know. They're brought up in the area and naturally all the kids will know [because] they all know their mother.

In this last statement, we find Veronica spatializing race for the third time. The first instance was in her localization of a particular phenotypic configuration. If her sister's children were to go to another town claiming to be Black, they would experience a painful rejection. The local, as I argued in chapters 6 and 7, is a spatial category that names and, in so doing, naturalizes cultural difference, resulting always in Liverpool's a priori disconnection from national society, except as the very embodiment of what England/Britain is not. Liverpool, then, is a port of call for very light Blacks with blondy brown hair; elsewhere, they confound. Second, Veronica suggested, albeit with ambivalence, that Blackness might not be a visual property after all; sometimes, it can be found inside the body (which is where Gary, earlier in this chapter, also located it). The third instance is in her retreat to Blackness as bodily—only now, its visibility is once removed. As in the case of Peter, who picks up his son at school, Veronica suggests that the racialized body of her sister—whether through "knowledge" of it or through its physical presence in the posh White neighborhood where she lives—determines the way her sister's children will be racially identified by others.

The various concerns about bodily matter expressed above bespeak the ambivalences and contestations surrounding the visible and the invisible as locations of racial identity and markers of racial belonging. These debates prompt the questions, How is vision racially constituted? And to what degree are racial experience and selfhood likewise a function of optics—as opposed, for example, to other techniques of power? Franz Fanon explored such questions in *Black Skin, White Masks* (1967). While many Black artists and intellectuals have regarded "invisibility" as paradigmatic of racial experience, Fanon gives that status to *visibility*.[12] In order to analyze it, he consulted phenomenology, which stresses that the perception of the external world provides access to truth, paving the way for one's transcendence. With irony, though, Fanon takes phenomenologists to task for being oblivious to the racial constitution and implications of perception and embodiment. The epigraph to this chapter quotes the lead-up to Fanon's famous "Look, a Negro!" passage. There he offers what can only be read as a mocking critique of this philosophical approach which, for its accent on perception and bodily experience, he nonetheless found useful:

> In the white world the man of color encounters difficulties in the development of his bodily schema. Consciousness of the body is solely a negating activity. . . . Below the corporeal schema I had sketched a historico-racial schema. The elements that I used had been provided for me not by "residual sensations and perceptions primarily of a tactile, vestibular, kinesthetic, and visual character," but by the other, the white man, who had woven me out of a thousand details, anecdotes, stories. (110–11)[13]

The warp and woof of such "details" consisted of "tom-toms, cannibalism, intellectual deficiency, fetichism [*sic*], racial defects, slave-ships, and above all else, above all: 'Sho' good eatin'" (112). Race, then, materializes in the form of powerful ideas about culture and civilization, not bodies. Those rhetorics precede perception, leading inevitably to the objectification of his body. In turn, when he is "in the world," he can only experience his body as a trigger of others' fantasies:

> "Look, a Negro!" It was an external stimulus that flicked over me as I passed by. I made a tight smile. "Look, a Negro!" It was true. It amused me. "Look, a Negro!"

The circle was drawing a bit tighter. I made no secret of my amusement. "Mama, see the Negro! I'm frightened!" Frightened! Frightened! Now they were beginning to be afraid of me. I made up my mind to laugh myself to tears, but laughter had become impossible. (111–12)

Fanon goes on to suggest that the self indelibly associated with his body, thus "perceived," can only be misrecognized: "I am given no chance. I am overdetermined from without. I am the slave not of the "idea" that others have of me but of my own *appearance*" (116, emphasis added). In that statement, he divorces the body from the "idea" that produced it, leaving us with the "fact" of his blackness. Fanon's racial critique of phenomenology enables that eminently phenomenological conclusion about race. Ideas may (mis)define him, but his appearance is what traps him. He implicates vision as the ultimate producer of racial experience, embodiment, and selfhood.[14] Fanon cannot himself be a perceiving subject in and of the world, as phenomenologists would have it. For being hypervisible, he cannot be just one human being among others. While the phenomenologist argues that truth can be revealed to the self through the perception of external objects, others' gaze turns Fanon into one of those objects, thwarting his own transcendence. In the White world, there can be no unmediated view of his body, though he does long for one. And his self becomes fragmented, damaged—a poignant concern for Fanon, as a psychiatrist and aspiring psychoanalyst.[15] These roles inspire his examination of race in relation to selfhood and desire: the desire to have one's self apprehended truly rather than in distorted form, the desire to be *just* a self (and a whole self), not the embodiment of others' categories and fantasies, not an object of others' gaze.

In the preceding ethnography, LBBs discussed the role of phenotype in determining what Fanon called "the fact of Blackness." Framed in terms of "in/visibility," the material shows the uneasy traffic between the visible and the invisible as criteria of racial belonging. It bears repetition in this context that, as I have argued in reference to place, the form of power called "race" is not reducible to the visual.[16] Fanon's useful contribution in this respect is to isolate particular aspects of racial experience and subjectivity that derive from the reification of the visual as a purveyor of truth. As a vehicle of racial power, the visual is never about what something looks like ("blondy brown hair") but about what the visual is meant to establish, the truth value handed over to it. Such "truth" owes to "the primacy of vision in Western culture" (Wiegman 1995: 10) and to the specific ideological imperative of the gaze itself. From that perspective, the transformation of bodily markers is not the engine of change in Liverpool/Britain; that status belongs to the very investment in the body as a marker of Blackness. LBBs' references to the phenotype of children should not be taken to mean, for example, that "light-skinned" Blacks with "blondy brown hair" are a novelty. Rather, these children are only the reference points for thinking through the contradictions—or imperatives—of an identity discourse produced in the context of a social movement spearheaded by Blacks (often the parents of said children) who themselves defied the visual boundaries of that category, as arbitrarily set by others.

LIST OF EXHIBITS

Concerns about how far the phenotypic boundary can be pushed betray a broader concern about the stability of the visual itself as a criterion for racial belonging. The vagueness of the dividing line between Black and White, and of what the line itself comprises (parentage? politics? phenotype? inside? outside?), means that the "fact" of Blackness can only be established on a case-by-case basis, one objectified body at a time. To some extent, then, racial experience consists of being perceived by the friendly and less friendly gazes of Veronica and Jean, respectively. For Fanon, the Black body signified a set of racially inscribed, cultural traits (tom-toms and the like). The "historico-racial schema" that overdetermines the Black body in Liverpool begins, at the very least, with the half-caste pathology and the assumption that Blacks are the offspring of illicit unions between White prostitutes and African seamen. But in view of LBBs' highly successful efforts, the Black body also comes into being through the gaze of other Blacks born here. Hence racial selfhood consists of the desire to be recognized, visually, as "just" Black and not to be misrecognized as White. Various skin/hair configurations and their association with White parentage signify that one's Blackness probably came about through trauma, an "identity crisis." It signifies that such a person was not always already Black, despite their phenotype. Despite the reification of the visual, then, phenotype itself is a moving target rather than a reliable indicator of one's politics or parentage, as mentioned earlier. "Light-skinned" people are not necessarily "mixed race." Hence, Veronica itches to ask a litany of cheeky questions. That impulse arises not from a person's ambiguous appearance but from the dynamics that make such questions cheeky in the first place. The politics of phenotype have changed more than phenotype itself. As Fanon suggests, narrative both precedes perception and creates the mandate for it.

People whose phenotype is perceived to disturb the already shaky boundaries of "race" may very well have their Black belonging questioned, even if silently. But, interestingly enough, that perceived ambiguity is the key to their local belonging. The boundary-confounding body and the self associated with it is welcomed in Liverpool 8 which, for that very reason, is the subject of "a thousand details, anecdotes, stories" (including the present ethnographic depiction). I was often likened to a "local girl." Gary insisted that because I *appear* to be mixed race, I would be perceived as a homegirl around Granby. Veronica implied that her niece and nephew would only be accepted as Blacks in Liverpool. Yet and still, in the posh neighborhood where they actually live, the Black parent's body must appear in the space of the child in order for the "fact" to be established. The word *visibility*, it bears mention, means "the ability to be viewed." A gaze can only occur somewhere. Even Fanon stressed his "appearance" as opposed to his phenotype, which can be interpreted—in line with a phenomenological approach—as a reference to his physical insertion into an environment racially structured in particular ways. His presence was clearly a surprise to the child who yelped, "Look, a Negro!" Along similar lines, the fact that particular phenotypic configurations are explicitly referred to as normative in Liverpool—*as opposed to elsewhere*—shows once again that place shapes race fundamentally and that the local, or a space of imagined difference from the nation, has been fashioned into a racial category in its own right. That category, and the "complexity" attributed to it, then informs the construction of "Liverpool," the signifier.

WHITE WOMEN AND THE FACT OF BLACKNESS

Chatting one day with Scott, I expressed a desire to talk with more White mothers than I had to date. His response took me aback. Among the many research projects that have been undertaken about this Black community, he said, few if any likely focus on Black mothers. He is surely right. White women in and around Liverpool 8 have been given quite a bit of attention. They are the subjects of many a master's thesis. For the normativity of their presence in families defined as Black, White women are quite the curiosity.[17] In response to various public talks I have given on the present research (all in the United States), audiences have expressed a rather telling fascination with this city, which, despite all my efforts at nonchalance, they seem to picture as exotica in its purest form, a place where racial taboos are routinely violated in a bizarre twist on the natural order of things. Scarcely have I been able to get away with a quick reference to the fact that many, perhaps most, Blacks born in Liverpool have White mothers. No matter what the focus of my presentation, I have had to respond to questions about The White Women. For their part, Black people and "The White Women" expect researchers to unsettle such fixations.

How might it be possible, then, to represent White women in a way that they themselves encourage and define? How to write about White women without reducing them to the monumental category of The White Women? How to accomplish that task without eliding the social forces that produce them as racial subjects? Finally, and most seriously, How to show the instability of racial categories, which is, on the one hand, of great importance to students of race but which, on the other hand, is anathema to LBBs? As with the preceding section, this one stands in the shadow of Muriel's formidable ghost.

The racialization and redemption of White women have already been discussed. Here I turn to the contradictory effects of those processes. I focus on the dilemmas that arise for two White women, Barbara and Lisa, who are differently affected by the hegemony of LBB constructions of race. These women's experiences also show the consequences of treating Blackness either as a nonfact or as an all-determining one.

But I begin with Marien. My encounter with her serves as a parable of what Fanon describes as a chief consequence of race: the unfulfillable desire to be "just" a self.[18]

Marien

It was by accident that I met the first White woman I got to know. Her nineteen-year-old son, Ian, invited me to his home on a Sunday afternoon. When I arrived, Ian was not around. Marien invited me in and kept me company. I explained to her that I was a researcher studying the Black community, and our conversation flowed from there. As afternoon turned to evening, and thankfully with no sign of Ian, she offered to substitute for her son as the subject of my research. She began making Sunday dinner for me.

Marien is not from Liverpool. She moved there from another northern city in 1965 and has lived in Liverpool 8 ever since. Her favorite topic of conversation was how the neighborhood has changed all around her and how she has elected to stay right there, in the heart of it all and in spite of it all. She lives right on Granby, and it was this beleaguered street that her kitchen window faced. She gazed out of it as she cooked, all the while talking to me. Granby Street was her reference point visually, narratively, and experientially. She does not know much about Liverpool, she told me, adding proudly that she scarcely leaves her street, never mind the area. "Why should I?" she harrumphed. She does all her shopping right on Granby because that is where she can get saltfish and ackee, plantains and yams. Despite the loss of the shops that, before the 1981 riots, lined this street—which is now barren of stores except for an international food shop, a halal butcher, a Christian bookshop, a hairdresser, and a newsagent—she still does not conduct business in town. She lives every day around the roughnecks that hang about on the street, but who do not faze her. Friends have prevailed upon her to move away from Granby. "Why should I?" she asked with another rhetorical flourish. "This is my home. What goes on out there does not enter my home," she said. A last-minute decision to go to bingo, as Ian later told me, once spared her from a front-row seat to a shooting. Marien is only in her mid-fifties, but her face betrays the stress of many more years. She has seen a lot. The 1981 riots devastated her.

Chicken, peas and rice, and salad were on the evening's menu. It was all completely delicious. Marien poured a scary amount of salt on her plate. She put too much sugar in her tea. She was a chain smoker. I began worrying about her health as I sat at her kitchen table. Yet the spicing on her chicken was so exquisite, and the peas and rice so un-English, that I was moved to ask her where she had picked up these cooking skills. I expected to hear that her former husband, who was from the Caribbean, had taught her. Phenomenal culinary talents are often attributed to African and Afro-Caribbean men, many of whom were employed on ships as chefs. Another White woman I knew, whose ex-husband was from Trinidad, detailed to me his various shortcomings. After describing each one, she added a refrain: "But, oh God, he could cook." And adult LBB children who cook what my friend Claire called "cultural food" learned to do so from their fathers. So Marien's answer to my question disarmed me. "I taught myself," she replied.

Until Marien said that, I was busily trying to figure out what earth-shattering questions I should ask her. In my mind, her real significance, until that moment, was that she was an Afro-Caribbean man's ex-wife and two Black children's mother. Her plucky reply put a different set of terms on the table. She became independent. I might learn more about her if I did not ask her a set of questions overdetermined by weighty racial histories as lived through the gendered roles of wife and mother. Maybe if I just listened to her as she chatted on about topics equally weighty I might learn what *she* thought was important. I already learned, without asking a single question, that Granby Street is home. The people are friendly, she told me, and you can always go to somebody for help. Later, she proffered an analysis of Granby's problems: an indifferent national government and a cycle of housing construction and destruction on the street instead of attention to matters of equal opportunity and education. Many people have left because of the riots, she said, but the place is going to pick up. You just have to stick with it. In the meantime, she is concerned that her children have the same opportunities in life as the White kids who live in Allerton, a posh neighborhood, also in south Liverpool, less than two miles from Liverpool 8. She also thought that Liverpool 8 was the only place in the city where her sons were free from racial abuse. In Allerton, she said, they would be cursed.

Marien is a small-framed, diminutive woman. Like other White women of the Black community whom I came to know, she was self-possessed. And she implored me to be so. For example, in trying to cajole me out of what she perceptively noted was my reticence to ask her questions, Marien surmised that I might have been nervous because she was White and I was "colored." "Never mind that," she instructed me. "God made us all the same." So Marien believes that "coloreds" and Whites are the same—even if the local and national governments, and the people in Allerton and the rest of Liverpool, did not treat them as such. Somewhat similarly, Ian would passionately tell me that White women like his mother are "Black inside." By way of example, he said that they defend their sons—to a fault, Ian said—in the face of their criminalization by the police. One woman Ian and I knew was in the habit of boasting about the accomplishments of one of her sons. But Ian emphasized to me that her son is a "known criminal." Ian's other examples extended into the sphere of culture. His own mother inspired his love of reggae music. He remembered her playing loads of Caribbean records as he was growing up.

I never asked Marien whether she felt she was Black inside. It seemed like an obnoxious question. And, quite frankly, I thought that description did not give Marien and other White women credit for being able to transcend racial boundaries *as* Whites. The Black status her son granted her represented—to me, anyway—a missed opportunity to de-essentialize the very category, *White*, that Marien attached to herself. She said clearly that she was White and I was colored. Her way of transcending that meaningful social distinction was to remember that God made us the same. Yet, as the White woman she considered herself to be, she situated herself squarely within an entity called "the Black community." I defined my research with that phrase and she presented herself as a wholly appropriate person to talk to on that day when I made her acquaintance.

Some time later, I popped in on Marien for a visit, at which point she promptly announced that she was going to take me on a field trip for my research. This turned out to be an excursion up Granby to a Christian bookshop, where some of her friends often gathered to chat the afternoon away. On this day, these friends were other White women—and, hence, other fine candidates for the role of informant. That is where I met Greg's mother, who later introduced me to him. And that is where I witnessed White women of Liverpool 8 discussing the city's slave history.

But this excursion was also a field "trip." In our short travels up the road, we happened across another pair that looked just like us: a Black woman of my general age and an older White woman. Just as she was due to pass us, the Black woman eyed me briefly and smiled at me softly. Though she did not know me, she seemed to know all about me. Marien and I—White and colored, respectively—had a presumed relation through and across "race," just as I assumed that the other duo were mother and daughter. I felt myself becoming Marien's daughter in that surreal little moment. I felt myself being made into the "local girl" to whom I was so often likened. Earlier in this chapter, it was the Black mother's presence that made a seemingly White child Black. Here, it's the White mother's presence that made the anonymous Black person (me) local. The other Black woman's warm, if fleeting, reception of me—based, perhaps, on the assumption of White parentage—felt like an embrace, an affirmation.

God made us all the same. But Marien did recognize a distinction—as did, I assume, the Black woman on Granby Street. Since Marien's positioning as a White woman is central to the social relations that define Liverpool 8, it is impossible to treat her or other White women apart from their connection to the Black people whom they befriend, marry, and mother. Those relations are colored, in turn, by the heightened attention to race in the community that LBBs—in concert with others, including White women—effectively, if incompletely, radicalized.

Barbara

Barbara featured briefly in the previous chapter. A couple of young Blacks on Granby Street edified her about Columbus's role in the slave trade as she made her way home from the celebration of his "discovery" of America.

Barbara is fifty-nine years old, and was born and raised in Anfield, in the north end of Liverpool. She described Anfield as "a pure White area." Growing up, she never saw a Black person until one showed up in her school to give a presentation about racism. His influence on her was profound: his talk represented the only counter to the racist views that her brothers and her father routinely expressed at home. Barbara started working when she was sixteen years old and began to develop a social life outside of Anfield. In that period, she "got into meeting Black people," as she put it. She would travel several miles by bus to the dock areas in the south end and to the nearby neighborhood where Blacks lived. One of the Black sailors she met at the docks gave her his picture, which she promptly placed in a glass cabinet at home. While her mother admired the man for his smart, uniformed dress, one of her brothers was so outraged, both by the photo and by Barbara's shameless display of it, that he beat her up. Barbara had two daughters by two Black men, and she continued living in Anfield until the birth of her second daughter, after which she moved to Liverpool 8.

Barbara met her Nigerian husband, now deceased, at a party. He was an esteemed member of the Black community, she told me. "All the big families knew and respected him—even all the big families. Around here now, you get lots of big names in our area, like [she names some families] and they're all Black families. They all respected him. He probably knew them since they were little, and their dads all knew each other. They all looked up to him." And through her marriage to him, Barbara garnered a similarly high status. "[H]e used to take me everywhere. They used to have, like, house parties. These Nigerians have a lot of house parties. All the different tribes they get together, or they go to each others' houses, if it's somebody's birthday or whatever, and they have meetings and they all bring the wives, and I was mixing with all the wives and he was always dead proud of me." Her husband, she said, adored her, treated her well, and adopted her children as his own. He even sent them all to Nigeria to meet his family.

> Even when we went to Nigeria, they all thought that my children, especially [Jenny]—he used to write home about his wife and his children. So when we went home, they all just automatically thought [Jenny]—they thought she was his, 'cause he wrote so many letters home about his [Jenny]. Because she used to really get spoiled by him, they just thought that [Jenny] belonged to him, and I just had to go along with it! Because really, I had never been in contact with them. But you can see by looking at her—you couldn't even tell her nationality. I couldn't believe that they just took her as their daughter; but maybe they were just thinking about her like he was thinking about her. They can't really think it's his daughter, like, you know. But he had written home about us so many times, that when I got there, the whole room was decorated with pictures of us! Pictures here, there and everywhere. Oh yeah, he was good.

Barbara cannot—or more appropriately, does not want to—go home again to Anfield. Above, she actually refers to Nigeria as "home." The shift in her own racial positioning makes her feel alienated from the old neighborhood. As she put it, "I've been here so long, I class *this* as my community. I class *this* as my home. I don't class Anfield as my home. . . . Most of the things that happened to me—they weren't happy times for me. It was only that there was my mother who, if she was living there now, it would be like a happy time. But since she went, Anfield went as well." Anfield is just the sort of neighborhood that authors of Liverpool autobiographies have been memorializing since the 1960s. In chapter 6, Frank Unwin lamented the emigration of Scottie Roaders, who now make their homes "in other countries and other climes." He does not hint that some of them may have dropped anchor here, in Liverpool 8.

Like LBBs, Barbara also constructs place through race and kinship. Her mother's presence made Anfield "a happy time," home. But she could not live there with a child recognized as Black. The racism of her brothers and neighbors also ran her out. As a family, Barbara, her husband, and her children were not able to cross town and find kinship with her White family, but they were able to cross an ocean and be ceremoniously welcomed by her husband's people in Nigeria. I asked her how she perceives her own identity as a White woman in the Black community.

I don't think about it. I just feel I'm a part of the Black community. I could never live in Anfield. I just couldn't. . . . Maybe I just class myself, I don't know whether it's "Black" or not, but just as a person. I have my own identity. . . . And I don't, like, condemn those White people for the way they felt, like me brother and that. Maybe you were just ignorant like the way I was, but you are a different person than what I am. I couldn't look at a person and be looking at a color, white and black. Like kids, you just start off looking at them as kids and carry on looking at them like that through their life. . . . I feel like we down here in Liverpool 8, Black and White women, are closer down here, like when we all go down to the Carnival and that. I just think of them like as if they're the same. They're all my friends and nothing else, kind of thing.

Barbara has traveled a long way from Anfield. For her, that "pure White area" is the site of racism, while Liverpool 8 stands for interracial mixing. At one point, she narrated her journey across racial difference through the cultural marker that is food. Before she lived in Liverpool 8, she visited a friend of hers who lived there, a White woman married to a Black man. Her friend offered her some of the meat and rice dish that she had prepared. Barbara reported that she turned her nose up at it because it was so unfamiliar. "When I think about it now," she continued, "I should've eaten it. It's my favorite now!" Her view of herself as a White person has been transformed. She is not the same as she used to be, or like her brother still is. She feels part of the Black community, but does not feel the need to define herself as Black. She prefers to be "just a person," and likewise are her friends just her friends, and kids just kids. In refusing racial distinctions in favor, alternately, of mixing and of being just a person, Barbara articulated an upbeat outlook on Black community life. Black and White women are close, and she had a great marriage to a Nigerian, who was always dead proud of her. Everything seemed to be in place. She even noticed a transformation in the attitudes of Whites just beyond the Granby area.

Granby Street, which is about four blocks long, intersects on one end with a major road, Princes Avenue. On the other side of Princes Avenue, Barbara noted, lived Whites who were hostile to Black people. Barbara reported on the easing of tensions, noting that "now they're getting together a bit more. Black people let people understand who they are." Later, though, she discussed these changes more pointedly, especially in terms of how they affect her. Despite her longtime membership in the community, Barbara expressed confusion about why, considering that she does not "see" color, she must now use the term *Black* rather than *half-caste*. "You can't call them half-caste now. They really get vexed. It's just a name! I know a woman—we call her 'half-caste [Laura].' She wouldn't be called anything else! Why do we all of a sudden have to change? We have to start calling them Black! I don't care what I call them, really."

Barbara's ambivalence, if it can be called that, speaks back to the same LBB politics that served to redeem her own identity as a White woman in the Black community. Barbara does not see herself, her friends, or her children in terms of color, so she believes that this should be Blacks' outlook as well.[19] But here the context in which she made this argument tells all. She had been talking about her eldest daughter, who was once enrolled in one of the Black studies courses offered by a Black organization in Liverpool 8. As a result, her daughter "gets vexed when she sees what Whites have done." She would return home with new understandings of history and scoff at Barbara's responses to it by saying things like, "You don't know what they [Whites] are like." Moments earlier, Barbara observed that Whites on the other side of Princes Avenue had been put on notice: "Black people let people understand who they are." Whites on her own side of Princes Avenue seemed not to need this indoctrination. When Barbara perceived her daughter to be putting *her* on notice, she was prompted to respond, "*I'm* White; not everybody's the same." On the one hand, Barbara uses her own color blindness to suggest that her daughter should see her, as her mother, outside of dominant racial categories. On the other hand, Barbara has to constitute herself as White, not "just a person," in order to de-essentialize Whiteness; she does this in the hope that she can become "just a person" at home, which seems rather impossible.

Racialized knowledge has caused a rift between mother and daughter. Barbara implies that she has overcome the racism her daughter was analyzing in her studies. Speaking of her brother, Barbara suggested that perhaps he is as ignorant as she used to be. Her newly acquired taste for foods associated with Blacks served as a narrative benchmark for her own evolving identity as a White woman adopting a different way of life in the Black space that has become her home. However, her poignant commentary about the term *half-caste* is triggered by her discussion of her child's own evolving racial identity—which, unlike Barbara's own transformation, has not been conflict-free. From Barbara's perspective, her daughter was erecting racial boundaries, not crossing them.

As described earlier, it was by accident that Barbara acquired the very same kind of knowledge her daughter was seeking. A couple of lads on Granby Street edified Barbara about the city's history vis-à-vis slavery. She was forced to reckon with new knowledge concerning historical problems of race as she walked through her neighborhood. In that instance, she was quite willing to grapple with its implications. It was all abstract. It did not impinge upon her life or her status as a mother. She was embarrassed for not having known all that stuff. But otherwise, that knowledge did not affect her—unlike the kind that her daughter brought home, which, in Barbara's view, implicated her directly. At home, she is told that she does not know "what Whites have done" and "what Whites are like." And with such statements, her own color-blind view of the world goes on trial. The political injunction that is the price of Barbara's ticket into the Black community relates directly to that crisis. She is called upon not merely to replace the term *half-caste* with the term *Black* but to understand the critical difference between them. Barbara represented the issue in terms of semantics and in terms of the bother of "having to change" after all these years. But these waters run a lot deeper. *Half-caste* may very well be just a term. But *Black* is not. The latter was most certainly the term circulating in her daughter's classes. As well, that term names a position from which to expose and critique all the ideologies that produced Barbara's privilege. All of that visits Barbara at home, where she does not have the luxury of being "just a person."

In the early years of their activism, LBBs recognized that White women and their children were racialized jointly through their kinship relation. As well, LBBs acknowledged that White women were giving up their families as well as the privileges of Whiteness by entering into a community that would come to be called Black and by creating families also defined as such. LBBs' political innovation, I would argue, was to disassociate phenotype from political position in a way so radical as to incorporate these women into the distinctly racial (that is, political not phenotypical) identity they were claiming. The constitution of Black identity in such terms has a tenuous hold, though. On the one hand, Ian suggested that White mothers' political subjectivities and practices—defending their Black sons against criminalization, for example—made them Black inside. And Barbara recognized that she had the option of defining herself as Black: "I don't know whether it's Black or not." On the other hand, these meanings cannot seem to withstand the contradictions posed by other, *also* radical constructions of race— such as those articulated in her daughter's courses. Safe haven though Liverpool 8 may be, it is not cut off from the rest of the city and the country, where Barbara's Whiteness may be compromised, yes, but where she is still reckoned to be White after all. Even in Liverpool 8, people construct race through phenotypic difference. Marien and Barbara see themselves as members of the Black community; but they also distinguish who is White and who is Black (or colored), even as they work to make the difference socially insignificant. God made us all the same.

Barbara's dilemma underscores the unresolved tension over how to situate the heroic White mothers in relation to complex discourses on past and present racism—discourses that produce, respectively, phrases like "what Whites have done" and "what Whites are like." Moreover, the inclusion of White women into the category *Black* may actually be deleterious, insofar as it renders it impossible for White women to challenge racism while remaining categorically White, even inside. Just as seriously, the construction of Liverpool 8 as a safe haven from racism and the recognition of White women's racialization encourage the view that these women are totally above the fray, only victims of racial power, not beneficiaries of White privilege, never mind agents of it. Racism exists on the other side of Princes Avenue, for example, or in Allerton, or in Anfield, or in town.

Another White woman I knew told me a story. A member of her husband's Black family, someone with whom she had tense relations, accused her of being racist. The accused responded, "How could I be racist? Look what I married!"

Lisa

Barbara placed the problem of racism "out there"—always beyond herself and beyond Liverpool 8, a place she defines through harmonious interracial mixing. Barbara declares herself just a person, and so she cannot quite reconcile with the fact that people all around her are declaring themselves to be Black, Black, Black. Lisa, by contrast, has grappled with that fact all too well.

Like Barbara, Lisa is originally from the north end of the city. She was part of LBB organizing circles in their heyday. She engaged in antiracist teaching and later organized with Black women on feminist issues. She attributes "the fight in her" to her Irish background. In the early 1980s, Lisa taught the earlier version of courses like those that, in the 1990s, produced the racial knowledges Barbara's daughter was accessing. Lisa featured in chapter 4, where she described how she used the classroom to educate young people of mixed racial parentage about Black identity. She forbade them from using the term *half-caste* and sought to convince them that they could identify as Black without negating or otherwise compromising their relationships to their White mothers.

I met Lisa through her close friends, Cecelia and Yvette. In the social situations in which I first met her, Lisa exhibited the gift for storytelling that is a source of Scouse pride. I was privileged to witness her showing off that cultural endowment at one of Yvette's dinner parties. Her use of irony, the sharpness of the images she cut, her word play, self-deprecation, and deadpan delivery kept us all at her mercy. Her abilities to analyze language and to use it bluntly (another marker of Scouse) were also her calling cards in the educational arenas in which she worked, in town and in Liverpool 8.

In the late 1980s, Lisa pursued a university degree as part of an economic survival strategy. She had four children and was without work. Living off the dole did not sustain her financially. She realized that she would be paid more if she were to go to university, for that would allow her to live off one of the grants that were, then, automatically given to students. Lisa's degree was in race and ethnic studies. As part of her requirement, she produced a thesis about White women like herself, yet not in their role as Blacks' mothers but as their wives. Her research goal was to learn how White women understood their own racism and how it unfolded in their marriages.

But Lisa was ultimately disappointed in the way they narrated their lives: "Sometimes I found in talking to White women with Black men that they had— the majority of them weren't very articulate. They couldn't express themselves. You find yourself leading them, and you didn't want to lead them. Or they wouldn't tell the truth. They'd gloss over it." She went on:

> Some of them were useless; they had very little awareness of how racism worked in their lives. They knew how their relationships went. They put racism more "out there" and considered society was racist toward them. They really believed they were victims of racism, whereas of course you're not a victim of racism if you're a White woman. . . . I was trying to say, "Do you believe that you are racist, that you have grown up in a racist society, that you were saturated in racism from the day you were born?"

She formulated such questions as a result of contemplating her own upbringing: "My mother was racist, as was my father, so was all my family. So was I, very much so. I didn't realize for many years. You work it out of your system over many years, and then looking at it in yourself, and changing your way of thinking, and speaking in many ways." Lisa's own sophistication on race matters set

her up to be disappointed in her informants. As well, her penetrating, perhaps imposing, demeanor might have overpowered them.

I may as well confess that I find Lisa irresistibly quotable. Her vivid, fearless words reflect how thoroughly she has thought about the same issues that she pursued in her research. But her vulnerabilities seep through as well. In what follows she continues on the topic of her parents. Having a baby out of wedlock marked the beginning of the end of her relationship with them.

> I don't think I'd ever been all that close to them. I was a bit unconventional, a bit of a
> risk taker. I'd had a child out of marriage. And of course, that put me on the wrong
> side of the tracks for a start in a White, working-class, Catholic, Irish family. . . . No
> respectable boy would marry me. As it turned out, the boy who fathered my first child
> married me, so that was one in the eye for them [her parents]. But it never worked out.
> They more or less forced me to marry him. It was just too much for my folks. They always
> thought they were very respectable people. How can I put it? They thought they
> were somebody. Oh, good God, it was terrible for me to have that child! They couldn't
> get rid of me fast enough when I married [names her first husband]. My eldest child
> was two and a half. And then the next three years I had another three kids. I lived with
> them, with the baby, until I got married. That was pure hell. But I wasn't allowed to
> go out or anything else, until I got married. So [when] I moved to Liverpool 8, they
> weren't surprised. I'd already disgraced myself. That was the ultimate disgrace, you
> know. My mother used to say, "You must've thought about the worst way that you
> could've offended us, or hurt us, and done it." I didn't think like that at all.

Lisa's first marriage dissolved. Among other problems, her husband physically abused her. Since then she has been involved with one man for thirty years, Rick, who is Black. Lisa described her life with Rick as "interesting"—a word that she spoke with irony.

> In fact, I'll be perfectly honest with you. When I first met [Rick] it was a kind of a
> fling. I didn't think I'd last this long with him. I didn't think I'd have children with
> him and still be together thirty years on. I couldn't! It was too terrifying! I knew how
> people felt about Black people! It scared the shit out of me, you know! It was
> thrilling as well, at the time. You were stepping over the traces, you know. And I was
> always one for stepping over the traces. An attention seeker I guess you'd call it. But
> it backfired on me anyway, in the sense that it became a lifetime [sigh]. It wasn't a
> joke anymore. It wasn't "an experience." It wasn't a fling. I fell in love. And [sighs
> again] stayed in love for a very long time, if I'm not still in love now. I think I am in
> some ways. But I did fall for him, very very hard.

Her discussion of the initial excitement about being with a Black man gave way to ambivalence, as she began thinking about the "interesting" life she has had with Rick for all these thirty years. Her attraction to a Black man, she intimates, represented a sexy kind of danger, even if it gets tempered by the sober realization of what being partnered with a Black man meant.

Lisa sees the effects of race operating at every identifiable stage in her life, before she began associating with Black people and ever since. So I asked what first prompted her to think about racism. "Don't forget," she said, "the sixties were very much a time of Black Power and so on, and it did spread here as well. . . . It was impossible not to think about racism because of the Black Power movement." From those beginnings, she learned to analyze the implications of different race/gender arrangements:

I saw more of how racism worked after I met [Rick] obviously because it was open season on you, with White men. The White man saw you with a Black man, and they'd think they could just "take you" 'cause you were no good anyway; you were there for the taking as far as they were concerned. It's different for the White men. White men walk around with a Black woman on their arm, and they think they're a hell of a guy! All their mates will think they're a hell of a guy 'cause the Black women are usually elegant, beautiful, beautifully dressed, and "exotic." I don't think there's a White man living who hasn't lusted after a piece of black ass—to put it like that, if you don't mind. So it's a hell of a thing for a White man. But it'd be different for a White woman. You can tell by the look in people's faces as you walk past with your Black fella. Like that [gives a dirty look], you know? Shit under their foot. But if they wanted you, they'd come around and try and get you because you were available as far as they were concerned. If you're with a Black man, you're "loose."

She was blissfully in love with Rick, and after many years of being together they married. So when the first shoe fell, she was unprepared—which she also analyzes in racial terms. Here she alludes to one of her theories about White women's racism, now applying it to herself. She believes that White women, for being White, are too sure of themselves.

That point I made earlier about White women not believing that it's their racism that very often alienates them from their Black men? When I—oh, it was dreadful. He always had other women. Always had other women. I just refused to accept it. . . . But in 1985, I found out that he had had another child by someone. . . . And the relationship had been going on for a while, for about two years. And that woke me up. I had a complete breakdown. Totally broken-hearted. The girls will tell you. [Cecelia] will tell you. I went down to 8 stone [112 pounds]. I didn't eat at all. It was only through my women friends that I was—they used to coax me to eat. I wanted to die. I couldn't get my head around the fact that there was somebody else. He just thinks totally different about it. "It's no big deal. I'm with you; you're my wife. Ships that pass in the night," he'd say [about the other woman]. But it's not. [The mother of his other child] was with him for a long time. As far as she was concerned, he was living with *her*. He was living with two of us at the same time. . . . He was giving us both a terrible life quality. And [her voice trails off] a lot of physical violence as well.

With that, Lisa got lost in thought. She took this opportunity to go to the kitchen to make us more tea. From that safe distance, she initiated a return to a topic that seemed much easier for her to discuss. "You asked me how it was that I began thinking about racism?" she called out to me. Later she returned, on her own, to the topic of her marriage.

[Rick] didn't treat me very well at first. I think I was too much trouble, really. I had four children [the ones to her previous marriage]. He didn't want my children; he wanted me. . . . He wanted me to leave them behind. Don't forget he had a different culture; children were brought up by the family. It wasn't a nuclear thing. He told me, "Your parents are there." But it didn't work that way in this country. If you abandon your kids they go into care.

She took a deep breath and let it out with this: "I abandoned my children, and they went into care, and . . ." She just as quickly added, "I got them out after six months. I needed them more than they needed me. They've never forgiven me. I'm almost completely estranged from my daughter, my beautiful daughter." She pulls out her daughter's wedding picture and begins talking about the man she married.

Lisa alludes again to the way racism was affecting her thinking, although a gender analysis seems to be struggling to get out: "Regardless of what man I had, I should've handled it differently. I should not have been so submissive, not been so terrified of losing the man. It was my fault. I guess I did put him first. . . . I put [my children] on hold when he came. He'd come for a weekend, maybe once a fortnight. And they would just be left to fend for themselves more or less. I'd concentrate on him." "I was *besotted* with him," she admitted with exasperation. "[Names her eldest son] is still extremely bitter. Now, when I take him to task and tell him, 'You're racist,' he says, 'I'm not racist about [Rick] being Black. What I hate about [Rick] is the way he's *treated* you.'"

Lisa's passion for analyzing the effects of racism may have been her undoing. She could not see Rick as "just" a man—one that her son seemed to suggest was not worthy of her. To Lisa, he was always a *Black* man. I hesitated to ask Lisa why she stayed in the marriage in spite of the physical abuse: "Why did you stay with [Rick]? If this is too personal . . ." She interrupted me. "As personal as you'd like. I've got nothing to hide."

I'm telling you the abuse I'd received from my Black husband; I also received abuse from my *White* husband. So there's no difference there, you know. And naturally I thought "it must be me" 'cause, you know, he's White, he's Black, and it's got to be me. There's something wrong with *me*. And the reason I stayed with [Rick], I'd tell myself, is that I'd seen the problems of four children growing up without their father. And I was determined that, with all the problems [her youngest son] would have in his life as a Black child, he wouldn't have that one. At least he'd be able to say, "I know my father; my father lives in the same house as I live in." I wanted him to be different from the majority of Black kids in Liverpool who have very little contact with their father because—sometimes, it isn't the father's fault. Sometimes it's because the women fall into this "serial relationships" thing. Some women have two, three kids to different Black men. I was determined that that was never going to happen to me. I would not be passed from one Black man to the next. I was going to stay with that one, impose my values onto the relationship. Now I accept responsibility for the problems, because . . . [she interrupts herself]. He's a very strong-willed man, stronger-willed than I am. He ruled the roost; whatever he said went.

At first she sees her way clear to dismiss race: it does not explain domestic vi-olence. But in other respects, she was blinded by the race analysis. She trapped herself in it. She was going to be heroic. She was "telling herself" that her Black child needed a father. After first dismissing race, it comes back. Her son is Black, and Rick also remains decidedly so, as do the men whom she was determined not to be passed among.

Along with LBB feminists, Lisa has been active in generating programs in Liverpool 8 targeted to young women, giving them exposure to career possibili-ties in a variety of fields, therein discouraging them from becoming "baby moth-ers." In her community work, the complicated matters of Lisa's wifely love and motherly duty are held safely at bay. But at home, her deep concern about racial issues seems to thwart the feminist sensibility she enacts in the public arena. When Lisa invokes a gender analysis in her own life narrative, it is to indict White women for their complicity in the sexual and marital practices of men—who, throughout, remain just Black. Cecelia, Yvette, and her other women friends, though, have been pleading with her for years to just leave Rick.

Can White women be "just mums"? Can their Black partners be "just men"? Their kids "just kids"? Race scarcely allows "just" sorts of positions, identities, or outlooks—although it does produce the desire and, sometimes, the urgent need for them. The ambivalences and contradictions in this chapter show the pro-found shift in milieu that has occurred since LBBs made their presence known both as Blacks and as Blacks *born here*. What once seemed unremarkable has become remarkably complicated and intense. The positive effects of the LBB revolution are being outpaced by the paradoxes it created. Ambiguity—rather than the stability that LBB activists sought—is one of the cornerstones of how race is lived. White women's racial positionings are shaped not only by the fact of Blackness but by the variable positions of their LBB children. Veronica sees her mother as just her mum, Ian sees his mother as Black inside, and Barbara's daughter (by Barbara's account) sees her mother as decidedly White.

For the anthropologist haunted by the ghost of Muriel Fletcher, geography is just a wound, not a port of call. Anthropological audiences, it seems to me, al-ways demand that ethnography be an anchorage, that it put the cultural flesh on social phenomena like race. We are called upon—or we take it upon ourselves—to inform our readers about what's going on for people X in location Y. That being our unique charge (tell us about The White Women!), it seems preposter-ous to ask the reader to imagine this chapter in particular as not really being about Liverpool after all. Every reference to dynamics that are, admittedly, par-ticular to Liverpool—such as the geographic "fact" that most Blacks born in Liverpool are of mixed racial parentage—undercuts my ability to destabilize the uniqueness narrative that turns Liverpool into "Liverpool" (wink-wink). Yet, it is hard to imagine that the issues described here, stripped of their localist reference points, do not also resound across Britain and countless other societies. To wit, even a cursory survey of Black diasporic literature, past and present, will reveal anxieties about skin/hair typologies and the blurry boundaries of Blackness. The dilemmas and unresolved questions surrounding Blackness *and* Whiteness, as described above, defy resolution not because Liverpool is so "complex" but because race is so insidious. As W.E.B. Du Bois brilliantly concluded a few generations ago, race is best understood as "a group of contradictory forces, facts, and tendencies" (1940: 133). At any given historical moment, or in any reputedly "particular" milieu, a plethora of mutually contradictory "truths" about race coexist. In the end, the ethical conundrum posed by Muriel's ghost stands as poignant illustration that place and localness shape race in Liverpool/Britain, and that race gives meaning to these in turn.

Local Women and Global Men:
The Liverpool That Was

> The real voyage of discovery consists not in seeking new land-
> scapes, but in having new eyes.
>
> —Marcel Proust

As SCOTT AND I stood on the corner where Pitt Street used to be, he brought its global milieu back to life by instructing me to visualize African, Chinese, and Arab people walking around in traditional garb. Veronica, Scott's junior by thirty years, also conjured a spectacular internationalist vision of the Black community's past. But she placed it around the Granby Street of her youth. As we strolled through Liverpool 8 running some of her errands, Veronica pointed out the row of modern, prefab council houses along Selbourne Street. Waving at them dismissively, she informed me that those didn't used to be there. In fact, the whole area had changed completely since she was a child, she said. With that, she summoned the Liverpool That Was. It used to be so alive "back when all the ships were coming in." Shops on Granby Street, where we were headed, stocked goods from everywhere on earth, she continued. There was even an organ grinder on the street. Expressing a distaste for having to go into town to shop nowadays, Veronica made a casual little remark that floored me: "It was so cosmopolitan around here, you never had to leave your street." How could she, as a member of a community that credited its very existence to global seafaring, be so indifferent to the world beyond her neighborhood? Her statement, I thought, represented the end of the line of a historical trajectory that unfailingly begins with the venerated African seaman sailing the seven seas. Now Veronica is ambivalent at best about having to leave the neighborhood created, seemingly, by sailing ships—even though, clearly, Selbourne Street and Granby are no longer what they once were.

For the deep sense of longing that Veronica and others express for the global age—the golden age of sail—I refer to the world they conjure as "the Liverpool That Was." That Liverpool is worth returning to not least because people considered it so worthy of recall, but also because it presents the opportunity to see landscapes previously visited in this ethnography with new eyes.

The Liverpool That Was is a critique of Black Liverpool. Places symbolize the gulf between them. As Scott warned me early on, I should not confuse Granby Street for the real Liverpool, located on the invisible Pitt Street. I would get a hopelessly distorted picture of Blacks' history if I were to search it out in Liverpool 8.

People there would occlude the sea's essential role, or fail to remember it. They would tell me that the Black presence begins in the 1950s with Caribbean immigration (in fact, I was never told that). Journeys back to Pitt Street are also motivated, at least in part, by what older Blacks decry as the disunity and disharmony within the "multiracial, multicultural, whatever community" of Liverpool 8. In revisiting Pitt Street or, alternatively, the Granby Street of the 1960s, they render present-day Granby a fake and throw into relief its unfathomable transformation from a haven of cosmopolitanism to an area commonly defined in singularly Black terms or, similarly, as a ghetto. Middle-aged and elderly Blacks and Whites lament young Blacks' reticence to leave their neighborhood. "Their fathers sailed the world," Caroline told me. But, she continued, Black youth nowadays "are afraid to venture out."

Because such disappointments inspire people's joyful reminiscences about the way Liverpool was, it would be tempting to dismiss that Liverpool as a fantasy world that never really existed. Instead, my analysis inhabits the milieu they so often conjured. Inspired by the energy people expended in getting me to visualize it, I even take a few leaps of the imagination with them. Interpreted liberally, their stories suggest alternative histories of race in Liverpool/Britain, while also exposing the racial, national, and gendered politics of Liverpool's local-as-global seaport identity and the cosmopolitanism associated with it.

In scholarly circles, cosmopolitanism has become *the* progressive ideal, despite the political problems associated with defining it. As Appadurai notes, any definition of cosmopolitanism would smack of universalism, which is never progressive (2000). Its advocates generally agree, though, that cosmopolitanism transcends the provincialism and absolutism of Identity. Racial, ethnic, religious, and especially national solidarities are *dis*abling of coalitional social movements, it is argued, because those affinities articulate the interests of individual groups. Yet as a singular resolution to a knotty set of predicaments, cosmopolitanism has been greeted with some circumspection.[1] What generally emerges in these debates, and to some degree in spite of them, is the view that a cosmopolitan politic is in effect when people successfully move "beyond" hegemonic, narrow, and rigid forms of social identification—perchance to become "just" selves, whose transcendence makes possible solidarity with other "just" selves.

One set of debates has gathered around the question, Can a cosmopolitan subjectivity emerge out of the one called *place*? Or must one be *out* of place? Is place in the way? What is to be done about place? With a passion, David Harvey, Paul Gilroy, and Doreen Massey have weighed in on these questions. In view of this book's focus on the mediating role of place in British cultures and politics, it is hard not to notice that, among all the scholars writing on cosmopolitanism, only the ones from Britain worry over the place of place. Moreover, the various foci of Harvey, Gilroy, and Massey illustrate the point I argued in chapter 1: all social categories, identities, and hierarchies in Britain articulate, in some way, with place. Harvey's critical analysis of place and cosmopolitanism is routed through class, Gilroy's through nation and race, and Massey's through gender.

Harvey argues that the revived politic of cosmopolitanism must proceed on better moral footing than it has in the past. Its proponents must specify their position on the "different geographies and spatialities (and local loyalties)" in which the world's people are situated (2000: 545). Otherwise, he so rightly argues, an ostensibly progressive politic could degenerate into yet another powerful discourse that consigns some to the margins of modernity, rationality, and morality. Later in his exegesis, however, Harvey takes a much harder position on "local loyalties" for fetishizing places and spaces in reactionary, exclusionary ways, and for being hopelessly incapable of resisting capitalism, especially in view of its new spatial organization (2000: 555).[2] Paul Gilroy's call for cosmopolitanism—or what he calls a "planetary humanism"—grows out of his principled critiques of nationalism, which has often been built on racist exclusions. The latter, whether they have articulated with nationalist ideologies or not, have spawned faulty political responses in the form of racial identity (1987, 1993a, 2000, 2003). Place comes under attack for valorizing and naturalizing sovereignty, territory, and kinship. In light of these concerns, his work has long ennobled the traveler—perhaps to a fault. If virtue attaches to the displaced, what becomes of the *em*placed? While the phrase "planetary humanism" resolves this problem by evoking a cosmopolitanism that does not require one to dig up her passport, it still strikes a rather placeless image. Doreen Massey is alone in arguing that a progressive sense of place, defined by a globally oriented social consciousness, is entirely possible. While admitting that place can breed all manner of reactionary politics, she also argues that it has more than one political potentiality (1994). For present purposes, her comments about the gender of localness and place are even more instructive:

> [S]ome culturally specific symbolic association of women/Woman/local persist[s]. Thus, the term local is used in derogatory reference to feminist struggles and in relation to feminist concerns in intellectual work (it is *only* a local struggle, only a *local* concern). Neither, it is often argued, possesses the claim on universalism made by a concern with class. . . . That bundle of terms local/place/locality is bound in to sets of dualisms, in which a key term is the dualism between masculine and feminine, and in which, on these readings, the local/place/feminine side of the dichotomy is deprioritized and denigrated. (1994: 10)[3]

This incisive critique forces attention to the political construction of categories that might otherwise pass for objective, analytical descriptors of, for example, geographical scale. The global and its supposed opposite, the local (generally conflated with place), are differently imbued with value, agency, and historical significance through their discrepant gendering. Does cosmopolitanism have a gender?

This chapter shows people variably challenging the politics of nation, race, and gender through appeals to cosmopolitanism—a stance transcending identity and, indeed, predating it. Liverpudlians imbue that quality to place and therefore to themselves. In some respects, then, we see place as an enabler of that ostensibly radical worldview. Alas, although its expressions inspire, that sensibility is still far afield of the promised land. Beneath its glowing exterior, the Liverpool That Was appeals to the same forms of power that it gets called upon to criticize.

For present purposes, I draw on Bruce Robbins's definition of cosmopolitanism as an ethical worldliness (1998), not because I want to stake a claim on how it should be conceptualized but because that definition so perfectly captures what people evoke through the Liverpool That Was. In the first section, I paint a general picture of the age of sail, as glimpsed from the port. The second section presents a full-length story that exposes the critical differences between Black Liverpool and the Liverpool That Was. The subsequent section presents the abbreviated life narrative of an elderly Black ex-seaman, since his travels are firmly ensconced as part and parcel of Black Liverpool's history. There we see the way place enables a cosmopolitan outlook and then disables it. Pursuing themes raised in the previous section, the final one studies the racial and gender implications of the sea and the port as sites of cosmopolitanism—and, indeed, as sites that, for their discrepant gendering, enjoy different degrees of visibility in narrations of Black Liverpool's history.

THE AGE OF SAIL

Pitt Street is an era as much as a place. It refers to the first half of the twentieth century. Pitt Street was bombed in World War II but managed to survive through to the dawn of urban regeneration in the 1950s, when many slums in the south end were razed. Older people, obviously, can remember the 1930s, while their younger peers' memories would refer to the 1950s—which does not imply discrepant memories across generations. Anything but. Pitt Street is uniformly remembered for its national heterogeneity. Although it was at the center of Chinatown, more than Chinese people lived there. As Black people often said, on Pitt Street they lived "cheek to jowl" with Arabs, Chinese, Poles—the lot. In view of historical and autobiographical accounts of those times, as treated in chapter 6 for example, the expression "cheek to jowl" might conjure images of Pitt Street as an unsanitary slum. But Blacks I knew evoked physical closeness to emphasize social closeness. Those old enough to remember Pitt Street situated themselves fluidly and harmoniously among all the world's people resident there. They formed meaningful, everyday relationships unencumbered by ideologies of racial, ethnic, or national difference—which were themselves unclear and in flux in the early twentieth century (Tabili 1996). People described a shared class positioning with their neighbors, beholden as they all were to the exploitative political economy of the shipping industry. With seamen away on voyages for months and months at a time, their families depended on allotments of their salaries, which they were to pick up monthly at a shipping office in town. But they could not rely on the allotments to actually be there. Black people frequently mention receiving loans from next-door neighbors, and in the same breath that they mention their neighbors' trust and generosity in times of scarcity, they make special reference to the nationality of those neighbors. As seventy-six-year-old Morris, an ex-seaman, recalled,

> I grew up in the heart of what they called Chinatown at that time. That was Pitt Street. And that neighborhood, even though I traveled quite some places, I've never

met a neighborhood like that. It was an international neighborhood. I think every nationality in the world was represented in Pitt Street. And everybody intermingled and
helped each other. I can remember myself, being asked by my aunt who reared me at
the time, to go to a certain Chinaman and ask him for the loan of a shilling. Now
this is a man who come from way over the other side of the world, who settled in
Liverpool, but he understood the difficulties of everybody else beside himself.

The ethic Morris describes is found in people's propensity to help each other
in view of their shared poverty, while worldliness is clear in the ability of the
"Chinaman" to understand the difficulties of people of a different background
than his own. As well, Morris attributes this cosmopolitanism to place in two
ways: Liverpool was a site of settlement for people from the world over, and Pitt
Street was defined by mutual affinity and cooperation across nationality.

Pitt Street always appears in stories as a dockside neighborhood—full of
portness—and, correspondingly, the families who lived there were defined by
their common relationship to seafaring. Everyone I knew with a seafaring father
indicated that these men were always away. Some said that they never really
came to know their fathers. By dint of their occupation, seamen contribute to the
construction of Liverpool's traditional identity. And, as indicated in chapter 1,
the global wanderings of their fathers gave Blacks access to local identity. But
that same occupation kept them away from Pitt Street for months on end. Hence
it was the families actually present on Pitt Street who made it cosmopolitan, insofar as their acts of neighborliness crossed what are constituted as the nonexistent lines of race and nationality. In stories about this era, people's backgrounds
come to bear only to point out that they were not salient. "This was a seaport and
they all mixed," one woman said of the plethora of groups that she knew growing
up around Pitt Street. "Everyone moved together; it's altogether different now,"
another woman, Susan, said. Place makes kinship relevant in a very particular
way, then. Since Liverpool is first and foremost a seaport, people describe
familyhood in *its* terms rather than in terms of ethnicity, race, and/or nationality.

The social arena that Blacks and Whites in the south end most frequently
recall and mourn is the club life that this seafaring milieu produced. It would not
be possible to overstate the unrestrained glee with which middle-aged and
elderly people I knew spoke of Liverpool's glamorous nightlife in the age of sail.
As Theresa, an eighty-eight-year-old Black woman, who owned a very popular
club with her husband, said of the Liverpool 8 area, "It was club land." The club
scene had an international flavor, and it was centered around Upper Parliament
Street and Princes Road—both in Liverpool 8, where many people relocated
after Pitt Street was razed. Although some of these clubs had thematic names,
like the Fortune Club (where gambling took place), many others announced the
nationality of the owners—but not necessarily the clientele. These clubs were
frequented as much by barristers and other political elites as by sailors docked in
Liverpool. There was the Nigerian Club, the Yoruba Club, and the Sierra Leone.
And there was also the legendary club, Dutch Eddie's, named for the owner
(Theresa's husband), a citizen of Dutch Guyana. An ex-seaman himself, Dutch

PART

I

Introduction to Intellectual Property

Eddie became so prosperous as a club owner that he was able to launch a side business in which he floated loans to people in the Granby area who could not get them from banks. He is remembered for facilitating homeownership in that neighborhood. And when, in this era, two White women club owners in Liverpool 8 could not get a liquor license from the city, the owner of the Fortune Club—a Jamaican who got to Liverpool via London by stowing away on a ship—interceded on their behalf through a Greek club owner he knew who had connections.

Though such stories are peppered with the details and plotlines of an individual's life, everyone I knew conjured a Liverpool That Was defined by harmonious heterogeneity. The variety of national backgrounds that come into play celebrate an era before identity became a battleground. Blacks' descriptions of this era reveal the meaningful presence in their lives of people from everywhere, not just the places of the storytellers' own ancestral pasts. Just about any national referent could pop up in the Liverpool That Was. Black people I knew betrayed no effort or desire to minimize the presence of non-Blacks in the essential, authentic Liverpool. Moreover, people's stories feature the array of nationals actually resident in south Liverpool—not just those sailing in and out of it. In the stories relayed above, two key players were from Greece and Dutch Guyana. People's stories, then, actually exceed the conventional boundaries of even the most enlightened accounts of British history, which trace the rise of a multiracial and multi-ethnic society through the nation's colonial past.

Scholarly histories document that racism was rife in early and mid-twentieth-century Liverpool and that Pitt Street was a ghetto very much in need of razing—which is what some people said about present-day Granby Street. But those who lived on or around Pitt Street suggested that a vital form of community—one that they might like to have back—was also razed in the process. Through their stories about Pitt Street and the early Granby Street, they restore what they consider the authentic nature of those places. In so doing, they imbue place with a different kind of agency vis-à-vis race than they did in producing the narratives of a previous chapter, where they rendered that city a slave to history. Both narratives depend on Liverpool's port status. But the eighteenth-century slave merchants whose sinister presence is still felt around town represent the continuance of Liverpool's racial past, while the Liverpool That Was bespeaks a tragic rupture. The next section, then, is about mourning.

In Memory

In the late summer of 1992, eight Black women ranging in age from early forties to mid-eighties, all born and raised in Liverpool, produced a collective piece of art to represent their memories. Every Thursday afternoon, for a few weeks, the women met in a room provided by Lodge Lane Library in Liverpool 8. Variously called a quilt, a banner, and a wall hanging, the piece eventually consisted of eight panels, each produced by one woman. Over many pots of tea and countless cigarettes, these women helped each other conceptualize their panels. The meetings also provided a pretext for them to reminisce about the Liverpool That Was. The organizers of the project included a White woman, Marie, who was a historian for one of the city's museums, and Cecelia. Over the years, both women had been involved in various projects to document the Black community's historical presence in the city. Between my first trip to Liverpool in 1989 and my last in 1999, there have been a wide array of such projects, most of them seeking to correct the longtime invisibility of Liverpool-born Blacks. The women at the library belong, at least nominally, to that group. But what their art makes most visible is the difference between Black Liverpool and the Liverpool That Was.

One panel featured a map of Africa, carved out of brown printed African cloth, inset with a smaller map of Ireland, represented in white cloth. Within that image was an even smaller inset of a four leaf clover. A ship was pictured sailing sweetly around West African shores. Interracial marriage was represented through the pictorial image of places. Another image was of Stanley House, the legendary community center. Its status as a cherished yet invisible place is matched only by that of Pitt Street and the early Granby Street. In what follows, I focus on two other panels and the women who produced them, in addition to the small stir that erupted one day about the women's collective approach to their topic.

The first panel depicted Pitt Street, which was "pictured" through a list of the actual surnames, written in gold shimmery letters, of people who once lived there. With the happy assistance of the other quilt-makers, a sixty-two-year-old woman, Susan, compiled the names of the families who lived on or near the fabled street. Claire, who was in her late fifties, took up the next historical epoch by depicting the Granby Street of the 1950s and 1960s. On her panel, the street is a lively place where figures represented in different shades of brown, pink, and beige strike the same joyful gesture as they stroll past all the shops. One session at the library was absorbed with a cheerful debate over which international shop was next to which other. These women's panels posited a radical break between past and present. The past that is at work here does not forge a sense of continuity between then and now. The past is what is, sadly, dead and gone.

One Thursday afternoon, Claire and I spent some time together at her house, and this made us tardy for that week's meeting. On our arrival, we found the usual discourse being disrupted. Two new people were there, neither of whom was known to us nor the other women. One was Leslie, a Black woman perhaps in her mid-fifties, and the other a Black man in his twenties, Omar.

"There's no actual history of Black Liverpool," said Omar, as I began tape recording. "Yes there is!" retorted one of the quilters. Omar continued, "There is no history like there is in America. In fact, you could spend your whole life reading the history of Black America." He went on to suggest the form that such a history should or should not take: "I didn't really come here to—If you're representing Black Liverpool history, it should be something more in-depth. I didn't know you were making a quilt. Someone could go and see that quilt and it's sort of—if you go to see what's happened in terms of Black people living here over the centuries and what you see is a quilt, it's just really sort of stunning. It just seems ridiculous."

One of the women interjected in disagreement, only to be drowned out by Susan, who said, "But you don't know what's going on the quilt! It's not like a quilt you'd put on a bed. It's going to have all illustrations and photographs on it." Marie adds, "It's up to the group to decide what they want to do. It's certainly not up to me to tell Black women what to do. . . . It's up to the group to decide what their history is." "I understand what you're saying," responded Omar, "but in fact it's not the history of the group; it's the history of the Black Liverpool community. And it's not a question of a few people saying, 'We're going to get together and make a quilt.' I think there's a lot more to it than that. Who was the first Black councillor, or the first Black person admitted to Liverpool University or a British university? Or during the First World War with the Black soldiers. Or the Second World War, or the Crimean. There's a number of things."

A few exchanges later Claire suggested, with sharp annoyance in her voice, that "if people want to do a quilt on the past *you're* talking about, that is fine! What *we're* doing is areas of Liverpool 8 [Susan interrupts her to add, "They're knocked down now!"] which have disappeared, such as—one person is doing a panel that is a collage, somebody is doing Granby Street from Selbourne to Upper Parliament Street, which has disappeared. And somebody's going to do Pitt Street." Again Susan, who is representing that place through a list of surnames, chimes in saying, "Right from the bottom." Omar interrupts, "But what do you think is more important? Having something that can be of use to people, to individuals who can draw some kind of strength from something that says, 'This is how things have been going all this time.' But with a quilt it's not like that, is it?"

Leslie offered to speak for Omar. "What he's saying is that he doesn't see much of the history going down." Omar took up the point, "What I'm saying is that this is a group which, if it was a group of individuals doing something for themselves that would be one thing; but if it's a group that is claiming to represent the community—."

"They don't! They don't claim to represent the community!" Marie rebutted strenuously. Another woman said in refrain, "We're not representing the community." "So, it's not a Black women's group?" Omar asked. "It *is* a Black women's group!" I added my voice in frustration. "*These* are Black women!" Omar responded, "But I thought it was supposed to be representing—." I interrupted him.

"I think it's really a tricky question when you talk about 'representing' because it's only what people bring from their experience. I interview people all over the city, and yesterday I was just with a young woman, my age, who was recalling her memories of growing up on Granby Street [this was Veronica], and it made me think of what Claire is doing. And Pitt Street! I've talked to people about Pitt Street as the most harmonious experience of their lives as Black people in this city. That is, growing up on Pitt Street. [Leslie added, 'That's Chinatown,' and Claire corrected her, 'It *used* to be Chinatown']. Obviously it's important because people keep bringing it up! And that comes across without people claiming to represent the whole community."

"If you're going to produce something, like a book or something like a book that people can relate to, then that would actually be for everybody. That's all I was saying," Omar retorted. Marie told Omar that she appreciated his point but that there are Black organizations in the city that are conducting that kind of work: "There's a whole stream of activities going on that is extremely exciting, representing, in their way, Liverpool 8 and its history—or Black people, I should say, not Liverpool 8. There are people who are older who cannot be here, who feel that this is something they can do. It's working in textiles. They're not being asked to go to libraries, but to just dip into their own memories. And they're being respected and are putting that on a panel."

Leslie interrupted her. In a self-important tone that tried to be unassuming, she again attempted to explain Omar's position: "You're talking to the young generation now that is impatient to see Liverpool Black people being—." With that Claire fought back, exclaiming, "*You* do that! You get *your own* group together! You get *your own* anthology together!"

Leslie asked, "Could he do that if he wanted to?" Marie responded, "Anybody can do it!" "Where would he go?" Leslie asked. Claire offered, "To the library. And he gets loads of photographs and information—."

"Photographs?! What would I do with photographs?" Omar asked, incredulously. Claire responded, "What do you want? A book with photographs or a book with no photographs? Or a story, or—." "A story?! I want a history!" Omar cried.

Susan turned to me and asked, "That's what you're doing isn't it?" At first I directed my answer to her and then to the whole group as they focused their attention on me.

"Yeah, but it's history as people tell it. History as people talk about it. Because I'm—like Marie, I'm dedicated to the history. But there are things that I'm interested in that people don't bring up. And I feel sometimes that I can't bring them up because I really want to get at what people think is important to talk about. So I take from what people say; that's where all my questions come from, just how people talk."

Omar expressed concern about this methodology: "Then what you get is a very sort of gossipy view of the past. . . . What I'm saying is—and actually, I've tried it—if you set out to get a Black history of Liverpool, you can't get it. There are little bits, different histories of different things, and so on, but there isn't actually a Black history of Liverpool. . . . It's important to know how Black people fit into the larger structures of the history of the city and the country."

Marie concurred, and a discussion ensued about Black seamen and war heroes. Leslie joined Marie and the women of the quilt-making group of Lodge Lane Library in a resounding chorus of agreement about the Black men of Liverpool who served in the Merchant Navy but are never acknowledged in public narrations of national wartime history. This is the history that Omar seemed to want told, or written.

If Omar was skeptical about these women's visual—and "gossipy"— narratives, Susan was irked by his repeated references to Black people. In the midst of the commotion, she began looking around for the key to a closet in the room where all the panels of the quilt were stored. She whispered to me that she wanted to get her panel representing Pitt Street, to show Omar that "it's not just Black people's names what I'm writing. I've got—it's not just Black people. It's just areas from the city—from Toxteth to here, Parliament Street. I'd just like to show him it's not just Black. Look at them names [she points to some notes she has written]. Not many of them are Black names. They're every nationality."

As the young Omar searched for the history of *Black* Liverpool, most of these Black women were constituting it in a decidedly internationalist and racially mixed frame, for which the juxtaposition of Africa and Ireland, joined in matrimony by a ship, served as the inaugural event. The images of Pitt and Granby Streets followed suit. "Look at them names," Susan instructed me, referring to the "sketch" for her portrait of Pitt Street. She was proud to clarify that not many of them belonged to Blacks. "They're every nationality."

To my infinite regret, I did not appreciate the significance of Susan's work then, for it only struck me in retrospect that her panel is the ultimate instantiation of English/Liverpudlian cultures of place. What I learned from her about place and cosmopolitanism was completely accidental. In an interview, Susan described her inspiration for her Pitt Street panel. In all her years at school, she told me, "nobody called us names because we were really a cosmopolitan area. As you can see from that list, all the difference was everywhere. You got every nationality there." She continued, "The community on Pitt Street was very close. Everybody moved together. It's entirely different now. It was all harmony. Every nationality." In the formulation "*we* were really a cosmopolitan *area*," people and place are one and the same, just as they are on her panel. She could depict the street "right from the bottom" completely through surnames. Place *equals* identity—as in English cultural logics previously discussed. But she goes one further: in this case, place equals a radical non-identity. "Everybody moved together," she told me, referring to the people of Pitt Street. "It's entirely different now," she lamented. Pitt Street, she went on to say, has been gutted. And so, too, were the cosmopolitan social relations that she memorialized on her panel. The city/self isomorphism in Susan's panel mirrors the memory work of Whites in the north end of Liverpool. In fact, it was only in studying Liverpool autobiographies that I came to appreciate the poignancy of Susan's use of surnames to depict Pitt Street. In those texts, the loss of people is equated with the loss of place—the death of Scottie Road. And so, those authors' work is replete with the names of the everyday people who made that legendary street. Through her depiction of Pitt Street, Susan does the same, conjuring a form of sociality that is also, by all accounts, dead. The difference, though, is that here in the south end, the names Susan memorialized are marked "local" by their global origins. "They're every nationality."

Susan did not share Omar's concern for a unitary racial narrative centered around a fixed Black identity. Even as a member of a Black women's group, she saw no contradiction in drawing others, represented in international terms, into her vision of the Liverpool That Was. She even gave the latter multitude pride of place on her panel: "not many of them are Black names." Again in retrospect, I think that I, like Omar, was looking for The Black History of Liverpool and missed the opportunity to ask her why the international character of Pitt Street was so important to her and, perhaps, how she understood the relationship between race and nationality. In her comment, "Not many of them are Black names. They're every nationality," there seems to be a little slippage. What is clear, however, is that cosmopolitanism is not located simply in the Pitt Street era. Here in 1992, Susan is so steeped in her own ethical worldliness that she is at cross purposes with Omar's more limited vision. She wants to show him that the names are not just Black ones, even though Blackness is precisely what Omar wanted and expected.

The Pitt and Granby Street panels represent the past in ways that counter popular and scholarly historical narratives. For its centrality to British imperial politics in the metropole, the category *half-caste* is ubiquitous in accounts of racial formation that are, however rightfully, dignified as the kind of authoritative history that Omar sought. As well, LBBs who had been politically active since the late 1970s narrated the rise of Black identity as a high point, a watershed moment when they finally countered the pathologized half-caste inscription. Indeed, younger LBBs' investments in the politics of race, racism, and identity overdetermined my own view about Black Liverpool's past, making it seem as if the only possible trajectory to trace was that from *half-caste* to *Black*. And, given the premium that now existed on unequivocal Blackness, some people were understandably reticent to engage a question that hinged on the prior construction. I once asked Claire what the term *half-caste* meant to her in those days, and she responded: "It meant having a Black father and a White mother full stop." That was the end of that discussion. Importantly, though, her curt response suggests that it was just a term, rather than some deep and meaningful way of understanding one's personhood.

Claire and Susan would have been considered half-caste in the old days, just as they are interpolated as LBBs in the present. But they remember something different about the era from which their younger counterparts distinguish themselves. They make it possible to imagine a world before identity. That is, their senses of self in relation to others, along the lines of sameness and difference, may have operated on a completely different, nameless plane—one that transcended race and nation. After all, people of mixed parentage born in Liverpool were excluded from the racial categories deemed stable (Negro and White), as well as from Britishness. From the margins they occupied, though, they fashioned forms of identity and community that crossed over the lines of difference being drawn, however murkily, by British ideologies and Liverpool institutions of the time (see chapter 1). Perhaps the blanks in Claire's response to my question can be filled in by the differently colored figures that grace her Granby Street panel, which depicted a form of community that went beyond race. Her panel portrays a community that was produced by and then lost with the international shops that the women struggled in one session to remember.

So often did Claire reminisce about Granby that I was compelled to ask her why she was so enamored by it. Her response cut the tail end off of my question:

I remember walking along Granby Street. Granby Street was a haven of joviality, music, liveliness, nice people. And you'd walk along Princes Avenue, Upper Parliament Street, and as soon as you turn onto Granby Street, it was a cosmopolitan area of wonderfulness. The people were nice. It was just a wonderful, lively place. It's gone! It's dead! It's a shame. I would like to do from Upper Parliament Street to Selbourne Street to bring back that memory of that liveliness that was there.

Claire once lived on Selbourne Street and loved it because the joyful sounds of Granby Street would drift up to her flat: "Now, you would hang out the window of your room on Selbourne Street and see myriads of people walking past lovely houses along Selbourne Street. Lovely. And you would hear the sounds coming from Granby Street and it was so close and so you wanted to be there." It was not just the sound of music that would call her:

There was a community there that was together. People would meet each other, you know. It was a meeting place. It seemed to be like the inner core of Liverpool 8: Granby Street. Granby Street was where people seemed to meet and, when they were doing their shopping people would just go there to meet people, people they hadn't seen. It was wonderful!

I asked Claire about the time frame for this liveliness. "I'd say the fifties and six-ties. Do you know, I don't even know when those houses were built, when they cut off Granby Street. I don't know the year." "What houses?" I asked. "When you're walking on Selbourne Street and suddenly on your left there's a housing estate which reaches to Upper Parliament Street. I don't know when that was built. I don't know how old that is. I hope I find out." This is the same con-temptible housing estate that Veronica waved at and summarily wished away, as she conjured the Liverpool That Was. "What is it about that housing estate that's significant to you?" I asked. "It's not!" Claire retorted.

It's *in*significant because it seems to have taken the guts out of the community by slicing Granby Street the way it did. When the housing estate appeared, then you got an influx of people who became—they weren't the nice people. . . . And hundreds of people left Liverpool 8 and moved to the outskirts, which was awful. So we lost quite a lot of people. And we were losing the guts, the inner core of the community just disappeared.

So in doing that piece for the wall hanging, I want to make that area of Granby Street to portray the liveliness that was there. And in my mind it will be bringing all the people back into this wonderful, cosmopolitan area as it was. Because Black peo-ple and White people were mixing together. All races of people were mixing to-gether. . . . it was a nice feeling, which is gone.

The death of Granby Street is marked both by the intrusion of a set of council houses and by the "influx of people" who were to occupy them. Claire wants to

know the exact year when they were built, but that time frame is already suggested in her narrative. They must have come after the 1960s, precisely when the
"influx" of immigrants started to receive national(ist) attention.

In the analysis of White Liverpudlians' memoirs, I suggested that Liverpool, as
place, is understood through an essential Liverpudlian soul. Out-migration, accordingly, animates their desire to bring Scottie Road back to life. Some of the authors
strained to list as many folks from the old neighborhood as they possibly could. In
so doing, I suggested, they were putting all the people lost through death (many
merchant seamen died at sea) or migration back where they really belong. Likewise did Claire say that she chose the visuals for her panel—multiply colored
figures happily strolling down Granby Street—in order to bring all those people
back. She brings them back to the place that their presence made cosmopolitan.

In her vision, those folks are the "guts" and "inner core" of Liverpool 8's *real*
community, which is gone. While Scottie Roaders have apparently moved out
of Liverpool, Claire's old neighbors have migrated to the city's outskirts. Claire
attributed the tragic loss of this soul, partially, to a growing poverty that was
creeping into Liverpool 8: "Suddenly everything changed." The lack of neighborliness, she opined, owed to the fact that "people for the first time in their lives
had heavy bills to pay. They didn't have all that. They lived in flats. All they had
was the payment for the rooms, bedsits. . . . Because of that, people changed.
They were getting worried. They didn't have the money. All the good times
seemed to go because they couldn't afford it." These were the people whom
Claire suggested left the area, heading for the outskirts. In another, more telling
respect, Claire attributed the decline of Granby to a growing racial divide. Here
she is talking about the rents that were charged to people in the flats and bedsits
that started appearing in the Granby area. Speaking of White women landlords in
the area, she says:

> You get very strange White women. When they were married to Black they would try
> to turn their men, give their men White ways. They would try and seclude their Black
> men friends away from the Black area. And it was only the Black men who were
> proud to be Black and all that, saying, "No, you know, if you don't like it you can get
> lost!" But you did get a few Black men who did adopt the White ways, which was
> sad. It was mainly West Indian men—called Caribbeans, now. And sometimes
> African men, and that was the hardest thing to do, cause you'd assume that once you
> had a Black landlord, you're okay.

I would direct attention here not to Claire's critique of White women, and African
and Afro-Caribbean men, but to the ways that her critical comments are cast: in
tones that bespeak racial divisiveness, as facilitated through class. Suddenly,
Granby went from being cosmopolitan to racially divided. She struggles to make
sense of the rupture. Maybe if she finds out when those *in*significant council
houses were built on Selbourne Street, she will be able to fully apprehend the
causes of the devastating loss that they symbolize. In the meantime, she brings all
"races of people"—whom she depicts as "mixing" rather than "mixed"—back to
life through her panel.

As Claire and the other quilt-making women were representing (and reliving) their collective past, Omar was busily searching for Liverpool's Black history and, through that, his own local identity. Despite his concern to find something "which can be a source of strength" for Blacks in Liverpool, his was a decidedly personal project.

I met with Omar a few days after making his acquaintance at the library. In describing his background to me, Omar joked that he was not at all "representative" and that he could never speak as "an authentic Black Liverpudlian." LBBs (who never use the term *Black Liverpudlian*) would likely affirm him on this point. Omar did not have a Scouse accent. His Nigerian father was a successful professional, not connected to the seafaring history on which LBBs commonly say their community was founded. His mother, also Nigerian, was a nurse. He lived in Aigburth, which is one of a few areas in the city where the professional, ex-colonial Africans lived. Housing in Aigburth is more expensive than in Liverpool 8, but the area is still working class on the whole. Aigburth lay just beyond what are considered the authentic boundaries of Black community life. No one would likely depict a scene from Aigburth, for example, on a quilt depicting Black Liverpool's past. As well, Omar's education included continuing university training, and hence it already far exceeded that attained by most Black Liverpudlians. Omar had social and familial networks that connected him to middle-class Africans not only in Aigburth but across Britain. Omar came to realize, though, that his own material well-being was based on his parents' economic status, and hence he sought a form of security independent of them. That desire motivated him to find a place for himself within the city's Black community, a goal that led him to search for its history. That urgent search, so vociferously pursued at Lodge Lane Library, is why I found him so interesting. Omar was also intrigued by me. He latched onto me as someone who would, of course, affirm his view that this community exists on the nether end of modernity. "Coming from America," he asked me poignantly, almost desperately, "don't you think this place is backward? You must! It is a terrible place in fact. It's like a third world country! In Black America you have all of those things and that's what you've been fighting for going back to the sixties, going back to *The Souls of Black Folk*! That's going back to the turn of the century. And we're coming up to the year 2000 and this *still* isn't done in Liverpool!"

Until his appearance at the library, he had given up his search for the history of Black Liverpool, realizing that it could not help him understand something much more complex than who the city's first Black councillor was. It could not help him understand the ineffable and utterly queer quality that he attributes to Liverpool Blacks. To Omar, there is something mysterious and peculiar, almost dark, about them. Something that actually overrides history. Whatever it is, it creates a puzzling social fabric that he was at pains to describe:

> What I'm trying to do is look at the Black history of Liverpool itself. Liverpool and Bristol have got sort of the same, almost the same sort of history. But actually Black people and the community in Bristol, and the *attitude* of Black people in the community in Liverpool, is absolutely different! I'm just saying, it's completely different.

It's amazing! And this stunned me. I'm talking about the nature of their, sort of, "psyche." Which is not something to do with personal—it's like the city characteristic of Liverpool. Someone can have the same personal background in Bristol and Liverpool, and they'll be different. When I say "different" I mean a different psyche. . . . There's something particular about Liverpool. And even that I should assert with some importance, "Right. I'm Black Liverpudlian"—it's ridiculous that I should have even thought like that.

At the library, he insisted that a proper history of Black Liverpool would show how it fits into the larger structures of the city and the country. But he insists above that Blacks in Liverpool are not like those in Bristol, despite having a similar history. Liverpool Blacks are also a century behind Black Americans who appear here, in the form of W.E.B. Du Bois's 1903 masterpiece, to be the diaspora's standard-bearers of Black progress. Omar's wide knowledge and experience of the Black world beyond Liverpool inspire his critique of the city. Yet even as a critic of localism, he participates in it. Liverpool is exceptional. It is like a third world country, not a city. National histories about Blacks in Britain would not suffice for his purposes; he is searching for Black Liverpool's "unique" history.

The narratives that the quilters produced about the past, as well as my own research material on that Liverpool, were too personal, or "gossipy," to be authoritative. To be sure, the seaport lives these women were documenting—on behalf of the whole dockside community, not just the community of Black women— will never show up in the History that Omar sought. Instead, it will likely center on Black seamen's wartime heroism—a concern that brings the nation right back onto center stage. Susan's Pitt Street panel interrupts the masculinist bent of Blacks' critical concerns about their absence from national History. Without her panel, the cosmopolitanism of *women* and *families* would be lost in a sea of narratives that privilege oceans as sites of global, manly adventure. These links already pervade the growing literature on seafaring in the Atlantic world, where the port is important only as the place continually left behind (Bolster 1997; Rediker 1987; Gilroy 1993a). If the sea is masculine, the port, by the insidious power of default, is feminized, rendered stable, awaiting penetration via the arrival of men and ships.[4] Susan's panel counters these logics by documenting the participation of families in a cosmopolitanism that could only be represented through place—not simply in material, physical terms, but as a basis of knowledge and subjectivity. As for the competing perspectives on race and history articulated at the library, the women were reaching almost as far back in time as Omar was, in order to suggest that contemporary Black Liverpool— notwithstanding its historic, heroic triumphs in the public arena of race, racism, and identity—has yet to surpass the achievements of the Liverpool That Was.

Indeed Black Liverpool and the Liverpool That Was present the opportunity to compare and contrast diaspora, as a framework for theorizing race and identity, and the one on cosmopolitanism that has been advocated in recent years. Both concepts productively point to the limits of the nation as a basis of community, identity, and group interest. Very often, diaspora frameworks push past n.p., n.d.). It is indeed a big problem when the abuse of faculty discretion is suspected. That happens when a student's work with very strong potential is rated as substandard while some real "minimum" job by any standard is given a high grade. The sociology of science suggests that this is not a paradise free from problems. Unfortunately, the best the scientific and educational community can do is to use faculty members as the gatekeepers, although they are far from perfect. And you are supposed to be aware of the potential "human" factor involved. You should try to get along with your advisor as well as your thesis/dissertation committee to prevent an academic matter from turning into a political issue by either party's mistake. Here a pious attitude on your part in learning and in showing respect is not enough. A thorough understanding and effective communication is also important. Preventative measures should also be taken to protect yourself by avoiding a person with a problematic personality or uncertain academic quality.

You need not be dismayed by knowing the fact that there is no absolutely objective standard in the academic world. From your past experience you understand that you always should do your part. Now the good news is that you need to do your best since you never know for sure and in detail what necessarily constitute an acceptable work (although you have sample works from some of your classmates). You are freed from worrying about the exact "minimum" requirements since you would rather aim higher in order to increase your odds of getting your thesis/dissertation passed. This would be good for you if you believe in the truth that "the higher your goal, the faster you grow." And the fact is that with the various limits the students have to face, some have produced really nice work and made significant contributions to the enterprise of science. It seems that there should be some aspiration in your thesis/dissertation. Otherwise, you are likely to produce just one more thing to waste paper and readers' time. Here a more aggressive approach to the thesis/dissertation will be helpful to bring about high quality results. And this is not necessarily associated with the prolongation of the time spent on the thesis/dissertation. Taken as a general rule, the requirement is a high-quality effort within reasonable limits of time and other resources. Later, we will talk about writing your thesis/dissertation for publication as a journal article or even as a book.

You may have no such ambition, or still feel uncomfortable with the uncertainty associated with the thesis/dissertation process. You need not worry too much since there are ways to handle those issues. Fortunate indeed, you are often allowed to choose and/or change your advisor and your committee members. You

nation-state thinking by showing how groups link themselves to others transnationally. Yet diaspora, as it concerns Blacks worldwide, still centers on racial identity for all intents and purposes. Meanwhile, the value of searching out what Robbins has called "actually existing cosmopolitanism" (1998) among Blacks is that it would show the conditions of possibility for Blacks' identifications beyond national *and* racial community. The very lack of racial and national allegiances is what people in south Liverpool construe as authentically local, back when the local was global by definition.

Just as Omar searched for Liverpool's Black history, others seek an explanation for the radical break they posit between past and present. As I hinted earlier with reference to Claire's periodization of Granby's decline, the limits of their cosmopolitanism are exposed in the explanations they come up with.

NATIONALIST COSMOPOLITANISM?

Despite their different investments in national belonging, Blacks in Liverpool agree on one point: there is a pronounced, calculated silence on how central African, Afro-Caribbean, and Black Liverpudlian seamen were to Britain's military victories in two world wars. With the extended narrative that follows, I make a modest contribution to Black people's goal of having their heroic story told—with the caveat that the provision of this story for such a purpose gives credence (like "birth here" claims) to the nationalist politic that these selfsame stories are meant to challenge.

Below, Morris may very well be sailing a ship on the high seas, but those seas do not constitute global space. *Pitt Street* is global. The sea—or better, the ship—is national.

All together I was thirty-six years at sea, and that includes the war years when I was in the Merchant Navy. Because I left—I was in another shipping company going to Brazil at the time and two of the ships were required by the Navy. So when we arrived in port we were told that the ship was going to be taken over by the Navy, so we were given the option of either staying on as merchant seamen or going with the ship. Because of our experience, the Navy would welcome us going with the ship into the Navy. Our Merchant Navy pay would still be the same, as opposed to the Royal Navy man who got a lower wage rate than us; but because merchant shipping life was our whole life kind of thing, our wages stayed the same. In fact they used to call us "the big money men" because we were getting more than the military people.

Apart from our money we were similar to the Royal Navy. We were in uniform and our station, as regards the war, we were more or less in the front, the same as all the other warships. But what they did then with the ship that they took [was] they converted it into a ship whereby we sailed under the red ensign, even though our flag was the white ensign. We sailed as merchant men. In other words, we were a spy on the high seas!

I always remember as we were being commissioned, we were going down the river going to our station. Our captain cleared all the deck and had us on the deck and gave us the "Articles of War." And one particular item that he taught us, and that didn't please us at all, was the fact that if we were captured in any way—if the ship was torpedoed and we were captured—we would not be treated as prisoners of war; we would be treated as spies, and dealt with accordingly. That didn't please us at all, you know? Because we had no defense at all. Whenever we went out on patrol or anything like that, all of our uniforms were locked up.

   . . . . [D]uring our duty at sea, we flew the white and not the red ensign. The red ensign is the merchant ship. The white is the military, or Royal Navy ship. So that if we had flown the merchant flag we would've been treated differently—or we were hoping to be treated differently by the enemy—if we were captured. But as I say, that didn't please us at all but they said, "You signed on" and that was it.

From that ship, I was torpedoed off the Irish coast going to pick up a convoy and all that kind of thing, you know? I had a spell at survival leave, and then I was given another ship, and that was an experimental ship, and I was on that for two years. Again, I was the only Black man throughout. From there, I went on an aircraft carrier out east, and as I told you it was 1,674 men on that ship. And I was on that ship for three years! That was the end of the war then. The end of the German war, and I got involved in the aircraft carrier in the Japanese war. I saw the end of the whole thing, out east.

Born in Liverpool in 1915 to a White English mother and a Barbadian father, Morris spent thirty years as a seaman. Earlier in this chapter, he waxed joyous about Pitt Street. He said he traveled to "quite some places" but he never "met a street like that." I was introduced to Morris by his adult son, who recommended his father because of his experience as a seaman and, therefore, his ability to speak about the definitive male experience in the city. And, quite frankly, that is why I was interested in him: he occupied a very important cultural category. And I did want to know what it was like to be a seaman. Yet Morris interpreted my interest in "history and identity in the Black community" to mean that I was studying racism. Accordingly, he used his seafaring stories to convince me that all this talk about racism in Liverpool was overblown. Morris obviously thought I would greet the Liverpool That Was with skepticism, so he worked especially hard to conjure it. Yet the further back his stories went in time, the more deeply enmeshed they became in the contemporary era. Ultimately, Morris's concerns show how easily a cosmopolitan subjectivity can morph into a nationalist one.

Like many others I knew, Morris was very disturbed about what he perceived as the degenerate state of affairs on present-day Granby Street—so much so that it and its contrary, Pitt Street, seep into stories about his life at sea. He indicated that on many a voyage, particularly while sailing during wartime, he was the only Black person on his ship. Twice he sailed as the sole Black crew member on an aircraft carrier with a crew numbering over 1,600 men. He told me the number, quite specifically, several times. And he was adamant that though he was a Black man sailing for months at a time on ships that were always overwhelmingly White, he never experienced racism. Not once. It bears note that I never actually asked him whether he had. In what follows, he contextualizes the harmonious relations among the crew members at sea via a quick detour through Pitt Street. "Well, the relationship as regards the crew was quite normal. There was no racism or anything like that. And I might add in those days, from the time

I grew up, and—I grew up in the heart of what they called Chinatown at that time. That was Pitt Street." Years later, Morris lived in the Granby area, when it was still home to doctors, lawyers, and shipping magnates. Now, he says, the people of Granby Street "are looking for this racism and all that kind of thing." Morris explained that in the postwar era, the Granby area changed fundamentally. Here is how he describes and explains Granby's fall:

> After the war it just deteriorated, you know? I could never understand why that attitude developed around Granby Street 'cause it didn't come from the original international area of Pitt Street. It didn't come from there. My belief, really speaking, is that it came from the West Indies. The poorer type of the West Indies came over with a chip on their shoulders, and unlike the Arab, unlike the Chinaman, the Indian, and the Jewish person, they didn't seem to want to make way of their own accord. By that I mean they didn't seem to want to help themselves because among them, I'm sure there were people amongst them that could've started businesses, you know? And employed some of their own type? By "some of their own type" I mean people from the West Indies. But they came over and right away, they didn't seem to want to seek employment of any description. . . .
>
> He came and went on DHSS [Department of Housing and Social Security] or something like that! Which didn't sit well with the rest of the people because some of them went into factories or something like that—like myself, I went into Ford's [the American automobile company] after sea life. A couple of the West Indies fellows seemed to come in. But most of the fellows, most from Jamaica it seemed, they came and they gave a bad image—I'll put it that way. Because they didn't seem to—I believe that when this immigration started in the West Indies, the Italians advertised just to get their shipping popularized by the passengers coming across. I was told that they had vast adverts in the island of Jamaica and various other small islands telling the people that the streets of England were lined with gold more or less and the people that hadn't been to the island fell for this, sold everything at home and came over here. They found it totally different from what they were told. I believe it was purely the Italian shipping magnates who encouraged them to pack up and come over to England, "they were British and they were able to come over to England" and all that sort of thing.
>
> Yes I feel very strongly about this because of the name that has been given to them owing to the fact that the brush has been dirtied and it seems to go all around. Everybody gets tainted with the same brush. As the people in that area—the Granby Street area, the White people—have always said, "There are good people amongst the Black people, but the few renegades are causing the other people to be tainted." And it's all wrong.

Morris's use of World War II as a turning point is important because it separates the seafaring-based Black community from later histories of movement that center on immigration—a phenomenon which, rather stunningly, is "blamed" on Italian shipping magnates rather than the British government. It is immigrants, not people of the Caribbean writ large, who are the subject of his critique. At another moment, for example, he expressed a sense of ethnic affinity with other "West Indies children" with whom he sailed. So it is not that he disparages Afro-Caribbean people as a whole—just those who had high expectations of England, did not want to make way of their own accord and open up businesses like other groups, did not want to engage in the cosmopolitanism already established in Liverpool, did not manifest English forms of class-based respectability, and, as he goes on to argue below, did not abide by law and order.

> In Granby Street they have an area that they made through themselves, a no-go area. And they were able to get away with quite a lot of disturbances and that because of the fact that they had this attitude to law and order they wouldn't abide by. *They only wanted the difference to be maintained.* . . . [T]hey wanted an area on their own, kind of thing. I didn't believe in ghettos yet they want them. And that's what they did: they made a ghetto out of Granby Street. I don't believe in ghettos at all. (Emphasis added)

Postwar Caribbean immigrants to Liverpool are the source of the race *and* place problems. His analysis of the disastrous effects of their immigration resounds so thoroughly with nationalist discourse of the 1960s and beyond that it is hard to imagine that it does not derive from it—except that for Morris, the focus is distinctly local. The historical postwar period serves as the rupture between, on the one hand, the international community that he and others use to define Pitt Street and, on the other hand, the more narrowly racial, or "Black," community of present-day Granby. The latter, in his view, went abruptly from cosmopolitan glory to a localized ghetto, where people are overly focused on racism and the maintenance, jointly, of racial and spatial separatism.

Morris's critiques of Blacks' racial politics informed his representation of his life at sea in ways that produced a series of contradictions. With every "um" and "you see?" he utters, Morris is at pains to avoid admitting that racism explained the different opportunities open to Black and White men back in the 1930s, when he first went to sea.

> From school the jobs were very difficult—especially for, um, Black people. The only channel open to us was sea life, you see? I did try to get an apprenticeship at various places, like Fosset and Preston's, a foundry—a big iron foundry and draughtsmanship—and there was nothing open for us. I went into Elder Dempsters [a big shipping company] which employed Black people down in the engine room and the stokehold and Whites on deck, you see? Also the catering was done by Black people. You know, the stewards waiting on—but at a different wage rate than the rest of the crew. Because of the fact that we weren't in a union. We weren't unionized. But the White people were unionized and we weren't, and of course the money was just a touch lower than the White people were getting.

Morris struggled to present these details matter-of-factly, as if it should not really be a matter of concern that sea life was the only channel open to Black men, or that there was nothing open for him and other Blacks at the foundry where he sought an apprenticeship, or that unionized Whites worked on deck, while Blacks, who were not unionized, worked in the grimy occupations below deck or as "stewards waiting on . . . [Whites?]," and were making wages that were "just a touch lower" than the wages White seamen earned. Morris's gingerly representation seems conditioned by his concern for how Whites view contemporary Granby Street and how this tar brush paints him.

Morris's memories of the seafaring life are not confined to shipboard experience and global adventures. His narrative sails the high seas in order to puzzle over the shift in sensibilities that marked Blacks' movement from Pitt Street to Granby, which he explains through the migration of new attitudes from the West Indies. He condemns contemporary forms of identity and community, as well as their narrow and fixed relationships to race and place. Whereas the sites of pre-war community life were defined by their internationalism, postwar Granby Street is defined by the new arrivals' refusal to participate in the racial, ethnic, and national mixing that defined the authentic Liverpool.

Morris's critical views of immigration are not his alone. He shares it with the group that he implicitly derides, LBBs—the people who are "looking for all this racism and that kind of thing." These are the same people who consider his experience their history. LBBs also distinguish prewar and postwar in order to resist being drawn into what became, on a national level, the singularly despised phenomenon of immigration. The seafaring origin story works wonders here, for it effectively counters the discourse on immigration, the form of movement applicable to postwar Caribbeans as well as to middle-class Africans who settled in Liverpool after independence. Seafaring is, quite simply, never assimilated into a general immigration history in Liverpool. Conveniently, the history of global wandering is too fluid. Unlike immigration, there is no "beginning" to seafaring, just as there is never a historical starting point for the Black presence in Liverpool. That presence is immemorial. It goes back "generations and generations," or "hundreds of years."

Seafaring has featured prominently in Paul Gilroy's laudatory treatments of the traveler and his automatic internationalism. Eighteenth-century sea travel apparently promoted a fundamentally different "ecology of belonging" than would be found on land, where territorial sovereignty reigned. The ship allowed *some* Blacks to assert a defiant "rootlessness," which he sees as the starting point of their cosmopolitan, outward-bound orientations and identifications—beyond both race and nation. The "sublime force of the ocean" (2000: 121) counteracts "the fundamental power of territory to determine identity," he suggests in rather phenomenological fashion (123). If place produces identity, as English cultural premises suggest, then the ostensible nonplace of the sea must erase it. Similarly, he hails diaspora as a "ready alternative to the stern discipline of primordial kinship and *rooted* belonging," an alternative created, again, by travel (123, emphasis added). In his fairly romantic depiction of all matters related to ships and the sea, Gilroy evokes a placeless, antinational, global realm that resists kinship, produces hybridity, and thwarts Identity.

Gilroy imbues the seagoing life with a magical aura unknown to seamen whom I knew. Granted, he is concerned with the eighteenth century; yet and still, because his account is meant to instruct and inspire us in the present day, the correctives that the twentieth century provides seem permissible. The Liverpool That Was shows fluid racial and national identifications operating in dockside neighborhoods—among women and families. But such affinities were not found on sailing ships. According to Black ex-seamen, differences of race, ethnicity, and nation were not bridged and blurred on ships, but redoubled. Seafaring was often shot through with a particular brand of racial terror. It bears emphasis in this context that a ship is characterized just as much by confinement as by movement. Crews could number in the hundreds, and were often composed almost completely of White men. The bonds among seamen were formed through race, not across it. One Black seaman I knew, Louis, described altercations that he said were initiated by White men. Fights onboard ship occurred all the time, he told me, and they were very dangerous affairs. Once a fight erupted, one's adversaries might just throw him overboard and report that he had fallen. He went on to detail a story in which his White shipmates continually threatened to assault him. As soon as their ship would dock, though, these same men would attempt to make amends with him. All their ports of call were in the Caribbean and the southern United States. His White shipmates desired a Black escort. Within the structure of sea life, then, Black men navigated tense race relations. Morris's son told me a story that illuminates his father's strident defense of ideologies of Englishness. When Morris first went away to sea, he sailed on a ship with an African and White English crew. The African men took an immediate disliking to Morris; to them, he was English. When Morris took severely ill, the Africans were prepared to leave him to die, while his English shipmates took care of him.

An African ex-seamen I knew provides another corrective to depictions of the sea as a liberating, global space. He told me that the very first thing any seaman wants to know as his ship pulls away from a port is how long it will take to get to the next one. The sea is interminable. Sean described it as depressing. It brought many a sailor to suicide, he said. One lived for letters from back home.[5]

Because Liverpool is always defined as an international seaport, African seafarers' global movements have pride of place both in the origin story and official history of this local Black community. In the next section, I analyze the gendering of that history, exposing its various elisions and offering a few alternatives for how Black Liverpool's glorious relationship to the sea might be understood.

LOCAL WOMEN, GLOBAL MEN?

Veronica conjured Liverpool's cosmopolitanism by remembering the flow of worldly commodities into Granby, back "when all the ships were coming in." All the world's men were also coming in, often carrying exotic commodities as gifts. I earlier quoted Muriel Fletcher on the point. She wrote that

> it is a significant fact that whenever there was a ship in port with coloured men on it practically none of the [young "half-caste"] girls would come to the club but they returned the following week displaying scarves, necklaces, wrist watches, etc., while two invariably brought money to be saved up for them. . . . [O]wing to the persistence

of the men it is practically impossible for the coloured girls to remain pure. (1930: 32)

Cecelia told me about a friend of hers who became something of a legend. Back when all the ships were coming in, this woman had the world's goods at her doorstep. And like the girls who so scandalized Fletcher, she did not buy them from international shops on Granby. This woman was affectionately known as "Shipping Times [Stella]" because of her penchant for reading the trade newsletter, *Shipping Times*. That paper kept her apprised of when ships would be docking in Liverpool, and from where. She always knew exactly where her next sexual adventures would be coming from. In what follows, Barbara, whom we have met before, tells briefly of her own adventures. It is her movements, I argue, not just those of seafaring Black men, that tell us how Black Liverpool was born.

In the previous chapter, Barbara said she was from "a pure White area" in the north end. In her youth, she would go down to the Pier Head, the central point of the dock area, where she would meet sailors in what is a neat inversion of the flaneur whose movements Anne McClintock (1995) and Judith Walkowitz (1992) analyze in exquisite detail. A flaneur is a would-be bourgeois male voyeur who walks the city, surveying its exotic life forms, especially working-class women— therein constructing their own masculinity and their own middle-class subjectivity. In what follows, it is Barbara who was the privileged urban spectator. She goes beyond the confines of her safe experience in Anfield to gaze upon the men down at the docks, in all their various—perhaps exotic—splendor. It is she, a working-class woman from a "pure White area" who travels across town to take in the jointly cosmopolitan and sexual pleasures that the city's port offered. She said,

When I was nearly seventeen [1950], I got into meeting Black people. I'd come down to the Pier Head with me friend. . . . There were, like, these uniformed sailors, and they'd all come down from somewhere or another, like, you know. And I used to have to get the bus back home at ten o'clock every night from the Pier Head, at the main bus station and get home. . . . At them days, with the big merchant ships— nobody was allowed to go on them you know—but we used to stand in the Pier Head, and girls all used to be there seeing the sailors, and everybody used to be taking pictures. But that's the first real big—there were all these Black people there, and to me like, God!, you know!

Her brothers would condemn her trips to the Pier Head, accusing her of "going up there to see niggers." Eventually, Barbara decided that since she was old enough to work, she could also do what she wanted. She could do it in relative peace if she stayed away from home as much as possible. "And they were very prejudiced, like, but it wasn't going to stop me from doing what I wanted to do. I'm seventeen now, and they tried beating me and whatever but I thought you know, you're not going to carry on. And the escape route was [to] get out, and I started coming down to this area, meeting people down here." "This area" was Liverpool 8. For Barbara, trips to the Pier Head meant meeting Black men. The docks were a place of desire totally defined by their presence. And a dangerous desire it was, for she had to escape home—the site of masculine power—in order to enjoy it. She escaped not via the sea, but the port.

Barbara had two daughters by Black men, and she continued living in Anfield until the birth of her second daughter, after which she moved to Liverpool 8. This is how she narrated that movement:

> When my first daughter was born she was really light, and all the family was saying, "God, she's lovely isn't she? I didn't think she'd be White." But they were made up [elated] with her—maaaaade up with her! [She slaps the table.] Then the next one come on the scene, and she took the color, like; they loved her like, you know, but it'd be one of them showing that I was mixing with Black. That was what it was like. [Speaking in a hushed, gossipy tone, she adopts the voice of her neighbors.] "Oh, you hear that [Barbara] is mixing with a Black fella? You seen that little girl?" It was like that in that area, and I couldn't take that. So I just come down here then. I got a flat, and me mum was always good. She used to come down here and mix with us all.

Barbara *had* to move. She became the subject of gossip when the second, darker-skinned daughter appeared on the scene, racializing Barbara herself. Her positioning as a woman from a "pure White area" was compromised by her sexual practices. Barbara moved to the place where other interracial families were confined but which was also, for that reason, relatively safe. And it is her very movement, and that of myriad White women like her, that produced Liverpool 8 as a place where jointly racial and sexual practices such as hers were not scorned but normalized, indeed, by the antiracist discourses that, as we saw in chapter 4, increasingly wrapped themselves around her.

Official historical narratives written about the Black community of Liverpool, while noting White women's membership, tend to erase their considerable agency. The community currently associated with Liverpool 8 was born of these women's desires, which were fulfilled by *their* movements—first from the outskirts of the city to the docks and, ultimately, to Liverpool 1 (the Pitt Street area) and Liverpool 8. The silence on White women's movements may owe to the masculinist emphasis on the sea rather than the port. As well, international seafaring had lascivious connotations that antiracist historical narratives in and about Liverpool nobly struggle to play down, not deconstruct, as I show momentarily. Moreover, the role of White women's desires and movements in producing Black Liverpool may be occluded, despite the fact that they hide in plain sight, because Blacks are the more racialized group. More crucially, it seems, they are occluded because the movement of men across *national* borders is perceived as more consequential. Untold numbers of women just like Barbara were migrating from the north end to the south end, fulfilling desires that ultimately produced "Black Liverpool." But apparently they were not moving *far enough* out of place to have their travels—motivated by arguably cosmopolitan desires—recognized as momentous and transformative.

All of these elisions are evident in the work of a contemporary scholar who here explains the role of seafaring in giving birth to the Black community: "Transient work patterns that derive from the nature of seafaring . . . led to short-term relationships with *local women*. Permanent and long-standing relationships with *local women* through marriage (formal or common-law) usually occurred when these seamen became permanently domiciled in Liverpool or in some cases this became a reason for gaining domicile" (Frost 1995/96: 51, emphasis added). In such narratives—and there are many like them—women are de-racialized. They are no longer "White," as in the *Fletcher Report* and, indeed, in Barbara's own narrative. Rather, they are marked "local," and thus are their sexual desires completely naturalized. In a way reminiscent of how the local has sometimes been constituted in contemporary cultural theory, here it is gendered in a way that renders it the inert—and, as it were, "feminine"—receptacle for the masculine category nominated the global. White women, being "local," just happen to be there, so they form the natural sex partners of Black seamen. At least in the *Fletcher Report*, the White women (and "half-caste" girls) were having "adventures," a term that carried unmistakable sexual connotations in Fletcher's original context; she argued that some younger White women consort with African men "*in a spirit of adventure* and find themselves unable to break away" (1930: 22). Fletcher's phrasing is especially provocative for present analytical purposes, considering that seafaring is often studied in terms of *male* adventure. In the local/global space of this port, it is White women who were having maritime adventures.

The port was racialized and sexualized by the movement of Black men into it—and, just as crucially, by their continuing movements *out of it*. The racial inscriptions that attached to the Pier Head referred not just to these men's presence but to the utter transience of it. Thus antiracist historical narratives like the one cited above tend to couch Black seamen's mobility in a respectable register, first by referring to the dictates of their seaborne livelihood and then by domesticating them—"localizing" them—through the pronounced emphasis on their eventual domicile in Liverpool. Yet Barbara's own emphasis lay in the fact that Black men were always "coming in from somewhere or another." These global men would come in and out with the tide. And the "local women"? Not only did women like Shipping Times Stella stay, but they would reappear at the Pier Head to greet the next ship. Liverpool's port, then, facilitated "local/global intersections" of a rather fleeting nature. Globalization studies that focus on race and migration never take the variety of movements that Barbara enacted into account. Although they were undeniably born of the colonial politics of race, relocations like Barbara's did not take place on the global, world-historical stage. They were "just" local.

Barbara's movements and the desires that animated them have additional racial implications to which I shall return. First, I want to examine the gendered relationship between the sea and the port, as mediated by race, nation, and kinship. Again, Gilroy's comments are provocative. In placing (mostly) men at sea, he liberates them from territory, nation, kinship, and all that goes with it—including, it seems, women and whatever demands women make in the realms of "hearth and home" with which they are ideologically linked.[6] By implication, the women left back at the port become synonymous with the insularity, stasis, and fixity of locality, while also embodying the parochial world of race, ethnicity, and nationality.

Instead of dignifying these probably unintended associations, I want to respond by presenting other ways of thinking about race, nation, and kinship, again through the gendered sea/port relationship. In real life, women restore to Black men the masculinity that was denied to them onboard ship. Black sailors' manhood was often compromised at sea, for they were routinely consigned to feminized occupations, such as that of cook. As scholars of seafaring have shown, such positions were denigrated in the context of the ship because they did not require nautical skill (Bolster 1997; Lane 1986). But this was not part of Blacks' narratives. In their loving depictions about the seafaring men in their families, Blacks would proudly volunteer information about the actual jobs these men held. My oldest informant, eighty-five-year-old Mrs. Smith, told me that her father was a chief chef on board a ship. "Chief!" she excitedly repeated to me, just in case I hadn't heard her the first time. As well, Black people at the port situated these men within their families—not as exiles from them—and accorded them an absolutely exalted status as *seamen*, one that never equivocated based on the gendered distinctions, as motivated by racism, that obtained onboard sailing ships. In short, Black women keep the stories of heroic Black seamen (many of whom died at sea) alive. When a researcher comes to town looking for Black Liverpool's history, it is the heroic tales of Black seamen that these women unfailingly rehearse.

In chapter 2, I discussed a family I called the Ewings, an "old Black family" whom Greg arranged for me to meet. Clara, in her sixties, warmly and anxiously greeted me on my arrival at their home. Barely had she introduced herself before embarking upon the fairly standard narrative. She apprised me, while shaking my hand, that her grandfather served heroically in World War I. His name appears on a memorial in town, I learned as I sat down. Her uncle, she continued, applied for entry into the Royal Navy at age seventeen, and did so because his own father had served in it. Her uncle was initially rejected, and so he entered the Merchant Navy, which did accept Black men. All of this I learned during the first five minutes of our acquaintance, before I could even make a little small talk or tell them what my project was about, much less ask a question.

One of the most disquieting moments in my research occurred in the context of an interview with a stunningly beautiful, frail, but intense eighty-eight-year-old Black woman, Theresa. I actually met her in 1999, and although I did not consider myself to be doing fieldwork on that trip, I could not resist the opportunity to interview her. Her fascinating life included having co-owned Dutch Eddie's, one of the clubs of Granby's heyday mentioned earlier. She also worked in a munitions factory on the outskirts of town during World War II. When Liverpool suffered a three-day bombing blitz in 1941, Theresa continued to go to work. I was enthralled to hear her describe—as if it were no big deal—waiting at a bus stop while bombs were dropping. Having heard many stories of Black men's heroism at sea, I asked whether she considered herself a hero. She never answered that question. Instead, she seized the opportunity it presented in order to correct some

Introduction to Intellectual Property Law

CHAPTER OVERVIEW

Intellectual property law protects the results of human creative endeavor. Intellectual property is generally thought to comprise four separate fields of law: trademarks, copyrights, patents, and trade secrets. A *trademark* is a word, name, symbol, or device used to identify and distinguish one's goods or services and to indicate their source. Rights in trademarks are created by use of a mark; registration with the U.S. Patent and Trademark Office is not required, although it offers certain advantages. *Copyright* protects original works of authorship, including literary, musical, dramatic, artistic, and other works. Just as trademarks are protected from the moment of their first public use, copyright exists from the moment of creation of a work; registration of a copyright with the U.S. Copyright Office, while affording certain benefits, is not required. A *patent* is a grant from the U.S. government that permits its owner to exclude others from making, selling, or using an invention. Patents exist only upon issuance by the U.S. Patent and Trademark Office. A *trade secret* consists of any valuable commercial information that, if known by a competitor, would provide some benefit or advantage to the competitor. No registration or other formalities are required to create a trade secret, and trade secrets endure as long as reasonable efforts are made to protect their secrecy.

INTELLECTUAL PROPERTY LAW BASICS

Intellectual Property Defined

There are three distinct types of property that individuals and companies can own: *real property* refers to land or real estate; *personal property* refers to specific items and things that can be identified, such as jewelry, cars, and stock; and *intellectual property* refers to the fruits or product of human creativity, including literature, advertising slogans, songs, or new little detail I had earlier gotten wrong about the Black men of the Merchant Navy. With that, Theresa seemed to relegate her own "just local" travels across town to the realm of insignificance, and indeed invisibility.

Even though seamen commonly spent twelve to eighteen months at a time away from home, it would be a mistake to consider them exiles from family life or indifferent to it. Another woman, Lucille, lovingly recalled her father's global adventures in "local" and "domestic" terms. She grew up in Anfield, the "pure White area" that Barbara hailed from. Here Lucille describes how she was afforded a measure of pride through her father's seafaring activities. Importantly, though, she also credits her mother and grandmother for producing her sense of well-being:

> Now my father, he was a seaman. . . . Obviously when I think about it now I was a lot better off than the White children because my father went to sea. My mother also worked, my grandmother worked. I benefited in many ways because I had nice clothes. My father brought me clothes home. And there was a lot of children that didn't have what I had, not just in food but in the upbringing that I also had. I went to church, and me mother dressed me nice, and there was times my mother would send food to people in the streets because obviously with my father being a merchant seaman, when the ship used to dock all the goodies used to come. There'd be sugar, and there'd be fruit and there'd be meat. Probably my mother was thinking, "Oh god!" So my mum used to share. I was probably looked on for different reasons.

Never do scholarly accounts of Black seamen's worldly adventures depict them shopping around in exotic ports of call for little girls' clothing. That might be construed as too familial, too domestic, too concerned with matters "just local," nay feminine.

In all, then, the sea and the port are no more separable than the local and the global. The use of kinship, in particular, to distinguish categories of space or place—even if for the purpose of challenging racial and national hegemonies—is itself an *enactment* of a gendered politic rather than being an objective statement about the intrinsic qualities of the local, the global, or the port or the sea.[7] This comment applies as much to Gilroy's account as to those that my informants rehearsed to me, and those that circulate in official and less official histories of Black Liverpool. With that, we may return to the racial implications of the global-cum-cosmopolitan space of the Pier Head.

Barbara's Liverpool That Was evoked a sense of excitement and desire that might otherwise be associated with seafaring. The Pier Head comes back to life through images of big merchant ships, Black uniformed sailors from wherever, and dolled-up girls taking pictures. In narrating her journey from "a pure White area" to Liverpool 8, Barbara told of her triumph over "the stern discipline of primordial kinship and rooted belonging." She defies her brothers' racist attacks on her and escapes the disciplinary tactics of her neighbors. She *had* to leave Anfield. That move, in her view, was the starting point of an ethical worldliness that defied the racial strictures of home. But as I suggested in the previous chapter, that narrative traced a dubious trajectory, ending in a color-blind, power-evasive view of race. Liverpool 8 is racism-free, in her view, and so is she. Her would-be cosmopolitanism is racially inscribed in another way. The desires she fulfilled at the Pier Head were premised on well-established ideologies of racial difference that worked through sexuality. Muriel Fletcher certainly did not invent the view of "Negro" men as hypersexual. But in her report, sex with them represents an adventure. Barbara echoes that perception here: "We used to stand in the Pier Head, and girls all used to be there seeing the sailors, and everybody used to be taking pictures. *But that's the first real big—there were all these Black people there, and to me like, God!, you know!*" These sailors were exciting for being Black. Since Liverpool was an international seaport, the Pier Head must have played host, on any given day, to a dizzying variety of the world's men. But she focused on the Black ones. In the previous chapter, Lisa also intimated that what made Black men sexually attractive was the danger and hence excitement of "stepping over the traces." The colonial politics of race and sexuality, here in the eminently global space of the port, shaped at least *some* White women's "cosmopolitan" desires—desires steeped in the same racism that the women believe themselves to be overcoming.

CONCLUSION

The alternative histories above show the cosmopolitan possibilities of place, a subjectivity that manifests in an inspiring rejection of racial and national allegiances and identifications. As well, these histories show that one need not physically leave a place to go beyond race and nation. Indeed, by defining the local as global, the Liverpool That Was contradicts the identity imperatives of LBB hegemony, which sutures Blackness to locality via a nationalist idiom of place. In the Liverpool That Was, one didn't have to be "born here" to be authentically local. Just the reverse: having links to elsewhere is what made one local. Such a possibility should encourage us to disentangle "place" from *all* received associations with the local, for only then can we inquire into how those two ideologically loaded abstractions come to be defined through each other—and through race, nation, and gender.

Yet place also *dis*abled the same cosmopolitan revisions of race and nation that it inspired. The death of Pitt Street and the early Granby is traced to the influx of immigrants. Rather than serving as an indictment of place, this contradiction invites further study of its inherent instability. Place acquires its fluid and contradictory political potentialities through its imbrication in the mobile discourses of race, nation, and, inextricably, gender.

Similarly, the local and the global in this analysis did not refer to scope, scale, or scapes but instead named the roles that men and women are differently allowed to play in historical narratives of various description. Remembering, again, that "geography" means "the writing of the earth," the spatial knowledge indexed by the terms *local* and *global* point up the gendered implications of *where* people are placed both in authoritative and counterhegemonic histories, as well as the forms of visibility and invisibility that result. The ethnography above showed additional ways that the local and the global are bound to race and gender ideologies: White women are racialized through their association with traveling, transient "global" Black men and through their occupation of the Pier Head, a place racialized and sexualized for playing host to men bearing no connection to hearth and home. As a consequence, Black seamen get narrated into History in a way that domesticates and desexualizes them, hence restoring, at least narratively, White women's respectability. In short, as Doreen Massey earlier suggested, the categories called *place*, *local*, and *global* are not abstract, objective, neutral spatial constructs. Rather, the particular ways in which they get invoked and naturalized—both textually and in actual social life—are directly implicated in the subject positions we know as gender, race, and nation.

Finally, although I join Liverpudlians in their enthusiasm for the Liverpool That Was, I do not offer up cosmopolitanism as a model of radical political subjectivity. Liverpudlians exalt it so much, invest it with so much hope and possibility, that it actually becomes yet another way of creating outsiders—just as David Harvey warned above.[8] Some scholarly versions of cosmopolitanism are in danger of doing the same thing—particularly in their consistent gendering of the (provincial) local as feminine, and the (adventurous) global as masculine.

The Leaving of Liverpool

"THE LEAVING of Liverpool" is a traditional song that dates to 1885, when a sailor was overheard singing it on a ship. The song has been recorded many times since. One version of the lyrics comes with the instruction to sing "expansively." In any event, the song begins like this:

> Farewell to Prince's landing stage
> River Mersey Fare thee well
> I am bound for California
> A place I know right well
> So fare thee well my own true love
> When I return united we will be
> It's not the leaving of Liverpool that grieves me
> But my darling when I think of thee.

Kim was one of my best friends in Liverpool. I often went out to parties with her and her friends and socialized with them all at her home. She told me details of her intimate relationships, and she counseled me on mine. On my first return trip to Liverpool in 1997, we got together and caught up with each other's lives. When I arrived at her home, I found her packing up house. She was in a new relationship, and she was ecstatic. Her new beau was a Black American in the armed forces. He was stationed at a base in southern England, where she was now headed. For the last several years, Kim had held a variety of jobs in race-oriented organizations, but none of them sustained her financially or offered any manner of advancement. On the night of our reunion, she told me of her recent epiphany: "I realized that I didn't want to wake up at thirty-five and realize that all I have is Liverpool." Essentially, Kim had asked herself, "Why Liverpool?" Failing for an answer, she decided to migrate south. At thirty-two years old, Kim had now developed a plan: she was going to live on the base and attend university, with the goal of becoming a professional counselor. The next night, we went dancing at the African to celebrate her future. As we danced, she noted the distinct lack of movement among the other partiers. "You see these people?" she asked me. "They're not going anywhere. They don't do nothing with their lives. You see the same ones here every week. They're scared to go out of the area. I don't want to live like that."

> I'm off to California
> By the way of the stormy Cape Horn
> And I will send you a letter, love,
> When I'm homeward bound.
> Farewell to Lower Frederick Street

Anson Terrace and Park Lane
Farewell, it will be some long time
Before I see you again.

The people whom I had the privilege to study never let me forget that I was accountable to them. Their frequent references to the *Fletcher Report* and myriad other examples of Liverpool racial exotica were explicit statements about the inseparability of power and knowledge. When I first met Greg, he confessed, "When you said 'anthropology' I got a fright. But anything you can do to mash down the misinformation would be positive." One of the very first interviews I conducted, during exploratory research in 1989, ended with my informant, Abraham, telling me sternly: "I want to see what you write about us." He seemed to think it would be just as insulting as everything that had ever gone before. I ran into him in 1997. He noted, again sternly, that I had failed to send him whatever it was I had written.

Black people and White women alike were sometimes guarded in their initial interactions with me. They seemed to expect that I would say something objectionable, or that I harbored views of them as weird and strange. They were critically attuned to the genealogies of any question of mine that even hinted at the topics of interracial marriage, romance, procreation, parentage, and sexuality. "Knowledge" produced on these topics, as the *Fletcher Report* dramatizes, has never been innocent. And the people constructed by that knowledge are, in a word, exhausted of being rendered curiosities. I, for my part, think that there are much more interesting things to say about Black people in Liverpool than the fact that many are of mixed racial parentage. I have struggled to write this ethnography in a way that might preempt questions fixated on that single fact— especially since I, following my informants in Liverpool/Britain, am transfixed by the issue of place.

I've shipped on a Yankee clipper ship,
Davy Crockett is her name
And Burgess is the captain of her
And they say she's a floating hell.
It's my second trip with Burgess in the Crockett,
And I think I know him well.
If a man's a sailor, he can get along.
But if not, he's sure in hell.

This book has struggled from the outset not to enact what it describes—that is, not to reproduce in ethnographic-analytical form all that goes into the making of "Liverpool" as the "self-pity city." Yet ultimately it does privilege Liverpool's point of view on its marginality and its renegade outsiderism. In response to a draft of chapter 6 ("My City, My Self"), an English friend asked me: What makes *them* so special? Another English friend charged that I was being Liverpool-centric for not showing, for example, that lots of other British places can lay claim to marginality. He added that people in every hamlet, town, and city in Britain that is not the metropole holds London in rather low esteem—a point that

I've heard many times. These friends were essentially asking me, Why Liverpool? Their helpful challenges compel me to reiterate one of my main points—indeed, the one point that shows the gulf between my view and that of my informants. Liverpool is not unique. Although this text reflects the dominant view in Liverpool about the city's wholesale alienation from the nation—and I admit that chapters 6 and 7 do defend Liverpool, even if toward interventionist ends—I have made a point of letting White Scousers, LBBs, and other Britons make all the uniqueness claims about that city. My goal has been to show the racial effects of those claims. In fact, I see "Liverpool" as a production of national political culture concerning place—a production that implicates positioned subjects and historical processes both within and beyond the city. To the degree that I succeeded in making that argument, this becomes a book about England/Britain as glimpsed from the vantage point of Liverpool.

Admittedly, it has only been in the leaving of Liverpool that Liverpudlian perspectives were thrown into clearest relief for me. Independently, those same two friends pointed out that the very qualities that are recognized in the rest of England as irreducibly Scouse—such as irreverence and impertinence—are actually admired by at least some other English people precisely because these stances express such round contempt for middle-class respectability, elite pretensions, and other status structures of English society. That excellent point acknowledged, I invite further controversy by suggesting that my non-Liverpudlian friends' critical responses to the issue of Liverpool's marginality are no less positioned than the views to which they so spiritedly responded. In anticipation of similar critiques, I cite the reflections of Patrick Wright, who here defends his own defense of Hackney, a London borough:

> [O]ne of the things you have to think about really carefully when writing about a place like East London is the habitual condescension of the better-placed onlooker.
>
> I found out more about this when I started writing for the Guardian...after [*A Journey through Ruins*] was published. I would be asked for an article whenever anything ghoulish or disastrous had happened in Hackney—the place could only achieve national interest under the rubric of monstrosity. I wasn't aiming to minimize the horrors that do indeed occur in the inner city, but if you're looking for a place where tolerance and reciprocal humanity are to be found at their best, you would probably do better in Hackney than in Tunbridge Wells. (2000: 480)

> The tug is waiting at the pier head
> To take us down the stream.
> Our sails are loose and our anchor secure,
> So I'll bid you goodbye once more.
> I'm bound away to leave you,
> Goodbye, my love, goodbye
> There's just one thing that grieves me,
> That's leaving you behind.

I risk a thousand clichés by suggesting that "The Leaving of Liverpool" truly expresses something essential about that place. After all, and as the song itself gives evidence, Liverpudlians have been folklorizing their city and themselves with a passion for generations. Rather than joining in, I have tried to deconstruct that practice—most radically, I think, by questioning the city's absolutely-beyond-question inscription as a seaport. Yet, I draw on this sailor's song and its evocation of nonstop movement to suggest that we would be mistaken to define Liverpool's mobility solely in globalist terms—a conceit encouraged both by the city's undying identity as an international seaport of world renown and by the ironically myopic scholarly fixation with all things global.

As we have seen since chapter 1, lots of people have set sail either from Liverpool's constituent locales or from the city itself. Black women left, as did the Yanks. The families memorialized on Susan's Pitt Street panel are now gone. In the 1960s, the "core" and "inner guts" of Liverpool 8 disappeared into the city's outskirts, Claire said. After the riots, Cecelia told me, still more people left. Caroline added a value judgment: "All the smart ones got out." Caroline's children all live and prosper in London, she was proud to tell me. Some White women moved from the city's north end—the environs of the much-memorialized Scottie Road—down to Liverpool 8. Years ago, as Black women were riding buses to get to the dances on the American bases near Manchester, White women were crossing town, also on buses, to meet men down at the Pier Head. White Scousers have migrated south to "genteel" places like Bournemouth. My friend Kim has followed them. During my 1997 visit, I stayed with Yvette, with whom I lived for several months in 1992. When I returned again in 1999, she had disappeared. Cecelia, her great friend, had no idea where she had gone off to. Yet many people, like Marien, who lives on Granby Street, remain. She refuses to leave. "Why should I?!" Nonstop movement—not just of the global variety—creates the mobility of place.

Hugh Raffles, whose ethnography on Amazonia is an exquisite meditation on place, has written that places, after they have disappeared from maps and landscapes, live on through story (2002). As people move, they carry places with them, materializing them as they narrate their own lives. This ethnography shows that the opposite also happens. Those who stay in a place that others have left continually bring those people back. This book began with Scott's tour of an invisible Liverpool inhabited by lots of ghosts. The loss of the city's raison d'être and the dispersal of the "real" Liverpool, as embodied in seafaring families, have produced a pronounced sense of displacement. After all, since the essential "being" of place—according to their folk phenomenology—produces the very being of its inhabitants, rendering people and place one and the same, the simultaneous departure of the port and the souls produced by it could only result in very intense longings. What's left? And what am I still doing here? "Why Liverpool?" Kim essentially asked herself. From the moment she shared it with me, her epiphany has always struck me as poignant beyond words. Of all the ways that she could have expressed her fears of an unfulfilled life, she said that she wanted to avoid waking to the realization that all she had was Liverpool.

During my last visit Cecelia insisted that my book must address what the future holds for this Black community. I cannot follow that injunction. But what

I can do is address the concern that Blacks express about that future. Cecelia was a mover and shaker in the late 1970s and 1980s. She narrated her own political practice and that of other LBBs in spatial and racial terms. They took their new politics of race into the streets of town in the hope of opening up a brave new world for Blacks as a whole, so that they might become part of the mainstream located there. So that they might be able to work there. LBB politics had the effect of creating employment opportunities—mostly within and around Liverpool 8, though, and all of them in race-oriented community institutions.

But, like the shipping industry before it, the race relations industry sank in the 1990s. By 1997, a few race relations bodies had disappeared, most notably the Merseyside Community Relations Council, where Cecelia had introduced me to her sister and other politicos years before. Cecelia was sanguine about this development. They had to go, she argued. Produced out of a specific set of political circumstances, they had run their course. Black people needed to move on. And *she* certainly had. Cecelia is a successful professional whose work is not connected to the voluntary sector. Scott also thought that Black people should expand their horizons, which he locates outside the safe haven of Liverpool 8. Scott has been involved in the development of equal opportunity policies in the local authority. When young Black men go into town to interview for construction jobs with the Liverpool City Council, Scott told me, all the bravado they manifest on Granby Street evaporates. When asked a question by a prospective employer, the respondent typically mumbles a reply into the top button of his shirt. Young Black women, for their part, do not apply for construction jobs.

When I first met Ian in 1991, he had a modest job in Liverpool 8's flagship Black institution. His mother, Marien, once told me that among her sons, Ian would probably go farthest in life. She lauded the institution where he worked and others like them for giving young men like her son the opportunity to work. His place of employment, though, was one of the doomed ones. Ian used to tell me about what he would do with his life if just given an opportunity. He might like to become a social worker, for example. One of our conversations took place in the canteen at his workplace. Overhearing our conversation, a middle-aged African woman who worked there injected her opinion: "He's a dreamer."

When I saw Ian in 1999, he spoke with great admiration of a mutual friend of ours, a Black man about ten years older than himself, who had recently attained a doctorate in the United States and had a promising future—likely in that country. All three of us knew that his future would not take place in Liverpool. Our friend's path is the one Ian wanted to follow. If only he were offered an opportunity he would seize it, he assured me. Ian's brother was on another path. He had been given what he considered an opportunity. For years, Blacks protested against racial discrimination in employment, particularly their exclusion from visible jobs in town. Now construction companies were finally, in 1999, training Black youth to do building work. Ian's brother was very excited to be a trainee. It did not concern him that his work would keep him within Liverpool 8, where construction and destruction of housing occurs with cyclical regularity, as Marien complained to me years before.

One day in 1992, taking a cigarette break from their work, Ian and a Black coworker of his, Lizzie, wondered aloud whether Europe was a place of possibility for Black people. The European Union was in formation. In the abstract, the dissolution of national borders was an intriguing prospect to them. The subtext of this conversation was that their future would not take place in Liverpool—or at least they hoped that it would not. Maybe America, Lizzie said. Then, after asking me whether I could ever live in Liverpool, she told me she really does not fancy living in the States at all. The possibility of venturing into town or into the rest of Britain for "opportunities" or as a passport to a better life never came up. When they projected themselves into the future, it was as immigrants. In 1999, I found Ian and Lizzie working in the same place. But come 2001, that institution, so identified with Black Liverpool's emergence as such, became defunct. It closed due to lack of funding, Veronica told me in a letter. But Cecelia's historical analysis, noted above, suggests it might have closed for lack of political raison d'être.

Initially, the motivation of my research was to understand Blacks' relationship to the racialized categories *British* and *English*. Following the path set forcefully by Paul Gilroy's inspiring *There Ain't No Black in the Union Jack*, I did not want to begin, as many studies of the time did, by treating Black people as always already ethnic subjects. Inquiring into their possible Britishness and Englishness would expose the intersection of race and nation in Black people's experience. I could not have been more surprised and, in the end, happy to find "Liverpool" sitting in the middle of everything. That discovery has allowed me to suggest the political importance of theorizing place: it can contribute to the always crucial project of denaturalizing race. The latter is not an autonomous preexisting essence housed in the bodies, selves, and worldviews of Black people or anyone else. This book has shown the specific conditions under which Black identity emerged. It has also suggested that in the generations prior, more fluid, "cosmopolitan" (for lack of a better term) identifications prevailed, ones that did not recognize or otherwise depend on race. And in the end, what continues to fascinate me is this: seemingly, about ten minutes after Black identity made its powerful appearance, "Liverpool-born" was placed right on top of it—as if it had been laying in wait for just the right racial signifier, one truly worthy of it. Why not Black Liverpudlian? Or Black British? Or British-born Black? I remain convinced that *place* not race was the more pronounced, palpable "structure of feeling" among the folks who eventually became Black. In its appropriation of "birth," the term *Liverpool-born Black* shows place dominating race. One is not "born" Black; one is *Liverpool*-born. That place is the more powerful category, I earlier claimed, is suggested by its total naturalization in people's subjectivity. Everyone in Liverpool 8 can tell you how they became Black. But "Liverpool-born"?

Why emphasize place rather than localness in this context? Why not analyze these as dynamics of "local identity"? First, because Liverpool is reified through discourses on place. For example, it is always a particular kind of place: an international seaport. As well, Liverpool places produce matching souls. Liverpudlian discourse—being, in the end, very English—attributes agency to place and gives it a particular job to do: producing identities and selves. Place acts—and it always does so first. Place *explains*. "Liverpool was a slave port and therefore . . ." I have been referring to such uses of place as a folk phenomenology because they link the pure, perceptible—even if invisible—truth of place to that of self. Second, I emphasize place over "local identity" in the construction of "LBB" because ultimately Liverpool is not reducible to localness. This work sought to question the common conflation of place with the local, a conflation that, at least in some academic discourses, devalues both. The local as hopelessly provincial and retrograde, for example. In this case, the local's most authentic, traditional content consists of Liverpool's often fraught engagement with the world—and not only through the constant comings and goings of men and commodities. Worldly encounters occurred in the context of international settlement and community formation on Pitt Street. Hence place.

Let me offer one final postscript—truly via the leaving of Liverpool. An American friend once suggested that my interest in theorizing place owes to my New York City origins. That city is, after all, a very place-y place. The unlikely validity of that hypothesis aside, I would suggest that an ethnography of the city in terms of place could make a desperately necessary contribution to the (nonexistent) anthropology of American nationalism. New York City has long been in the business of folklorizing itself. It probably beats out any other city on earth with respect to its relentless production of totally self-congratulatory narratives. Not long ago I watched (admittedly with great interest) a documentary about the history of the elevator in New York City—not an esoteric topic, as it turns out. Skyscrapers were fundamental to the city's growth as a global city defined by finance and commerce. Hence, the pivotal role of the elevator. But New York City history is also very social, often centering around immigration (think Ellis Island and the Statue of Liberty). That narrative enables another one about America as the land of opportunity, which is easily parlayed into a premature celebration of racial and ethnic tolerance and equality. New York City constantly constructs itself as the ultimate in worldliness. After all, the foods, arts, and culture of the world's people are, on any given day, available for consumption in the countless restaurants, museums, and recital halls of the city. This view of New York City silently creates complacency both in regard to racism in the city (as if racism only exists in the south and in small-town America) and to American dominance of the very same world that New Yorkers use to construct their cosmopolitanism.

In the aftermath of the tragic events of September 11, New York City became iconic in a whole new, extremely nationalist way. "America" was inscribed everywhere on the city's landscape. There were flags in the windows of apartment buildings and on every single bus and subway car. Signs in store windows read, "I love New York now more than ever." Overnight, this reputedly cosmopolitan place, previously held in low esteem by much of the nation (like London in Britain), became its symbol. Place is mobile not fixed. Liverpool/Britain is not unique. In New York City/America—and "now more than ever"—place is central to the making of race, nation, and empire.

inventions. Thus, property that is the result of thought, namely, intellectual activity, is called **intellectual property.** In some foreign countries, intellectual property is referred to as **industrial property.**

Many of the rights of ownership common to real and personal property are also common to intellectual property. Intellectual property can be bought, sold, and licensed. Similarly, it can be protected against theft or infringement by others. Nevertheless, there are some restrictions on use. For example, if you were to purchase the latest bestseller by John Grisham, you would be entitled to read the book, sell it to another, or give it away. You would not, however, be entitled to make photocopies of the book and then distribute and sell those copies to others. Those rights are retained by the author of the work and are protected by copyright law.

The Rationale for Protection of Intellectual Property

Intellectual property is a field of law that aims at protecting the knowledge created through human effort in order to stimulate and promote further creativity. Authors who write books and musicians who compose songs would be unlikely to engage in further creative effort unless they could realize profit from their endeavors. If their work could be misappropriated and sold by others, they would have no incentive to create further works. Pharmaceutical companies would not invest millions of dollars into research and development of new drugs unless they could be assured that their inventions would enable them to recover these costs and develop additional drugs. Thus, not only the creators of intellectual property but the public as well benefit from protecting intellectual property.

On the other hand, if the owner of intellectual property is given complete and perpetual rights to his or her invention or work, the owner would have a monopoly and be able to charge excessive prices for the invention or work, which would harm the public. Intellectual property law attempts to resolve these conflicting goals so that owners' rights to reap the rewards of their efforts are balanced against the public need for a competitive marketplace. Thus, for example, under federal law, a patent for a useful invention will last for only twenty years from the date an application for the patent is filed with the U.S. Patent and Trademark Office (PTO). After that period of time, the patent expires and anyone is free to produce and sell the product.

TYPES OF INTELLECTUAL PROPERTY

The term *intellectual property* is usually thought of as comprising four separate, but often overlapping, legal fields: trademarks, copyrights, patents, and trade secrets. Although each of these areas will be discussed in detail in the chapters that follow, a brief introduction to each discipline is helpful. (See chart on inside front and back covers of text comparing and contrasting the various types of intellectual property.)

Trademarks and Service Marks

What Is Protectable. A trademark or service mark is a word, name, symbol, or device used to indicate the source, quality, and ownership of a product or service. A **trademark** is used in the marketing of a product (such as REEBOK® for shoes), while a **service mark** typically identifies a service (such as STARBUCKS® for restaurant services). A trademark or service mark identifies and distinguishes the products or services of one person from those of another.

CHAPTER 1: SETTING SAIL

1. This is a unique perspective on shipping companies' position.

2. Because the presence of Africans—either as seamen or as children of African elites who were sent to Liverpool for British education—goes back centuries, one can never discount the possibility of a Black female presence, however small, in places like Park Lane.

3. But see Hartigan 1999, Gregory 1998, Wade 1993, and Jackson 2001. Of course, my use of the phrase "Black folk here and there" alludes, with reverence, to St. Clair Drake's study that goes by that title (1987).

4. Akhil Gupta and James Ferguson suggest, "Though anthropologists often picture themselves as specialists in 'the local,' we suggest that the idea of locality in anthropology is not well thought out. Clearly geographical contiguity and boundedness are insufficient to define a 'local community'; otherwise, high-rise buildings in urban metropolises would automatically qualify. . . . Is the idea of the local a way of smuggling back in assumptions about small-scale societies and face-to-face communities that we thought we had left behind?" (1997a: 15). See also their seminal statements on place and culture (1992, 1997b).

5. Yet one might quibble with his conclusion that the politics of race are most significantly engaged situationally. "Situations" may very well be the contexts in which Whites in Detroit come to perceive themselves as racial subjects. If that is the case, they are reaping the benefits of White privilege, their class positions notwithstanding. Being members of the dominant group, they have the luxury of not having to think about race until a situation is presented. Another limitation of "situations" as an all-embracing approach to the anthropology of race is that racial power is too deeply embedded in institutional practices and subjectification processes to be reduced to the interpersonal encounter—which, of course, is not to discount the latter as an important site of investigation.

6. Pile and Keith 1993, 1997; Massey 1984, 1994; Gupta and Ferguson 1992, 1997b; D. Moore 1998, 1999; Moore, Kosek, and Pandian 2003; Harvey 1993; Low and Lawrence-Zúñige 2003; Raffles 2002.

7. I find Harvey 1993 very useful in regard to place as primarily a construction and in his elaboration of the use of place in the exercise of power—even if he ultimately explains that power in terms of the "mediating power of money" (20). He writes, "To write of 'the power of place,' as if places (localities, regions, neighborhoods, states, etc.) possess causal powers, is to engage in the grossest of fetishisms: unless that is, we confine ourselves rigorously to the definition of place as a social process. In the latter case, the questions to be posed can be rendered more explicit: why and by what means do social beings invest places . . . with social power; and how and for what purposes is that power then deployed and used across a highly differentiated system of interlinked places?" (21). See Gupta and Ferguson 1992 for a similar analysis of the local.

8. In an essay for the Encyclopedia Britannica, Edmund Husserl also defined it as "a new kind of descriptive method which made a breakthrough in philosophy at the turn of the century, and an *a priori* science derived from it" (1996 [1929]: 15, original emphasis). Heidegger defines science as "the totality established through an interconnection of true propositions" (1996a: 32).

9. Husserl 1996 [1912] provides a similar roadmap.

10. This quote is from the commonly used Macquarrie and Robinson translation of *Being and Time* (Heidegger 1967), as anthologized in Kearney and Rainwater 1996. A more recent translation of this quotation reads, "In *which* being is the meaning of being to be found; from which being is the disclosure of being to get its start? Is the starting point arbitrary, or does a certain being have priority in the elaboration of the question of being? Which is this exemplary being and in what sense does it have priority?" (Heidegger 1996a: 5, original emphasis) The quotation I used in the text is arguably clearer for using the word *entities* as opposed to *being*. But in the translation above Heidegger uses *being* to refer both to the *phenomenon* (whose appearance prompts reflection and transcendental experience) as well as to the question of being, whose mysteries are at the heart of the enterprise. This translation, with its two *beings*, captures the desired oneness between subject and object characteristic of phenomenology. Without wishing to mediate or otherwise stake claims in debates among phenomenologists, it might also be noted that Heidegger did not mean for "being" to be conflated with the self. The latter construct, though, is prevalent in the work of present phenomenologists such as Sokolowski. As well, I use the self in the present work because it bears on cultural constructions of Englishness vis-à-vis place.

11. See Harvey 1993 for a great discussion of Heidegger on matters of place.

12. This line of analysis may wreak of essentialism. I pursue it precisely because it highlights forms of essentialism that produce Englishness itself.

13. See Said 1978; Bell, Butlin, and Heffernan 1995; Gregory 1994; Blunt and Rose 1994; and Driver 1992, 2000. In an interview at the University of California, Berkeley, Michael Watts was asked to explain "for an American audience" what a geographer does. He responded, "Well, that's a question that geographers often get asked in this neck of the woods. I suppose I'd start from the following observation, which is the fact that you're asking that question, and it gets asked so frequently here, says a great deal about the fact that geography is not institutionalized as an academic discipline in the United States in the same way that it is in other parts of the world. So, for example, in Europe, one is taught geography from the age of five, and geography is a part of the national curriculum. In academic settings, in universities in Britain, let's say, geography departments have the size and the stature of history [departments]. Most geography departments are larger than most sociology and anthropology and history departments in British universities" (http:// globetrotter.berkeley.edu/people/Watts/watts-con3.html).

14. Transplanted to colonies, though, this view also held, as Baucom goes on to show. Cricket fields abounded in India and the Caribbean. English colonists of the seventeenth-century New World reproduced England by planting cottage gardens—and boundary-defining hedges and fences (Seed 1995). In India, English colonists reproduced the idyllic England pastoral—the village churches, cottages, and gardens of their memory or imagination (Kennedy 1996).

15. In *Albion: The Origins of the English Imagination*, Peter Ackroyd discusses Ford Madox Ford's 1912 dismissal of the racial paradigm in favor of place. "[Ford] noted in particular the descent of the English 'from Romans, from Britons, from Anglo-Saxons, from Poitevins, from Scotch . . .' which is perhaps the best antidote to the nonsensical belief in some 'pure' Anglo-Saxon people. In its place he invoked the spirit of territory with his belief that 'It is not—the whole of Anglo-Saxondom—a matter of race but one, quite simply, of place—of place and of spirit, the spirit being born of the environment' " (2002: xxi).

16. England's natural environment is also a premier idiom through which Englishness is defined. Descriptors that link Englishness to nature abound. Greenery has already been discussed, but there is also "English weather." On the one hand, England, surrounded mostly by sea and ocean, would of course have characteristically cold and cloudy weather

patterns. Conceived as jointly natural and national, "English weather" is readily available for racializing purposes, as Aihwa Ong argues (1998: 144–45).

17. I really do not mean to be condescending here. I have to make these points clear because, in my concrete, lived experience, I have learned that many Americans do not know the difference between Northern Ireland and the Republic of Ireland, or between Wales and England, etcetera. For the politics of Englishness vis-à-vis Celtic groups of Ireland, Wales and Scotland, see Lunn 1991; A. Taylor 1965; Kearney 1994; Hecter 1975; Nairn 1977; Eagleton 1995; and R. Williams 1973. For Northern Ireland, see Aretxaga 1997; Feldman 1991.

18. Yet, for a period in the nineteenth century, and again between 1914 and 1948, the nationality of White British women (but not that of men) was revoked upon their marriage to a non-British subject. Hence, the territorial principle was not quite so immemorial, or at least not uniformly so. See Baldwin 2001.

19. I refer to state legitimation in order to stress that the state does not monopolize the power to imbue Britishness with meaning. Though state actions have often denied Black people Britishness, Blacks nevertheless participate in the cultural practices that define that category. My use of Scott's formulation about "place," which this section is enlarging upon, is but the first of many instantiations of this point.

20. This is not to refute her argument but to add British scholarship in geography into the scope of Henrika Kuklick's argument about British social anthropology. Kuklick analyzes sixty years of British anthropological inquiry, ostensibly into the nature of political systems in *other societies*, in terms of debates about hierarchy and political authority wracking British society itself. She concludes that "anthropologists' observations were refracted through cultural lenses. Thus the history of British anthropological thought demonstrates the extraordinary persistence of the folk tradition of British political theory. This conclusion is in some sense ironic, for the demonstration of continuities in political argument impacted in British anthropology illustrates . . . the value of the anthropological notion of culture" (1984: 78–79). We might reread the classic works of British social anthropology in this light. E. Evans-Pritchard's work in Nuerland (1940), and Edmund Leach's on the Kachin Hills (1977) emphasized the same link between territorial and lineage principles that we find in British cultures.

21. The Act's deployment of these ideologies may explain why some rank-and-file White Britons, of whatever political stripe, could happily defend White British nationalist premises by asserting, like Raymond Williams did, that it is only through "long experience" and "actual and sustained relationships" that one can become British (see Gilroy 1987: 49).

22. For a powerful case study of Northern Ireland, where "spatial ethnic divisions . . . were also divisions between life and death," see Aretxaga 1997: 37.

23. For the history of RP, see Rawnsley 2000. For the contemporary sociolinguistics of it, see Trudgill 2001 and Wales 1994. And for an exquisite articulation of the jointly class- and place-based elitism of it, see Leach 1977. There he made a point about language in highland Burma by drawing an analogy to England, outlining its politics of place authoritatively: "[T]he average Englishman is keenly alert to differences of dialect and even of accent; but the values that he attaches to such differences are not those of the grammarian. . . . Firstly unity of language can be used as a badge of social class. In England the 'public school accent' is a highly sensitive criterion in this respect. Of this English upper-class speech we may note (a) that *it is not localised in any one place*, (b) that though the people who use this speech are not all acquainted with one another, they can easily recognise *each other's status* by this index alone, (c) that this elite speech form tends to be imitated by those who are not of the elite, so that other dialect forms are gradually eliminated" (47, emphasis added).

24. Jeanette Edwards makes the same connection in her ethnography on place and kinship in Bacup. "The statement '[I'm] Bacup born and bred' embraces two significant aspects of English kinship. It juxtaposes what is perceived as an immutable place of birth with the effects of a variable upbringing: it is not enough to be born in Bacup, one also needs to be reared in Bacup" (2000: 84).

25. Not all queries of provenance, though, are met with such responses. I also met a White man from Liverpool in London, where he worked as a bouncer for a popular club in the trendy Stoke Newington neighborhood. His Scouse accent was quite strong. In chatting him up, I referred to his Liverpool accent, and he seemed quite happy to talk about being from there and why he had moved to London—where he did not feel stigmatized and where he very much enjoyed living. But London is far more hospitable than Bath to diversity and difference.

26. Rob Shields warns that although stark divisions between the North and South are very real, economic and political analyses have treated them as internally coherent monoliths (1991). Liverpool provides a good example here. Although it is in the North, Liverpool never built heavy industry and manufacturing concerns, as did many other towns and cities. Liverpool was primarily a commercial city, specializing in regional and international transport, as well as finance. For these and other reasons, historian John Belchem suggests, rightly in my view, that Liverpool is in the North, but not of it (1992). Along similar lines, the Lake District, one of the most powerful symbols of Englishness, is physically located in the North.

27. The images of Manchester, fictionalized as "Milton" in the county of "Darkshire," in Elizabeth Gaskell's 1855 *North and South*, could compete with Dickens's descriptions of Preston. Friedrich Engel's description of Manchester in *The Condition of the Working Class in England* (1987) is also worthy of note. Stuart Rawnsley provides a vivid example of the conflation of place and selfhood in his study of 1930s photojournalism: "A photograph of an unemployed Wigan miner, slumped against the wall, head bowed, dejected and helpless, was one of the most important images created [in this period]. Northernness secreted out of the clothed body—a flat cap hiding most of his face, a muffler tucked into a grimy waistcoat, clogs supporting the human frame; two children . . . stare away from the man and broaden the sense of human tragedy. The photograph was titled 'Wigan,' and thus the archetypal northern town was collapsed into the human figure" (2000: 17).

28. Blake Morrison, "Children of Circumstance," *The New Yorker*, February 14, 1994, p. 48.

29. The history of British colonialism overflows with fascinating stories of racial classification. The term *Lascar* provides one example. Prior to the mid-nineteenth century, it referred to an "Eastern seaman" and afterward included "Burmese, Bengali, Malay, Chinese, Siamese, and Surati" (Salter, quoted in Myers 1995: 9). By the 1870s, it had expanded to include British merchant sailors from East Africa and Arabia. Norma Myers notes, "[I]t would appear that the term Lascar was applicable to a broad spectrum of nationalities and it is interesting to note that the British employed the single category of 'Lascar' for such a heterogeneous collection of people" (1995: 9).

30. Thanks to the work of Diane Frost, the Kru of Liberia is the most thoroughly researched of all the African groups hired by British shippers (1999).

31. For Wootton's death and the 1919 riots, see Murphy 1995 and Evans 1995.

32. Also see Evans 1995 for the enormous scale of colonial agitation in the single year 1919, at least some of which might have been inspired by Bolshevism. He also makes the intriguing suggestion of possible links between political mobilization in British colonies and a series of riots that took place in the United States in 1919.

33. Evans 1995 explores the effects of the imperial imperative on the politics of race in Britain. Here he quotes the secretary of the Anti-Slavery and Aborigines' Protection Society, who made the connections quite bluntly in an interview with the *Liverpool Courier* in 1919: "it is well to recognise, however, that this question of the colour bar is going to be the great post war problem in all the overseas territories. The thing the British public does not recognise adequately is that we are a coloured Empire. . . . What we have got to make up our mind on is whether we are going to solidify the Empire or disrupt it. Ours being a coloured Empire, legislation resting on colour is unthinkable, except at the risk of the dissolution of the Empire—or as I prefer to call it the Commonwealth. Think of Great Britain restricted to a white Empire!" (76).

34. Although I am framing these questions in local/global terms, the scholars whose work I have been citing all along have blazed this trail by analyzing Britain and the empire as a single social space. See also Hall 2000.

35. See Rich 1986 for anthropology's rise in this era of imperial expansion and its involvement in the burgeoning "science" of race. Douglas Lorimer (1996) also highlights the complex history of racial science in this period, emphasizing the contradictory nature of the field.

36. Fletcher is here quoting from a study by another scholar whose findings, based on research in various ports, were reproduced in a pamphlet called *Anthropological Studies of Children*, for which a full citation is not given.

37. See Myers 1996 for a review of the historical literature that has attempted to provide such a count.

CHAPTER 2: BLACK LIVERPOOL, BLACK AMERICA,
AND THE GENDERING OF DIASPORIC SPACE

1. I use the term *Black American* as opposed to *African American* for several reasons. First, it is the term that I, as a Black American, prefer. It calls attention to our racialization and our continuing resistance to it. "African American" depoliticizes our historic positioning in a society structured in racial dominance by rendering us an ethnic group. Second, and thankfully, this is also the term that people in Liverpool use—when they don't use "Yanks," that is.

2. This should not be taken to mean that Black men never partnered Black women; even in the data I have presented thus far, there is evidence of such unions. Laura Tabili documents early cases but does so in a way that actually corroborates the dominant narrative articulated in Liverpool. She writes: "Owing to a scarcity of Black women, couples typically comprised a Black husband and a white wife. Still, there were some Black women in Britain's seaport neighborhoods, and as in other racially mixed societies Black men married them when they were available. Although numerically small, their presence serves as tacit repudiation of the stress on Black and white men competing for white women, racist in its view of Black women as less desirable and sexist in its view of all women as passive in gender relations" (1994: 145). My emphasis is on the way Black Liverpudlians commonly tell their story.

3. See, for example, Lord Gifford, Brown, and Bundey 1989; Frost 1995/96; and Christian 1995/96.

4. A few recent ethnographic and historical accounts manage to break up the homeland/diaspora binary. Daniel Linger (2001) uses diaspora to refer to Japanese Brazilians who immigrated "back" to Japan from Brazil. At once he shows that they have no one home, while nicely avoiding the usual focus on existential crises of identity. Avtar Brah has suggested that diasporic groups' "homing desires" may not be for the land imagined as

the original home (1996: 192–93). Also see Henry Goldschmidt's innovative work on Lubavitcher Hasidim, who locate the authentic Jewish homeland in Crown Heights, Brooklyn, not Israel (2000). Likewise, Charles Piot (2001) and J. Lorand Matory (1999) chart new waters by showing how African cultural practices and identities have been influenced by Blacks in the Americas, rather than the reverse.

5. Khachig Toloyan theorizes diaspora in relation to stateless power and "the transnational moment" (1996). Accordingly, Black America is deemed a problem case, fitting awkwardly in the new set of terms that globalism has provided. See Mintz 1998 and especially Tsing 2000 for indispensable critiques of academic discourse on globalization for fetishizing newness and futurism. Whatever credence we might lend such globalism, it should not be allowed to set universalist terms for what will count as diaspora. Ironically, the ostensibly new conditions of globalization encourage reliance on a set of ancient terms. Black America has been studied in much more provocative ways than its apparently exceptional status would lead us to predict. See Edwards 2001; Gaines 2001; Ebron 2002; Piot 2001; Campt 2003; and Gilroy's classic discussion (1987).

6. He also discusses diaspora in *Between Camps* (published in the United States as *Against Race*), but I find that discussion less useful for its retreat to the migration model.

7. Gilroy defines ethnic absolutism as "a reductive, essentialist understanding of ethnic and national difference which operates through an absolute sense of culture so powerful that it is capable of separating people off from each other and diverting them into social and historical locations that are understood to be mutually impermeable and incommensurable" (1993b: 65).

8. Here he also echoes the important observations of the late St. Clair Drake, who argued that Black movements in which African descendants formed links with Africans were motivated by a "struggle against racial derogation and for some degree of autonomy from white control, *not a common admiration for African cultures*" (1982: 353, my emphasis).

9. Brent Edwards (2001) and Kevin Gaines (2001) show that diaspora was conceptualized similarly in the context of internationalist political movements among Blacks and Africans in the 1960s. See also Drake 1982.

10. In conversation with colleagues, I have often heard arguments against assigning *The Black Atlantic* in anthropology courses because of its emphasis on biography. Again, St. Clair Drake offers a view affirming Gilroy's approach. "Comparative biography should be an important component of diaspora studies" (1982: 349). "At a subliminal level we must remember [figures] in the diaspora and the homeland . . . [including] black Americans who did not feel that they could live and work in the United States. We are not discussing any of our exiled, detained, imprisoned or silenced intellectuals, but there is an obligation upon us to keep their names alive in our footnotes at least. They must not be forgotten as living examples of some aspects of black history—diaspora and homeland—working themselves out over centuries" (356).

11. For more on Black and White American GIs in England and the racial politics of that presence, see Reynolds 1995; Enloe 1989; and G. Smith 1987. These studies focus on the relations between Black GIs and White British women, rather than with Black British women as in the present study.

12. It is not my intention to normalize heterosexuality through the solitary focus on male-female sexual relations. Here, as elsewhere, I chose to follow the various paths that my informants opened up. I did not ask about homosexual sex and/or relationships because these topics were not germane to the issues at hand—and because I wished to maintain good relations with the ex-seafarers I knew (all married with children) and, indeed, with everyone else. Heterosexual relations were difficult enough to probe, given the longstanding use of

discourses on sexuality to racialize and pathologize this community. In view of these circumstances, I cannot comment on homosexual relationships of any kind, despite the fact that I did look for signs of contemporary Black gay life there.

13. Like Kathleen, Caroline noted that the Black Americans also dated White women and that they indeed felt liberated by their ability to do so without the taboo that accompanied such pairings in the United States. Caroline, though, expressed all that with her characteristic flair: "Oh! They were made up, weren't they?!!" ("Made up" means elated). The Yanks' racial politics of desire can be contextualized further, for here was a city where the overwhelming majority of Black women had physical features historically preferred by Black American men: light skin.

14. Liverpool's post-shipping economy retains what one study calls "a legacy of a relatively unskilled workforce." This is reflected in the city's sobering unemployment rate, which has for decades exceeded national averages. In 1986, 55 percent of the city's unemployed population had been without work for more than a year, compared to 41 percent nationally. Twenty-nine percent had been without work for over three years, and 8,500 people on the register of unemployed people had not worked in over five years (Liverpool City Council 1987: 15). Going further back to the era under discussion, it is notable that between 1974 and 1980 the unemployment rate in Liverpool had increased by 120 percent, a figure that becomes even more alarming when "race" is specified. The same study indicates that the number of Black unemployed workers increased by 350 percent over the same six-year period. The unemployment rate among Black youth was 32.5 percent in 1971 (compared to 19.5 percent for White youth) and by 1980 had jumped to 47 percent (Merseyside Area Profile Group 1980: 12).

15. Kathleen eventually settled in London, where I interviewed her. I first made her acquaintance in Liverpool at the Walker Art Gallery. Kathleen features in an incident that unfolded there, as described in chapter 7.

Chapter 3: 1981

1. As Paul Gilroy has wonderfully documented, young Whites in the 1980s were shouting down "Labor Party Capitalist Britain" as they rocked against racism in solidarity with Rastas chanting down Babylon (1987: 117–130).

2. Classics in cultural studies, focusing on youth subcultures, come out of this period, including Hebdige 1979 and Hall and Jefferson 1976.

3. See also Hall 1980 for the historical roots of Thatcherite authoritarianism.

4. As the cover photograph on the important volume *The Empire Strikes Back: Race and Racism in 70s Britain* illustrates, the police seemed not only to be protecting the National Front but "demonstrating" with them (CCCS 1982).

5. Also see Kathleen Paul's analysis (1997) of the ways various immigrant groups were racially categorized and differently positioned vis-à-vis Britishness in the context of government debates, and in relation to an overwhelming set of concerns including population decline, labor recruitment, and control over a declining empire.

6. The Labour Party, for its part, had long been forced into a defensive position. In the 1964 general election, for example, a Conservative candidate from Birmingham rallied voters with the slogan, "If you want a nigger neighbor, vote Labour." The left could not be counted on for reasonable discourse on race, since it was too busy trying to harness the popularity and political legitimacy the right had been gaining. As time wore on, some Labour-controlled local authorities (i.e., local governments) such as the Greater London Council did try to create antiracist and otherwise liberal programs. But the press under

Thatcher relentlessly made a caricature out of these (Murray 1986). These local authorities, along with liberal or radical groups operating outside of official politics, were dubbed "the loony left." Gilroy's analysis of this general period is indispensable, of course (1987). In fact, he emphasizes the stunning likenesses between the discourses of the right and the left, particularly on the question of nationalism. Importantly, his discussion exceeds the boundaries of official politics. Also see the prognosis that Stuart Hall proffered for the left in view of the right's popularity in the 1980s (1988).

7. See Gilroy 1987 and Barker 1981 for subtle analyses of the strategic slippage between biology and culture in these discourses on nationhood. Barker offers a full-scale examination of the uses of biology in right-wing thinking.

8. See Ann Dummett and Andrew Nicol (1990) for a discussion of less public government debates on immigration that occurred in the 1940s, also centering on fears of degeneration. Chapter 6 of the present book discusses those same fears in the context of mid-nineteenth-century Irish immigration to England.

9. As Martin Barker documents, even the most shamelessly sensationalist and conservative tabloid, *The Sun*, offered front-page condemnations of the NF (1981).

10. In her memoir, Margaret Simey, then councillor for Liverpool's Granby ward, recalled her constituents' anxious responses to Powell's speech: "Setting out on my housing visits the morning after that outburst, I was immediately aware of the shiver of excited apprehension which his speech had provoked . . . 'Had I heard, . . .' I was asked tentatively. . . . The spectre of racial prejudice had lurked at the back of people's minds for long enough. Previously only discussed behind closed doors, now it stalked openly about our streets. What next?" (1996: 126).

11. This really is an arguable point. On the one hand, the effect of such public events, and the press's role in shaping popular opinion on them, cannot be counted out as forces in the production of racist discourse and sentiment. That is, the press, as Hall has argued, created racial animosities that it claimed simply to be reporting on (1980). Some argue that government panics about Black immigration preceded widespread negative public opinion about it (Paul 1997). On the other hand one would not want to assume that popular racism was not already in play prior to the intervention of the press. For example, Margaret Simey recalled that Powell's speech stirred anxieties that had not been given such voice hitherto, suggesting that racism was already there, if mute.

12. Since the Industrial Revolution, the countryside has been identified with quintessential Englishness—not only to the exclusion of urban areas, but in hostile opposition to them and the processes of industrialization that created them. Yet the countryside was not completely abandoned as a symbol of Englishness in the era under discussion. Indeed, this historical juncture—which, to reiterate, is characterized by economic, imperial, and social decline—also witnesses the National Heritage Act of 1980, which represented an unprecedented enshrinement of the nation in rural, idyllic terms. See Wright 1985, Hewison 1987, and Lowenthal 1985, 1991 for critical analyses of the National Heritage Act. For more on the invention of the English countryside broadly speaking, see Baucom 1999, Short 1992, P. Williams 1973, and Frake 1996. For the racial constitution of such sites, see Ingrid Pollard's photographic essays about the Lake District (2004) as well as Edward Said's discussion of Jane Austen's *Mansfield Park* (1993).

13. In his ethnography about rural East Anglia, Charles Frake highlights the importance of the quality of "pleasantness" to constructions of place, as well as East Anglians' attribution of ultimate Englishness—a racially inscribed one—to their corner of England: "My more cynical local friends tell me that this show of pure, white Englishness is, as much as the appeal of the countryside, what makes rural East Anglia such an attractive retirement

area for British city dwellers. If one's place is 'lost,' perhaps all those foreigners and ethnics that one used to confront in London, Liverpool, and Manchester will not be able to find it" (1996: 230).

14. Although the present discussion concerns the postwar era, characterized by decline and culminating in the 1981 rebellions, these issues have relevance to later periods. See Ian Baucom's wonderful analysis of mourning and melancholy inspired by, or projected onto, place in the late 1990s.

15. The descriptions of the riots presented here are drawn from CARF Collective 1981/82; "Trigger Happy: Police Open Fire on Civilians," *New Statesman* 102(2626): 2, 6–7; Mike Phillips, "Rage That Shattered Thatcher," *New Statesman* 102(2626): 8–9; and Michael Williams, "The Tents at the Gate of the City," *New Society* 57(974): 98–100.

16. CS is a common abbreviation for O-chlorobenzylidene malonontrite.

17. This point is reminiscent of a poignant moment in the film *Handsworth Songs*, about the riots in Birmingham. One woman responds to a journalist searching for "the story" of those riots by saying (to paraphrase), "There is no story here. There is only the ghost of other stories."

18. This figure is provided in *Loosen the Shackles* (Lord Gifford, Brown, and Bundey 1989: 37) and includes the following groups: Black British, Chinese, West Indian, Arab, African, and Asian.

CHAPTER 4: GENEALOGIES

1. Decades of debate have centered on the question of who counts as Black and what kinds of elisions accompany the inclusive, "political" version of that category (Modood 1988). As Julia Sudbury's work shows, the very fact that African descent, as *one* criterion for reckoning Black identity, is so fiercely contested in Black women's organizations in Britain means that the descent idiom is not hegemonic there (1998: 109–17). In the United States, by contrast, such a debate would be fundamentally impossible because Americans have been naturalizing descent since the slavery era. This is not to say that Blackness is any less contested in the United States, but that "African descent" would scarcely appear at the center of such contentions. Interestingly, Jayne Ifekwunigwe explicitly adopts the American "one drop" criterion in her work in Bristol (1999), while France Winddance Twine uses the culturally specific notion of "African-descent" in her work in Leicester (1998a, 1999). Both authors seem intent on carving out a space to legitimately study people who would be categorized as Black in the United States, preempting criticisms of those who, contra Tariq Modood, insist that every reference to Blacks in Britain must be based on the inclusive version of *Black*. Chapter 5 of the present work shows why that version is not operative in constructions of Liverpool-born Blackness.

2. Faye Harrison describes the significance of descent in American racial politics in multidimensional terms: "Stigmatized in an especially dehumanizing manner, African origins and 'blood' have symbolized to many Euro-Americans the social bottom and an ever-threatening contagion to white purity. In my case as well as that of many other black people, the greater social salience of my African heritage relative to my other ancestral origins is consistent with a cultural logic that anthropology has helped me understand. . . . Individuals with any sub-Saharan African heritage have historically been incorporated into the category to which their racially subordinate ancestors were assigned. This classificatory praxis has relegated people of any known African origins to precarious life chances and structural positions" (2002: 146).

3. Granted, the body is at the forefront of myriad societies' notions of race. Deconstructing race through its main signifier is warranted. Yet the price of focusing solely on bodies and biologies is that we unwittingly reinforce the views of race that we struggle to dismantle. We neglect attention, for example, to the ways that race works without regard to phenotype, blood, or genes. Peter Wade's study of Colombia shows that qualities attributed to the physicality of place work to construct populations in racial terms (1993). Ann Stoler argues that ideas about culture and civilization are really the stuff of racial ideology, the "visible" body being only a trigger (1997a). Edward Said's *Orientalism* shows racialization processes working through ideas about distance in addition to civilization (1978). Goldberg also notes the importance of geography to early formulations about race in the West (1993). In the colonial era, the English racialized the Irish by referring to the "wildness" of Ireland's landscape (Eagleton 1995). The arbitrary nature of *all* racial constructions—but especially those that work through bodies—is best dramatized by illuminating forms of racialization that have nothing to do with phenotype.

4. That said, a history of Liverpool's recent Black movement would certainly be welcomed. I know of only two such accounts. One is the unpublished manuscript by David Clay, a local historian who is not a professional academic but who participated in many of the events discussed in this chapter and the next. The value of Clay's manuscript (which I do not actually refer to or rely on here) is that it is restricted to the period from 1981 to 1991. Most histories of Black Liverpool end well before the contemporary era. Another excellent, detailed account of an important episode in recent Black politics—an event not covered in the present text—is found in Liverpool Black Caucus 1986. This account describes the yearlong protest that followed the appointment of Sampson Bond, a Black Londoner and reputed mouthpiece for the far left political party, Militant Tendency, to the position of race relations advisor to the Liverpool City Council. An excruciatingly brief account of Liverpool's Black movement in the late 1970s and 1980s is found in the 1996 memoir of Margaret Simey, councillor of the Granby ward. Without intending to write "History," she does offer fascinating snippets of insight and information about local Black resistance in that era. Many of her observations are consistent with LBBs' own narratives, as presented in this chapter and the next.

5. Similar phraseology appears in Liverpool Black Caucus 1986, in which the authors state one of the objections to the appointment of a Black Londoner, Sampson Bond, to the position of race relations advisor to the Liverpool City Council. "[H]e showed no awareness of different minorities in the city, their particular histories etc., particularly the unique nature of the Liverpool born Black community" (1986: 74).

6. BBC (British Broadcasting Corporation), "On the Mersey Beat," *Listener*, November 12, 1978, p. 11.

7. The high moralism that suffused Liverpool and other urban centers of Victorian Britain might account for the conflation (Walkowitz 1980; Walton and Wilcox 1991). Along different lines, the masses in Liverpool were impoverished during the shipping industry's heyday and contemporary stereotypes about Liverpudlians' propensity toward criminality (see chapter 6) date back to that era, when feckless foreign seamen were their usual victims (O'Mara 1933). On a different note, Laura Tabili offers this analysis: "Many Black men earned even less than white workingmen, impugning their masculinity and thereby their wives' respectability, as women were compelled into wage labor and even into casual prostitution to supplement household incomes. Wives' exceptional public visibility and their families' 'low standard of life' were thus due to racial discrimination" (1996: 176).

In addition to words, trademarks can also consist of slogans (such as THE KING OF BEERS® for Budweiser beer), designs (such as the familiar "swoosh" that identifies Nike products), or sounds (such as the distinctive laugh of Woody the Woodpecker).

Trademarks provide guarantees of quality and consistency of the product or service they identify. Thus, upon encountering the golden arches that identify a McDonald's restaurant, consumers understand the Big Mac they purchase in Chicago will be the same quality as one purchased in Seattle.

Companies expend a great deal of time, effort, and money in establishing consumer recognition of and confidence in their marks. Yet not all words, phrases, or symbols are entitled to protection as trademarks. A chain of stores that sells electronic goods could not obtain a registered trademark for "Electronic Goods" inasmuch as the name is generic, yet CIRCUIT CITY® is a nationally recognized mark for the retail sale of electronic goods, equipment, and appliances. Marks may not be protectable if they are generic in nature or merely descriptive of the type of products or services they identify. Generally, marks that are protectable are those that are coined (such as KODAK®), arbitrary (such as SHELL® for gasoline), or suggestive (such as STAPLES® for office supplies).

Federal Registration of Trademarks. Interstate use of trademarks is governed by federal law, namely, the United States Trademark Act (also called the Lanham Act), found at 15 U.S.C. § 1051 *et seq.* See Appendix E. Additionally, trademarks are provided for in all fifty states so that marks that cannot be federally registered with the PTO because they are not used in interstate commerce can be registered in the state in which they are used.

In the United States, trademarks are generally protected from their date of first public use. Registration of a mark is not required to secure protection for a mark, although it offers numerous advantages, such as allowing the registrant to bring an action in federal court for infringement of the mark. Applications for federal registration of trademarks are made with the PTO. Registration is a fairly lengthy process, generally taking anywhere from twelve to twenty-four months or even longer. The filing fee is $335 per mark per class of goods or services covered by the mark.

A trademark registration is valid for ten years and may be renewed for additional ten-year periods thereafter as long as the mark is in use in interstate commerce. Additionally, registrants are required to file an affidavit with the PTO between the fifth and sixth years after registration and every ten years to verify the mark is in continued use. Marks not in use are then available to others.

Trademarks are among the most visible items of intellectual property, and it has been estimated that the average resident of the United States encounters approximately fifteen hundred different trademarks each day and 30,000 if one visits a supermarket. A properly selected, registered, and protected mark can be of great value to a company or individual desiring to establish and expand market share. There is perhaps no better way to maintain a strong position in the marketplace than to build goodwill and consumer recognition in the identity selected for products and services and then to protect that identity under federal trademark law.

Copyrights

What Is Protectable.   Copyright is a form of protection governed exclusively by federal law (17 U.S.C. § 101 *et seq.*) granted to the authors

8. That is about as much as I will say about Black women and White men in this book. I focus on the Black male/White female relationship—or the ideological uses of it—because it comes to bear most often and most profoundly in the matters that really concern this analysis as a whole. For example, it is key to the origin stories of Black Liverpool and to racial formation broadly speaking. The clear double standard that Abraham articulated with reference to Yvette's partnering choice stands in for numerous other instances. Black women I knew who were partnered with White men referred to it quite often.

9. Some Blacks in Liverpool have Black American fathers who were GIs. This matter does not bear upon the central issues of the present study.

10. Black Liverpudlians one generation older are more generous. Claire was matter-of-fact in relaying to me that her father, who was from Sierra Leone, had changed his surname to a Christian one, which he took from one of the White English captains of a ship he sailed. Claire made no explicit judgment about this. Her generational peer, Caroline, lovingly described her father's occupation of two cultural worlds, English and Yoruba, as I discussed in chapter 2. His affinity for Englishness inspired no critique on her part. And Mrs. Smith, who is another generation older still than Caroline and Claire, spoke of the Africans of her younger days in the 1930s and 1940s as culturally African through and through. She gave no inkling of any Englishness about them, nor did she pronounce upon or otherwise express wonder about their politics.

11. I chose not to interview "the old Africans" on this issue, nor on the other, fairly critical point about how these men positioned their children racially. In fact, among the people I knew with African fathers, only Howard's was still alive. I knew his father and I was part of a social circle in which his father had been adopted as a revered elder. His father would inevitably be at informal social gatherings with this group of friends, one that did not include Howard himself. Despite multiple opportunities, I never took up these issues with him, for I did not think that he should have to respond to others' perceptions of him and his peers. Moreover, this ethnography is really focused on racial constructions that Liverpool-born Blacks have responded to and those that they have produced in turn.

12. The other two were Leroy Cooper, whose attempted arrest in 1981 sparked three days and four nights of rioting, and Sampson Bond, (see Liverpool Black Caucus 1986) who was appointed to an important race relations post after the riots.

13. The Home Office is a department of the British state that deals with internal affairs, including criminal law, the prison system, and policing, as well as community relations, race relations, and immigration and nationality law and policy.

CHAPTER 5: DIASPORA AND ITS DISCONTENTS

1. This is a pseudonym.

2. I tend to be less reflexive than many anthropologists. At the risk of underplaying the effect of my own positioning on the matters being "observed" and selected for discussion and analysis, I do not think that my subjectivity or the ways that people perceived me really illuminates much—or not to a degree that warrants interrupting discussions about them to talk about me-and-them. However, in view of my concerns about British nationalism, this chapter presents certain difficulties. Writing it was an excruciating exercise in what Diane Nelson describes as "fluidarity" (1999), a position that entails being in solidarity with one's informants in ways that require one to be, indeed, less "solid," or less rigid and fixed. It encourages a fluid approach to analyzing oppressed people's answers to some of life's toughest questions. Through fluidarity, we recognize that people who have been historically subjugated may assert agency in ways that surprise and confound us, and

sometimes trouble us. Lisa Rofel deals powerfully with a similar dilemma when she describes heated arguments she had with her Chinese informants, in full knowledge of her greater power as a Western scholar (1999). The beauty of anthropology is that we struggle, at the very least, to make our informants' perspectives and political practices comprehensible, despite what we might think of them; perhaps, as Rofel's work shows, we even stand to learn from them. The anthropologist's difficult charge is also to explain people's responses to their subordination, even while attending to the power asymmetries further unleashed in the name of resistance to it. By contrast, politically engaged scholars in other disciplines often pronounce upon analogous predicaments in self-congratulatory ways; since they, as intellectuals, have been able to see through and triumph over what has come to be demonized as "identity politics," they assume that everyone else should be disposed to following them on that path to enlightenment. Critics of anthropology often seem to declare themselves exempt from Foucault's power/knowledge problematic, writing about the world from a privileged location that they scarcely acknowledge as such.

3. The preoccupation with authenticity leads these scholars to attend less to diaspora, per se, than to the question of culture. That concern, rather unnecessarily, leads them to essentialize anthropology, which they render outside the flow of history. Gilroy, for example, names hybridity as the only possible route to understanding diasporic cultural formations—and all cultural formations for that matter (2000: 271). In this context, he identifies anthropology's fatal flaw: it treats culture as bounded. Culture must be studied in its "postanthropological" sense, which entails tracing culture's many origins and further travels (roots and routes). The entirety of this critique implies that anthropology has been completely unaffected by postmodernism—a mind-boggling proposition indeed. Scott's critique implies that anthropology has been oblivious to the poststructuralist revolution (1999). He, too, is concerned about anthropology's mistakes in the study of culture. The discipline's self-appointed role, he argues, has been to adjudicate Caribbean people's truth claims about the African basis of their culture. Yet this critique is based on the work of two scholars (only one is an anthropologist) who rely on the work of anthropologist Melville Herskovits. Back in the 1940s, Herskovits did actually pronounce upon the degree of "Africanism" manifested in Caribbean cultures (1990 [1941]). So, yes, Herskovits had his day; but is his approach to diasporic cultures still the menace Scott makes it out to be?

4. Antagonism and affinity are not the only options, nor are these necessarily dichotomous. The material of this chapter lends itself to this framing. In chapter 2, there is more traffic between the two positions. Black Liverpudlians were able to draw from the Yanks because they perceived affinities (analogous experiences of racism) and could therefore be inspired in spite of their many criticisms of them. Tina Campt's fluid rendering of the tensions of diasporic relation in Black German subjectivity provides a similar, elegant model (2004).

5. Of course, a community need not be based in a locality, even though in the case under discussion it is. Historian Brent Edwards's discussion of the Pan-Africanist movement would provide an internationalist example of a nonterritorialized diasporic community (2001). Also see Julia Sudbury's excellent study of Black women's political organizations across Britain (1998). My concern about place is animated not only by its great relevance to politics of all kinds in Liverpool/Britain, but also by the tendency to treat diaspora solely as a transnational relation.

6. Black scholars from Liverpool describe the role of place in the constitution of racial groups in ways that resonate with the present analysis. For example: "In Liverpool there is a racialisation of community identity. The black community exists with its own sense of identity, networks, structures, history and contemporary experiences, consolidated by the excluding process of racism. It is identified by two main elements. The primary one is

'racial' criteria imposed by racism in the white community (*which defines black as any physically evident sign of not being white*), and the secondary is 'area'. The geographic area is usually 'Granby' but Toxteth is also used" (quoted in Christian 1997: 67, original emphasis). Here the Black community is defined through the geography of racial experience: "[A]ny assumptions concerning the nature of the 'Black community' in this context will have to be justified by economic argument. To make an assumption that people from South and East Asia, Africa, the Caribbean, Arabia and Somalia are members of the 'Black community' can be justified, even though they are not culturally, ethically [*sic*] and religiously homogeneous. A generalisation concerning the local 'Black community' can be made because they share the experience of living in a geographical area—Granby Toxteth—which has for a long time suffered from social and economic decline due to racism" (Chukwuemeka 1997: 43). Claire Alexander notes another territorialization of Black identity in London: "The 'black community' can be seen to function on two levels: first, at an ideological, non-territorial level; and secondly, at a territorial level, internal to an imagined black community, which is opposed to other perceived 'black' areas" (1996: 61). Here one might ask whether the latter, territorial function is also ideological.

7. Asian/American studies, mostly of the feminist anthropological variety, is an inspiration. Scholars in this field examine the production of a political community called *Asian American* across lines of class, nation, and history. As Lisa Lowe states, "The articulation of an 'Asian American identity' as an organizing tool has provided a concept of political unity that enables diverse Asian groups to understand *unequal* circumstances and histories *as being related*" (1996: 70–71, emphasis added). Others, like Yanagisako (1995), Kondo (1997), and Visweswaran (1997), spotlight the elisions to gender and class that result in the process of building such unity. Along these lines, a fine model for what I am urging can be found in Kamala Visweswaran's work on how capital (disguised as "Culture") participates in the "Asianization" of varied immigrant groups. Rather than focusing on Asians' varied relationships to their roots and authentic traditions, she shows how class formation in the United States proceeds through the ways these groups are racialized *vis-à-vis each other* (1997). Asian/American studies provides a useful analogy and source of inspiration for the case at hand, which is concerned with the construction and deconstruction of the *counter/part* in the larger context of political community formation and in view of economic and other inequalities—or the "vis-à-vis" relation. In African diasporic worlds—or, rather, in social scientific scholarship *about* them—class and political-economy do not exist (but see Ebron 2002; Brown 1998). Gender does, if only to a small but growing extent (Ifekwunigwe 1997, 1999; Campt 2004; Rassool 1997).

8. Historian Carlton Wilson, who has studied Black Liverpool in the interwar years, notes the same propensity for report writing. He refers here to political actions on the part of local officials in 1942, which eventually resulted in the establishment of Stanley House: "For the first time officialdom was willing to aggressively attack the problems facing the residents of Liverpool's south end by implementing a specific program rather than merely conducting studies and surveys" (1992: 470).

9. The National Dwelling and Housing Survey's report provides the following information on how it collected data on "ethnic minorities": "Respondents to the survey were shown a card listing the main ethnic groups in this country and asked to which of the groups listed each member of the household belonged. Less than one in a thousand respondents refused to answer this question but a few insisted on being recorded as British, English etc rather than one of the specific groups listed—White, West Indian and so forth. Overall less than 1 per cent of persons were recorded as 'other (please state)': analysis of the details given indicates that many of these persons belonged to one of the groups listed. However, because there was insufficient information to recode most of these persons—often the

only information recorded was English or British—no attempt has been made to do so in these results. The 'other' category [presented in accompanying tables] is thus very heterogeneous since it contains not only persons recorded as 'other (please state)' but also persons recorded as 'Chinese', 'Other Asian', 'Arab', and persons of 'Mixed Origin'" (Department of the Environment 1978: 15).

10. Although other ethnic centers use social rather than national terms, this one is the Pakistan Centre, not the Pakistani Centre.

11. See Julia Sudbury's analysis of White feminist appropriations of this phraseology, which she critiques for favoring the ethnic part of the equation (1998: 206–14).

12. Only rarely did I hear a Black person include himself or herself, much less LBBs as a whole, under the rubric of English culture. But this is precisely what the speaker does, and pointedly so. Yet and still, s/he stops short of describing LBBs as English.

13. A prominent Black scholar from Liverpool uses the following definition for the term *Black*: "people who have claim to African descent and who have British citizenship" (Christian 1998: 305). And in the previous chapter, Greg made the same point: for being born in Britain, he was Black. His father was African. Steven Small writes that "in Liverpool the notion of 'British born Black' is usually taken as synonymous with mixed origins" (1991: 515).

14. It may be clear by now that the term *Liverpool-born Black* does not include people of Asian, Arab, and Chinese background. A few LBBs I knew did use the term Black to refer to those groups, but *Liverpool-born Black* emerges out of a "specific" set of debates that effectively rerouted that inclusive usage. Peter's narrative in the previous chapter, for example, shows that LBB was formed in resistance to Africans' usage of the term *half-caste*. Along similar lines, a senior lecturer at Liverpool's Charles Wootton College here uses a jointly local and diasporic framework to explain the narrower conception of Blackness operative in the city: "The local context has played an important role in the contested nature of Black identity in Liverpool. The unique terminology 'Liverpool Born Black' (LBB) is indicative of processes that have taken place which have bound certain groups of Black people together, but which can also present a barrier or boundary to other groups of Black people seeking to forge links with the local 'Black community.' . . . Hence Blackness in the local contexts can serve as both 'fences' and 'bridges'. The 'fences' are the local signifiers or identification marks that keep other people out, whereas the 'bridges' are the signifiers of blackness that unite people of African descent across the world" (Ackah 1997: 57). Of course, the argument of the present book is that the reification of the local is the key process at work in the forms of Black identification he describes. The local is no mere "context."

15. For a politically committed, personal account of the invisibility of Black Liverpudlians in this era, Margaret Simey's memoir is indispensable (1996). Describing the response to the state's war on politics, Simey alludes to the LBO: "Gradually, for lack of nourishment, the willingness of local residents to cooperate with officialdom gave place to a tide of protest which increasingly verged on open hostility. Community councils city-wide found themselves elbowed aside by a mushroom growth of pressure groups from which they were excluded by reason of the long-standing embargo on political activity as a condition of grant aid" (142).

16. The merits of the reports are not the likely problem, of course. The same could be said of the vast race relations literature, both theoretical and policy-oriented, and as it concerns both Britain in general and Liverpool in particular. I confess to being alienated from scholarship in the race relations policy vein. To cite it anyway would be a meaningless gesture. Studies of racial politics in Liverpool that I have found very useful include Nelson 2000; Small 1991; Simey 1996; Liverpool Black Caucus 1986; Arline Wilson 1998; Christian 2000; Murphy 1995; and Law and Henfry 1981.

17. The political scene in and around Liverpool 8 included a group of Afrocentric Blacks, male and female, in their twenties and thirties. They were Afrocentric in the strict sense of the term, arguing for an African-centered Black politic. They were well-read on Afrocentric literature. Most important, they were the most articulate and organized critics of Liverpool-born Blackness. Their critique did not take the form of direct confrontation, per se, but in the many events that they produced. They commonly brought Afrocentric speakers such as Professor Leonard Jeffries to speak in Liverpool. Afrocentrism had tremendous appeal among young Blacks (in their teens and twenties) in particular: the Afrocentric speakers were extremely charismatic, and their discourse included Blacks of mixed racial parentage as Blacks *and* as Africans in ways that their fathers often did not. I regret not being able to dedicate more space to Afrocentrism in Liverpool.

18. According to Yvette and Cecelia, the LBO died a natural death in the aftermath of the 1981 riots, in which many people were arrested. The LBO was replaced by the Liverpool 8 Defense Committee, which was better equipped to deal with the police and the criminal courts. Many LBO members were involved in the Defense Committee, but the latter incorporated solicitors (lawyers) to defend those arrested. The Defense Committee later became the Liverpool 8 Law Centre, which still exists.

19. Although this state project came into full flower in the post-1981 era, the process of individuating Blacks into Asians and Afro-Caribbeans (Africans tend to drop out of sight in discussions of Black Britain writ large) had started well before (Sivanandan 1982a, 1985). Between 1966 and 1981, the state made similar attempts to depoliticize grassroots community work. The mid-1970s saw the emergence, for example, of the Inner City Partnership Program, funded by the central government and to be administered by selected local authorities. On the one hand, the state could thus appear to be supporting "community" projects including ethnic ones, while on the other hand quietly imposing a disabling set of guidelines for that support (Bridges 1981/82: 180–81).

20. Mervyn Alleyne notes that the slavery-derived tripartite racial division described in reference to Jamaica is generalizable to the Caribbean, and that presently, the Jamaican categories "white," "brown," and "black" correlate to socioeconomic positions. More significant, "In Jamaica, 'brown', signifying the 'highest' shade of mulatto, has become the more active pole of opposition and antithesis to black" (2002: 193). On the one hand, that point may provide a bit more context to the politics of difference under discussion, even if as a possible intensification of the racial constructions that informed Reese's remarks in 1981. On the other hand, it is vital to stay focused on the ethnographic context of Liverpool in the early 1990s. Jamaicans and other Afro-Caribbeans in present-day Liverpool or even 1990s Liverpool should not be equated with those who live in the Caribbean now. Reese's remarks, however, bore such distinct traces of his past that the historical and ethnographic trip back to Jamaica—admitting that he may not have even been Jamaican—seemed in order.

Another caveat. Neither Reese's remarks, nor the positions of the Afro-Caribbean men at the center, nor Alexander's ethnographic material should be taken to indicate that Afro-Caribbeans in Liverpool, or Britain more broadly, did not marry and have children with Whites. However, that collective material could suggest the kind of criticism that might have greeted Afro-Caribbeans who did. An elderly Afro-Caribbean man I knew expressed great injury at having been castigated by his sister for having married a White woman. She did not want his children to refer to her as their aunt, and she referred to his children as "brown"—which offended him very much. I mention this man's case to make the point that, though this chapter and the book at large is about LBBs, the contestations being described are more cross-cutting and have affected others as well.

21. Carlton Wilson notes that although this organization was not radical (it had a Christianity-inspired conciliatory approach to politics), it at least attended to the entire community of Blacks (1992: 458–65).

22. Of course, the huge silence in this analysis concerns the role of Rastafarianism as a point of identification and inspiration for young Blacks in particular. Since I would only be able to proffer superficial observations on this matter, I prefer to just acknowledge the gap.

CHAPTER 6: MY CITY, MY SELF

1. Most famously Defoe (1971) and Priestly (1984 [1934]).

2. My selection of these books, with the exception of one (Pat O'Mara's), was completely random. They are the ones I happened to collect while in Liverpool. I bought them along with myriad other artifacts that one mindlessly gathers in the field and then peruses back at home. I took no notice whatsoever of anything about these books when I bought them. I didn't realize, for example, that all the authors were of Irish background. More seriously, I didn't notice that all the authors were men. If I had had any inkling that these books were going to become so important to this one, I certainly would have made a point of collecting some written by women.

3. In the quotation that opened this chapter, Caryl Phillips draws on the same English premise but self-consciously and subversively. In view of the historical exclusion of Black people from both Britishness and especially Englishness, he uses the symbol of place—the iconic white cliffs of Dover which, for Britons, mark homecoming—to constitute his identity as British. To be clear, that passage is a performance of English culture, even though it is British identity that place produces in Phillips's case.

4. Ernest Marke's autobiography might also fit in the genre (1986).

5. See Anna Tsing's productive critique of globalization literature and her helpful suggestion that we instead study the global as a set of scale-making projects (2000). Another interesting critique comes from the anthropology of law (Wastell 2001).

6. For example, Howard Winant has argued that a set of whirlwind processes associated with late capitalism are "globalizing racial space. . . . [R]acial identities are transnational and some form of racial difference nearly universal" (1994: 112). In then adding that global generalizations should not replace "detailed analyses of local racial formations," he implies that "the local" is important only as a data collection site (123). It provides "detail." See Massey (1994: 125–45) for a critique of that logic.

7. In political-economic accounts of globalization, capitalism is a highly masculinized agent. Stuart Hall invokes gender in arguing against the discourse of "hyper-globalization" in which "everything is transformed; everything is an outcast in the same way by the global processes. . . . The whole world comes as a sort of kaleidoscope of ever-migrating folks. So localism is very important and is indeed the only point of intervention against the hegemonic, universalizing thrust of globalization" (1999: 15). For more on the gendering of global theory see Massey 1994; Freeman 2001; and Kondo 1997.

8. For example, "The tendency of much of the literature on globalization is to focus on the macro scope of the phenomenon, thinking of it principally in terms of very large-scale economic, political, or cultural processes. Anthropology, on the other hand, is most concerned with the articulation of the global and the local, that is, with how globalizing processes exist in the context of, and must come to terms with, the realities of particular societies, with their accumulated—that is to say historical—cultures and ways of life. . . .

What anthropology offers that is often lacking in other disciplines is a concrete attentiveness to human agency, to the practices of everyday life, in short, to how subjects mediate the processes of globalization" (Inda and Rosaldo 2002: 5).

9. Theorizations of the local must also avoid the reductionism that would simply associate it with the kinds of places that actors often use to symbolize it—like neighborhoods (Appadurai 1996).

10. The essays in Doreen Massey's *Space, Place and Gender* offer great guidance and inspiration. She theorizes the global as "part of what constitutes the local, the outside as part of the inside" (1994: 5). Along similar lines, she suggests that the local need not refer to insularity; it can express extroversion and refer to a "global sense of place." I agree with these views, although my concern is to study the production and implications of these very inscriptions. As well, her discussion of locality studies in Britain outlines debates in that country about how to think about place politically. In that context, she provides a corrective to some of the views and assumptions about the local that I have argued characterize some globalization discourse.

11. As chapter 2 showed, contemporary Blacks make a similar move, constituting Liverpool as a very African city. Within Liverpool (and possibly without), the city is variously imagined as utterly working class, utterly Irish, and utterly African; any one of these inscriptions would be enough to set Liverpool apart from dominant, elite constructions of Englishness. The fact that all three condense into Liverpool fascinates.

12. Without wishing to theorize history's relationship to memory, I do want to mark that Liverpool has valid claims to a certain global history, while also acknowledging that the very interest in invoking such a history is discursively produced. As Lisa Rofel writes in a related context, it is as if "the dynamics of capitalism could be grasped apart from the dynamic construction of knowledge about it, or as if attention to narrative form alone can resolve the dilemmas of cultural power" (1999: 33).

13. Martin Lynn (1998) shows that Liverpool's slave traders of the late eighteenth century became the palm oil traders of the nineteenth century. To procure the oil, they used the same networks and methods as they had before. Lynn also presents a compelling analysis of the role of salt in the trading network that linked West Africa to Liverpool, before and after slavery.

14. As is well-known, Liverpool also provided passage for hundreds of thousands of European, especially Irish, immigrants to the New World. As Hyde writes, "Of the estimated $5\frac{1}{2}$ million emigrants departing from Britain between 1860 and 1900, just over $4\frac{3}{4}$ million went from Liverpool" (112). As important as passenger liners were, the real money was in cargo shipping. Their discrepant statuses were reflected spatially: passenger liners occupied the docks farthest from the Pier Head, while cargo ships sailed right into the center of town (1971: 127–28).

15. The work of Laura Tabili is an exception, even though her major study (1994) is not about Liverpool's shipping industry, per se, but about colonial seamen and other workers. Also see the fascinating work of Martin Lynn (1998).

16. In 1945, the British government passed the Distribution of Industry Act. Its primary objective was not to diversify any locale's economy, but to ensure that no town's population was left so utterly vulnerable to the collapse of its single or major industry (Hyde 1971; HMSO 1948).

17. One public health official worried that "the native inhabitants are exposed to the inroads of numerous hordes of uneducated Irish, spreading physical and moral contamination around them. . . . By their example and intercourse with others they are rapidly lowering the standard of comfort among their English neighbours, communicating their own

vicious and apathetic habits, fast extinguishing all sense of moral dignity, independence and self-respect" (quoted in Belchem 1998: 9).

18. These effects can be seen in the key arenas of labor organizing and political party affiliation (Belchem 2000).

19. Many of the histories of Liverpool sold in its present-day bookshops seem targeted to a popular audience. See, for example, Lane 1987 and Chandler 1973. Presumably, these histories and the Liverpool autobiographies to be discussed shortly would not be published were it not for a well-developed market of readers. The popular histories that concern the Black presence or questions of race are simply excellent. These include Murphy 1995, Cameron and Crooke 1992, and Law and Henfrey 1981. A contemporary Liverpool-born Black activist, David Clay, should be added to the pantheon of lay historians, even though his manuscript, "Ten Years On, 1981–1991: Looking Back over the Years," is unpublished. In 1994, Scouse Press reissued *Liverpool and Slavery*, originally published in Liverpool one hundred years earlier. A person who wished to remain anonymous authored the study, using the pen name "Dicky Sam" (a forerunner to "Scouser"). In his opening he says, "When I appear in print, if I should have the audacity to do so, some may be trying to find out who I am. However, I may say, to satisfy all concerned, that I am an every day common-place being, with a strong predilection for things not generally known" (1984 [1884]: 2). Since histories always have a purpose, it is worth noting the goals of Scouse Press in republishing *Liverpool and Slavery*: "In recent years it has become fashionable among some sections of the Liverpool community to tar all Liverpool merchants of the 18th and 19th centuries with the same brush. Some unruly individuals recently have even carried their hate-fed ignorance so far as to deface, or mindlessly destroy, monuments to the very men who worked tirelessly for the abolition of the slave-trade, merely because they were Liverpool worthies of the past. It is hoped that this book will help to spread greater awareness of their noble work as well as that of the wicked slave-traders" (iv). A book about slavery is meant both to discipline Black people in the present and rehabilitate "Liverpool."

20. This section draws heavily on John Darwin, *The End of the British Empire: The Historical Debate* (1991). This is not the place to deliberate over the finer points of this complex history. Yet since I enter this topic via Liverpool, it is important to at least register disagreements over whether Britain's empire was maritime or territorial. See Armitage (2000).

21. The access that the Suez Canal gave to Liverpool shippers allowed them an edge in the worldwide cotton market in the late nineteenth century. In one period, Liverpool exporters provided more Indian cotton to Europe than did India itself. They also upset the market for American cotton, even if they never surpassed it (Hyde 1971: 96).

22. Between 1920 and 1921, the unemployment rolls in Liverpool grew from 15,000 to 30,000 (Murphy 1995: 73). See Hyde for a discussion of the fall in trade (1971, chapter 8).

23. Andrea Murphy's *From the Empire to the Rialto: Racism and Reaction in Liverpool, 1918–1948* (1995) is an indispensable account of these processes. See also Tabili 1994 and Rich 1986, who proffer rival analyses of the causes of the riots, as well as May and Cohen's pioneering study, which situates the 1919 riots in transnational colonial context (1974).

24. Liverpool was still a functioning port at the time of my fieldwork, and it remains so. In fact, in the mid-1990s the docks reached a level of traffic it had not seen since the 1960s. But the difference between now and then is that changes in the nature of the entire shipping industry (in terms of the rise of other big ports, the geography of trade, and automation) have resulted in a greatly reduced need for workers. In 1995, the Mersey Docks and

Harbour Corporation employed 500 dockers (329 of whom were fired that year) down from a height of 25,000 in the industry's earlier years (Keiller 2000: 448).

25. By way of caveat, let me say that henceforth, this chapter is an enactment of what it describes, and unavoidably so. It expresses a critical concern about the effects of Liverpool's marginality from the nation; but in so doing, it may provide fodder for the kinds of critiques that other Britons make about Liverpool.

26. For a perspective from striking dockers and their families, consult Lavalette and Kennedy (1996). Also see Allan Sekula's beautiful essay analyzing Liverpool workers' resistance in a transnational political-economic context. For example, "Trace a line of dockers' solidarity across the Pacific, from Freemantle and Sydney to Los Angeles. Set that line against the heavier line of transnational corporate intrigue, the line that seeks to strangle and divide and endlessly cheapen the cost of labor, the line that respects only the degradation of the 'bottom line.' . . . Trace the thin line of resistance further in reverse, crossing America and the Atlantic to Liverpool, great city of working-class toil, departure, refusal, and enjoyment" (2000: 414). A bit romantic and also steeped at the end in all the signs of Liverpool exceptionalism, but at the very least it offers a rejoinder to perspectives that give no credence to the mere *possibility* of worker exploitation.

27. Margaret Thatcher would have been one unsympathetic observer. As she put it, "Trying to cure the British disease with socialism is like trying to cure leukemia with leeches." See Martin Weiner's classic study for a culturalist analysis of the so-called disease (1981).

28. Erlend Clouston, "Grievous Bleasdale Harm," *Guardian*, June 14, 1991, p. 19; Sarah Baxter, "National Power: Militant again threatens to dirty Kinnock's Image—the National Party is determined it Won't," *New Statesman and Society*, July 27, 1990, p. 6; Patrick Wintour, "Clogged by the Deterius of Ideology," *Guardian*, April 27, 1991, p. 5; David Selbourne, "Rotten Borough," *Sunday Times*, January 6, 1991, sec. 3, p. 1.

29. In this context it is also worth considering the way Charles Dickens used Liverpool in his novel *Hard Times* (1854). Dickens is known to have loved the city. It was among his favorite places to give readings. In *Hard Times* Liverpool plays a brief but intriguing role. When it is discovered that Thomas Gradgrind, the son of a banker, has committed a crime that had been pinned on the novel's working-class hero, the disgrace is so huge that he must leave England—further supporting the point that to be English is to be law-abiding. Dickens makes a point of having Thomas exit from Liverpool, which signals two things. First—and here we might recall the opening of O'Mara's autobiography—once you hit Liverpool, you're already out of England. Second, Liverpool is criminality, and is hence a perfectly suitable place to send his fallen character.

30. The urban historian of Britain P. J. Waller counters such popular, cultural, phenomenological logic, writing that "[t]he human spirit is not predictably crushed by mean-looking towns any more than it is always elevated by paradisiacal landscapes" (1983: 100).

31. John Belchem makes these arguments most stridently, indicating that Scousers contribute to their own negative image in the national eye. He urges them to cease whining and ally themselves with the "trademark Britain" movement being spearheaded by capitalists seeking to modernize the country's image (1992, 2000).

32. As many Britons have been quick to tell me, all Britons who are not Londoners hold such views about London. I do not claim an exceptional status for Liverpool on this or any other score. I have suggested, instead, that Britons outside of Liverpool constitute the city's identity in particular ways: through labor union militancy, localism, insularity, and phenomena to be treated in the next two chapters. My purpose is to deconstruct such claims, not to reinforce or otherwise validate them.

CHAPTER 7: A SLAVE TO HISTORY

1. Because this chapter analyzes whiteness as a set of representations, it goes without capitalization here. This move avoids conflating actual White people, on the one hand, with critical conceptualizations of historical and contemporary power relations on the other hand. As well, it is the very connection between the two that is being forged and contested in this chapter.

2. In the vein of historical anthropology, see Mintz and Price (1992 [1976]) as an exception. In literary studies, see Toni Morrison's powerful *Playing in the Dark: Whiteness and the Literary Imagination* (1992).

3. Anthropologists have most commonly elaborated slavery's legacy in American and African cultural contexts. See, for example, Alexander 1984; R. Shaw 1997; Hale 1997; Holsey 2003; Bruner 1996; and Gable and Handler 1992, 1996. This chapter will elaborate Britain as a site of abolitionism, but it is also worth noting that Frederick Douglass visited Liverpool as part of his antislavery activities and, more notably perhaps, Ida B. Wells found it important to go to the city to further her anti-lynching campaign.

4. For Liverpool's history vis-à-vis the slave trade, see Hyde 1971; Fryer 1984; Cameron and Crooke 1992; Dicky Sam 1984 [1884]; Drescher 1988; and Anstey and Hair 1976.

5. I mark this boy's racial positioning for the sake of consistency; every person in this ethnography gets racially marked.

6. I choose to sidestep questions of truth, although I do occasionally pit different "truths" against each other in order to illuminate the operative tensions. The tunnels in particular prompt the questions, Do they actually exist? And were they used to store human beings? The "truth"—as I have perhaps wrongly apprehended it—is not nearly as important as the ethnographic fact at hand: these questions are the stuff of active debate in Liverpool. In any event, and as Rosemary Coombe suggests in a similar context, "[T]he practices involved in spreading a rumor, reporting it, commenting on it, and analyzing it necessarily collapse into one another" (1997: 271).

7. The evidence for that point is well worth quoting: "Black people across the nation are at great disadvantage, but with signs of marginal improvements in employment, the development of businesses, education and political representation; while they are still far from achieving parity, many significant inroads have been made and a base established which can be consolidated. . . . In Liverpool, however, there is a dearth of educated and professionally qualified black people, few black people in the professions—only a handful of individuals constitute the seeds of a black middle class—and even fewer black businesses" (1991: 516).

8. The family features in another common explanation for racism in Liverpool. Some argue that the shipping industry thrived on nepotism and that the practice survives in the present, affecting all sectors of employment. In a city of chronically high unemployment, Whites reputedly avert the usual hiring procedures and place their own family members into available jobs.

9. See M. Smith 1991 and Ogude 1981 for examples of the former argument, and Price 1983 for the latter. D. Scott (1991) offers a cogent critique of Price's suggestion that the Saramacca of Surinam have the truest, purest form of historical consciousness among Blacks in the Americas.

10. I cannot emphasize enough that the antebellum slave narratives to be discussed here draw Britain, the Caribbean, and the United States together; the texts may refer to slavery in the United States, but the authors themselves—such as Douglass, who opened this chapter—traveled around Britain, as this section will make clear. I make this point because previous readers have suggested to me that this material seems "out of place" for not

of original works of authorship, including literary, dramatic, musical, artistic, and certain other works. See Appendix E. Thus, books, songs, plays, jewelry, movies, sculptures, paintings, and choreographic works are all protectable. Computer software is also protectable by copyright.

Copyright protection is available for more than merely serious works of fiction or art. Marketing materials, advertising copy, and cartoons are also protectable. Copyright is available for original works; no judgment is made about their literary or artistic quality. Nevertheless, certain works are not protectable by copyright, such as titles, names, short phrases, or lists of ingredients. Similarly, ideas, methods, and processes are not protectable by copyright, although the expression of those ideas is.

Copyright protection exists automatically from the time a work is created in fixed form. Thus, similar to trademark law, securing a registration for a work (with the U.S. Copyright Office) is not required for a work to be protected, although registration does provide significant advantages, such as establishing a public record of the copyright claim and providing a basis upon which an infringement suit may be brought in federal court and in which statutory damages and attorneys' fees may be recovered.

The owner of a copyright has the right to reproduce the work, prepare derivative works based on the original work (such as a sequel to the original), distribute copies of the work, and to perform and display the work. Generally, violations of such rights are protectable by infringement actions. Nevertheless, some uses of copyrighted works are considered "fair use" and do not constitute infringement, such as use of an insignificant portion of a work for noncommercial purposes or parody of a copyrighted work.

Federal Registration of Copyrights. Neither publication nor registration of a work is required for copyright protection, inasmuch as works are protected under federal copyright law from the time of their creation in a fixed form. Registration, however, is inexpensive, requiring only a $30 filing fee, and the process is expeditious. In most cases, the Copyright Office processes applications within four to five months.

Copyrighted works are automatically protected from the moment of their creation for a term generally enduring for the author's life plus an additional seventy years after the author's death. After that time, the work will fall into the public domain and may be reproduced, distributed, or performed by anyone. The policy underlying the long period of copyright protection is that it may take several years for a painting, book, or opera to achieve its true value, and, thus, authors should receive a length of protection that will enable the work to appreciate to its greatest extent.

Patents

What Is Protectable. A **patent** is a grant from the U.S. government that permits its owner to prevent others from making, using, or selling an invention. There are three types of patents: utility patents, which are the most common patents and which cover useful inventions and discoveries (such as the typewriter, the automobile, and genetically altered mice); design patents, which cover new, original, and ornamental designs for articles (such as furniture); and plant patents, which cover new and distinct plant varieties (such as hybrid flowers or trees).

Patent protection is available only for useful, novel, and nonobvious inventions. Generally, patent law prohibits the patenting of an invention that is merely an insignificant addition to or alteration of something already known. Moreover, some items cannot be protected by patent, such as scientific principles.

Federal Registration of Patents. Patents are governed exclusively by federal law (35 U.S.C. § 100 *et seq.*). See Appendix E. To obtain a being about Liverpool. I beg to differ. This book is dedicated to deconstructing Liverpool's ostensible uniqueness. If it were to restrict itself to what has happened within Liverpool's physical space, it would conspire in Liverpudlians' and other Britons' view that the city is best treated on its own, as a perpetual exception to every rule, as an isolated realm existing on the outside of the larger histories that, indeed, *connected* places (Britain, its constituent locales, the Caribbean, the United States, and Africa).

11. The analysis to follow has been inspired by the brilliant work of John Sekora (1987) and Frances Foster (1994).

12. See Sekora 1987 and Davis and Gates 1985 for testimony as to the popularity of slave narratives among the book-buying American public. Frances Foster (1994), though, states the case for their popularity most exquisitely: "Most of the slave narratives were not intended for exactly the same audiences as Thoreau's, Melville's, or even Hawthorne's works. Yet a comparison between sales figures for their works and those of slave narratives which were published during the same period shows that the contemporary audiences of Douglass, Brown and [Father] Henson were far larger than those of three of the literary figures most revered today. . . . Their popularity is astounding when one considers how precarious their situation was" (23).

13. See Sekora 1987 for an exhaustive analysis of White abolitionists' effective ownership of, and influence on, slave narratives. See Foster 1994 for the paucity of antebellum slave narratives written by women.

14. Vron Ware (1992) argues that the distribution in Britain of *Uncle Tom's Cabin* and the agitation for abolition in the Caribbean paved the way for the positive reception of Black abolitionists and the morality they espoused.

15. With the continuing rise of empire in the nineteenth century, however, motherhood would become increasingly, and profoundly, racialized in Britain. See, for example, Davin 1997.

16. Also see Twine (1998b) for a provocative and productive connection between the slave narratives' construction of motherhood and contemporary analyses of White women as mothers of Black people.

17. For example, Adrian Mellor (1991) notes that in 1988 alone the Albert Dock received 3.5 million visitors, making it the third most popular free tourist attraction in Britain. Vron Ware and Les Back express concerns similar to mine, suggesting, "A commemorative site is likely to become a potential feature of a tourist itinerary, which will in turn influence the way that it is presented to the public. This requires an interpretation of historical evidence that is sensitive to the line between entertainment and education. How does this story 'fit' into the bigger picture of the nation's invincible seafaring past?" (2002: 216).

18. See Ware and Back 2002 for a brief analysis of Britain's history vis-à-vis slavery that is set somewhere other than Liverpool, in Devon.

CHAPTER 8 : THE GHOST OF MURIEL FLETCHER

1. The 39 percent figure must also reflect transracial adoption. Admitting, for the sake of argument, that only half of that percentage refers to birth parentage, that would still create a significant number of Black people of mixed racial background in Britain. Liverpool's larger proportion of Blacks of dual racial parentage cannot be skewing these figures because the city's Black population (6,786 in 1991) is too small.

2. Paul, Barker, "Liverpudlians Are Very Proud of Their Heritage. But the City Stopped Winning the Pools, or the New Industries, a Long Time Ago," *New Statesman* 126, no. 4320 (1997): 540.

3. In 1985, an important "report" on racial disadvantage in Britain (known as the Swann Report) focused on Blacks in Liverpool. It went to special pains to describe the Black population in a section called "Definition of Liverpool Blacks." The need for such a title is indicative of the perceived burden of explanation that discourses on Black Liverpool bear. Liverpool is so unique within Britain that the city's relationship to the category *Black* seems to require careful elaboration. This is how Liverpool Blacks are defined: "There is a long-established community in Liverpool of African, mixed African and English, or African and Liverpool-Irish descent, with some of Asian descent as well. The mixed community characteristic of the modern city grew from the end of the nineteenth century onwards, mainly through the settlement of African seamen. By the late 1940s the ethnic minority population of Liverpool was recorded as coming mainly from West Africa and the West Indies. It is this group of long-established families that we call 'Liverpool Blacks'" (DES 1985: 42).

4. France Winddance Twine, "Is Transracial Motherhood Transformative?: Racial Consciousness among White Mothers of African-Descent Children," (talk presented at Stanford University, February 18, 1999). See also Twine 1999.

5. See Sherry Ortner's discussion of "ethnographic refusal" (1995).

6. Given the proliferation of literature and scholarship on the politics and experience of *mixed-race* identity in the United Kingdom and the United States, and given the conventional association of Liverpool with people of "mixed race," some readers might be disappointed to realize that this chapter is not really about that category, per se. Although it is very much at issue in this chapter, I do not aim to theorize it or the related issues of interracial marriage, procreation, or sexuality. Nor do I aim to provide an exhaustive ethnographic treatment of these issues—ones that I have instead tried to weave into the larger, singular concern of this book. That concern is the intersection of two axes of power called *place* and *race*—or, put differently, localization as racialization. The present chapter is about the construction of the racial category and identity called *Black*. Readers interested in mixed-race identity and related matters should consult the classic and still growing literature in Britain (and perhaps the United States). Although I discuss interraciality toward different ends than might be expected, I freely admit that consulting the larger British literature (which I do not do here) would be an important step in refusing the selfsame uniqueness problematic that I am trying to deconstruct. Highlights of the relevant British literature include: Christian 2000; Ifekwunigwe 1997, 1999; Alibhai-Brown 2001; Alibhai-Brown and Montague 1992; Parker and Song 2001; Tizard and Phoenix 2001; Phoenix and Owen 1996; Anne Wilson 1987; and Twine 1998a, 1999, 2000.

7. Greg's words raise issues that I do not deal with here. In short, he is echoing the contestations between Afro-Caribbeans and LBBs discussed at length earlier, although he speaks with none of the vitriol that characterizes older LBBs' positions. Growing up, though, his friends were other children of West African background because all of his fathers' friends were West African. At the present point in his life, though, he was thinking through what other forces caused divisions among children of West African and West Indian backgrounds.

8. And herein lies a major difference between racial categorization in Britain and the United States. In the latter, the same answer, "Both my parents are Black," absolutely never satisfies. My interrogators start poking around in the further reaches of my genealogy, searching for the drop of "white" blood that would explain my appearance.

9. This phenomenon is not unique to Liverpool, obviously. Virginia Dominguez's classic *White by Definition* (1986) describes the unreliability of phenotype and the malleability of ancestry in the construction of racial identity in Louisiana. Another link to the Liverpool

case is in Dominguez's analysis of the role of the civil rights movement in putting a premium on Black identity over Creoleness.

10. France Winddance Twine (1998a, 1999) similarly studies the parenting practice of White mothers of Black children in Leicester. She notes Blacks' assumption that White women are not racially equipped, so to speak, to raise their Black children.

11. In her book, Jayne Ifekwunigwe cites one of her Black Liverpudlian informants expressing the same point as Veronica: "I remember going to Wolverhampton and being in this pub with a friend and this Black guy sittin' on the pool table sayin' to me that I was like a White woman. That I wasn't Black, I was White. All this shit being hurled at me, I was thinkin', 'What's goin' on here?' It was like a complete contradiction to what was happenin' at home. That brought in the whole thing about how light I was, and me mother being White. I didn't feel like it was a real big issue for me prior to that, but now it was becoming this issue. Whereas in Liverpool, I didn't find it was a big issue" (1999: 107).

12. Classic statements include W.E.B. Du Bois's analysis of the veil in *The Souls of Black Folk* (1985 [1903]), Ralph Ellison's *Invisible Man* (1953), Hazel Carby's "White Woman Listen! Black Feminism and the Boundaries of Sisterhood" (1982), and Michele Wallace's *Invisibility Blues: From Pop to Theory* (1990). The artist Fred Wilson portrays Black invisibility in his installation piece about security guards in museums (Berger 2001). For the exact inverse of Wilson's statement about invisibility, see Ingrid Pollard's equally wrenching photographic analysis of Blackness and *visibility* in her acclaimed series *Pastoral Interludes* (2004). Echoing Franz Fanon ("Look, a Negro!"), Pollard includes the following text with her photographs of Black people vacationing in the English Lake District: "The owners of these fields, these trees and sheep, want me off their GREEN AND PLEASANT LAND. No Trespass, they want me DEAD. A slow death through eyes that slide away from me" (2004: 29).

13. David Macey clarifies Fanon's phenomenological allusions with the help of Merleau-Ponty; "a corporeal schema is a 'resume of our bodily experience' and 'a way of expressing the fact that my body is in the world.'" (2000: 166).

14. There is some contemporary enthusiasm for a phenomenology of race. See Alcoff 2001; Bernasconi 2001. While I admire the ways that such scholars, following Fanon, have injected much-needed racial analysis into that philosophical school, I do not share their enthusiasm for it. Ultimately, I reject all totalistic approaches to and interpretations of race. Phenomenology focuses too much on the (admittedly important) visual and experiential aspects of race—to the exclusion, for example, of its structural dimensions. And as chapter 2 suggested, the very category of *experience* should be approached with caution (J. Scott 1992). For non-totalistic and hence far-reaching theorizations of race, the introduction to *Race, Nature, and the Politics of Difference* is without peer (Moore et al. 2003).

15. Macey clarifies that Fanon only had rudimentary training in psychoanalysis. *Black Skin, White Masks* (and "The Fact of Blackness" in particular) reflects his reading in the area, rather than any formal education (2000: 135).

16. As Ann Stoler argues, "Racism is commonly understood as a visual ideology in which somatic features are thought to provide the crucial criteria of membership. But racism is not a visual ideology at all; physiological attributes only signal the non-visual and more salient distinctions of exclusion on which racism rests" (1992: 521; see also 1997b). This is not to discount the visual but to suggest that its precise role and nature should be analyzed rather than assumed as the all-determining foundation of race. And since the visual is generally understood to refer to the body, Robyn Wiegman's contribution is especially helpful. She goes beyond the corporeal, while situating it—or showing how it is situated—within particular "economies of visibility." She writes, "What does it mean,

for instance, that the visual apparatuses of photography, film, television, and video (as well as the many offshoots of computer technologies) serve as our primary public domain, our main shared context for the contestations of contemporary cultural politics? And perhaps more important, what does it mean that within these technologies, the body is figured as the primary locus of representation, mediation, and/or interpretation?" (1995: 7). Paul Gilroy's *Against Race* (2000) is an extended meditation on the visual, as it appears (or disappears) as a basis of racial truths, and as it manifests in a variety of guises (filmic, mass-mediated, scientific, and technological). While attuned to such "novel racial imaginaries," Moore, Kosek, and Pandian remind us that "a key question remains the relationship between new technologies of imaging race and the embodied politics and social relations in bars, buses, and Babylons, near and far" (2003: 26).

17. As far as I am concerned, the real unanswered question of the present work concerns African fathers, not White mothers. As was suggested in chapters 2 and 4, Black people themselves describe these men's subjectivities as cryptic at best. Veronica put it best: "These African men—these old ones what come from back home—they have some heavy mentality that is very difficult to understand."

18. It should go without saying that the White women of the Black community are as diverse as members of any other racialized group. Most are either Irish or English. Some are Catholic and some are Protestant. They hail from all parts of Liverpool, including its north end, Liverpool 8, the dock area of Liverpool 1 (Pitt Street), the suburbs, as well as from other cities altogether. They come from working-and middle-class backgrounds. Some of their families—or members of them—were very supportive of their marriage to Blacks, some were indifferent, and others were hostile.

19. Of course, the pathbreaking ethnography on the color-blind and hence power-evasive discourse constitutive of whiteness is Ruth Frankenberg's *White Women, Race Matters* (1993). But see also the earlier-cited literature on whiteness, especially Wiegman (1999).

CHAPTER 9: LOCAL WOMEN AND GLOBAL MEN

1. The interest in cosmopolitanism stems from, and is embroiled in, the intersecting discourses of globalization, modernity, and multiculturalism/identity politics. The debates outlined below appear in various forms and to varying degrees in Harvey 2000; Diouf 2000; Abbas 2000; M. Cohen 1992; Lee 1995; Robbins 1995, 1998; Mignolo 2000; and Pollack et al. 2000. The debates that surround cosmopolitanism, which I shall not mediate here, center on the following issues: whether it is outside of the politics in which it seeks to intervene; whether it can be meaningful without being unifying, and if it attempts to unify, can it do so without privileging the West; whether it necessarily depends on Western notions of modernity; whether its goals of superceding nationalism would merely put in place some other equally systemic and problematic ideology and, similarly, whether it is indeed nationalism that must be overcome in order to achieve a progressive internationalist sensibility; whether cosmopolitanism can—or should—answer the varieties of localisms popping up around the world as a critical response to globalization, and whether that is indeed what localisms are; and whether the term carries too much historical baggage to be useful for the liberatory tasks at hand. All of the scholars who invest any manner of possibility in cosmopolitanism go to great pains to specify either what needs to be overcome, or otherwise accomplished in order for it to work as a viable basis of progressive politics. Clearly, cosmopolitanism is as hopeful a field as it is a contested one.

2. With this, he appropriately cites his earlier work, *The Condition of Postmodernity* (1989), where he made similar arguments. On a different note, Harvey's discussion of

cosmopolitanism opens with a fine lesson on the racial implications of different deployments of geography, as evident in Immanuel Kant's original treatment of cosmopolitanism. But by the end of the article race has disappeared, having been replaced by class.

3. For more on the gendering of local/global theory, see Freeman 2001 and Massey 1994, chapter 10.

4. By stark contrast, historian Laura Tabili (1994) spins a decidedly unromantic tale of the lives of Black seamen of late imperial Britain. Her analysis barely travels to sea. When it does, it is devoid of the masculinist adventure idiom that suffuses the accounts of male scholars. The port is neither a site of absolute difference from the sea nor the site of provincialism. Rather, it is the site where various actors—from the British state and labor unions, to colonial and White seamen and shipping bosses—fought fiercely ideological battles that served in turn to produce Black seamen's experiences at sea *and* in British ports.

5. Tony Lane corroborates this point (1986).

6. He does discuss the Black poet Phyllis Wheatley as a sea traveler. We might also add Ida B. Wells and Mary Seacole as other famous examples.

7. See Collier and Yanagisako 1987 for the classic statement on the mutual imbrication of gender and kinship.

8. I am also convinced by James Clifford's critique of cosmopolitanism (1998). He favors a focus on discrepant cosmopolitanisms, which at once respect "different forms of encounter, negotiation and multiple affiliation" without disparaging others for being skeptical of coalitional politics that assume that people should necessarily want to engage in these encounters.

Abbas, Ackbar

2000 "Cosmopolitan De-scriptions: Shanghai and Hong Kong." *Public Culture* 12(3): 769–86.

Abu-Lughod, Janet

1989 *Before European Hegemony: The World System A.D. 1250–1350*. New York: Oxford University Press.

Abu-Lughod, Lila

1990 "The Romance of Resistance: Tracing Transformations of Power through Bedouin Women." *American Ethnologist* 17:41–55.

Ackah, William

1997 "The Fact of Blackness: Identity in Context." In *Black Organisation and Identity in Liverpool: A Local, National and Global Perspective*, ed. William Ackah and Mark Christian, 55–61. Liverpool: Charles Wootton College Press.

Ackroyd, Peter

2002 *Albion: The Origins of the English Imagination*. London: Chatto and Windus.

Alcalay, Ammiel

1993 *After Jews and Arabs: Remaking Levantine Culture*. Minneapolis: University of Minnesota Press.

Alcoff, Linda

2001 "Toward a Phenomenology of Racial Embodiment." In *Race*, ed. Robert Bernasconi, 267–83. Oxford: Blackwell.

Alexander, Claire

1996. *The Art of Being Black*. Oxford: Oxford University Press.

Alexander, Jack

1977 "The Culture of Race in Middle-Class Kingston, Jamaica." *American Ethnologist* 4(3): 413–36.

1984 "Love, Race, Slavery and Sexuality in Jamaican Images of the Family." In *Kinship Ideology and Practice in Latin America*, ed. Raymond T. Smith, 147–80. Chapel Hill: University of North Carolina Press.

Alibhai-Brown, Yasmin

2001 *Mixed Feelings: The Complex Lives of Mixed-Race Britons*. London: Women's Press.

Alibhai-Brown, Yasmin, and A. Montague

1992 *The Colour of Love: Mixed Race Relationships*. London: Virago.

Alleyne, Mervyn C.

2002 *The Construction and Representation of Race and Ethnicity in the Caribbean and the World*. Kingston, Jamaica: University of West Indies Press.

Anstey, Roger, and P.E.H. Hair, eds.

1976 *Liverpool, the African Slave Trade, and Abolition*. Transactions of the Historic Society of Lancashire and Cheshire. Vol. 125.

Appadurai, Arjun

1987 "Putting Hierarchy in Its Place." *Cultural Anthropology* 3(1): 36–49.

1989 "On Moving Targets." *Public Culture* 2(1): i–iv.

1996 *Modernity at Large: Cultural Dimensions of Globalization*. Minneapolis: University of Minnesota Press.

2000 "Spectral Housing and Urban Cleansing: Notes on Millennial Mumbai." *Public Culture* 12(3): 627–51.

Aretxaga, Begona

1997 *Shattering Silence: Women, Nationalism and Political Subjectivity in Northern Ireland*. Princeton: Princeton University Press.

Armitage, David

2000 *The Ideological Origins of the British Empire*. New York: Cambridge University Press.

Baldwin, M. Page

2001 "Subject to Empire: Married Women and the British Nationality and Status of Aliens Act." *Journal of British Studies* 40 (October): 522–56.

Barker, Martin

1981 *The New Racism: Conservatives and the Ideology of the Tribe*. London: Junction Books.

Basch, Linda, N. Glick Schiller, and C. Szanton Blanc

1994 *Nations Unbound: Transnational Projects, Postcolonial Predicaments, and Deterritorialized Nation States*. Langhorn: Gordon and Breach Science Publishers.

Basso, Keith H.

1988 "'Speaking with Names': Language and Landscape among the Western Apache." *Cultural Anthropology* 3(2): 99–130.

1996 *Wisdom Sits in Places: Landscape and Language among the Western Apache*. Albuquerque: University of New Mexico Press.

Baucom, Ian

1999 *Out of Place: Englishness, Empire, and the Locations of Identity*. Princeton: Princeton University Press.

Belchem, John

1992 "Introduction: The Peculiarities of Liverpool." In *Popular Politics, Riot and Labour: Essays in Liverpool History, 1790–1940*, 1–20. Liverpool: Liverpool University Press.

1998 "Liverpool in 1848: Image, Identity and Issues." *Transactions of the Historic Society of Lancashire and Cheshire*. 147:1–26.

2000 *Merseypride: Essays in Liverpool Exceptionalism*. Liverpool: Liverpool University Press.

Bell, Morag, Robin Butlin, and Michael Heffernan, eds.

1995 *Geography and Imperialism, 1820–1940*. Manchester: Manchester University Press.

Berger, Maurice

2001 *Fred Wilson: Objects and Installations, 1979–2000*. Baltimore: Center for Art and Visual Culture, University of Maryland.

Bernasconi, Robert

2001 "The Invisibility of Racial Minorities in the Public Realm." In *Race*, ed. Robert Bernasconi, 284–99. Oxford: Blackwell.

Bhabha, Homi

1986 "Remembering Fanon." Foreword to *Black Skin, White Masks*, by Franz Fanon. London: Pluto Press.

Birth, Kevin

1997 "Most of Us Are Family Some of the Time: Interracial Unions and Transracial Kinship in Eastern Trinidad." *American Ethnologist* 24(3): 585–601.

Blackett, R.J.M.

1983 *Building an Antislavery Wall: Black Americans in the Atlantic Abolitionist Movement, 1830–1860*. Ithaca: Cornell University Press.

Blunt, Alison, and Gillian Rose, eds.

1994 *Writing Women and Space: Colonial and Postcolonial Geographies*. London: Guildford Press.

Bolster, W. Jeffrey

1997 *Black Jacks: African American Seamen in the Age of Sail*. Cambridge, MA: Harvard University Press.

Booth, William

1890 *In Darkest England and the Way Out*. New York: Funk and Wagnalls.

Brah, Avtar

1996 *Cartographies of Diaspora: Contesting Identities*. London: Routledge.

Bridges, Lee

1981/82 "Keeping the Lid on: British Urban Social Policy, 1975–81." *Race and Class* 23(2/3): 171–85.

Brontë, Emily

1993 [1850] *Wuthering Heights*. New York: Barnes and Noble Books.

Brown, Jacqueline Nassy

1998 "Black Liverpool, Black America and the Gendering of Diasporic Space." *Cultural Anthropology* 13(3): 291–325.

Bruner, Edward M.

1996 "Tourism in Ghana: The Representation of Slavery and the Return of the Black Diaspora." *American Anthropologist* 98:290–304.

Bunyan, Tony

1981/82 "The Police against the People." *Race and Class* 23(2/3): 153–70.

Butler, Judith

1993 *Bodies That Matter: On the Discursive Limits of "Sex."* New York: Routledge.

Cameron, Gail, and Stan Crooke

1992 *Liverpool: Capital of the Slave Trade*. Liverpool: Picton Press.

Campt, Tina

2004 *Other Germans: Black Germans and the Politics of Race, Gender, and Memory in the Third Reich*. Ann Arbor: University of Michigan Press.

Carby, Hazel

1982 "White Woman Listen! Black Feminism and the Boundaries of Sisterhood." In *The Empire Strikes Back: Race and Racism in 70s Britain*, ed. Center for Contemporary Cultural Studies, 212–35. London: Routledge.

CARF (Campaign Against Racism and Fascism) Collective

1981/82 "The 'Riots.'" *Race and Class* 23(2/3): 223–50.

Casey, Edward

1987 *Remembering: A Phenomenological Study*. Bloomington: Indiana University Press.

1996 "How to Get from Space to Place in a Fairly Short Stretch of Time: Phenomenological Prolegomena." In *Senses of Place*, ed. Steven Feld and Keith Basso, 13–52. Santa Fe: School of American Research Press.

CCCS (Center for Contemporary Cultural Studies), ed.

1982. *The Empire Strikes Back: Race and Racism in 70s Britain*. London: Routledge.

Chandler, George

1973 *The Merchant Venturers*. Liverpool: Rondo Publications.

Channel 4 Television Corporation.

1999. *Riot*.

Christian, Mark

1995/96 "Black Struggle for Historical Recognition." *North West Labour History* 20:58–66.

1997 "Black Identity in Liverpool: An Appraisal." In *Black Organisation and Identity in Liverpool: A Local, National and Global Perspective*, ed. William Ackah and Mark Christian, 62–79. Liverpool: Charles Wootton College Press.

1998 "An African-Centered Approach to the BlackBritish Experience with Special Reference to Liverpool." *Journal of Black Studies* 28(3): 291–308.

2000 *Multiracial Identity: An International Perspective*. London: Macmillan.

Chukwuemeka, Angus

1997 "The Economic Dimensions of Local Black Community Organisation." In *Black Organisation and Identity in Liverpool: A Local, National and Global Perspective*, ed. William Ackah and Mark Christian, 42–51. Liverpool: Charles Wootton Press.

Clay, David

n.d. "Ten Years On: 1981–1991, Looking Back over the Years." Unpublished manuscript.

Clifford, James

1988 "On Ethnographic Authority." In *The Predicament of Culture: Twentieth Century Ethnography, Literature and Art*. Cambridge, MA: Harvard University Press.

1994 "Diasporas." *Cultural Anthropology* 9:302–38.

1997 *Routes: Travel and Translation in the Late Twentieth Century*. Cambridge, MA: Harvard University Press.

1998 "Mixed Feelings." In *Cosmopolitics: Thinking and Feeling beyond the Nation*, ed. Pheng Cheah and Bruce Robbins, 362–70. Minneapolis: University of Minnesota Press.

Cohen, Anthony P., ed.

1982a *Belonging: Identity and Social Organization in British Rural Cultures*. Manchester: Manchester University Press.

1982b "A Sense of Time, a Sense of Place: The Meaning of Close Social Association in Whalsay, Shetland." In *Belonging: Identity and Social Organization in British Rural Cultures*, 21–49. Manchester: Manchester University Press.

1986 *Symbolising Boundaries: Identity and Diversity in British Cultures*. Manchester: Manchester University Press.

Cohen, Mitchell

1992 "Rooted Cosmopolitanism: Thoughts on the Left, Nationalism, and Multiculturalism." *Dissent* 39(4): 478–83.

Collier, Jane F., and Sylvia Yanagisako, eds.

1987 *Gender and Kinship: Essays toward a Unified Analysis*. Stanford: Stanford University Press.

Collings, Rex, ed.

1981 *Reflections of a Statesman: The Writings and Speeches of Enoch Powell*. London: Bellew Publishing.

Colls, Robert, and Bill Lancaster, eds.

1992 *Geordies: Roots of Regionalism*. Edinburgh: Edinburgh University Press.

Coombe, Rosemary

1997 "The Demonic Place of the 'Not There': Trademark Rumors in the Postindustrial Imaginary." In *Culture, Power, Place: Explorations in Critical Anthropology*, ed. Akhil Gupta and James Ferguson, 249–74. Durham: Duke University Press.

Cooper, Frederick, and Ann Laura Stoler, eds.

1997 *Tensions of Empire: Colonial Cultures in a Bourgeois World*. Berkeley: University of California Press.

Creighton, Margaret S., and Lisa Norling
1996 *Iron Men, Wooden Women: Gender and Seafaring in the Atlantic World, 1700–1920.* Baltimore: Johns Hopkins University Press.

Darwin, John
1991 *The End of the British Empire: The Historical Debate.* Oxford: Basil Blackwell.

Davin, Anna
1997 "Imperialism and Motherhood." In *Tensions of Empire: Colonial Cultures in a Bourgeois World*, ed. Frederick Cooper and Ann Laura Stoler, 87–151. Berkeley: University of California Press.

Davis, Charles T., and Henry Louis Gates, Jr.
1985 "Introduction: the Language of Slavery." In *The Slave's Narrative*, xi–xxxiv. Oxford: Oxford University Press.

de Certeau, Michel
1984 *The Practice of Everyday Life.* Berkeley: University of California Press.

Defoe, Daniel
1971 [1714] *A Tour through the Whole Island of Great Britain.* Middlesex, UK: Penguin.

Dennis, Ferdinand
1988 *Behind the Frontlines: Journey into Afro-Britain.* London: Victor Gollancz.

Department of Education and Science
1985 *Education for All* (The Swann Report). London: Her Majesty's Stationery Office.

Department of the Environment
1978 *National Dwelling and Housing Survey.* London: Her Majesty's Stationery Office.

Dickens, Charles
1958 *The Uncommercial Traveller and Reprinted Pieces.* London: Oxford University Press.
1980 [1854] *Hard Times.* New York: Signet.

Dicky Sam
1984 [1884] *Liverpool and Slavery.* Liverpool: Scouse Press.

Diouf, Mamadou
2000 "The Senegalese Murid Trade Diaspora and the Making of a Vernacular Cosmopolitanism." *Public Culture* 12(3): 679–702.

Dominguez, Virginia
1986 *White by Definition: Social Classification in Creole Louisiana.* New Brunswick, NJ: Rutgers University Press.

Douglass, Frederick
1986 [1845] *Narrative of the Life of Frederick Douglass, an American Slave.* New York: Penguin.
1994a [1855] *My Bondage and My Freedom.* In *Frederick Douglass: Autobiographies.* New York: Library Classics of America.
1994b [1893] *Life and Times of Frederick Douglass.* In *Frederick Douglass: Autobiographies.* New York: Library Classics of America.
1997 [1852] "What to the Slave Is the Fourth of July?: An Address Delivered in Rochester, New York, on 5 July 1852." In *The Norton Anthology to African American Literature*, ed. Henry Louis Gates, Jr., and Nellie Y. McKay, 379–91. New York: Norton.

Drake, St. Clair
1982 "Diaspora Studies and Pan-Africanism." In *Global Dimensions of the African Diaspora*, ed. Joseph Harris, 341–404. Washington, DC: Howard University Press.
1987 *Black Folk Here and There: An Essay in History and Anthropology.* Los Angeles: Center for Afro-American Studies, University of California.

patent, an inventor must file an application with the PTO (the same agency that issues trademark registrations) that fully describes the invention. Patent prosecution is expensive, time-consuming, and complex. Costs can run into the thousands of dollars, and it generally takes over two years for the PTO to issue a patent.

Patent protection exists for twenty years from the date of filing of an application for utility and plant patents and fourteen years from the date of grant for design patents. After this period of time, the invention falls into the public domain and may be used by any person without permission.

Patents promote the public good in that patent protection incentivizes inventors. In return for fully describing the invention in the patent application, the inventor is granted an exclusive but limited period of time within which to exploit the invention. After the patent expires, any member of the public is free to use, manufacture, or sell the invention. Thus, patent law strikes a balance between the need to protect inventors and the need to allow public access to important discoveries.

Trade Secrets

What Is Protectable. A **trade secret** consists of any valuable business information that, if known by a competitor, would afford the competitor some benefit or advantage. There is no limit to the type of information that can be protected as trade secrets; recipes, marketing plans, financial projections, and methods of conducting business can all constitute trade secrets. There is no requirement that a trade secret be unique or complex; thus, even something as simple and nontechnical as a list of customers can qualify as a trade secret as long as it affords its owner a competitive advantage and is not common knowledge.

If trade secrets were not protectable, companies would have no incentive to invest time, money, and effort in research and development that ultimately benefits the public. Trade secret law thus promotes the development of new methods and processes of doing business in the marketplace.

Protection of Trade Secrets. Although trademarks, copyrights, and patents are all subject to extensive statutory schemes for their protection, application, and registration, there is no federal law relating to trade secrets and no formalities are required to obtain rights to trade secrets. Trade secrets are protectable under various state statutes and cases and by contractual agreements between parties. For example, employers often require employees to sign confidentiality agreements in which employees agree not to disclose proprietary information owned by the employer.

If properly protected, trade secrets may last forever. On the other hand, if companies fail to take reasonable measures to maintain the secrecy of the information, trade secret protection may be lost. Thus, disclosure of the information should be limited to those with a "need to know" it so as to perform their duties, confidential information should be kept in secure or restricted areas, and employees with access to proprietary information should sign **nondisclosure agreements.** If such measures are taken, a trade secret can be protected in perpetuity.

Another method by which companies protect valuable information is by requiring employees to sign agreements promising not to compete with the employer after leaving the job. Such covenants are strictly scrutinized by courts, but generally, if they are reasonable in regard to time, scope, and subject matter, they are enforceable.

Other Intellectual Property Rights

Although the most common types of intellectual property are trademarks, copyrights, patents, and trade secrets, other intellectual property rights exist and will be discussed in the

Drescher, Seymour
1988 "The Slaving Capital of the World: Liverpool and National Opinion in the Age of Abolition." *Slavery and Abolition* 9(2): 128–43.
Driver, Felix
1992 "Geography's Empires: Histories of Geographical Knowledge." *Environment and Planning D: Society and Space* 10:23–40.
2000 *Geography Militant: Cultures of Exploration and Empire*. Oxford: Blackwell.
DuBois, W.E.B.
1940 *Dusk of Dawn: An Essay toward an Autobiography of a Race Concept*. New Brunswick, NJ: Transaction Publishers.
1974 [1928] *Dark Princess: A Romance*. Millwood, NY: Kraus-Thomas Organization.
1985 [1903] *The Souls of Black Folk*. New York: Penguin.
Dummett, Ann, and Andrew Nicol
1990 *Subjects, Citizens, Aliens and Others: Nationality and Immigration Law*. London: Weidenfeld and Nicolson.
Eagleton, Terry
1995 *Heathcliff and the Great Irish Hunger: Studies in Irish Culture*. London: Verso.
Ebron, Paulla
2002 *Performing Africa*. Princeton: Princeton University Press.
Edwards, Brent Hayes
2001 "The Uses of *Diaspora*." *Social Text* 19(1): 45–73.
Edwards, Jeannette
2000 *Born and Bred: Idioms of Kinship and New Reproductive Technologies in England*. Oxford: Oxford University Press.
Eichstedt, Jennifer, and Steven Small
2002 *Representations of Slavery: Race and Ideology in Southern Plantation Museums*. Washington, DC: Smithsonian Institution Press.
Ellis, Richard, and Aaron Wildavsky
1990 "A Cultural Analysis of the Role of Abolitionists in the Coming of the Civil War." *Comparative Studies in Society and History* 32:89–116.
Ellison, Ralph
1953 *The Invisible Man*. New York: New American Library.
1964 *Shadow and Act*. New York: Random House.
Engels, Friedrich
1987 *The Condition of the Working Class in England*. Harmondsworth, Middlesex: Penguin Books.
Enloe, Cynthia
1989 *Bananas, Beaches and Bases: Making Feminist Sense of International Politics*. Berkeley: University of California Press.
Evans, Neil
1995 "Across the Universe: Racial Violence and the Post-War Crisis in Imperial Britain, 1919–25." In *Ethnic Labour and British Imperial Trade: A History of Ethnic Seafarers in the UK*, ed. Diane Frost, 59–88. London: Frank Cass.
Evans-Pritchard, E. E.
1940 The Nuer: *A Description of the Modes of Livelihood and Political Institutions of a Nilotic People*. New York: Oxford University Press.
Fanon, Franz
1967 *Black Skin, White Masks*. New York: Grove Press.

Feld, Steven

1996 "Waterfalls of Song: An Acoustemology of Place Resounding in Bosavi, Papua New Guinea." In *Senses of Place*, ed. Steven Feld and Keith Basso, 91–135. Santa Fe: School of American Research Press.

Feld, Steven, and Keith Basso, eds.

1996 *Senses of Place*. Santa Fe: School of American Research.

Feldman, Allen

1991 *Formations of Violence: The Narrative of the Body and Political Terror in Northern Ireland*. Chicago: University of Chicago Press.

Fletcher, Muriel

1930 *Report on an Investigation into the Colour Problem in Liverpool and Other Ports*. Liverpool: Liverpool Association for the Welfare of Half-Caste Children.

Foster, Frances

1994 *Witnessing Slavery: The Development of Ante-Bellum Slave Narratives*. Madison: University of Wisconsin Press.

Foucault, Michel

1977 *Discipline and Punish: The Birth of the Prison*. New York: Pantheon.

1978 *The History of Sexuality*. Vol. 1. New York: Random House.

1980 *Power/Knowledge*. Brighton: Harvester.

Frake, Charles

1996 "Pleasant Places, Past Times, and Sheltered Identity in Rural East Anglia." In *Senses of Place*, ed. Steven Feld and Keith Basso, 229–57. Santa Fe: School of American Research.

Frankenberg, Ruth

1993 *White Women, Race Matters: The Social Construction of Whiteness*. Minneapolis: University of Minnesota Press.

1997 "Local Whitenesses, Localizing Whiteness." In *Displacing Whiteness: Essays in Social and Cultural Criticism*, 1–33. Durham: Duke University Press.

Freeman, Carla

2001 "Is Local:Global as Feminine:Masculine? Rethinking the Gender of Globalization." *Signs* 26(4): 1007–37.

Frost, Diane

1995a Introduction to *Ethnic Labour and British Imperial Trade: A History of Ethnic Seafarers in the UK*, 1–6. London: Frank Cass.

1995b "Racism, Work and Unemployment: West African Seamen in Liverpool, 1880s–1960s." In *Ethnic Labour and British Imperial Trade: A History of Ethnic Seafarers in the UK*, ed. Diane Frost, 22–33. London: Frank Cass.

1995/96 "West Africans, Black Scousers and the Colour Problem in Inter-war Liverpool." *North West Labour History* 20:50–57.

1999 *Work and Community among West African Migrant Workers since the Nineteenth Century*. Liverpool: Liverpool University Press.

Fryer, Peter

1984 *Staying Power: The History of Black People in Britain*. London: Pluto Press.

Gable, Eric, and Richard Handler

1992 "On the Uses of Relativism: Fact, Conjecture, and the Black and White Histories at Colonial Williamsburg." *American Ethnologist* 19:791–805.

1996 "After Authenticity at an American Heritage Site." *American Anthropologist* 98:568–78.

Gaines, Kevin

2001 "Revisiting Richard Wright in Ghana: Black Radicalism and the Dialectics of Diaspora." *Social Text* 67, 19(2): 75–101.

Gallagher, Tom

1985 "A Tale of Two Cities: Communal Strife in Glasgow and Liverpool before 1914." In *The Irish in the Victorian City*, ed. Roger Swift and Sheridan Gilley, 106–29. London: Croom Helm.

Gaskell, E.

1973 [1855] *North and South*. Ed. A. Eason. London: Oxford University Press.

Gilley, Sheridan, and Roger Swift

1985 Introduction to *The Irish in the Victorian City*, 1–12. London: Croom Helm.

Gilroy, Paul

1987 *There Ain't No Black in the Union Jack: The Cultural Politics of Race and Nation*. London: Hutchinson.

1993a *The Black Atlantic: Modernity and Double Consciousness*. Cambridge, MA: Harvard University Press.

1993b "Nationalism, History, and Ethnic Absolutism." In *Small Acts: Thoughts on the Politics of Black Cultures*, 63–73. London: Serpent's Tail.

1993c "Art of Darkness: Black Art and the Problems of Belonging to England." In *Small Acts: Thoughts on the Politics of Black Cultures*, 74–85. London: Serpent's Tail.

1994 "'After the Love Has Gone': Bio-politics and Etho-poetics in the Black Public Sphere." *Public Culture* 7(1): 49–76.

1995 "Roots and Routes: Black Identity as an Outernational Project." In *Racial and Ethnic Identity: Psychological Development and Creative Expression*, ed. Herbert W. Harris, Howard C. Blue, and Ezra E. H. Griffith, 15–30. London: Routledge.

2000 *Between Camps: Race, Identity and Nationalism at the End of the Colour Line*. London: Penguin.

2003 "After the Great White Error . . . The Great Black Mirage." In *Race, Nature, and the Politics of Difference*, ed. Donald Moore, Jake Kosek, and Anand Pandian, 73–98. Durham: Duke University Press.

Goldberg, David

1993 *Racist Culture: Philosophy and the Politics of Meaning*. Oxford: Blackwell.

Goldschmidt, Henry

2000 "'Crown Heights Is the Center of the World': Reterritorializing a Jewish Diaspora." *Diaspora* 9(1): 83–107.

Gramsci, Antonio

1971 *Selections from the Prison Notebooks*. Ed. and trans. Quentin Hoare and Geoffrey Nowell Smith. New York: International Publishers.

Gregory, Derek

1994 *Geographical Imaginations*. Oxford: Blackwell.

Gregory, Steven

1998 *Black Corona: Race and the Politics of Place in an Urban Community*. Princeton: Princeton University Press.

Grewal, Inderpal, and Caren Kaplan

1994 *Scattered Hegemonies: Postmodernity and Transnational Feminist Practices*. Minneapolis: University of Minnesota Press.

Gupta, Akhil, and James Ferguson

1992 "Beyond 'Culture': Space, Identity, and the Politics of Difference." *Cultural Anthropology* 7(1): 6–23.

1997a "Discipline and Practice: 'The Field' as Site, Method, and Location in Anthropology." In *Anthropological Locations: Boundaries and Grounds of a Field Science*, 1–46. Berkeley: University of California Press.

1997b *Culture, Power, Place: Explorations in Critical Anthropology*. Durham: Duke University Press.

Hale, Lindsay Lauren

1997 "Preto Velho: Resistance, Redemption, and Engendered Representations of Slavery in a Brazilian Possession-Trance Religion." *American Ethnologist* 24:392–414.

Hall, Catherine, ed.

2000 *Cultures of Empire, A Reader: Colonizers in Britain and the Empire in the Nineteenth and Twentieth Centuries: A Reader*. Manchester: Manchester University Press.

Hall, Stuart

1978 "Racism and Reaction." In *Five Views of Multi-Racial Britain*, ed. Commission for Racial Equality, 23–35. London: Commission for Racial Equality.

1980 *Drifting into a Law and Order Society*. London: Cobden Trust.

1988 *The Hard Road to Renewal*. London: Verso.

1990 "Cultural Identity and Diaspora." In *Identity: Community, Culture, Difference*, ed. Jonathan Rutherford, 222–37. London: Lawrence and Wishart Press.

1999 "A Conversation with Stuart Hall." *Journal of the International Institute* 7(1): 15–18.

Hall, Stuart, and Tony Jefferson, eds.

1976 *Resistance through Rituals: Youth Subcultures in Post-war Britain*. London: Routledge.

Hall, Stuart, C. Crither, T. Jefferson, J. Clarke, and B. Roberts

1978. *Policing the Crisis: Mugging, the State and Law and Order*. London: Macmillan.

Hamer, Mary

1996 "'Black and White?' Viewing Cleopatra in 1862." In *The Victorians and Race*, ed. Shearer West, 53–67. Ashgate: Scolar Press.

Handler, Richard, and Eric Gable

1997 *The New History in an Old Museum: Creating the Past at Colonial Williamsburg*. Durham: Duke University Press.

Haraway, Donna J.

1997 *Modest_Witness@Second_Millennium. FemaleMan_Meets_Onco Mouse*. New York: Routledge.

Harris, Cheryl

1993 "Whiteness as Property." *Harvard Law Review* 106(8): 1709–91.

Harrison, Faye

2002 "Unraveling 'Race' for the Twenty-first Century." In *Exotic No More: Anthropology on the Front Lines*, ed. Jeremy MacClancy, 145–66. Chicago: University of Chicago Press.

Hartigan, John

1997 "Locating White Detroit." In *Displacing Whiteness: Essays in Social and Cultural Criticism*, ed. Ruth Frankenberg, 180–213. Durham: Duke University Press.

1999 *Racial Situations: Class Predicaments of Whiteness in Detroit*. Princeton: Princeton University Press.

Harvey, David

1989 *The Condition of Postmodernity*. Oxford: Blackwell.

1993 "From Space to Place and Back Again: Reflections on the Condition of Postmodernity." In *Mapping the Futures: Local Cultures, Global Change*, ed. Jon Bird, Barry Curtis, Tim Putnam, George Robertson, and Lisa Tucker, 3–29. London: Routledge.

2000 "Cosmopolitanism and the Banality of Geographical Evils." *Public Culture* 12(2): 529–64.

Hayden, Dolores

1995 *The Power of Place: Urban Landscapes as Public History*. Cambridge, MA: MIT Press.

Hebdige, Dick

1979 *Subculture: The Meaning of Style*. London: Methuen.

Hechter, M.

1975 *Internal Colonialism: The Celtic Fringe in British National Development, 1536–1966*. Berkeley: University of California Press.

Heidegger, Martin

1967 [1953] *Being and Time*. Trans. J. Macquarrie and E. Robinson. Oxford: Blackwell.

1977 "Building Dwelling Thinking." In *Martin Heidegger: Basic Writings*, ed. D. Krell, 319–39. New York: Harper and Row.

1996a [1953] *Being and Time*. Trans. Joan Stambaugh. Albany: State University of New York Press.

1996b "From the Introduction to 'Being and Time'." In *The Continental Philosophy Reader*, ed. Richard Kearney and Mara Rainwater, 27–47. London: Routledge.

Helmreich, Stefan

1993 "Kinship, Nation and Paul Gilroy's Concept of Diaspora." *Diaspora* 2(2): 243–49.

HMSO (Her Majesty's Stationery Office)

1948 *Distribution of Industry*. London: Her Majesty's Stationery Office.

Herskovits, Melville

1990 [1941] *The Myth of the Negro Past*. New York: Beacon Press.

Hesse, Barnor

1993 "Black to Front and Black Again: Racialization through Contested Times and Spaces." In *Place and the Politics of Identity*, ed. Michael Keith and Steve Pile, 162–82. New York: Routledge.

2000 *Unsettled Multiculturalisms: Diaspora, Entanglements, Transruptions*. New York: Zed Books.

Hewison, Robert

1987 *The Heritage Industry: Britain in a Climate of Decline*. London: Methuen.

Hobsbawm, E. J.

1969 *Industry and Empire*. Harmondsworth, Middlesex: Penguin.

Holmes, Colin

1988 *John Bull's Island: Immigration and British Society, 1871–1971*. London: Macmillan.

Holsey, Bayo

2003 "Routes of Remembrance: The Transatlantic Slave Trade in the Ghanaian Imagination." Ph.D. diss., Columbia University.

hooks, bell

1991 "Representing Whiteness in the Black Imagination." In *Cultural Studies*, ed. Lawrence Grossberg, Cary Nelson, and Paula Treichler, 338–46. New York: Routledge.

Husserl, Edmund

1996 [1929] "Phenomenology." In *The Continental Philosophy Reader*, ed. Richard Kearney and Mara Rainwater, 15–22. London: Routledge.

Hyde, Francis E.

1971 *Liverpool and the Mersey: An Economic History of a Port, 1700–1970*. Newton Abbot, UK: David and Charles, Ltd.

Ifekwunigwe, Jayne O.

1997 "Diaspora's Daughters, Africa's Orphans? On Lineage, Authenticity and 'Mixed Race' Identity." In *Black British Feminism*, ed. H. Mizra, 127–52. London: Routledge.

1999 *Scattered Belongings: Cultural Paradoxes of "Race," Nation and Gender*. New York: Routledge.

2002 "Re-Membering 'Race': On Gender, 'Mixed Race' and Family in the English-African Diaspora." In *Rethinking "Mixed Race,"* ed. David Parker and Miri Song, 42–64. London: Pluto Press.

Inda, Jonathan Xavier, and Renato Rosaldo

2002 "Introduction: A World in Motion." In *The Anthropology of Globalization: A Reader*, ed. Jonathan Xavier Inda and Renato Rosaldo, 1–36. Oxford: Blackwell.

Jackson, John

2001 *Harlemworld: Doing Race and Class in Contemporary Black America*. Chicago: University of Chicago Press.

Jacobs, Harriet [Linda Brent]

1986 *Incidents in the Life of a Slave Girl*. Boston.

Jewell, Helen M.

1994 *The North-South Divide: The Origins of Northern Consciousness in England*. Manchester: Manchester University Press.

Kaplan, Caren

1996 *Questions of Travel: Postmodern Discourses of Displacement*. Durham: Duke University Press.

Kearney, H.

1994 *The British Isles: A History of Four Nations*. Cambridge: Cambridge University Press.

Kearney, Richard, and Mara Rainwater, eds.

1996 *The Continental Philosophy Reader*. London: Routledge.

Keiller, Patrick

2000 "Port Statistics." In *The Unknown City: Contesting Architecture and Social Space*, ed. Lain Borden, Iain Borden, Jane Rendell, Joe Kerr, and Alicia Pivaro, 442–57. Boston: MIT Press.

Keith, Michael

1993 *Race, Riots, and Policing: Lore and Disorder in a Multi-racist Society*. London: University College London Press.

Kennedy, Dane

1996 *The Magic Mountains: Hill Stations and the British Raj*. Berkeley: University of California Press.

Kerr, Madeline

1958 *The People of Ship Street*. *London*: Routledge and Kegan Paul.

Kidd, Alan J.

1998 "'Local History' and the Culture of the Middle Classes in North-west England, c. 1840–1900." *Transactions of the Historic Society of Lancashire and Cheshire* 147:115–38.

Kirk, Neville, ed.

2000 *Northern Identities: Historical Interpretations of "The North" and "Northernness."* Aldershot, UK: Ashgate Publishing.

Kondo, Dorinne

1997 *About Face: Performing Race in Fashion and Theater*. New York: Routledge.

Kuklick, Henrika
1984 "Tribal Exemplars: Images of Political Authority in British Anthropology, 1885–1945." In *Functionalism Historicized: Essays on British Social Anthropology*, ed. George Stocking, 59–82. Madison: University of Wisconsin Press.

Lane, Tony
1986 *Grey Dawn Breaking: British Merchant Seafarers in the Late Twentieth Century*. Oxford: Alden Press.
1987 *Liverpool: Gateway of Empire*. London: Lawrence and Wishart.
1995 "The Political Imperatives of Bureaucracy and Empire: The Case of the Coloured Alien Seamen Order, 1925." In *Ethnic Labour and British Imperial Trade: A History of Ethnic Seafarers in the UK*, ed. Diane Frost, 104–29. London: Frank Cass.

Lavalette, Michael, and Jane Kennedy
1996 *Solidarity on the Waterfront: The Liverpool Lock Out of 1995/96*. Liverpool: Liver Press.

Laverty, Kevin, ed.
2003 *National Statistics: Annual Abstract of Statistics*. London: Her Majesty's Stationery Office.

Lavie, Smadar, and Ted Swedenburg, eds.
1996 *Displacement, Diaspora and Geographies of Identity*. Durham: Duke University Press.

Law, Ian, and J. Henfrey
1981 *A History of Race and Racism in Liverpool*: 1660–1950. Liverpool: Merseyside Community Relations Council.

Leach, Edmund
1977 *Political Systems of Highland Burma: A Study of Kachin Social Structure*. London: Athlone Press.

Lee, Benjamin
1995 "Critical Internationalism." *Public Culture* 7:559–92.

Linger, Daniel
2001 *No One Home: Brazilian Selves Remade in Japan*. Palo Alto, CA: Stanford University Press.

Liverpool Black Caucus
1986 *The Racial Politics of Militant in Liverpool*. Liverpool: Merseyside Area Profile Group and Runnymede Trust.

Liverpool City Council
1987 *Past Trends, Future Prospects: Urban Change in Liverpool, 1961–2001*. Liverpool: Liverpool City Council.
2002 "Local Public Service Agreement between Liverpool City Council and the Government, 2002–2005." Liverpool: Liverpool City Council.

Liverpool Echo
1991 Letters to the Editor. September 6, p. 8.

Lord Gifford, QC, Wally Brown, and Ruth Bundey
1989 *Loosen the Shackles: First Report of the Liverpool 8 Inquiry into Race Relations in Liverpool*. London: Karia Press.

Lorimer, Douglas
1978 *Colour, Class, and the Victorians: English Attitudes to the Negro in the Mid-Nineteenth Century*. Leicester: Leicester University Press/Holmes and Meier.
1996 "Race, Science and Culture: Historical Continuities and Discontinuities, 1850–1914." In *The Victorians and Race*, ed. Shearer West, 12–33. Aldershot, UK: Scolar Press.

Low, Setha M., and Denise Lawrence-Zúñiga
2003 *The Anthropology of Space and Place: Locating Culture*. Oxford: Blackwell.
Lowe, Lisa
1996 *Immigrant Acts*. Durham: Duke University Press.
Lowenthal, David
1985 *The Past Is a Foreign Country*. Cambridge: Cambridge University Press.
1991 "British National Identity and the English Landscape." *Rural History* 2(2): 205–30.
Lunn, K.
1991 "Reconsidering Britishness." In *National Identity in Contemporary Europe*, ed.
   B. Jenkins and Spyrus A. Sofos, 83–100. London: Routledge.
Lynn, Martin
1998 "Liverpool and Africa in the Nineteenth Century: The Continuing Connection."
   Transactions of the Historic Society of Lancashire and Cheshire 147:27–54.
Macey, David
2000 *Franz Fanon: A Biography*. New York: Picador.
Malchow, H. L.
1996 "The Half-Breed as Gothic Unnatural." In *The Victorians and Race*, ed. Shearer
   West, 101–11. Aldershot, UK: Scolar Press.
Marke, Ernest
1986 *In Troubled Waters: Memoirs of Seventy Years in England*. London: Karia Press.
Martinez-Alier, Verena
1974 *Marriage, Class and Colour in Nineteenth-Century Cuba: A Study of Racial
   Attitudes and Sexual Values in a Slave Society*. Ann Arbor: University of Michigan
   Press.
Massey, Doreen
1984 *Spatial Divisions of Labor: Social Structures and the Geography of Production*.
   London: Macmillan.
1993 "Power-Geometry and a Progressive Sense of Place." In *Mapping the Futures:
   Local Cultures, Global Change*, ed. Jon Bird, Barry Curtis, Tim Putnam, George
   Robertson, and Lisa Tickner, 59–69. New York: Routledge.
1994 *Space, Place and Gender*. Minneapolis: University of Minneapolis Press.
2000 "Living in Wythenshawe." In *The Unknown City: Contesting Architecture and
   Social Space*, ed. Lain Borden, Iain Borden, Jane Rendell, Joe Kerr, and Alicia Pivaro,
   457–74. Boston: MIT Press.
Massey, Doreen, and Richard Meegan
1982 *The Anatomy of Job Loss: The How, Why and Where of Employment Decline*.
   London: Methuen.
Matory, J. Lorand
1999 "The English Professors of Brazil: On the Diasporic Roots of the Yoruba Nation."
   Comparative Studies in Society and History 41(1): 72–103.
May, Roy, and Robin Cohen
1974 "The Interaction between Race and Colonialism: A Case Study of the Liverpool
   Race Riots of 1919." *Race and Class* 16(2): 111–26.
Mays, John Barron
1964 *Growing Up in the City: A Study of Juvenile Delinquency in an Urban Neighbor-
   hood*. Liverpool: Liverpool University Press.
McClintock, Anne
1995 *Imperial Leather: Race, Gender and Sexuality in the Colonial Contest*. New York:
   Routledge.

Mellor, Adrian
1991 "Enterprise and Heritage in the Dock." In *Enterprise and Heritage: Crosscurrents of National Culture*, ed. John Corner and Sylvia Harvey, 93–115. London: Routledge.
Mercer, Kobena
1994 "Introduction: Black Britain and the Cultural Politics of Diaspora." In *Welcome to the Jungle: New Positions in Black Cultural Studies*, 1–32. London: Routledge.
Merseyside Anti-Racialist Alliance
1979 *Merseyside against Racism: First Annual Report of MARA* [Merseyside Anti-Racialist Alliance]. Liverpool: Merseyside Anti-Racialist Alliance.
Merseyside Area Profile Group
1980 *Racial Disadvantage in Liverpool—An Area Profile*. Liverpool: Merseyside Area Profile Group.
1983 *Equal Opportunities and the Employment of Black People and Ethnic Minorities on Merseyside*. Liverpool: Merseyside Association for Racial Equality in Employment.
Mignolo, Walter
2000 "The Many Faces of Cosmo-polis: Border Thinking and Critical Cosmopolitanism." *Public Culture* 12(3): 157–87.
Mintz, Sidney
1998 "The Localization of Anthropological Practice." *Critique of Anthropology* 18(2): 117–33.
Mintz, Sidney, and Richard Price
1992 [1976] *The Birth of African American Culture: An Anthropological Perspective*. Boston: Beacon Press.
Modood, Tariq, ed.
1988 "'Black,' Racial Equality and Asian Identity." *New Community* 14(3): 397–404.
1997 *Ethnic Minorities in Britain: Diversity and Disadvantage*. London: London Policy Studies Institute.
Moore, Brenda L.
1996 *To Serve My Country, To Serve My Race: The Story of the Only WACs Stationed Overseas during World War II*. New York: New York University Press.
Moore, Donald S.
1996 "Marxism, Culture and Political Ecology: Environmental Struggles in Zimbabwe's Eastern Highlands." In *Liberation Ecologies: Environment, Development, and Social Movement*, ed. Richard Peet and Michael Watts, 125–47. New York: Routledge.
1998 "Subaltern Struggles and the Politics of Place: Remapping Resistance in Zimbabwe's Eastern Highlands." *Cultural Anthropology* 13(3): 344–75.
1999 "The Crucible of Cultural Politics: Reworking 'Development' in Zimbabwe's Eastern Highlands." *American Ethnologist* 26(3): 654–91.
Moore, Donald, Jake Kosek, and Anand Pandian, eds.
2003 *Race, Nature, and the Politics of Difference*. Durham: Duke University Press.
Morrison, Toni
1992 *Playing in the Dark: Whiteness and the Literary Imagination*. Cambridge, MA: Harvard University Press.
Muir, Ramsay
1907 *A History of Liverpool*. London: Williams and Norgate.
Murphy, Andrea
1995 *From the Empire to the Rialto: Racism and Reaction in Liverpool, 1918–1948*. Merseyside: Liver Press.

Murray, Nancy
1986 "Antiracists and Other Demons: The Press and Ideology in Thatcher's Britain."
Race and Class 27(3): 1–20.
Myers, Norma
1995 "The Black Poor of London: Initiatives of Eastern Seamen in the Eighteenth Centuries." In *Ethnic Labour and British Imperial Trade: A History of Ethnic Seafarers in the UK*, ed. Diane Frost, 7–21. London: Frank Cass.
1996 *Reconstructing the Black Past: Blacks in Britain, 1780–1830*. London: Frank Cass.
Nadel-Klein, Jane
1991 "Reweaving the Fringe: Localism, Tradition, and Representation in British Ethnography." *American Ethnologist* 18:500–517.
Nairn, Tom
1977 *The Break-up of Britain: Crisis and Neo-nationalism*. London: New Left Books.
Nayak, Anoop
2003 "Last of the 'Real Geordies'? White Masculinities and the Subcultural Response to Deindustrialisation." *Environment and Planning D: Society and Space* 21:7–25.
Nelson, Diane
1999 *A Finger in the Wound: Body Politics in Quincentennial Guatemala*. Berkeley: University of California Press.
Nelson, William E.
2000 *Black Atlantic Politics: Dilemmas of Political Empowerment in Boston and Liverpool*. Albany: State University of New York Press.
Ogude, S. E.
1981 "Slavery and the African Imagination: A Critical Perspective." *World Literature Today* 55(1): 21–25.
O'Mara, Pat
1933 *Autobiography of a Liverpool Irish Slummy*. New York: Vanguard Press.
Omi, Michael, and Howard Winant
1994 *Racial Formation in the United States: From the 1960s to the 1990s*. New York: Routledge.
Ong, Aihwa
1998 "Flexible Citizenship among Chinese Cosmopolitans." In *Cosmopolitics: Thinking and Feeling beyond the Nation*, ed. Pheng Cheah and Bruce Robbins. Minneapolis: University of Minnesota Press.
OPCS (Office of Population Censuses and Surveys)
1992 County Monitor. 1991 Census: Merseyside. Government Statistical Service.
Ortner, Shelly
1995 "Resistance and the Problem of Ethnographic Refusal." *Comparative Studies in Society and History* 37:73–93.
Palmie, Stephan, ed.
1995 *Slave Cultures and Cultures of Slavery*. Knoxville: University of Tennessee Press.
Parker, David, and Miri Song
2001 *Rethinking Mixed Race*. London: Pluto Press.
Paul, Kathleen
1997 *Whitewashing Britain: Race and Citizenship in the Postwar Era*. Ithaca: Cornell University Press.
Phillips, Caryl
2000 *The Atlantic Sound*. New York: Knopf.

chapters that follow. Some of these rights include semiconductor chip protection, plant variety protection, the right of publicity, and rights relating to unfair competition, including passing off, misappropriation, and false advertising.

Additionally, intellectual property rights often intersect and overlap. Thus, the formula for Coca-Cola is a trade secret, while the distinctive script in which the words COCA-COLA® are displayed is a trademark. Generally, computer programs are protectable under copyright law, patent law, and as trade secrets, while the name for a computer program, such as WINDOWS®, qualifies for trademark protection. Jewelry may be protected both under copyright and design patent law. Legal practitioners in the field of intellectual property law must fully understand how the various types of intellectual property intersect so that clients can achieve the widest possible scope of protection. For example, although an item of jewelry can be protected as a design patent, securing a patent is complex and expensive. Moreover, a design patent lasts only fourteen years from the date of grant of the patent. In contrast, securing copyright protection for the same article of jewelry is easy and inexpensive. More importantly, copyright protection endures during the life of the work's creator and for seventy years thereafter. Trade secrets that are properly protected can endure perpetually. Thus, intellectual property owners need to consider the complementary relationships among trademark, copyright, patent, and trade secrets law so as to obtain the broadest possible protection for their assets.

AGENCIES RESPONSIBLE FOR INTELLECTUAL PROPERTY REGISTRATION

United States Patent and Trademark Office

The agency charged with granting patents and registering trademarks is the **United States Patent and Trademark Office (PTO)**,

one of fourteen bureaus within the U.S. Department of Commerce. The PTO, founded more than two hundred years ago, employs nearly seven thousand employees and is presently located in eighteen buildings in Arlington, Virginia. Its official mailing address is Commissioner of Patents and Trademarks, Washington, DC 20231. The PTO is physically located at 2900 Crystal Drive in Arlington, Virginia. Its web site is http://www.uspto.gov. The PTO web site offers a wealth of information, including basic information about trademarks and patents, fee schedules, forms, and the ability to search for trademarks and patents. Since 1991, under the Omnibus Budget Reconciliation Act, the PTO has operated in much the same way as a private business, providing valued products and services to customers in exchange for fees that are used to fully fund PTO operations. It uses no taxpayer funds. The PTO plans to move all of its operations to Alexandria, Virginia, by mid-2005.

The PTO is one of the busiest of all government agencies, and as individuals and companies begin to understand the value of intellectual property, greater demands are being made on the PTO. For example, over the past five years the PTO has seen a 50 percent increase in the number of trademark and patent applications. In 2002, the PTO issued 162,221 patents and registered 113,225 trademarks.

Legislation passed in 1997 established the PTO as a performance-based organization that is managed by professionals, resulting in the creation of a new political position, deputy secretary of commerce for intellectual property. Changing the PTO from a mere governmental agency to a governmental corporation made the PTO equivalent to other similar organizations, such as the Tennessee Valley Authority and the Federal Deposit Insurance Corporation. Performance-based organizations have considerable flexibility in personnel matters and set specific goals and objectives to achieve. In brief, the PTO operates more like a business with

Phoenix, Anne, and Charlie Owen
1996 "From Miscegenation to Hybridity: Mixed Relationships and Mixed Parentage in Profile." In *Children, Research and Policy*, ed. B. Bernstein and J. Brannen. London: Taylor and Francis.

Pile, Steve, and Michael Keith, eds.
1993 *Place and the Politics of Identity*. London: Routledge.
1997 *Geographies of Resistance*. London: Routledge.

Pinar, William
1993 "Notes on Understanding the Curriculum as a Social Text." In *Race, Identity and Representation in Education*, ed. Warren Crichlow and Cameron McCarthy, 60–70. New York: Routledge.

Piot, Charles
2001 "Atlantic Aporias: Africa and Gilroy's Black Atlantic." *South Atlantic Quarterly* 100(1): 155–70.

Pollack, Sheldon, Homi K. Bhabha, Carol A. Breckenridge, and Dipesh Chakrabarty, eds.
2000 "Cosmopolitanisms." *Public Culture* 12(3): 577–89.

Pollard, Ingrid
2004 *Postcards Home*. London: Autograph.

Portelli, Alessandro
1991 *The Death of Luigi Trastulli and Other Stories: Form and Meaning in Oral History*. Albany: State University of New York Press.

Power, M. J.
1992 "The Growth of Liverpool." In *Popular Politics, Riot and Labour: Essays in Liverpool History 1790–1940*, ed. John Belchem, 21–37. Liverpool: Liverpool University Press.

Pratt, Mary
1992 *Imperial Eyes: Travel Writing and Transculturation*. London: Routledge.

Price, Richard
1983 *First-time: The Historical Vision of an Afro-American People*. Baltimore: Johns Hopkins University Press.

Priestley, J. B.
1984 [1934] *English Journey*. Chicago: University of Chicago Press.

Raffles, Hugh
2002 In *Amazonia: A Natural History*. Princeton: Princeton University Press.

Rassool, Naz
1997 "Fractured or Flexible Identities? Life Histories of 'Black' Diasporic Women in Britain." In *Black British Feminism: A Reader*, ed. Heidi Safia Mirza, 187–204. London: Routledge.

Rawnsley, Stuart
2000 "Constructing 'The North': Space and a Sense of Place." In *Northern Identities: Historical Interpretations of "The North" and "Northernness,"* ed. Neville Kirk, 3–22. Aldershot, UK: Ashgate.

Rediker, Marcus
1987 *Between the Devil and the Deep Blue Sea: Merchant Seamen, Pirates, and the Anglo-American Maritime World, 1700–1750*. Cambridge: Cambridge University Press.

Reeves, Frank
1983 *British Racial Discourse: A Study of British Political Discourse about Race and Race-Related Matters*. Cambridge: Cambridge University Press.

Reynolds, David
1995 *Rich Relations: The American Occupation of Britain, 1942–1945*. New York: Random House.

Rich, Paul
1986 *Race and Empire in British Politics*. 2nd ed. Cambridge: Cambridge University Press.

Richmond, Anthony
1954 *Colour Prejudice in Britain: A Study of West Indian Workers in Liverpool, 1941–1951*. London: Routledge and Paul.

Robbins, Bruce
1995 "The Weird Heights: On Cosmopolitanism, Feeling and Power." *Differences: A Journal of Feminist Cultural Studies* 7(1): 165–87.
1998 "Actually Existing Cosmopolitanism." In *Cosmopolitics: Thinking and Feeling beyond the Nation*, ed. Bruce Robbins and Pheng Cheah. Minneapolis: University of Minnesota Press.

Roberts, Ken, Michelle Connolly, and Glenys Parsell
1992 "Black Youth in the Liverpool Labour Market." *New Community* 18(2): 209–28.

Roberts, K., S. Dench, and D. Richardson
1987 "The Changing Structure of Youth Labour Markets." Department of Employment Research Paper 59, London.
1998 "Actually Existing Cosmopolitanism." In *Cosmopolitics: Thinking and Feeling beyond the Nation*, ed. Pheng Cheah and Bruce Robbins. Minneapolis: University of Minnesota Press.

Rodman, Margaret
1992 "Empowering Place: Multilocality and Multivocality." *American Anthropologist* 94(3): 640–56.

Roediger, David
1991 *The Wages of Whiteness: Race and the Making of the American Working Class*. London: Verso.

Rofel, Lisa
1999 *Other Modernities: Gendered Yearnings in China after Socialism*. Berkeley: University of California Press.

Said, Edward
1978 *Orientalism*. New York: Pantheon.
1993 *Culture and Imperialism*. New York: Knopf.

Sanjek, Roger
1994 "Intermarriage and the Future of Races." In *Race*, ed. Roger Sanjek and Steven Gregory, 103–30. New Brunswick, NJ: Rutgers University Press.

Sartwell, Crispin
1998 *Act Like You Know: African-American Autobiography and White Identity*. Chicago: University of Chicago Press.

Sassen, Saskia
1991 *The Global City: New York, London, Tokyo*. Princeton: Princeton University Press.

Scott, David
1991 "That Event, This Memory: Notes on the Anthropology of African Diasporas in the New World." *Diaspora* 1:261–83.
1999 *Refashioning Futures: Criticism after Postcoloniality*. Princeton: Princeton University Press.

Scott, Joan

1992 "Experience." In *Feminists Theorize the Political*, ed. Judith Butler and Joan Scott, 22–40. New York: Routledge.

"Scouse Equals Louse in Genteel Bournemouth."

1991 *The Independent*, September 1, p. 5.

Seacole, Mary

1988 [1857] *Wonderful Adventures of Mrs. Seacole in Many Lands*. New York: Oxford University Press.

Seed, Patricia

1995 *Ceremonies of Possession: Europe's Conquest of the New World, 1492–1640*. Cambridge: Cambridge University Press.

Sekora, John

1987 "Black Message/White Envelope: Genre, Authenticity, and Authority in the Antebellum Slave Narrative." *Callaloo* 32:482–515.

Sekula, Allan

2000 "Freeway to China (Version 2, for Liverpool)." *Public Culture* 12(2): 411–22.

Shaw, Frank

1971 *My Liverpool*. Liverpool: Gallery Press.

Shaw, Rosalind

1997 "The Production of Witchcraft/Witchcraft as Production: Memory, Modernity, and the Slave Trade in Sierra Leone." *American Ethnologist* 24:856–76.

Sherwood, Marika

1995 "Strikes! African Seamen, Elder Dempster and the Government 1940–42." In *Ethnic Labour and British Imperial Trade: A History of Ethnic Seafarers in the UK*, ed. Diane Frost, 131–45. London: Frank Cass.

Shields, Rob

1991 *Places on the Margin: Alternative Geographies of Modernity*. London: Routledge.

Short, Brian, ed.

1992 *The English Rural Community: Image and Analysis*. Cambridge: Cambridge University Press.

Simey, Margaret

1951 *Charitable Effort in Liverpool in the Nineteenth Century*. Liverpool: Liverpool University Press.

1996 *The Disinherited Society: A Personal View of Social Responsibility in Liverpool during the Twentieth Century*. Liverpool: Liverpool University Press.

Sivanandan, Ambalavaner

1982a "From Resistance to Rebellion." In *A Different Hunger: Writings on Black Resistance*, 3–54. London: Pluto Press.

1982b "Race, Class and the State: The Black Experience in Britain." In *A Different Hunger: Writings on Black Resistance*, 101–25. London: Pluto Press.

1985 "RAT and the Degradation of the Black Struggle." *Race and Class* 26(4): 1–33.

1987 *A Different Hunger: Writings on Black Resistance*. London: Pluto Press.

Small, Stephen

1991 "Racialised Relations in Liverpool: A Contemporary Anomaly." *New Community* 17(4): 511–37.

1994 *Racialised Barriers: The Black Experience in the United States and England*. New York: Routledge.

Smith, Graham

1987 *When Jim Crow Met John Bull: Black American Soldiers in World War II Britain*. London: I. B. Travis.

Smith, M. van Wyk
1991 "Writing the African Diaspora in the Eighteenth Century." *Diaspora* 1(2): 127–42.

Smith, Neil
1992 "Geography, Difference and the Politics of Scale." In *Postmodernism and the Social Sciences*, ed. Joe Deberty, Elspeth Graham, and Mo Malek, 57–79. Houndsmills, Basingstoke, Hampshire, UK: Macmillan.

Smith, Raymond T.
1988 *Kinship and Class in the West Indies: A Genealogical Study of Jamaica and Guyana*. Cambridge: Cambridge University Press.

Sokolowski, Robert
2000 *Introduction to Phenomenology*. Cambridge: Cambridge University Press.

Stewart, Kathleen
1996 *A Space on the Side of the Road: Cultural Poetics in an "Other" America*. Princeton: Princeton University Press.

Stoler, Ann Laura
1989 "Rethinking Colonial Categories: European Communities in Sumatra and the Boundaries of Rule." *Comparative Studies in Society and History* 31(1): 134–61.
1997a "Racial Histories and Their Regimes of Truth." *Political Power and Social Theory* 11:183–207.
1997b "Sexual Affronts and Racial Frontiers: European Identities and the Cultural Politics of Exclusion in Colonial Southeast Asia." In *Tensions of Empire: Colonial Cultures in a Bourgeois World*, ed. Frederick Cooper and Ann Stoler, 198–237. Berkeley: University of California Press.

Strathern, Marilyn
1982 "The Village as an Idea: Constructs of Village-ness in Elmdon, Essex." In *Belonging: Identity and Social Organization in British Rural Cultures*, ed. Anthony Cohen, 247–77. Manchester: Manchester University Press.

Sudbury, Julia
1998 *Other Kinds of Dreams: Black Women's Organisations and the Politics of Transformation*. London: Routledge.

Tabili, Laura
1991 "The Construction of Racial Difference in Twentieth-Century Britain: The Special Restriction (Coloured Alien Seamen) Order, 1925." *Journal of British Studies* 33:54–98.
1994 *"We Ask for British Justice": Workers and Racial Difference in Late Imperial Britain*. Ithaca: Cornell University Press.
1996 "'Women of a Very Low Type': Crossing Racial Boundaries in Late Imperial Britain." In *Gender and Class in Modern Europe*, ed. Laura Frader and Sonya Rose, 165–90. Ithaca: Cornell University Press.

Taylor, A.J.P.
1965 *English History, 1914–1945*. Oxford: Oxford University Press.

Taylor, Jenny Bourne
1992 "Re:Locations—from Bradford to Brighton." *New Formations* 17:86–94.

Ten.8
1992 *Critical Decade: Black British Photography in the 80s* 2(3).

Tizard, Barbara, and Ann Phoenix
2001 *Black, White, or Mixed Race?: Race and Racism in the Lives of Young People of Mixed Parentage*. New York: Routledge.

Toloyon, Khachig
1996 "Rethinking *Diaspora*(s): Stateless Power in the Transnational Moment." *Diaspora* 5(1): 3–36.

Trudgill, Peter
2001 *Sociolinguistic Variation and Change*. Edinburgh: Edinburgh University Press.
Tsing, Anna
1993 *In the Realm of the Diamond Queen: Marginality in an Out-of-the-Way Place*. Princeton: Princeton University Press.
2000 "The Global Situation." *Cultural Anthropology* 15(3): 327–60.
Twine, France Winddance
1996 "Brown Skinned White Girls: Class, Culture and the Construction of White Identity in Suburban Communities." *Gender, Place and Culture: A Journal of Feminist Geography* 3(2): 205–24.
1998a "Managing Everyday Racisms: White Mothers of African-Descent Children in Britain." In *Everyday Inequalities: Critical Inquiries*, ed. Jodi O'Brien and Judith Howard, 237–51. London: Blackwell.
1998b "The White Mother: Blackness, Whiteness and Interracial Families." *Transition* 73:144–54.
1999 "Transracial Mothering and Anti-racism: The Case of White Mothers of African-Descent Children in Britain." *Feminist Studies* 25(3): 729–46.
2000 "Bearing Blackness in Britain: The Meaning of Racial Difference for White Birth Mothers of African-Descent Children." In *Ideologies and Technologies of Motherhood: Race, Class, Sexuality, Nationalism*, ed. Helena Ragone and France Winddance Twine, 6–108. New York: Routledge.
Unwin, Frank
1983 *Reflections on the Mersey: Memoirs of the Twenties and Thirties*. Leighton Banastre, Parkgage South Wirral, UK: Gallery Press.
van Helmond, Marij, and Donna Palmer
1991 *Staying Power: Black Presence in Liverpool*. Merseyside: National Museums and Galleries on Merseyside.
Visweswaran, Kamala
1994 *Fictions of Feminist Ethnography*. Minneapolis: University of Minnesota Press.
1997 "Diaspora by Design: Flexible Citizenship and South Asians in U.S. Racial Formation." *Diaspora* 6(1): 5–29.
1998 "Race and the Culture of Anthropology." *American Anthropologist* 100(1): 70–83.
Wacquant, Loic J. D.
1997 "For an Analytic of Racial Domination." *Political Power and Social Theory* 11:221–34.
Wade, Peter
1993 *Blackness and Race Mixture: The Dynamics of Racial Identity in Colombia*. Baltimore: Johns Hopkins University Press.
2002 *Race, Nature and Culture: An Anthropological Perspective*. London: Pluto Press.
Wales, Katie
1994 "Royalese: The Rise and Fall of 'The Queen's English.'" *English Today* 39, 10(3): 3–10.
Walkowitz, Judith R.
1980 *Prostitution and Victorian Society: Women, Class and the State*. Cambridge: Cambridge University Press.
1992 *City of Dreadful Delight: Narratives of Sexual Danger in Late-Victorian London*. Chicago: University of Chicago Press.
Wallace, Michele
1990 *Invisibility Blues: From Pop to Theory*. London: Verso.

Waller, P. J.
1983 *Town, City and Nation: England, 1850–1914*. Oxford: Oxford University Press.
Walton, John K., and Alastair Wilcox, eds.
1991 *Low Life and Moral Improvement in Mid-Victorian England: Liverpool through the Journalism of Hugh Shimmin*. Manchester: Manchester University Press.
Ware, Vron
1992 *Beyond the Pale: White Women, Racism and History*. London: Verso.
Ware, Vron, and Les Back
2002 *Out of Whiteness: Color, Politics, and Culture*. Chicago: University of Chicago Press.
Wastell, Sari
2001 "Presuming Scale, Making Diversity: On the Mischiefs of Measurement and the Global:Local Metonym in Theories of Law and Culture." *Critique of Anthropology* 21(2): 185–210.
Weiner, Martin J.
1981 *English Culture and the Decline of the Industrial Spirit*, 1850–1980. London: Penguin.
Wells, Ida B.
1970 *Crusade for Justice: The Autobiography of Ida B. Wells*. Chicago: University of Chicago Press.
West, Cornel
1993 "The New Cultural Politics of Difference." In *Race, Identity and Representation in Education*, ed. Cameron McCarthy and Warren Crichlow, 11–23. New York: Routledge.
Wheeler, Roxann
2000 *The Complexion of Race: Categories of Difference in Eighteenth-Century British Culture*. Philadelphia: University of Pennsylvania Press.
Wiegman, Robyn
1995 *American Anatomies: Theorizing Race and Gender*. Durham: Duke University Press.
1999 "Whiteness Studies and the Paradox of Particularity." Boundary 2, 26(3): 115–50.
Williams, Brackette
1991 *Stains on My Name, War in My Veins: Guyana and the Politics of Cultural Struggle*. Durham: Duke University Press.
Williams, Raymond
1973 *The Country and the City*. New York: Oxford University Press.
Wilson, Anne
1987 *Mixed Race Children: A Study of Identity*. London: Allen and Unwin.
Wilson, Arline
1998 "The Cultural Identity of Liverpool, 1790–1850: The Early Learned Societies." *Transactions of the Historic Society of Lancashire and Cheshire* 147:55–80.
Wilson, Carlton
1992 "A Hidden History: The Black Experience in Liverpool, England, 1919–1945." Ph.D. diss., University of North Carolina, Chapel Hill.
Winant, Howard
1994 *Racial Conditions: Politics, Theory, Comparisons*. Minneapolis: University of Minnesota Press.
Woods, John
1989 *Growin' Up: One Scouser's Social History, 1925–42*. Preston, UK: Carnegie Press.

Wright, Patrick
1985 *On Living in an Old Country: The National Past in Contemporary Britain*. London: Verso.
2000 "The Last Days of London: A Conversation with Joe Kerr." In *The Unknown City: Contesting Architecture and Social Space*, ed. Lain Borden, Iain Borden, Jane Rendell, Joe Kerr, and Alicia Pivaro, 476–91. Boston: MIT Press.
Yanagisako, Sylvia
1995 "Transforming Orientalism: Gender, Nationality and Class in Asian American Studies." In *Naturalizing Power: Essays in Feminist Cultural Analysis*, ed. Sylvia Yanagisako and Carol Delaney, 275–98. New York: Routledge.
Young, Martin
1978 "On the Merseybeat." *Listener*, November 2, 1978.
Young, Robert J. C.
1995 *Colonial Desire: Hybridity in Theory, Culture and Race*. London: Routledge.

greater autonomy over its budget, hiring, and procurement. Additionally, the PTO web site's searchable database includes information about all U.S. patents from the first patent issued in 1790 to the most recent, with full information for all patents since 1976 and the text and images of more than three million pending and registered federal trademarks. Users can view, download, and print the images of these patents and trademarks. The PTO is continuing its transition from paper to electronic filing for both trademarks and patents. In the last quarter of 2002, over fifty percent of all initial trademark applications were received electronically, and the PTO expects to achieve a full paperless patent process by the end of 2004.

The PTO is led by the Under Secretary of Commerce for Intellectual Property and Director of the United States Patent and Trademark Office (the "Director"), who is appointed by the President. The Secretary of Commerce appoints a Commissioner for Patents and a Commissioner for Trademarks.

Citations to many cases in this text will be to "U.S.P.Q.," a reference to *United States Patent Quarterly*, a reporter of cases decided by the **Trademark Trial and Appeal Board (TTAB)** as well as patent and copyright cases.

Library of Congress

The **Library of Congress,** sometimes referred to as "Jefferson's Legacy," was established in 1800 as a legislative library. It is America's oldest national cultural institution and is the largest library in the world. Thomas Jefferson is considered the founder of the Library of Congress, and his personal library is at the heart of the Library inasmuch as in 1814 the Library's three thousand volumes were burned by the British, and Jefferson sold his personal library collection of 6,487 volumes to the Library of Congress for $23,940 the next year.

The U.S. Copyright Office has been a part of the Library of Congress since 1870 and is in charge of examining the approximately 600,000 copyright applications filed each year, issuing registrations, and maintaining copyright deposits in its vast collection.

The Library of Congress is located at 101 Independence Avenue SE, Washington, DC 20559-6000, and its web site is http://www.loc.gov/copyright. Basic information about copyrights, forms, and other valuable information can be obtained for free and downloaded from the Copyright Office's web site.

INTERNATIONAL ORGANIZATIONS, AGENCIES, AND TREATIES

There are a number of international organizations and agencies that promote the use and protection of intellectual property. Although these organizations are discussed in more detail in the chapters to follow, a brief introduction may be helpful:

- **International Trademark Association (INTA)** is a not-for-profit international association composed chiefly of trademark owners and practitioners. More than 4,000 companies and law firms in more than 150 countries belong to INTA, together with others interested in promoting trademarks. INTA offers a wide variety of educational seminars and publications, including many worthwhile materials available at no cost on the Internet (see INTA's home page at http://www.inta.org). INTA is located at 1133 Avenue of the Americas, New York, NY 10036-6710 (212/768-9887).

- **World Intellectual Property Organization (WIPO)** was founded in 1883 and is a specialized agency of the United Nations whose purposes are to promote intellectual property throughout the world and to administer twenty-three treaties dealing with